Power Programming... the IBM XGA

by Jake Richter

MIS:
PRESS

A Subsidiary of
Henry Holt and Co., Inc.

First Edition—1992

Book ISBN 1-55828-127-4   Book/disk ISBN 1-55828-214-9

Printed in the United States of America.

10 9 8 7 6 5 4 3 2 1

MIS:Press books are available at special discounts for bulk purchases for sales promotions, premiums, fund-raising, or educational use. Special editions or book excerpts can also be created to specification.

For details contact: Special Sales Director
MIS:Press
a subsidiary of Henry Holt and Company, Inc.
115 West 18th Street
New York, New York 10011

Trademarks

AnimatorPro, AutoCAD, Autodesk, AutoShade, and 3D Studio are trademarks of Autodesk, Inc.
Apple, Apple II, and Macintosh are trademarks of Apple Computer Corp.
Cirrus Logic is a trademark of Cirrus Logic, Inc.
DesqView is a trademark of Quarterdeck, Inc.
DLD and DLD-XGA are trademarks of Panacea Inc.
DMQS, IBM, IBM-PC, Micro Channel, Personal System/2, PC-AT, PC-DOS, Presentation Manager, PS/2, and XGA
    are trademarks of International Business Machines Corp.
Hercules is a trademark of Hercules Computer Technology, Inc.
HiColor is a trademark of Sierra Semiconductor, Inc.
i386, i486, and Intel are trademarks of Intel Corp.
Inmos and SGS-Thomson are trademarks of SGS-Thomson, Ltd.
IIT is a trademark of Integrated Information Technology, Inc.
Lotus is a trademark of Lotus Development Corp.
Microsoft, MS-DOS, and Windows are trademarks of Microsoft Corp.
Motorola is a trademark of Motorola Corp.
OS/2 is a trademark of International Business Machines Corp. and Microsoft Corp.
Panacea is a trademark of Panacea Inc.
PharLap is a trademark of PharLap, Inc.
QEMM is a trademark of Quarterdeck, Inc.
TARGA is a trademark of Truevision, Inc.
386MAX is a trademark of Qualitas, Inc.
TIGA is a trademark of Texas Instruments.
UNIX is a trademark of Bell Laboratories
VBE, VESA, and VSE are trademarks of the Video Electronics Standards Association.

Note: Much of Chapter 2 originally appeared in an XGA article Jake Richter wrote for the February 1991 issue of BYTE magazine.

Dedication

To the whole gang at Panacea for putting up with me during my "Leave me alone! I need to write!" tirades, and to my wife for allowing me to occupy the living room with strewn paper, cables, and computer hardware, for nearly a year.

Acknowledgments

I'd like to thank the following, without whom this book probably would have appeared in the next century:

The Video Electronic Standards Association, for allowing me to participate in forming new industry standards, and to provide the VESA XGA Extensions Standard to XGA enthusiasts.

IBM, for aid in getting advance information about new products and interfaces, and for hardware support when I needed it most. Particularly Paul Mugge, for writing the foreword, and Graeme Dougal, Ed Eilbeck, and James Wilkinson, for providing the IBM DMQS standard that appears in Appendix N.

M&T Books, for allowing me to use the 8514/A-specific portions of the AI sections from *Graphics Programming for the 8514/A*.

Larry Coffey, my technical editor, for wielding a wonderfully fine-toothed comb to find technical inconsistencies that would have detracted from the usefulness of the book.

Elizabeth Gehrman, my editor, for saintly patience with me and my continually self-induced slipping schedules, and for a great contextual massage of the book.

Liz Misch, associate production editor, for laying out many pages and entering many corrections.

Contents

Foreword

It is a pleasure to write these opening comments for Jake Richter's *Power Programming the IBM XGA*. We here at IBM's Boca Raton laboratory believe that the Extended Graphics Array (XGA) represents a new and exciting graphics architecture rich in function and performance. Because of our internal commitment to expanding the XGA, as well as our licensing activities with business partners, we believe the XGA is destined to become an industry standard.

This book is aimed at engineers and programmers who will exploit the full potential of the XGA. It deals with the XGA at the register level as well as at the Adapter Interface level. It is rich in examples and sample source code. It is likely to become a thumb-worn reference on the desks of its owners.

To understand the XGA, one must first recall a little history of IBM's graphics adapters. In 1982, IBM introduced the Color Graphics Adapter (CGA), which was capable of a 320x200 resolution with four colors. IBM's second PC color graphics adapter, the Enhanced Graphics Adapter (EGA), was introduced in 1985 as a successor to the CGA. EGA expanded the resolution to 640x350 with sixteen colors. In 1987, IBM introduced Video Graphics Array (VGA), and made it standard on all the Personal System/2 (PS/2) platforms. VGA supported 640x480 resolution with sixteen colors, but became more significant for two other reasons. First, IBM made it resident on PS/2 system boards, giving all PS/2 users this graphics capability as part of their system. Second, VGA arrived at a time when the industry was deciding what was to follow the earlier adapters. VGA caught on and soon became a standard within the industry.

In 1990, IBM introduced XGA as its strategic graphics interface and successor to VGA. XGA also arrived at a time when the industry had been wrestling with a number of Super VGA modes, none of which has emerged as a standard. We believe that XGA is on its way to becoming pervasive in the industry.

Our experience with the 8514/A convinced us to publish the hardware register set for the XGA adapter. At the same time, we have continued to support the Adapter Interface to maintain compatibility with those applications written to it. But access to the hardware registers offers the opportunity to fully exploit performance. To clearly signal its intentions, IBM built the XGA into the system board in the PS/2 Model 90 XP/486 desktop system, in addition to providing the XGA graphics adapter card as a standard feature in the PS/2 Model 95 XP/486. Furthermore, the adapter card is sold as an option for upgrading PS/2 systems using 80386 processors.

To further promote the XGA as an industry standard, we have licensed its technology to several marketing and development partners. We are also actively supporting Independent Software Vendor (ISV) porting of their products to the XGA. And we are continuing to develop enhanced versions of it.

Recognizing the strong momentum of its VCGA predecessor, we ensured that XGA provided VGA hardware register capability, along with the new XGA high-resolution extended graphics modes. In addition, a 132-column text mode has been provided. These modes are all present in our XGA chip set.

The Extended Graphics modes of the XGA offer high resolution and lots of colors. The XGA provides resolutions up to 640x480 with 65,536 colors (16-bit direct color mode) and 1024x768 with 256 colors. With 64K colors available at the 640x480 resolution, photo-realistic images can be displayed.

Another significant benefit of the XGA is the hardware drawing assist capability in extended graphics modes. The XGA has a hardware graphics coprocessor to provide drawing assist functions. The hardware drawing assist functions are optimized for the OS/2 Presentation Manager and the Microsoft Windows windowing environments. These environments move large blocks of pixels around on the screen frequently in operations called Block Transfers (BitBLT). The XGA coprocessor has a hardware BitBLT function, which significantly increases screen performance that is readily apparent to the user. Two other major windowing functions, Line Drawing and Area Fill, have also been built into the XGA coprocessor hardware.

Jake Richter has provided a comprehensive reference for XGA video, and we believe this to be an important contribution to graphics literature. It is complementary to our efforts to make the XGA the graphics standard of choice in our industry.

Paul C. Mugge
Vice President, Systems and Technology
Entry Systems Technology
IBM Personal Systems Line of Business
Boca Raton, Florida

Preface

(Or, Why You Should Buy and Read This Book)

The purpose of this book is to provide, in one place, a complete reference to the IBM eXtended Graphics Array (or just **XGA**). The XGA seems destined to be one of only a couple of new PC graphics standards, and as such, will play an important role in the evolution of PC graphics hardware and software.

Included in this book are chapters about the history of the PC graphics industry, the evolution of the XGA, XGA architectural information, and extensive information on how to program the XGA, via both the hardware registers and the Adapter Interface. These later chapters offer both reference and tutorial information. Finally, full documentation of the recently passed VESA XGA Extensions standard is also provided.

You have the option of purchasing this book with a disk, which contains copies of all the source code, and includes files shown in this book.

The reference material presented here is oriented toward two groups:

- The marketer or analyst who needs technical insight into the current state of the PC, and, more specifically, needs to know more about the IBM XGA and its place in the PC graphics marketplace.

- The engineer/programmer who wishes to: (a) write device drivers that use the XGA, (b) write custom software that needs to access the XGA, and/or (c) understand the capabilities of the XGA in order to design software that can take proper advantage of its advanced features.

Introduction

Welcome to *Power Programming the IBM XGA*! This is the second book I've written about advanced PC graphics standards, in an effort to educate programmers everywhere about the exciting potential offered by hardware level graphics control. The first book, *Graphics Programming for the 8514/A*, unveiled the mysteries of the IBM 8514/A—mysteries because IBM had decided not to reveal the hardware specifications of the 8514/A.

With the XGA, IBM changed its position and offered technical documentation right off the bat. This means that the information in this book originated with the developer of the XGA architecture, but is presented here in a much more readable and usable format.

The XGA plays an important role in the evolution of PC graphics, and many companies are betting that the XGA will be the successor to the empire built by Super VGA boards over the past several years. This comes after some of these companies invested heavily and somewhat unsuccessfully in graphics board ventures based on 8514/A, TIGA (Texas Instrument Graphics Architecture), and proprietary graphics chip technologies. Considering, however, that Super VGA technology is peaking, and in some ways is even evolving into XGA-like realms, the bet that XGA will become a dominant force is probably a good one.

This book is meant to give you the complete XGA picture, from the origin of the XGA architecture as part of IBM's RS/6000 workstations, to its eventual cloning by over a half-dozen companies. More important, all technical information necessary to program an XGA-based device is contained herein, along with detailed tutorials that will show you how to access almost any portion of the XGA architecture.

What You Need

The largest audience for this book will be the programmer or engineer who wants to put an XGA-based device through its paces—be it through a driver, a fractal program, or a high-level application. As such, this book provides a lot of source code to allow you to play with XGA functions. This code has been developed and tested with Microsoft C version 5.1, and Microsoft Assembler (MASM) version 5.0. The environment used is real mode MS-DOS. So, if you plan to write some XGA programs based on the example this book, make sure you have development tools compatible with those listed above.

You can also benefit from this book even if you are not an avid programmer. If you are a software designer, this book can help you to analyze the graphics hardware capabilities your applications may start to depend upon in new PCs, including hardware clipping, masks, multiple pixel depths, and more. If you are an analyst or marketer, this book will help give you insight into current PC graphics technology, as well as trends that govern the graphics industry.

The Layout of This Book

To give you a better idea of where you might want to turn to first, let me provide you with a brief layout of the book.

The book is broken into three major sections. The first section, covering chapters 1 through 3, contains an overview of the XGA, including history, current market conditions, architecture, use in different environments and operating systems, and, finally, a look at the future of XGA.

The second section contains all the programming information. There are three sets of chapters in the second section. The first provides a tutorial on the XGA register set, as well as a register reference. The second does the same for the Adapter Interface. And the third provides some information on accessing the XGA in non–real mode DOS environments. (Additionally, Appendix B covers the VESA XGA Extensions standard.)

The last section of the book is a mishmash of reference, and includes about a dozen appendices, containing company addresses, program listings, register listings, function comparisons, and more. Also provided in the last section are an index and an extensive glossary of the terms used in this book.

So, if you want just the techie stuff, skip directly to chapters 2 and 8, which talk about the XGA architecture and use in different operating systems, and then continue on to the second section, which starts with Chapter 4 and XGA register information.

If you want background on the XGA, just start at the beginning.

Who Is the Author?

I am Jake Richter, a man with too many hats. Probably the biggest hat I wear is that of chief technologist of Panacea Inc., which is a midsized company that develops utility software and drivers that take advantage of the graphics hardware capabilities of PCs.

I also write for a variety of publications, ranging from the now-defunct *Programmer's Journal* and *Personal Workstation,* to *InfoWorld, PC Magazine, BYTE,* and *Computer Buying World.* My articles are almost always oriented toward PC graphics, in some form or other. Another hat I wear is that of a director of VESA, the Video Electronics Standards Association (about which you can read in Appendix B).

My involvement with the XGA started about six months before it was announced by IBM, which contacted Panacea about writing an AutoCAD driver for the XGA. After coming to an agreement, we developed a driver that directly accessed the XGA registers, and provided significant performance. Since then, we've written several more XGA-based drivers, including ones for AutoShade 2 w/RenderMan, 3D Studio, and Animator Pro. I am also involved in the VESA XGA technical committee, and have written several articles on XGA. The ultimate result of my XGA work is this book.

I try to make myself reasonably accessible, so if you have any questions, please feel free to contact me through (listed in order of preference): BIX or MCI Mail (ID: jrichter), America On-Line (ID: PanacJake), CompuServe (ID: 75130,2705), or U.S. Mail (Panacea Inc., P.O. Box 940, Londonderry, NH 03053-3376). Please provide some background on your question, and please do not phone, as your message will likely end up in among the other several dozen phone messages I receive every day, and thus I will not likely be able to answer your questions in a timely fashion.

Chapter 1

The Birth of PC Graphics Standards

O n October 30, 1990, three and a half years after introducing both the VGA (Video Graphics Array) and 8514/A graphics standards, IBM finally unveiled its next generation of PS/2 graphics hardware, namely the XGA (eXtended Graphics Array).

In this chapter, I'll give you a glimpse of how the PC graphics hardware industry has evolved, starting with the original PCs, and ending with a look at current technology and the XGA's place in the market.

Why Read This Chapter If You're a Programmer?

Although this chapter doesn't contain any real programming information, it should help give you a better idea of how new PC graphics hardware is developed in response to market trends, and how good graphic hardware can fail due to bad packaging. Since history does repeat itself, analyzing past trends helps give us insights into future developments, thereby allowing us to design software with the future in mind.

Why Do We Even Need Graphics?

Perhaps the most important component of any computer system is its output subsystem, whether it be a monitor, printer, paper tape, or computer cards. Without an output subsystem, a computer is almost useless because you cannot see the data produced by an application. The lack of output subsystems would also make it rather difficult to develop these applications in the first place.

Thus, we could infer that visually representing computer-generated data is second in importance only to the performance/productivity boost provided by using a computer. This visualization of data ranges from the output of spreadsheet information and the odds on the latest sports events, to the display of computer-generated photo-realistic images.

With the arrival of the first mass-market personal computers, more than a dozen years ago, graphical representation of data became easy to accomplish and afford. Unfortunately, these first PCs achieved resolutions of only 128x48 or 160x100. But over the ensuing years, PC graphics hardware technology has made large strides, making the PC a viable alternative to mainframes, minis, and even workstations in the graphical visualization of information.

In the Beginning (Before IBM's PC)...

First there were expensive, obscure, and cumbersome display systems. Then, in the late 1970s, the personal computer market was born, with the entry of mass-marketable computers from a number of companies, notably Apple Computer Corp., Radio Shack, and Commodore Business Machines (CBM). This new PC market also brought about the wide use of low-cost graphics displays.

These first mass-market display systems only sported resolutions of 128x48 or 160x100, and only in monochrome or a small number of colors. Nonetheless, the arrival of these machines caused an explosion in third-party hardware and software add-ons. This, in turn, increased sales of all products, computers and add-ons alike, thereby further reducing price and increasing both acceptance and proliferation of PC graphics.

Other companies—such as Ohio Scientific, CompuColor, SOL, and Exidy—helped contribute to the growth of the PC mass-market, often with excellent (for that time period) graphics, but Apple, Radio Shack, and CBM were the largest sellers. Each had a different approach toward desktop computing and displays; let's examine each briefly to see how it helped to shaped the industry.

Apple Computer Corp.

Apple approached the masses with graphics in 1978 with the Apple II, which minimized the cost of color graphics by using a standard television as a display device.

With its open architecture and color-display capability, the Apple II quickly grew to be the machine of choice for home computer hobbyists. Soon, composite video monitors appeared for the Apple II, refining the output quality, but not the resolution.

The graphics board was soon released as an additional hardware enhancement for the Apple II. Some of these boards were "Slot 7" RGB-output boards (hence the birth of Video Seven, one of the larger VGA-board companies around today), which allowed Apple II users to use the crisper TTL RGB monitors, but did not actually change the resolution. Other boards, such as those from Number Nine, increased the number of colors available from 8 to 256, while also increasing the output resolution and providing output to an analog RGB monitor.

Apple then released a new machine aimed at business users. The Apple III provided improved graphics, but because of the Apple II's reputation as a hobbyist's machine, the Apple III gained little business-community support and eventually flopped.

The next Apple machine was the Lisa, a high-resolution (back then) monochrome system with the first affordable Graphical User Interface (GUI). Unfortunately, the Lisa was rather bulky and expensive, and thus, Apple failed to gain entry into the business market a second time.

After the Lisa came the Macintosh. The Mac, as it became known, gained great support because of its small size, lower cost, and GUI. The Mac became an overnight success, appealing to people who didn't want to use the less-than-intuitive MS-DOS interface.

The Mac gained graphics hardware add-ins early on, as developers saw the need for full-page displays to aid in desktop publishing. Color displays were not far behind; Apple introduced its own, concurrent with the Mac II. The real benefit of the Mac was that the software effort was minimal; once the graphics board was integrated into the system, any Mac application would be able to run on it automatically.

The Mac has gained the leading position among PC graphics artists and desktop publishers. Applications such as True Color editing, color pre-press, and multimedia are commonplace among today's Mac users. And, as the base systems evolve with more powerful processors and add-in boards, photo-realistic rendering is becoming popular as well. But, as we'll see later in this chapter, the PC, combined with Microsoft Windows, is rapidly invading the niche markets previously held only by the Mac.

Commodore Business Machines

CBM introduced the PET, a one-piece system with an odd keyboard, in 1977. With its integrated monochrome display, it was able to display primitive character-based graphics. But the PET did not have enough support to sustain ongoing development, and it soon faded out of the picture.

Commodore tried again, introducing the CBM, a machine oriented toward small business. Because of the reputation the company earned with the PET, the CBM quickly failed.

Commodore then tackled a virtually untapped market: the low-end (under $300) home computer market. This market was dominated by video game units like the Atari 2600, and as yet was free of real computers. However, the low-end home market did have some pretty severe media requirements, such as lots of colors, good animation performance, and high-quality sound. Commodore's VIC-20 was the first computer to enter the low-end home market; its popularity was soon followed by the raging success of the Commodore 64 (C64).

In 1985—this time with the Amiga—Commodore again tried to enter the business market, and again failed. The game-playing image inspired by the C64 prevented Commodore from tapping into the more serious market; the Amiga did not flop, however. Instead, as the only machine with true multi-tasking, a color GUI, and phenomenal color, animation, and sound capabilities, it went on to capture the hearts and minds of a small set of users who gave it strong grass-roots support.

The Amiga has evolved into a true multimedia platform, and even today accomplishes things that still cannot easily be matched on either the PC or Mac without spending thousands of extra dollars. Newtek's VideoToaster is a shining example of these Amiga-specific capabilities.

Radio Shack/Tandy

Radio Shack's TRS-80 Model I, introduced in 1978, had a monochrome display and could support a graphics resolution of 128x48 using character graphics. Though it was not a spectacular machine, the TRS-80 shipped in large numbers because every one of the thousands of Radio Shack stores in the world carried them.

Like Apple and Commodore, Radio Shack tried to enter the business world with the TRS-80 Model II, a one-piece integrated unit with a high-resolution monochrome display and no backward compatibility with the Model I. The Model II was not a total flop, but it failed to entrench itself in the business world.

Radio Shack next introduced the Model III, which was basically an ergonomic Model I. Also, in trying to compete with Apple in the educational market and Commodore in the home market, Radio Shack introduced its Color Computer, known to aficionados as the CoCo.

The CoCo was Radio Shack's first color-capable computer, using a TV as a display. And again, because of Radio Shack's wide distribution network, the CoCo ended up in many households, but somehow still failed to get into the educational market.

Since the business market proved difficult for Radio Shack to break into, the company decided to shift its whole high-end computer product line over to the Tandy brand name. With this transition, the first new Tandy machine was the Tandy 2000, an IBM PC "wannabe." The Tandy 2000 offered superior graphics capability, but because it was not 100 percent IBM compatible, its success was limited.

Learning its lesson, Tandy developed the Tandy 1000 and 1200 product lines, the former of which is still being sold and offers better graphics and sound capability. Tandy systems now offer VGA capabilities as a base.

The Third Wave—IBM

If the first real wave of personal computers were the home-brew, home-built Altair and Imsai class of computers; the second wave was the one just described (Apple, Commodore, and Radio Shack); the third wave, therefore, must be the one created by IBM.

This latest computer revolution (though most people these days seem not to be aware of the earlier ones) began in 1981, when the IBM PC was introduced. Finally, a solid product was available from a company respected in the business community. Where Apple had failed with the Apple III, Radio Shack with the Model II, and Commodore with the CBM, IBM succeeded beyond even IBM's wildest hopes.

The early IBM PCs were not very impressive, graphically speaking. They were available only with a monochrome display (the Monochrome Display Adapter, or MDA) that had no graphics capability. IBM soon added a color display, the Color Graphics Adapter (CGA), capable of four colors at a resolution of 320x200, or two colors at 640x200.

IBM followed Apple's lead in providing an open architecture, and thus garnered a large amount of third-party support. Among the innovators supporting the IBM PC were several graphics hardware companies, including Plantronics and Hercules.

Plantronics created a CGA-compatible graphics board capable of 16 colors at 320x200 (the company left the PC graphics market in 1984, and is now a leading provider of hands-free phone headsets).

Hercules saw the gap that IBM left in the monochrome market by not providing graphics capability with the MDA, and produced the Hercules Monochrome Graphics Controller (MGC). The MGC board produced a graphics resolution of 720x348, using the existing IBM MDAs—the display with which most early IBM PCs were shipped. The MGC was a big hit, and is still the standard monochrome graphics adapter for PCs.

Other companies introduced "pseudocolor" (8-bit per pixel/256 color) and "true color" (24-bit) add-in boards around the same time.

The growth in the graphics hardware add-on market, both then and now, has been limited by the MS-DOS environment and the lack of a uniform interface. Traditionally, PC graphics-display subsystems have been geared toward specific environments or applications, such as AutoCAD or Ventura Publisher. An additional problem with these niche-market products was that they commanded a high price, usually for a board/ monitor combination. Acceptance of any of these high-end graphics hardware products as a standard was impossible because virtually no graphics hardware product was compatible with any other.

In 1984, IBM introduced the Enhanced Graphics Adapter (EGA), a 640x350, 16-color TTL (Transistor-Transistor Logic) display system, designed as a substantial upgrade to the CGA. Around the same time, IBM also introduced the Professional Graphics Controller (PGC), capable of 640x480 by 256 colors. The PGC, based on an Intel 8088 chip, was IBM's answer to the third-party high-end graphics board market. The EGA was a big success, but the PGC was not. Though it was one of the first intelligent PC graphics controllers on the market, its performance and resolution did not justify its substantially higher cost to business users.

The success of the EGA could be attributed to its lower price and better resolution; all the hardware developers started cloning it, thereby helping to make it a mass-market standard. Most of the cloners also took pains to "one-up" the others by offering EGA extensions, such as resolutions of 640x480 and 800x600. These higher resolutions would not have been possible without the release of NEC's MultiSync monitor, however. The MultiSync and its clones, capable of both TTL and analog operation, opened the gate for affordable higher resolution mass-market display systems.

Higher resolution display systems started appearing for CAD and DTP. PC CAD color graphics boards with resolutions of 1024x768 and 1280x1024 became common, as did full-page and dual-page monochrome monitors with a resolution of 1600x1200. Also, the TARGA (**T**ruevision **A**dvanced **R**aster **G**raphics **A**dapter) board made its debut, offering video capture and overlay capability at 16 bits per pixel. Many of these graphics devices were based on intelligent or semi-intelligent controllers, such as the NEC 7220, Hitachi ACRTC, TI 32010 DSP, Intel 82786, AMD QPDM, and TI 34010.

Unfortunately, the leaps in graphics board technology generally were not followed by similar leaps in software applications. Software applications just were not sophisticated enough to take full advantage of these powerful graphics devices.

Meanwhile, IBM was trying to catch up with the enhancements others made to its EGA standard, and introduced the Video Graphics Array (VGA) in 1987. The VGA sported a resolution of 640x480 at 16 colors on an analog RGB monitor. The VGA was also able to display 256 colors in a 320x200 resolution, and was built into the motherboard of the new MCA (**M**icro **C**hannel **A**rchitecture)—based PS/2 system. This was a first for IBM, which had traditionally sold video display systems as options.

The VGA followed in the footsteps of the EGA by being widely cloned and enhanced. Initially, resolutions of 800x600 by 16 colors were added, followed by 1024x768 at 16 colors, and then by numerous 256 color modes. Currently, Super VGAs, as they're called, sport resolutions as high as 1280x1024 at 16 colors, 1024x768 at 256 colors, and 800x600 at 32,768 colors.

Simultaneous with the introduction of the VGA, IBM unveiled the 8514/A graphics adapter, an option board apparently targeted as a competitor to the high-end CAD and DTP boards that had been on the market for a while. A flaw in this approach was that the 8514/A used an interlaced display, causing annoying flicker in CAD packages—a serious shortcoming.

The 8514/A could support resolutions up to 1024x768 by 256 colors, and was the first IBM graphics board to use VRAM (**V**ideo **RAM**) in its design. The 8514/A was based on a proprietary graphics coprocessor that allowed applications to tell it to draw lines, fill rectangles, and perform copies of image data. Unfortunately, IBM never disclosed the low-level register information for the 8514/A. Instead, the company chose to provide a software interface, called the Adapter Interface (AI), which was designed to make applications portable across both the 8514/A and future IBM graphics products.

The 8514/A wasn't in quite the same situation as the VGA as far as popularity and cloning. A number of companies tried to clone it, but were not successful, and to date only a handful of 8514/A clones have made it to market.

About two years after the introduction of the VGA and 8514/A, IBM unveiled its Image Adapter/A, an expensive, high-end graphics board. It was initially used for graphical document processing operations, and subsequently used for other imaging and graphical applications. The Image Adapter/A is based on a RISC (Reduced Instruction Set Computer) engine, similar in nature to TI's 34010, but, as with the IBM 8514/A, no detailed programming specifications were made available, with the exception of an AI for the board.

Then, in late 1990, IBM announced the XGA as its latest and greatest graphics standard. The XGA provides no greater resolution than the 8514/A, but has an integrated VGA mode, something the 8514/A lacked. Additionally, the XGA supports bus-master access on an MCA bus. The XGA also marks the first time that IBM has shipped drivers for third-party applications with its graphics platforms. The drivers shipped are for OS/2 Presentation Manager, Microsoft Windows (both 2.1 and 3.0), AutoCAD (developed by Panacea), and an AI interface. Essentially, the XGA is the result of blending the 8514/A and VGA technologies together, and then tossing in some additional functionality.

A number of companies have already quietly indicated that they are cloning the XGA, and since they have experience with both 8514/A and VGA, they should have an easier time of it. Among the companies that have made their XGA efforts public are Cirrus Logic, ULSI, and Integrated Information Technology.

Additionally, IBM has licensed the XGA technology to both Inmos/SGS-Thomson and Intel Corp., with SGS offering repackaged IBM XGA silicon, and Intel providing derivative products, such as a local bus XGA chipset.

Other Forces in PC Graphics

Though IBM's graphics products were the catalysts for new mass-market graphics standards, other companies were also trying to gain entry in the PC graphics hardware market in an attempt to form standards, or at least make a lot of money. Much of this activity started in the high end of the graphics market, but with the ever increasing niche-oriented demands of the high end, companies have started targeting their products more and more toward the mass market.

Texas Instruments

Most formidable of these graphics hardware forces is Texas Instruments (TI). In the early days of the PC graphics controller chip market, there was quite a bit of competition between companies like Intel, TI, AMD, NEC, and Hitachi. Some of the products had bugs, others were poorly supported. The net result was that TI came out on top, with its 34010 graphics system processor (GSP).

The TI 34010 GSP is a full processor with additional built-in graphics functions. This means that it can run standalone software without the intervention of the PC's CPU. This can be valuable in applications where multi-processing is required, but can significantly increase the complexity of supporting a more generic application.

To aid developers in supporting its graphics processors, Texas Instruments developed the TIGA (TI Graphics Architecture) software interface, which serves three purposes:

1. It allows software developers to write applications and drivers that will work across a wide range of graphics boards that are quite different from one another, and most likely completely incompatible.

2. Because TIGA is a standard interface, application developers can ship TIGA drivers for their applications, which in turn makes TIGA more of a standard.

3. TIGA is designed to be both portable and extensible. In theory and in practice, this allows developers to build code that will not have to change every few months in order to support a new TI 340x0–based graphics board.

With the help of good timing, a more solid product than the competition's, and TIGA, TI has remained virtually the sole supplier of advanced graphics silicon to the PC graphics industry.

In 1990, TI released a next-generation part, the 34020. The 34020 has started to appear on a rather large number of graphics boards, some of which are relatively inexpensive (as little as $795). Many companies that have had 34010 technology have migrated to the 34020 as a replacement, both to preserve margins and to gain the performance necessary to compete with newer fixed-function graphics coprocessors, such as the XGA and S3's 86C911.

Another reason for the recent spate of TI 34010/34020–based boards is the release of Microsoft Windows 3.1, which now has hooks that allow intelligent graphics boards to more completely utilize on-board memory for caching graphical data. Windows 3.1 also offers built-in TIGA support. Up until the recent Windows boom, most of the 340x0 boards were focused almost exclusively on supporting high-end CAD applications, and as such were high-price/low-volume.

The latest trend in TI 34020–based graphics boards is 24-bit per pixel true color support under Windows, with entries from companies like Truevision, VideoLogic, OPTA, and Number Nine.

Intel's i860

Intel introduced the i860 RISC processor in 1989 and touted it as a graphics engine beyond compare. Basically, Intel was right. The i860 RISC engine has excellent support for graphics operations requiring floating point. Though the i860 is not a great drawing engine, its computational ability is outstanding, especially in the areas of ray tracing, photo-realistic rendering, and shading.

Unfortunately, the i860 has had a difficult time entering the PC marketplace. Companies like IBM, Matrox, and Truevision have all introduced i860 processor cards, but with limited success. Part of the i860's problem in establishing a solid foothold is due to price. Another part is application support—most applications have no way of supporting an external floating-point device, and no i860 design was even remotely compatible with others, disallowing the chance for a TIGA-like interface to come into existence.

Perhaps the final nail in the i860 coffin is the news in March 1992 that Intel is going to halt all further development on the i860, meaning that the technology has come as far as it's going to.

Other Graphics Chips

During the past year, a number of companies have announced fixed-function graphics coprocessors intended to supersede Super VGA technology. The IBM 8514/A could be considered the first serious such product (even though it was announced coincident with the original VGA), with 8514/A clones from Western Digital Imaging, Chips and Technologies, and ATI Technologies. ATI is making quite a bit of headway with its Mach 8 8514/A clone chip, while the other two are struggling with their products.

Next to be released in this arena was the XGA. Its appearance of the XGA implied that the 8514/A was basically a dead product, and ultimately, IBM announced that it would cease shipping its 8514/A board. Companies like ATI were quick to remove the "8514/A" portion of their product name, and equally quick to start touting their products as "Graphics Accelerators" or "GUI Accelerators."

The argument for the label offered by companies with "GUI accelerators" was that with a few key graphical environments and applications becoming the dominant uses for graphics boards, as long as a given graphics hardware product offered support for these environments, it didn't matter what technology the product was based on. Therefore, the result was that the 8514/A was out, and the GUI accelerator was in.

The first product to be called a GUI accelerator right off the bat was S3's 86C911 (which, by the way, was code-named "Carrera" after the original Porsche 911). The '911 has had an amazing number of design wins. Within two months after it started shipping in small volumes, S3 had signed up over 40 customers to ship '911–based graphics boards. The performance of the '911–based products is quite respectable, but more important, the '911 has one important feature the 8514/A (and its clones) lacked: built-in VGA support.

Other accelerated VGAs/GUI accelerator chips have been announced by Western Digital Imaging (the 90C31), Avance Logic (the GUIEngine), Primus Technologies (the P2000), Trident (the GUI9400), and Tseng Labs (the ET4000-32X).

Why this sudden plethora of accelerated graphics solutions? It all has to do with resolution.

1024x768: The Up and Coming Resolution of Choice

With the high-end board market, the lowest common resolution among TI 340X0–based and similar graphics controllers appears to be 1024x768. Many TI boards run at 1280x1024, 1600x1200, or even 2048x2048, however. Once the resolution goes beyond 1024x768, display subsystem costs increase rapidly. Though you should be able to purchase a good 1024x768 monitor for well under $1000, a decent 1280x1024 monitor will run much closer to $2000. The same price disparity exists among graphics controllers.

From the other end of the spectrum, almost all Super VGAs are supporting a maximum resolution of 1024x768, with prices as low as $145 for a Super VGA capable of 1024x768 by 256 non-interlaced colors. This means you can purchase a full 1024x768 display subsystem (board and monitor) for just under $1000. This would tend to imply that the mass-market is heading toward a standard resolution of 1024x768, because once higher-end graphics solutions break the $1000 barrier from above (while maintaining backward compatibility), they usually become a standard within a short period of time. This is what helped both the EGA and VGA succeed initially.

I should point out that 1024x768 may not be the resolution of choice for niche markets, however. In many cases, these niche markets require higher resolutions in order to accomplish their tasks. Also, workstation vendors seem to have standardized 1280x1024 as the resolution for much of the color work on which their users focus.

However, higher resolution isn't necessarily all it's made out to be, because there is a hidden cost involved—namely, performance. As you increase the resolution of a system, you also increase the amount of data that has to be manipulated for the display of graphics. For example, a 640x480 VGA display, at 4 bits per pixel (16 colors), requires 153,600 bytes. If you go up to 1024x768 at 8 bpp, your display requires 786,432 bytes, more than five times the amount of the 640x480 display. This means that screen updates that occupy proportionally equal portions of the screen will require the system's CPU to do five times as much work, and hence take five times as much time.

Accelerated graphics hardware is the solution to this overhead dilemma. By off-loading some of the processing, such as line drawing, rectangle fills, block copies, and related graphics functions onto a device that can handle such things more efficiently than a general-purpose processor, you can dramatically speed up your graphics throughput. This becomes extremely useful as your resolution increases, both in the X and Y directions, as well as in color depth. Hence the appearance of nearly a dozen graphics accelerator chips on the market. And many of these chips support resolutions from 640x480 to 1280x1024, thereby filling demand in both the mass market and niche markets.

Other Types of Accelerators

One common fallacy is that you need acceleration hardware to increase your system's graphics throughput. This is only half right—you also need well-written software. For example, my company has made its mark on the PC industry because it develops and markets high-performance, software-only accelerators for AutoCAD and Windows. The "software-only accelerators" do require certain types of graphics hardware to function, but the key here is that intelligently written, well-tuned driver software (which is basically what our accelerators are) can make an enormous difference in graphics performance. And when you combine good driver software with a good graphics accelerator, you have a hell of a high performance graphics solution.

What We Have Learned from History

Perhaps the most important thing to be learned from the success and failure of various graphics architectures and devices is that compatibility—especially backward compatibility—is crucial. The sales of 8514/A clones did not pick up until companies started to add VGA compatibility to their boards. The so-called "GUI accelerators" learned that lesson well, as did IBM with the XGA, and TI has made decent inroads in providing cross-vendor compatibility with TIGA.

Another important thing is that the best graphics product in the world will fail if it's packaged and/or marketed incorrectly—witness the Apple III, the Amiga, and similar products. On the marketing side, which sells better these days: an 8514/A board or a GUI accelerator, even though both are exactly the same piece of hardware? (Hint: it's the one without the numbers)

For the PC side of the market, if IBM introduces a graphics standard, someone is bound to clone it and make it more of a standard. Unfortunately, in the cloning process, companies usually add additional functions that create long-term incompatibilities.

VESA: Shaping the Future

The future is certainly promising, because the number of graphics coprocessors coming out in the next year, both XGA clones and proprietary solutions, is rather large (nearly a dozen), which means more competition, and hence lower prices and better performance potential.

However, without some cooperation between these various graphics silicon companies in creating a baseline of compatibility in these products, it will be more difficult to sell them. Fortunately, this cooperation has started to take place. The Video Electronics Standards Association (VESA) was formed in 1989 to come up with standard display timing information for an 800x600 resolution. Since its inception, VESA has created nearly a dozen standards, ranging from monitor timings, to 8514/A register definitions, to a universal Super VGA software interface mechanism called VBE (VGA BIOS Extension).

So what does this all have to do with the XGA and the proprietary solutions?

The VBE is in the process of being further extended to encompass the capabilities of the new breed of XVGA products, while VESA's XGA Extensions Committee has produced a new standard called VXE 1.0 (**VESA XGA Extensions**), which allows the XGA to exist in ISA and EISA environments and allows software to more generically locate and use XGAs in all PC bus environments (the full text of the standard can be found in Appendix B).

Additionally, by the time you read this, VESA should have formalized the next epoch in high performance graphics, namely "local bus," which is a new bus tied in directly to the PC's CPU. By using a local bus interface, graphics hardware can eliminate the bandwidth problems incurred by traditional bus designs (such as ISA, MCA, and EISA), improving data transfer rates by as much as two hundred times. VESA's initial effort involves designing a standard connector for local bus support. Once such a connector is designed, motherboard and systems manufacturers can incorporate it into their hardware, while graphics board companies can design boards to use the local bus connector. It'll be a while before this interface becomes pervasive, but with its memory mapped architecture, the XGA architecture is an ideal fit for local bus.

The most remarkable thing about VESA is that it consists primarily of companies that are direct competitors, but that, under the guidance of VESA, work together to set standards for the industry.

One Final Thought

No matter what graphics device you support with your software, be it a proprietary solution or an XGA-compatible (I hope it's the latter, since you're reading this), make sure to write tight, solid, efficient, fast code. Hardware can only do so much.

Chapter 2

XGA: An Overview

Just as the VGA was shipped standard with the newly announced PS/2 systems back in 1987, the XGA is now shipped as the default graphics display platform with a number of IBM PS/2s, including the Model 90 XP 486, Model 95 XP 486, and Model 57SLC. In the desktop models 90 and 57, the XGA is on the motherboard, while in the Model 95—a tower unit—it is on a separate Micro Channel Architecture (MCA) add-in board. The board is also available for other 386– and 486–based PS/2s as the XGA Display Adapter/A.

Having the XGA replace VGA as a default graphics platform was a remarkable move for IBM. While rumors a in the late 1980s had been rampant about IBM implementing its 8514/A advanced graphics technology on PS/2 motherboards, the 8514/A lacked one major feature necessary for this to occur: backward compatibility. The XGA has full VGA hardware compatibility, thus eliminating this problem, and hence it's suitable for a motherboard implementation. In some ways, the XGA is a merger between the VGA and 8514/A graphics platforms.

Table 2.1 shows a feature comparison of the several mass-market graphics hardware platforms demonstrating how the XGA has evolved.

Table 2.1. Feature comparison of IBM-originated mass-market PC graphics standards.

	Resolution	Interlaced at 1024x768	Base compatibility	Graphics co-processor	Memory-mapped frame buffer	Works in 80286 and 8088 systems	RAM type
PS/2 VGA	640x480x16/256 320x200x256	N/A	VGA	No	Yes	Yes	DRAM
Super VGA	800x600x16/256 1024x768x16/256	No[1]	VGA	No	Yes	Yes	DRAM[2]
8514/A	640x480x16/256 1024x768x16/256	Yes[3]	None[4]	Yes	No	Yes	VRAM[5]
XGA	640x480x2/4/16/ 256/65536 1024x768x2/4/16/ 256	Yes[6]	VGA	Yes	Yes	No[7]	VRAM

1. Some Super VGAs are still interlaced at only 1024x768, though most allow you to switch between interlaced and non-interlaced.

2. A small handful of Super VGAs use VRAM instead of DRAM

3. Clone 8514/As offer 1024x768 non-interlaced.

4. VGA compatibility is achieved via a pass-through, requiring an actual VGA to still exist separately from the 8514/A.

5. ATI's Graphics Vantage is a DRAM based 8514/A clone.

6. The new IBM XGA NI and clone XGAs offer 1024x768 non-interlaced support.

7. Some clone XGAs will work in less than a 386SX.

There are several features that distinguish the XGA from other graphics hardware platforms. Among them are that it:

- Supports resolutions of 640x480 and 1024x768 at 2, 4, 16, and 256 colors, and 640x480 with 65,536 colors.
- Is compatible with all existing PS/2 monitors.
- Has a memory mapped interface and a frame buffer.
- Is compatible with 8514/A only via AI, not via the registers.
- Is 100 percent VGA compatible.
- Has a special 132-column VGA text mode.
- Has a sprite/hardware cursor of 64x64 pixels.
- Has bus-mastering capabilities.
- Works only in 386 and 486 systems.
- Is standard in new PS/2 Models 90 and 95.
- Has a base VRAM of 512KB, expandable to 1MB.

Furthermore, up to eight XGAs can be used in one system. Register specifications are available from IBM.

Where Does the XGA Come From?

The XGA was developed at IBM's Hursley Labs, in the United Kingdom, just like the 8514/A and the niche-oriented Image Adapter/A. It is therefore not surprising that the XGA maintains many of the features of the 8514/A in its design, although it accesses these features in a very different fashion. It is interesting to note that portions of the XGA can be found in the IBM RS/6000's graphics subsystem.

Some of the XGA's new features, such as bus-mastering, are designed to take advantage of the Micro Channel bus, standard in most PS/2s. Other features, such as a memory mapped frame buffer and hardware cursor, provide greater flexibility over existing designs while at the same time easing the burden for software developers. Another boon to software developers is that IBM has released full register specifications for the XGA. Also, an Adapter Interface (AI) comes with the XGA, to provide backward compatibility for applications that supported the 8514/A via this software interface.

Technicalities

VGA compatibility is only one of the three distinct modes of the XGA. The other two modes are a 132-column VGA-compatible text mode, and the extended graphics mode. The extended graphics mode is the most interesting of the three, since it is the one that provides higher resolutions and substantial graphics acceleration.

VGA Mode

In addition to maintaining full compatibility with the VGA standard it originally created, IBM learned some lessons from the vast number of VGA clones out there, and implemented a larger data path. The VGA portion of the XGA, though it still has only an 8 bit internal data path, supports a 32 bit wide bus, as well as an internal write cache that allows the chip to break down and write the bus data without holding up the rest of the system with unnecessary wait states. According to IBM documents, the XGA in VGA mode is up to 90 percent faster than the original VGA under DOS, and up to 50 percent faster under Windows.

Except for performance improvements, there is no change in VGA functionality in this mode. It is important to note, however, that while you can have up to eight XGAs in one system (the configuration software will support only up to six, however), you can have only one VGA active in the system at any one time. This means that if you switch an XGA into VGA mode, you must ensure that no other VGA is active in the system, otherwise the system might crash due to the I/O conflicts.

132-Column Text Mode

This mode is a VGA extension that allows you to display (and manipulate) 132 characters per line of text on the screen. The character width is 8 pixels, for a virtual horizontal resolution of 1056. Character height depends on the font used, which means that you can have text screen resolutions of 132x43, 132x50, or even 132x60. Initially, this mode will be accessible only by manually manipulating the XGA registers. Ultimately, however, this mode will be accessible by switching into video mode 14H. Figure 2.1 shows the frame buffer configuration in the 132 column text mode. Note that for all practical purposes, this is still a VGA mode, and the same multiple-VGA caveat applies. (See Appendix M for sample code to allow you to access the 132-column mode.)

Linear Address	Column

```
                              1 1 1 1 1 1 1 1
                              1 2 2 2 2 2 2 3 3
                0 1 2 3 4 5 6 8 9 0...4 5 6 7 8 9 0 1
B8000           CACACACACACACACACACA...CACACACACACACACA  Line 0
B8108           CACACACACACACACACACA...CACACACACACACACA  Line 1
B8210           CACACACACACACACACACA...CACACACACACACACA  Line 2
B8318           CACACACACACACACACACA...CACACACACACACACA  Line 3
B8420           CACACACACACACACACACA...CACACACACACACACA  Line 4
                     .
                     .
                     .
```

C = Character. This is a 1-byte ASCII value.

A = Attribute. This is the standard 1-byte character attribute.

Figure 2.1. Memory layout in 132-column text mode.

Extended Graphics Mode

The extended graphics mode has all of the exciting features—65,536 colors or a resolution of 1024x768, bus-mastering, drawing acceleration, and the hardware cursor. While some limited features of this mode are available in the other modes, most of the XGA registers and functions are for use in the extended graphics mode.

The XGA Registers

The XGA design consists of Video RAM, a type of dual-ported RAM designed for use in graphics display systems; glue logic; and two custom chips. The first chip is the graphics engine, which controls VGA compatibility, drawing functions, and memory management. The second is the display controller, which contains the RAMDAC (RAM Digital to Analog Converter with color look-up table), the CRT controller, hardware cursor support, and a VRAM serializer (a device that extracts data from VRAM for display). These two chips are the core of the XGA architecture.

Access to the XGA is accomplished through two sets of registers. One set is mapped into the system's I/O space, while the other set is mapped into memory. The addresses of these registers varies, primarily due to the configurability of the XGA. This also allows for multiple XGAs in the same system.

The I/O registers are mapped in at hex I/O address $21x0$, where x is the "instance" of the XGA. According to IBM, in systems with only one XGA, the instance is typically 6, resulting in a base I/O address of 0x2160. A list of the I/O registers is provided below.

Address	Register Name
21x0H	Operating Mode Register
21x1H	Aperture Control Register
21x2-3H	Reserved
21x4H	Interrupt Enable Register
21x5H	Interrupt Status Register
21x6H	Virtual Memory Control Register
21x7H	Virtual Memory Interrupt Status Register
21x8H	Aperture Index Register
21x9H	Memory Access Mode Register
21xAH	Index Register
21xB-FH	Data Register (the number of data registers allows for byte, word, or even double-word I/O)

The memory mapped registers occupy 128 bytes of memory in the last kilobyte of an eight KB chunk. This eight kilobyte chunk can reside on an 8K boundary, anywhere between PC addresses 0C0000H and 0DFFFFH. The purpose of having an 8KB chunk is that the first 7KB of the chunk will contain ROM data, but only on an XGA Display Adapter/A. The motherboard implementation of the XGA does not require its own ROM, as the main motherboard ROMs contain all the necessary information, such as initialization code. The location of the 128 bytes within the 8KB chunk is also determined by the XGA instance number. The XGA memory mapped registers are listed on the next page. The size definitions are as follows: BYTE = 1 byte, 8 bits; WORD = two bytes, 16 bits; DWORD = four bytes, 32 bits. Note that all undefined locations are reserved.

Address	Size	Register Name
00H	DWORD	Page Directory Base Address
04H	DWORD	Current Virtual Address
0CH	BYTE	State A Length
0DH	BYTE	State B Length
12H	BYTE	Control Register
13H	BYTE	Pixel Map Index
14H	DWORD	Pixel Map n Base Pointer
18H	WORD	Pixel Map n Width
1AH	WORD	Pixel Map n Height
1CH	BYTE	Pixel Map n Format
20H	WORD	Bresenham Error Term
24H	WORD	Bresenham Constant 1
28H	WORD	Bresenham Constant 2
2CH	DWORD	Short Stroke Register
48H	BYTE	Foreground Mix
49H	BYTE	Background Mix
4AH	BYTE	Color Compare Function
4CH	DWORD	Color Compare Color
50H	DWORD	Plane Mask
54H	DWORD	Carry Chain Mask
58H	DWORD	Foreground Color
5CH	DWORD	Background Color
60H	WORD	Operation Dimension 1 (Width)
62H	WORD	Operation Dimension 2 (Height)
6CH	WORD	Mask Map Origin X Offset
6EH	WORD	Mask Map Origin Y Offset
70H	WORD	Source Map X
72H	WORD	Source Map Y
74H	WORD	Pattern Map X
76H	WORD	Pattern Map Y
78H	WORD	Destination Map X
7AH	WORD	Destination Map Y
7CH	DWORD	Command Register

The I/O registers pertain predominantly to the display controller portion of the XGA, while the memory mapped registers refer primarily to the graphics coprocessor. The base addresses for both registers are set by the POST routines for the XGA, and can be determined by examining the PS/2 POS registers for the XGA in question.

A number of the memory mapped registers are 32 bits in size. This is because the XGA is designed to fit into 32-bit environments, like that of the Intel 386/486. Also, due to the software support IBM developed for the XGA, it will work only in a 386 or 386-based PS/2 (including 386SX based PS/2s). The XGA also offers Motorola format addressing (different byte ordering compared to an Intel format), which would allow a Motorola 68000 or similar processor (such as the RISC processor used in the RS/6000 workstation) to take advantage of the XGA, assuming that the XGA hardware was ported to such a hardware environ.

Using the XGA

There are several key areas of interest in the XGA extended graphics mode:

- Initialization
- The Display Controller—look-up tables and the sprite
- Defining drawing space (bitmaps)
- Drawing
- Task switching

Initialization

All graphics devices must be initialized before use. Initializing the XGA mainly involves setting it for extended graphics mode via the Operating Mode register, then generating the proper CRT control register data for the desired resolution, 640x480 or 1024x768. The table on the next page lists the various resolutions and pixel depths for the XGA in its two memory configurations.

The 16 bit per pixel (65,536 color) resolution provides almost perfect photo-realistic output. This means that you can scan or capture a full-color picture, display it in this 65,536 color mode, and see an almost exact replica on your XGA screen. The 16 bit pixel is laid out as 5 bits of red, 6 bits of green, and 5 bits of blue (5-6-5)—or 32 shades of blue, 64 shades of green, and 32 shades of blue—in each pixel. This varies from the PC standard TARGA format of 5-5-5 (1 bit is used for overlay), as well as the i860 format of 6-6-4. According to sources at IBM, the 5-6-5 approach was used because of similar implementations already in place in various IBM installations. Apparently, the eye is also more sensitive to variations in green than in red and blue. (The reason for the choice of red, green, and blue is that these are the three color guns found in all color monitors. The beams from the three guns combine to display just about any color, depending on the intensity of each gun.)

Resolution (x and y by colors)	512KB VRAM	1MB VRAM
640x480x2	Yes	Yes
640x480x4	Yes	Yes
640x480x16	Yes	Yes
640x480x256	Yes	Yes
640x480x65,536	No	Yes
1024x768x2	Yes	Yes
1024x768x4	Yes	Yes
1024x768x16	Yes	Yes
1024x768x256	No	Yes

The Display Controller

The display controller is used for initialization, but it has other uses as well, including the color look-up table (LUT) and the sprite.

The LUT is used to translate the 1,2,4, or 8 bit pixel value into appropriate R, G, and B values. The pixel value is used as an index into the LUT. The resultant R, G, and B values are then converted from digital levels into analog voltage levels via a built-in DAC. In the case of the XGA, as with the VGA and 8514/A, the LUT supports 64 levels (6 bits) of each primary color, for a grand total of 262,144 possible color combinations, also known as the **palette**. This means that in a 256 color mode, each one of the colors may be chosen from this palette.

The sprite is a 64x64 pixel block that overlays the screen. Each pixel in the sprite has four possible values: sprite color 0, sprite color 1, transparent, and complement. The sprite colors are defined via the Sprite Color *n* R,G,B registers, and passed directly to the DAC. This allows applications to fully modify the local color palette without having to save two entries for the cursor or worry about the cursor changing color as it goes over various portions of the display. The transparency setting allows cursors smaller than 64x64 to be defined; the complement setting is for applications that want cursors that are always visible.

Task Switching

One of the biggest headaches for systems software developers in creating a multitasking environment is saving the current state of the graphics hardware in order to allow another application to take over the graphics device. This state save also has to account for the possibility that the hardware might be in the middle of an operation or a palette update. The XGA was designed with task-switching in mind, because it has extensive facilities for saving and restoring the state of the hardware, including interrupt operations.

Defining Drawing Space

One XGA feature unique among current PC graphics standards is the use of bitmaps, which must be defined in order perform any drawing function. **Bitmaps** are linear regions of memory that are defined with a pixel width, height, and depth (or **bits per pixel**). As such, an 8 bit per pixel bitmap with a width of 10 and a height of 6 lines would require 60 bytes of memory. The last pixel of a given line of the bitmap is directly adjacent in memory with the first pixel in the following line.

The best feature of these bitmaps is that they can exist anywhere in the system's address and memory space. This means that if you define a bitmap that resides in your program's data area, the XGA can draw into it or read from it, saving you the effort of having to copy data to and from the XGA manually (with your system processor). The XGA VRAM is mapped into the system's address space, so when you want to specify it for a bitmap definition, you just need to use its address. The location of the VRAM is usually in the uppermost addresses of the 386/486 4-gigabyte address space, so as a result, there should never be a memory conflict. When the XGA accesses a bitmap, it determines whether the access is local (VRAM) or remote (system). For remote access, it arbitrates for the bus and starts accessing system memory. This is where the XGA's bus-mastering capability comes into play. This also means there is additional overhead in the use of system memory for bitmaps, beyond that for accessing local VRAM; but there are also the performance benefit of having the XGA processor manipulate memory while the system processor is doing something else.

This bus-mastering has some potential pitfalls. The 386 and 486 processors support virtual memory via an internal page-mapping table. The page-mapping table allows control applications, such as expanded memory managers, DOS extenders, and advanced operating systems, to virtualize PC addresses 4 kilobytes (or a page) at a time. So, while software thinks it is writing data to address WWWWW, the page-mapping table might translate that address to the physical address QQQQQ. In many cases, there is no way for an application to know that the address it is using is not the physical address. And, in order to properly bus-master, the XGA requires a physical address. Otherwise it may copy data to or from an incorrect address, and the results may be disastrous. There is a possible solution to this dilemma with some control software environments. If an application has access to the control software's page-mapping table, it can pass this information to the XGA, which will then make use of the page-mapping table and do its own virtual-to-physical address translations. Unfortunately, many control programs and operating systems do not provide access to the page-mapping table, so it's still a long shot. In any case, regular DOS applications have the best chance of being able to utilize the bus-mastering, because the first 640K of memory are generally the least likely to be virtualized. (See the bus mastering section in Chapter 5 for a more detailed discussion.)

In addition to always having the VRAM mapped into very high memory, software can also map the XGA into a 64K bank at either A0000H or B0000H, the standard PC video memory addresses. Accessing different 64K banks in the XGA's VRAM via this approach requires only that an index value be written into the Aperture Index register. This banking mechanism is very handy for real mode applications. Alternately, the whole 1MB chunk of VRAM may be mapped somewhere in the first 16MB of the system's memory, assuming there is no memory conflict. This type of mapping is useful only for protected mode applications.

The XGA has three generic bitmaps available for definition: Maps A, B, and C. These maps are then referenced when drawing commands are executed. The drawing commands may require a source bitmap, which contains the data you want to either copy or use as a tile; a destination bitmap, into which you want to draw or copy data; and a pattern bitmap, which contains a monochromatic (1 bit per pixel) pattern to be used as either an area pattern or a pixel exclusion pattern.

The XGA also supports an additional map referred to as the mask map. The mask map is a monochromatic bitmap that can be used to perform arbitrary clipping. When enabled, each 0 bit in the map indicates a pixel that should not be modified during a drawing operation, while a 1 bit is a signal to draw the applicable pixel. If the dimension of the mask map is smaller than that of the destination map for a given operation, then the outer edges of the mask map also define a clipping rectangle. The mask map is extremely useful in windowing environments where you have overlapping windows, because you can draw on underlying windows without having to manually pre-clip all the objects you're drawing. Instead, you just define a mask map that permits drawing only in the exposed area of the desired window. A full-screen 1024x768 mask map will occupy only 96KB of memory. A mask map may also be partially enabled so that it acts only as a clipping rectangle, and does not perform the arbitrary pixel-by-pixel clip.

All four maps are defined via the five pixel map registers. The first pixel in the bitmap, which is in the upper-left corner of a display bitmap, has a coordinate of 0,0. The mask map position over the destination map is defined by the mask map origin registers. All maps are limited to a height and width of 4096 by 4096.

Drawing with the XGA

Before you can draw anything with the XGA, you must define at least the destination map for the operation you want to perform. Some operations, such as a Bit BLock Transfer (**BitBLT** is an operation that copies bits from one place to another), will also require a source map. The available drawing operations on the XGA are:

- Lines
- Short vectors
- Filled rectangles
- BitBLTs
- Area fills

Unfortunately, drawing lines is not as simple as just providing an X,Y coordinate pair. The XGA uses a Bresenham line-drawing algorithm, but you have to calculate the initial Bresenham parameters first, which creates a bit of overhead when drawing short lines. Coincidentally, the method for calculating these parameters is virtually identical to that used in drawing lines on the 8514/A.

The XGA's short vectors are similar to the 8514/A's short stroke vectors. They can be up to 15 pixels in length, and can point in any direction that is a multiple of 45 degrees—horizontally, vertically, and 1:1 diagonally. The benefit of these vectors is that the definition for each one consumes only a byte, and up to 4 bytes can be passed at a time, allowing for a quick transfer rate, and therefore a quick drawing rate.

Filled rectangles are quite straightforward; you just specify a width, height, and position, and off you go.

BitBLTs are pretty much the same as a filled rectangle except that you have to specify a source map as well as a destination map. The XGA can also perform a simple color-expansion BLT, one in which the source is monochromatic and each 0 bit is converted to one color and each 1 bit to another. The destination map may be anything from 1 to 8 bits deep. This is useful for displaying rendered fonts on a high-color content screen or bitmap.

Area fills are modified rectangle fills in which the XGA graphics coprocessor uses the pattern map as a guideline for a scan-conversion fill. This type of fill uses 1-bit flags to toggle the fill state as it scans each line in the pattern bitmap. For each line, it initially does not fill. Upon hitting a 1 bit, each subsequent pixel (or bit) in the pattern map is filled until the next 1 bit is encountered. A description of this algorithm can be found in Foley and Van Dam's *Computer Graphics: Principles and Practice,* one of the bibles of graphics programming.

Lines, short vectors, and filled rectangles may also use both a source map and a pattern map. The pattern map is used for line patterns and area patterns, while the source map can be used for tiling a region in the case of a filled rectangle, or for providing a color line pattern for lines and short vectors.

All the drawing functions are also affected by four types of drawing modifiers: drawing colors, mixes, color compare, and the bit plane mask.

Drawing colors is simple. The foreground color specifies what color you normally draw in, while the background color specifies the color to be used in color expansions (for a 0 bit).

Mixes, known as raster operations or raster ops on other graphics platforms, provide a mechanism by which the destination pixel (the one in the destination map at the current drawing position) and the source pixel (the foreground color or source map pixel) are mixed. A typical mix is XOR, the exclusive OR operation, which is used for cursors and highlights. All the XGA mixes are listed on the next page. Objects are typically drawn in mode 3, Dst = Src.

The color compare is used during normal pixel updates to determine whether a given pixel should be updated, based on its color. The destination pixel value (or color) is compared to the Color Compare Color register using the compare operation set in the Color Compare Function. If the result of the comparison is TRUE, the pixel is not updated. There are eight compare conditions: always TRUE, always FALSE, greater than, less than, equal, not equal, less than or equal, and greater than or equal. This can be useful when you need to protect a range of colors from being updated, such as background and foreground objects in graphical scenery.

The bit plane mask controls which pits in a pixel can be modified and which can't. Its main use is in protecting binary color ranges and planes of color.

Value	Mix
00H	0 (all bits cleared)
01H	Src AND Dst
02H	Src AND NOT Dst
03H	Src
04H	NOT Src AND Dst
05H	Dst
06H	Src XOR Dst
07H	Src OR Dst
08H	NOT Src AND NOT Dst
09H	Src XOR NOT Dst
0AH	NOT Dst
0BH	Src OR NOT Dst
0CH	NOT Src
0DH	NOT Src OR Dst
0EH	NOT Src OR NOT Dst
0FH	1 (all bits set)
10H	MAXIMUM(Src, Dst)
11H	MINIMUM(Src, Dst)
12H	Src + Dst [with saturate]
13H	Dst - Src [with saturate]
14H	Src - Dst [with saturate]
15H	(Src + Dst) / 2

Src is the source pixel from the color registers or source map. *Dst* is the destination pixel that resides in the destination map. AND, OR, XOR, NOT are all bitwise binary operators. *Saturate,* as used above, means that the operations are bounded at 0 in the case of subtractions, or at the maximum pixel value in the case of additions.

Summary

From a technical standpoint, the XGA is a very elegant piece of work. It counters just about all the problems that the 8514/A has had, except interlaced displays (the new IBM XGA NI, discussed in Appendix G solves this problem) and simplified line drawing. The added features of the definable bitmaps, bus-mastering, memory mapping, and state saving are well thought out and should prove to be quite useful to software developers who want to get the most out of the XGA.

Chapter 3

The XGA Market: Past, Present, and Future

IBM has openly stated that it wants to make XGA the next PC graphics industry standard. Though it was successful in doing this with past graphics products, such as the EGA and VGA, IBM has not been pleased with the results of the standardization. Companies took the base hardware definition produced and developed by IBM, and extended it to cover the perceived needs of their customers—but without an extension of the standard. This was a major factor in the founding of VESA, the Video Electronic Standards Association.

With the XGA, IBM is taking a different route, which IBM hopes will allow the XGA architecture to evolve without creating the same splintering of compatible technology that the EGA and VGA suffered through.

IBM has taken several steps to promote a more universal graphics standard with the XGA. Let's look at each of these steps to see how it might contribute to making the XGA a mass-market standard.

An XGA Register Specification

Perhaps the biggest mistake IBM made with its 8514/A graphics coprocessor technology was that it didn't make the hardware definition public. Even today, it is available only under stringent nondisclosure agreements. As a result, both graphics hardware clone companies and software developers had a difficult time supporting it. The only IBM-approved way to support 8514/A hardware was through the Adapter Interface.

Conversely, the EGA and VGA were successful with hardware and software developers because both devices were quite well-documented by IBM.

IBM took a beating from a lot of people about the 8514/A hardware definition (or the lack thereof), so when it announced the XGA in 1990, IBM had full XGA register documentation available. Granted, the documentation isn't the easiest to use or read, but it is certainly a step in the right direction.

Current and Future Capabilities of the XGA

When the XGA was released, it offered the same base features (performance and resolutions) as an 8514/A, as well as some additional goodies, like the hardware sprite, bus-mastering, and 65,536 color support. Many of these features are now standard on many alternative graphics hardware platforms. The original XGA was probably most hurt by the fact that it still didn't support a non-interlaced 1024x768 graphics mode. This is partly because the silicon couldn't handle that fast a refresh rate, and partly because IBM had not come up with a 1024x768 non-interlaced refresh rate that it could sell in Europe—hence, no such monitor existed.

The XGA's performance is certainly quite good, especially compared to the type of hardware that existed when it was announced. The base XGA architecture is also very well suited to today's common protected mode applications, as well as vertical market applications that may require multiple graphics displays operating simultaneously.

Additionally, IBM released support for Windows 2.x and 3.0, OS/2 v1.3, AutoCAD, and an Adapter Interface with the XGA, so that all existing applications had a decent chance of supporting it.

Probably the best reason, however, for using the XGA as a core technology is its extensibility. It is obvious by looking at the XGA architecture that it can be extended to support local bus; 16-, 24-, or 32-bit per pixel (bpp) display and graphics coprocessing; and significantly higher resolutions.

As a step in extending the base XGA architecture, IBM has announced the IBM XGA-NI (non-interlaced), which offers, among other new features, 1024x768 non-interlaced support (at 70Hz refresh), coprocessed drawing for the 16 bpp graphics mode, and 8-bit DACs (which support a 16.8 million color palette instead of the original XGA's 256K palette). All original XGA software will work on the NI, but only newer software will support the 1024x768 NI resolution. (See Appendix C for more on this.)

Price Competitiveness and Availability

As almost anyone will tell you, IBM products are not cheap—you pay for the name. The initial XGA pricing was indicative of this. The XGA cost $1095 as a separate graphics board for a 512KB VRAM configuration, while an additional 512KB of VRAM was $350. Ten months later, IBM dropped these prices to $795 and $280, respectively—more in line with what graphics hardware companies were selling product for. Of course, the prices are still a bit high, but they're certainly competitive, and for a company that buys only IBM equipment, a couple of hundred dollars doesn't make that much difference.

Making the XGA available to more users is part of a standardization formula. Instead of just selling the XGA Display Adapter/A, IBM also incorporated the XGA as the base graphics platform for the new line of 486 systems it introduced on the same day as the XGA. Since then, the XGA has become the base graphics platform for several new IBM PS/2 systems, with no end in sight for its use. The XGA-NI will probably take the XGA's place in some of the higher end systems soon as well.

VESA Participation

Since VESA's business is to explain and standardize poorly understood and nonstandard approaches to PC graphics, IBM decided it would be a good venue for XGA standardization.

At VESA's quarterly meeting at the Fall COMDEX trade show in 1990, IBM unveiled the XGA architecture to a general audience for the first time. Spokespersons showed how the XGA could fit into the grand scheme of things, declared that IBM intended to make the XGA the next graphics industry standard, and promised that the company would help in any reasonable way it could to ensure that this would happen

Every time IBM releases a new PC graphics standard, companies start cloning it, and the XGA was no exception. At the next quarterly VESA meeting in February, 1992,

Cirrus Logic formed the VESA XGA Extensions technical subcommittee, with record member participation. The primary charter of this subcommittee was to solve a problem that cloning the XGA would create—namely, XGA support in non-Micro Channel systems. The subcommittee would also look at adding a custom extension mechanism to the core XGA architecture to allow for easy XGA chip and board vendor identification, as well as the addition of special manufacturer-specific features. Finally, a software interface to locate and initialize the XGA would also be examined.

With lots of work on the part of all the members of the subcommittee—including representatives from IBM, Cirrus Logic, IIT, Binar Graphics, Panacea, Brooktree, Inmos and many others—the VESA XGA Extensions standard (VXE 1.0) finally came into existence, and was approved by the VESA general membership on May 8, 1992, just over a year after the committee was formed. A copy of the VXE 1.0 standard can be found in Appendix B.

In order for VESA to even start looking at something to standardize, a few requirements must be met:

1. *There has to be a perceived need to standardize the subject.* Cirrus came up with the need, namely potential incompatibility in ISA and EISA systems, extensibility, and software support.

2. *There has to be industrywide interest in standardization.* More than three dozen companies participated in the XGA Extensions technical subcommittee at various times. This certainly indicates an enormous amount of industry interest.

3. *The standard must ultimately serve the end-user.* If no standard had been created, the XGA would cause end-users and vendors alike great headaches from a software support point of view; standardization minimizes compatibility problems and makes the device much friendlier for end-users.

Of course, there's nothing that says VESA cannot create standards that may appear to be conflicting. A classic example is VESA's ongoing standardization of its VGA BIOS Extension (VBE), which is designed to support arguably older technology that could be seen as a competitor to the XGA as SVGAs become XVGAs. This effort continues because the VBE meets VESA's three requirements. SVGA and XVGA boards are still being sold in droves, so vendor and end-user interest continues in supporting, developing, and using them.

The end result of IBM's VESA activities pertaining to the XGA is that the original XGA architecture is the base design upon which VXE 1.0 is centered, and as such, IBM has been successful in making the XGA an industry standard.

Assisting XGA Cloners with Compatibility

IBM has backed up its commitment to make the XGA a standard by helping potential competitors solve compatibility problems.

Key members of IBM's XGA technical staff frequently help XGA-clone silicon engineers to increase the compatibility of the clone XGA silicon with the XGA architecture. This process was also vital to providing a useful VXE 1.0 specification, since many extension issues couldn't be easily solved without IBM's insight into the XGA architecture.

Selling XGA Chip Sets

In September 1991, IBM announced a strategic partnership with Inmos, a division of SGS-Thomson Microelectronics, Ltd., headquartered in Bristol, England. Inmos is the developer of the Transputer processor used in many parallel processing and graphical rendering applications, as well as the original manufacturer of the DAC (digital to analog converter) used on many popular VGA boards and subsystems. As the XGA licensee, Inmos will manufacture and sell IBM-developed XGA chips.

As part of the licensing agreement, Inmos has the exclusive right (outside of IBM) to manufacture and remarket IBM's existing XGA chip set for a period of at least 18 months. Any extensions to the XGA architecture that IBM made would be made available to Inmos during the three years following the start of the license.

The initial parts offered by Inmos were the IMS G190 XGA Serializer Palette DAC and the IMS G200 XGA Display Controller, the same two chips you can find on the original IBM XGA Display Adapter/A. The price per chip set was $99 in quantities of 5,000, and at the time of the announcement, Inmos indicated that it had no intention of selling board level XGA products.

So, why did IBM sign the licensing agreement? Because it took the XGA one step closer to becoming an industry standard. With Inmos, IBM got a full sales, support, and distribution network, as well as a manufacturing facility, for the XGA chips. Inmos has sales offices worldwide, as well as many clients in the VGA industry due to its DAC business. Furthermore, Inmos is familiar with combining digital and analog technology, a requirement vital to producing the XGA serializer palette DAC.

IBM is attempting to make the XGA more prolific by making it available from a global source that knows how to deal with chip sales and the necessary design engineering.

This approach hasn't been as successful IBM had hoped; at the time of this writing, only five companies—AHEAD, Genoa, Infotronic, Radius, and AGT—had officially announced products based on the Inmos XGA parts. This is probably a result of both the chip set prices (rather high compared to competitive products like S3's 86C911) and the availability of an ISA bus-compatible chip set.

On the flip side, Inmos got to expand its PC graphics line, the most prominent member of which had been the Inmos VGA DAC. Overnight, Inmos became a player in the potentially lucrative graphics coprocessor marketplace.

Inmos has an opportunity to make a decent bit of money on the XGA chip sets. The IBM stamp of approval on the IMS G190 and G200 chips (and all subsequent ones as well), makes it easier to compete against upcoming XGA chip set clones, even if the clones are less expensive. The IBM name carries a lot of weight in corporate America.

The one potential drawback for Inmos, however, is that it is dependent on IBM's development schedule for new XGA derivatives. It is likely that XGA clone chips will be faster than what Inmos is currently offering, and Inmos has to make sure that IBM is on the ball in enhancing their XGA design in order to be performance- and feature-competitive with these new XGA clones.

What the rest of the graphics industry got out of this deal was varied. For companies that had been in the process of cloning the XGA, this licensing announcement validated their efforts, because it helped to propagate an XGA open standard. This is because the IBM XGA was suddenly available from a second source, and because the commitment was made by IBM to extend the XGA architecture to the ISA bus and non-interlaced displays.

On the other hand, those companies that were pushing proprietary graphics coprocessing technology as the ultimate solution faced slightly tougher times trying to convince customers to choose a proprietary architecture over an open standard. Technologically, there is no reason that a proprietary architecture can't do things better than an XGA (and some of these companies have proved that they can substantially outperform the XGA), but the age old IBM-related Fear, Uncertainty, and Doubt (FUD) always comes back to haunt companies—the XGA is just a safer bet for many people.

Perhaps more important was IBM's renewed commitment to "being in synch" with VESA's XGA Extensions standardization efforts.

The Second License

In order to try to speed up the standardization process a bit more, IBM announced in April 1992 that it had signed an XGA licensing agreement with Intel. This agreement seemed to use semantics to avoid infringing upon Inmos's exclusive eighteen-month right to develop XGA technology.

Intel and IBM will work jointly to expand the efforts to make the XGA an industry standard. IBM has licensed its XGA silicon design to Intel so that Intel "will develop, manufacture, and market new implementations of XGA chip sets". As I interpret it, this means that though Inmos retains the exclusive right to manufacture and market silicon developed by IBM, Intel must make changes in the silicon in order to market it without contractual conflict. Intel representatives indicated that such new XGA silicon might appear in the form of a local bus-capable XGA, while some analysts felt that Intel would integrate the XGA with its CPU technology to create a low-cost, high performance computer-on-a-chip with XGA graphics capabilities.

Intel has many strengths, its processor prowess being among them. Intel is also a major proponent of local bus technology, as well as a leading manufacturer of PC motherboards and peripheral cards. It is not difficult to see an Intel-developed XGA integrated into any one of these product lines, especially since Intel hasn't had any real or new graphics silicon technology since 1988's now-defunct Intel 82786 graphics coprocessor.

In any event, until Intel actually announces any XGA-based products, speculation is moot. The same applies to the long-term impact the Intel/IBM agreement will have on making XGA a household term. Intel must deliver for the agreement to have any real significance.

XGA Is a Registered Trademark

In a move that surprised many companies, IBM announced in late 1991 that it had trademarked the XGA, and would take legal action against any company that infringed upon it. This was surprising because IBM had never before done this with its mass-market graphics products; it had put a "TM" above "VGA," but never enforced it.

This change in philosophy was yet another way in which IBM decided to maintain XGA as a "clean" standard. If IBM controlled the XGA name, then IBM could say what could be called an XGA and what couldn't.

I discussed this with an executive in IBM's Entry Systems Division, who described three levels of legally using the XGA name:

- Level I: IBM can use the XGA mark in any way it chooses for its own products, including calling them "SuperXGA," "MegaXGA," "XGAPlus," and so forth.

- Level II: IBM's licensees and sublicensees (customers of the licensees) can use the XGA mark in their product name. A board company like Genoa, for example, can call their XGA graphics board the "Genoa XGA," but not "Genoa SuperXGA." If Genoa stops using IBM-originated XGA parts on those boards, however, it will have to stop using the XGA name.

- Level III: Anyone else who uses an IBM XGA-compatible part that is not actually an IBM-originated part (i.e. purchased from an IBM XGA licensee), cannot use XGA in their product name. In such situations, however, it's all right to describe the product as being "IBM XGA compatible."

In my mind this approach is limiting, since, in order for XGA to become a household word, a user has to be able to easily determine that he or she is buying or looking at an XGA-compatible device, even if it was built using non-IBM XGA clone chip sets. There is some talk that a seal might be created by VESA, and licensed to companies that are certified to be VXE 1.0 compatible. Until then, this trademark issue will create a hurdle in marketing non-IBM originated XGA products.

Aiding Independent Software Vendors (ISVs)

Another way to get mass acceptance of a graphics platform is to make sure that it supports as many graphics applications as possible. This can be accomplished in a number of ways:

- *Supply a large of number of drivers that support a variety of applications.* IBM supplies Windows 2.x and 3.0, OS/2 1.3, and AutoCAD drivers with the XGA.

- *Supply an industry-accepted software interface for your graphics board.* While some might argue about the Adapter Interface (AI) being "industry accepted," there's no question that it is widely supported by applications, and IBM supplies an AI for the XGA.

- *Provide ISVs with an easy means to obtaining XGA documentation, education, and hardware.* IBM is just starting to do this. In April 1992, IBM sponsored XGA Camp—two days of presentations designed to educate ISVs in XGA programming. Documentation for the XGA is becoming more readily available, and IBM documents can be obtained inexpensively by calling 1-800-IBM-PCTB and referencing the document numbers shown in the bibliography of this book. As for hardware, IBM has generally focused on large software companies, but at XGA Camp, even some smaller software and driver developers ended up with loaner XGA-NI boards. IBM also used the event to distribute an SDK (software development kit) that shows how to use DMQS (see Appendix N). This SDK should become available through the IBM PC Technical Books phone number one of these days. (Note: If you need loaner XGA hardware because you have an application that might interest IBM, try sending a letter describing the application to the IBM address listed in Appendix A; address it *Attn.: XGA ISV Program*, and use a mail-stop of 1716. Who knows? You might get lucky.)

Getting XGA Support in the Software Box

It's not difficult to get software companies to support a corporation the size of IBM. For example, Microsoft provides XGA drivers with Windows 3.1, while IBM's own OS/2 2.0 ships with XGA drivers as well. And even Autodesk will provide XGA support for its new AutoCAD Release 12, as well as for AutoShade 2 w/RenderMan, and 3D Studio.

IBM's size certainly helps, but IBM is also selling the hardware standard concept; that is, if a pervasive graphics platform exists, it makes sense to support it, especially if the alternative is supporting a range of proprietary solutions with multiple drivers.

The Big Picture

IBM has made some decent inroads into making XGA a name to be reckoned with in the PC industry, although things would probably move faster if IBM weren't encumbered by its sheer size.

Prior to the Intel/IBM announcement, Dataquest, one of the more prominent market research companies, forecast that by 1996, XGA-derived products would control more than 20 percent of the PC graphics hardware market. Thus, the XGA will be a dominant force in the PC graphics hardware market in the coming years, but real support is just starting to appear.

Chapter 4

The XGA Hardware

This chapter is the first in the section about programming the XGA hardware—the section where all the really interesting stuff happens. Please note, however, that it focuses on the extended-graphics portion of the XGA, not the VGA-compatible portion.

Of course, programming the XGA registers is not something everyone needs to do. In many situations, the AI will serve just as well, and will also give your software greater portability to non-XGA platforms.

You will want to write software that directly accesses the XGA hardware if:

1. You have an application that is graphics performance-sensitive, such as animation, CAD, or interactive paint software (tests I performed on the original 8514/A AI showed that using it took twice as long as directly accessing the hardware, and while clone AIs and the XGA AI have been improved, by nature they still exhibit noticeably slower performance than direct hardware access).

2. Your application runs in protected mode and/or under a non-DOS operating system (the XGA AI is available only in a real mode DOS environment).

3. You are willing to sacrifice the easy portability achieved by writing to the AI (a properly written AI-based application will work on the 8514/A, as well as on some Super VGAs and TIGA boards which have AI emulation).

4. You like to twiddle hardware bits.

5. You're just a speed freak at heart (aren't we all, really?).

While these may seem somewhat whimsical, they all are relevant. In my case, they are all true—but I'm rather biased toward wanting direct access to any and all graphics hardware I can get my hands on.

Assuming you have managed to convince yourself that going the hardware direct route is the way for you, continue reading this section. If you want AI documentation and tutorials, see the section commencing with Chapter 6.

In this chapter, I'll give you the complete overview of the XGA hardware, including full details on the XGA's architecture and in-depth coverage of the XGA registers.

By the time you read this, IBM probably will have released an extension to the base XGA architecture, called XGA-NI. This extension is fully documented in Appendix C.

The XGA Architecture

For those of you who are familiar with the architecture of Super VGAs, look at the XGA as being a high-end VGA with graphics assists. For those of you who deal with 8514/A-compatible solutions, the XGA is basically an 8514/A with memory mapped video memory and built-in VGA support.

The IBM XGA, initially designed to inhabit a Micro Channel–based IBM PS/2, takes a good part of its heritage from its environment. Its key system-related features are:

- It is VRAM-based
- It has memory mapped display buffer access
- Multiple XGAs can coexist in a system
- It supports both I/O and memory mapped registers
- It has bus mastering
- It has a 32-bit address and data path

An XGA board consists of two core chips, a graphics coprocessor, and a palette DAC/VRAM serializer. All communications with the host system are conducted via the graphics coprocessor, while the palette DAC's purpose is to fetch data from video memory, translate it from digital form to analog, and display a hardware cursor. All other functionality exists in the graphics coprocessor, including video timing control, VGA compatibility, memory management, and graphics assists.

At boot time, the system scans itself for all XGAs and configures them to use different memory addresses by assigning an **instance number**. The instance number then pretty much controls where in I/O and memory space a given XGA can be accessed.

Using a simple algorithm, the system determines which XGA, if any, will be initialized into its VGA mode. The VGA mode is fully compatible with the prior IBM VGA implementation. (Since these earlier VGA registers are widely documented, they will not be covered here. Check the bibliography at the end of this book for a listing of titles on VGA programming.)

While the XGA architecture allows for up to 4 MB of VRAM, IBM only ships versions with 512KB, offering an additional 512KB (for a total of 1MB) as an upgrade. When placed in a 32-bit MCA slot, an XGA always has its entire display memory address space (all 4MB of it) mapped in somewhere in the top 32 MB of the Intel 386/486 four gigabyte address space. The exact location depends on the XGA device's instance number. When placed in a 16-bit MCA slot, the memory is not directly accessible by the system CPU, but its potential address is still quite important, as we'll see later.

Additionally, under software control, the XGA memory can be mapped into PC address space for a 1MB window somewhere in the first 16MB of PC address space, or for a bank-switchable 64KB area where a VGA's graphics memory would reside at (physical segment 0A000H or 0B000H).

The I/O registers—used to initialize display frequencies, control the color look-up table (LUT), manipulate the hardware cursor/sprite, and map memory—are placed at I/O address 21x0H, where x is the instance of the XGA.

The memory mapped registers occupy a 128 byte section within a 1KB portion of memory at the top of the XGA's 8KB of ROM. Again, the exact location of the memory mapped registers is determined by the instance number.

Maps: A New PC Graphics Concept

Internally, the bus master capability affects the design of the XGA, starting with the XGA's **maps**. There are four maps, one of which is a **mask map**—used to indicate which pixels may or may not be modified in a given destination area. The other three maps, conveniently called A, B, and C, are used to define regions of memory (XGA or system) for graphics access, whether it be for writing or reading of graphical data. A map is defined as having an address (hence the importance of the address of the 4MB chunk at which the XGA is mapped), width, height, and depth (bits per pixel).

Typically, a map would be defined to access within the XGA a data area the size of a full screen, but by providing a PC memory address, a map may point to PC-based data, and this is where the XGA's bus-mastering capability comes into play.

The maps are used within the XGA's graphics operations, with each operation capable of accepting a source map, destination map, and pattern map, and optionally enabling a specified mask map. This means that you can treat XGA or PC memory as a graphical drawing area, and be able to define pretty much any type of map/memory configuration.

Suppose you were developing a GUI application, and you needed to save a rectangular part of the display to off-screen video memory. Your source map would typically be the full screen, while you would go and define a destination map that conformed exactly to the dimensions of the rectangle you wanted to copy. After the XGA performed the copy, the rectangle would have been copied to a linearly contiguous chunk of memory. See Figure 4.1 for a visual representation.

12	12	12	12	12	13	14	14	14	15	14	14	13	12	12	12	12
12	12	12	12	11	13	13	13	13	15	12	12	12	12	12	12	12
12	12	12	12	10	13	12	12	12	13	10	12	12	12	12	12	12
12	12	12	12	12	13	10	10	15	15	12	12	12	12	12	12	12
12	12	12	12	12	13	10	10	15	15	12	12	12	12	12	12	12
12	12	12	12	12	13	13	13	13	13	12	12	12	12	12	12	12

Map A

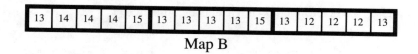

Map B

Figure 4.1. Maps of different dimensions can be used for screen save BitBLT operations. Map A represents the screen; each numbered block is a pixel and its value. Map B represents the destination map after a BitBLT from the highlighted area in Map A. Map B is 5 pixels by 3 lines, and, assuming an 8bpp mode, occupies 15 bytes.

This approach allows you to write reasonably simple memory-management software that can manage regular data and graphical data at the same time, without wasting memory, with the XGA understanding how it all works (with a minor bit of set up).

For those of you who have dealt with PC graphics for some time, you may notice that the map usage in the XGA closely resembles capabilities similar to that of the ill-fated Intel 82786 graphics coprocessor, released by Intel in 1986.

The LUT

The XGA's color LUT functions quite similarly to the one in a typical VGA, except that while it is still limited to 6 bits (64 levels) per red, green, and blue gun, the bits are all left-aligned within a byte, leaving room for the eventual expansion to a 16.8 million color LUT and DAC (digital to analog converter) with a full 8 bits per gun, like those found on high-end graphics boards. The LUT is also used to ensure that proper color values come out of the DAC in the 65,536 color mode the XGA supports.

The Hardware Sprite

The palette DAC/serializer chip contains a hardware sprite, or, as some refer to it, a hardware cursor (I use the terms interchangeably). The purpose of a hardware cursor is to allow for the display of a graphical icon (such as the arrow used as a cursor in Microsoft Windows) over the top of regular display information in such a way that software need not save/restore the area under the cursor, as it might when a cursor is driven entirely in software. This provides a significant performance benefit, because a software cursor may suck up as much as 15 percent of the graphics bandwidth of an application.

The XGA's hardware cursor implementation allows for a cursor of as large as 64x64 pixels, plus it supports 2 bits per pixel. Nicest of all is that two cursor colors may be defined as direct RGB values, bypassing the look-up table, and hence freeing software from having to allocate two colors out of the XGA's active palette.

The 2 bits of the XGA cursor are defined as follows:

Bit 1	Bit 0	Definition
0	0	Sprite color 0
0	1	Sprite color 1
1	0	Transparent (allows underlying pixel data to show through)
1	1	Complement (1's complement of underlying pixel data)

This bit definition is especially handy when dealing with AND and XOR cursor masks, such as those provided by Microsoft Windows and AutoCAD to their drivers. Sample code showing how to take advantage of this capability is offered in the next chapter.

The Register Reference

Now that I've covered some of the basics of XGA operation, let me present you with documentation on each of the XGA registers. Please note:

- Any register addresses or indices not defined below are to be considered reserved, and therefore should not be read or written.

- A chip reset is not guaranteed to initialize any registers. Register initialization must be done by software.

- You should not assume that an index register (such as the one used for the palette) will wrap to 0.

- XGA registers should not be accessed while the XGA is in VGA mode.

- VGA registers should not be accessed while the XGA is in XGA graphics mode.

Appendix D lists, by address, all the XGA registers with addresses, access, mnemonics, and name.

The Registers Themselves

Each of the following sections is dedicated to an individual register, with the POS registers being listed first, the I/O registers next, then the I/O Index registers, and finally the memory mapped registers, all sorted by ascending address.

Each register description section is formatted like the sample page that begins the section. Note the descriptors at the top, which tell whether the register is I/O or memory mapped; whether it is readable, writable, or both; and how many bits of data are significant.

After reading the register's description and the descriptions of registers referenced in the comments, you may still have questions about using a register. If so, look at the next chapter's programming examples, which should touch on most register usage issues.

I/Ox[1]   1234[2]   Sample Register Description[3]

Read Only,[4] 16 bits[5]

THIS_BIT
Description of the bit indicated.

THOSE_BITS
Description of the bits indicated.

Comments
Comments about this register, noting any special programming considerations.

Mnemonic[7]
SAMP_REG

1. This field describes the type of register, which will be POS I/O, Index, or Memory.

2. This field show the hexadecimal address of the register. For I/O and POS registers, it shows the I/O address; for Index registers, it shows the index to be used to access the register via I/O port 21xA; and for Memory registers, it show the byte offset of the register into the 128 byte memory register page.

3. The name of the register is shown here.

4. Shows the access to the register: Read Only, Write Only, or Read/Write

5. This field shows the width of the register: 8, 16, or 32 bits. Note that 16- or 32-bit registers can be written as multiple 8- or 16-bit values, just by incrementing the I/O or memory address in proportion to the amount of data written on the Intel access.

6. This whole area shows the layout of the bits in the register, as well as the mnemonic for each used bit or field in the register. For Memory registers, the bit/byte ordering is displayed in Intel mode. For Motorola mode, see the description of the Operating Mode register. The mnemonic for the bit/field is the same as that used in the ASM and C include files used by programs in this book. The function of these bits or fields is defined below the register layout. Comments about the register then follow the bit/field descriptors.

7. Finally, the mnemonic for the register itself is shown.

POS 100H   Identification Word Low Byte

Read Only, 8 bits

```
Bit          7  6  5  4  3  2  1  0
             1  1  0  1  1  0  X  X
```

Comments

This register contains the low byte of the board ID, which is normally defined to be 0DBH for XGA boards. By definition, it is possible for XGA boards to have Low ID values ranging from 0D8H through 0DBH; check for this range to determine whether an XGA is present. It is also necessary to check the high byte of the ID word (see next section). Note: The POS registers need to be enabled for access. See the next chapter for sample code to enable the POS registers.

VESA has extended the valid list of XGA-compatible POS I/Os with the following 1028 values:

0240H-027FH	0A90H-0BFFH
0830H-0A7FH	8FD0-8FD3 (reserved)

These values are intended for use with devices that are compatible with the VESA XGA Standard (shown in Appendix B).

Mnemonic

POS_ID_ LO

POS 101H   Identification Word High Byte

Read Only, 8 bits

```
Bit          7  6  5  4  3  2  1  0
             1  0  0  0  1  1  1  1
```

Comments

This register contains the high byte of the board ID, which is defined to be 08FH for XGA boards. The actual range of valid XGA IDs is documented above. Note: The POS registers need to be enabled for access; see next chapter for sample code.

Mnemonic

POS_ID_HI

POS 102H   XGA Configuration Register

Read/Write, 8 bits

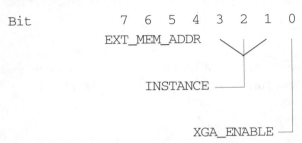

EXT_MEM_ADDR

This 4-bit field specifies one of sixteen possible locations for the 8KB of external XGA memory, which in normal implementations consists of 7KB of ROM, and 1KB dedicated to the memory mapped XGA registers. The values specified by these bits are as follows:

Bit 7	Bit 6	Bit 5	Bit 4	Physical PC Base Address
0	0	0	0	0C0000H
0	0	0	1	0C2000H
0	0	1	0	0C4000H
0	0	1	1	0C6000H
0	1	0	0	0C8000H
0	1	0	1	0CA000H
0	1	1	0	0CC000H
0	1	1	1	0CE000H
1	0	0	0	0D0000H
1	0	0	1	0D2000H
1	0	1	0	0D4000H
1	0	1	1	0D6000H
1	1	0	0	0D8000H
1	1	0	1	0DA000H
1	1	1	0	0DC000H
1	1	1	1	0DE000H

The external memory can be disabled by clearing the EXT_MEM_ENABLE bit in the Bus Arbitration register (POS register 103H).

INSTANCE

This is the instance number of the XGA board, which determines which set of I/O addresses the XGA device uses (this number replaces the x in the I/O base address), as well as which 128 byte register page of the last 1KB of the external memory is used for the current XGA's registers.

XGA_ENABLE

This bit enables/disables the XGA register decode. When this bit is cleared to 0, only the XGA POS registers can be accessed. This bit is normally used by the PC's POST (**Power-On Self Test**) code at boot time.

Comments

This register should not be written unless extreme circumstances warrant it. In actuality, all POS registers are writable, but that functionality is generally reserved for the POST code. Therefore, the values found in the POS registers were placed there by system initialization code. This means that things like the external memory address and the instance number were determined by the system initialization code to be safe locations (and possibly the best ones), which is why I recommend you don't alter them. Note: The POS registers need to be enabled for access. See the next chapter for sample code to enable the POS registers.

Mnemonic

POS_CONFIG

POS 103H   Bus Arbitration Register

Read/Write, 8 bits

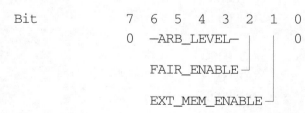

```
Bit          7  6  5  4  3  2  1  0
             0  —ARB_LEVEL—  |   |     0
                            |   |
             FAIR_ENABLE ———'   |
                                |
             EXT_MEM_ENABLE ————'
```

ARB_LEVEL

These bits contain the priority level of the XGA device for the purpose of bus mastering, and arbitration between bus masters. The priority level usage is documented in Micro Channel Architecture (MCA) technical reference materials available from IBM.

FAIR_ENABLE

This bit is used to control the MCA fairness protocol. If set, the fairness protocol is enabled. If cleared, the protocol is disabled.

EXT_MEM_ENABLE

This bit controls the decode of the XGA external 8KB memory block described in the previous section. If this bit is set, the external memory is accessible. If it is cleared, then the external memory (that is, the 8KB ROM) is not accessible, but access to the memory mapped registers remains unaffected.

Comments

If you need to write to this register, make sure that bits 7 and 0 are written as 0s. Note: The POS registers need to be enabled for access. See the next chapter for sample code to enable the POS registers.

Mnemonic

POS_ARBITRATE

POS 104H   Display Memory Base Address

Read/Write, 8 bits

```
Bit          7  6  5  4  3  2  1  0
             —— DISP_MEM_BASE ——    ⌐
                                    │
             DISP_MEM_ACCESS ———————┘
```

DISP_MEM_BASE

These specify the seven most significant bits (bits 31-25) of the physical address of the XGA display memory base in PC address space; the INSTANCE field in the XGA Configuration register supplies an additional 3 bits (bits 24-22). The XGA display memory base is therefore mapped on 4MB boundaries. If the XGA device is attached to the system via a 16-bit bus slot, however, the display memory will not be accessible to the PC CPU, since it is mapped above the 16MB mark. Normally, the display memory for the first XGA device located by the POST will be mapped to the second to last 4MB chunk of memory (0FF800000H), since the uppermost 4MB of memory is occupied by dually mapped ROM, in most systems. The 4MB also will never be 00000000H, since that would conflict with a PC's base memory.

If the XGA can be accessed with a full 32 bits of address by the CPU, knowing this address can enable protected-mode software to directly answer all of the XGA display memory as one contiguous chunk of memory. The base address of the display memory is required by the XGA initialization process.

DISP_MEM_ACCESS

This bit is used to control access to the display memory by the PC's CPU if it has full access to all 32 bits of address of the XGA device. If this bit is set, access is enabled; otherwise, access is disabled.

Comments

As with the other POS registers, don't write to this one unless you absolutely must. Note: The POS registers need to be enabled for access. See the next chapter for sample code to enable the POS registers.

Mnemonic

POS_DISPMEMBASE

POS 105H   1 MB Aperture Base Address

Read/Write, 8 bits

```
Bit           7 6 5 4 3 2 1 0
              —RESERVED—  —BASE_1MB—
```

BASE_1MB

These 4 bits determine where the XGA's 1MB aperture will be located in the PC CPU's address space (addresses 0100000H–0F00000H). A 0 value in this field indicates that the POST has not been able to locate a free 1MB memory area in the first 16MB of the PC's address space, and hence, the 1MB aperture is disabled.

Comments

Bits 7–4 are reserved, and may or may not return the values listed above. If you need to write to this register, however, make sure that bits 7–4 are written with a bit pattern of 1101. Note: The POS registers must be enabled for access. See the next chapter for sample code to enable the POS registers.

Mnemonic

POS_BASE_1MB

I/O 21x0   Operating Mode Register

Read/Write, 8 bits

REG_FORMAT

This bit sets the format for the Memory registers: 0 for Intel format, and 1 for Motorola format. These formats differ in the byte order of words and double words. Intel 80x86 class CPUs use a "little endian" format; Motorola (and PDP-11s) uses a "big endian" byte order. In the case of the Memory registers, this means that the byte order in each block of 4 bytes (on double-word boundaries) reverses, and the MSB changes as well:

	MSB			**LSB**
Intel Byte Order	3	2	1	0

	LSB			**MSB**
Motorola Byte Order	0	1	2	3

The exceptions to this byte ordering are the Short Stroke and Command registers, whose definitions remain unchanged regardless of the setting of the REG_FORMAT bit.

DISPLAY_MODE

These 3 bits select the display mode of the XGA:

Bit 2	Bit 1	Bit 0	Display Mode
0	0	0	VGA mode, disable XGA address decode
0	0	1	VGA mode, enable XGA address decode
0	1	0	132-column mode, disable XGA address decode
0	1	1	132-column mode, enable XGA address decode
1	0	0	XGA Extended Graphics mode
1	0	1	Reserved
1	1	0	Reserved
1	1	1	Reserved

Disabling the XGA address decode means that XGA-specific registers and memory will be inaccessible to software, until access is reenabled. Note that just setting the mode bits is not necessarily sufficient to enable the selected mode—additional Display Control registers will probably have to be set. See the XGA initialization examples in the next chapter.

Comments

The reserved bits in this register must be set to 0 when writing this register.

Mnemonic

OP_MODE

I/O 21x1   Aperture Control Register

Read/Write, 8 bits

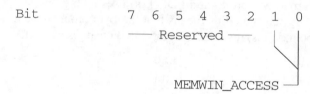

MEMWIN_ACCESS

This field controls access to the XGA 64KB aperture (or memory window). Via this memory window, real and protected mode software can directly access the XGA display memory, 64KB at a time. The two bits provide the following control:

Bit 1	Bit 0	Memory Window Access
0	0	Disable the 64KB memory window
0	1	Enable the 64KB memory window at 0A0000H
1	0	Enable the 64KB memory window at 0B0000H
1	1	Reserved

Note that enabling the memory window may cause an addressing conflict in your system if you have other adapters in it that are also in the process of using such memory. The location of the memory window in XGA display memory is controlled via the Aperture Index register.

Comments

The reserved bits in this register must be set to 0, even though their contents during a read might be different.

Mnemonic

MEMWIN_CTRL

I/O 21x4   Interrupt Enable Register

Read/Write, 8 bits

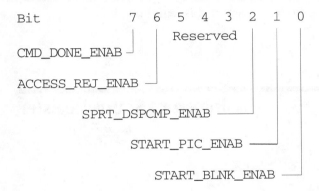

CMD_DONE_ENAB

This bit, if set, enables the command completion interrupt, which is issued whenever an XGA graphics command is completed (see the description of the Command register at the end of this chapter for details). If the bit is cleared, no hardware interrupt is issued.

ACCESS_REJ_ENAB

This bit controls the interrupt for the XGA access reject interrupt, which is issued if data is written to the XGA Memory registers while an XGA command is in progress. Writing data to the Memory registers during an active XGA command may corrupt the current command. If this bit is set, the interrupt is enabled.

SPRT_DSPCMP_ENAB

This bit enables the interrupt issued upon the completion of the display of the XGA hardware sprite.

START_PIC_ENAB

This bit controls the interrupt that occurs at the start of the picture display, which is also the end of the vertical blanking period. If set, the interrupt is enabled.

START_BLNK_ENAB

This bit will enable the interrupt issued at the start of the vertical blanking period, which also happens to be the end of the picture display.

Comments

The state of these bits has no effect on the interrupt status bits in the Interrupt Status register (see the next section). When an interrupt bit is enabled, and the XGA issues said interrupt, it comes in as IRQ 2, which results in interrupt vector 0AH being called. This means you need to set up an interrupt handler that can process the XGA interrupts, and determine which XGA state actually caused the interrupt to occur. Information on writing interrupt handlers is available in most PC programming books. The reserved bits are undefined on a read, and must be set to 0 on writes to this register.

Mnemonic

INT_ENABLE

I/O 21x5   Interrupt Status Register

Read/Write, 8 bits

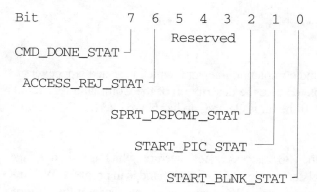

CMD_DONE_STAT

This bit indicates whether or not a command completion interrupt has occurred. If this bit is set, the interrupt has occurred. The status bit is cleared by writing a 1 to it.

ACCESS_REJ_STAT

This bit shows the status of the XGA access reject interrupt. If this bit is set, the interrupt has occurred. This bit may be cleared by writing a 1 to it.

SPRT_DSPCMP_STAT

This bit reflects the state of the sprite display completion interrupt. If it is set, the interrupt has occurred. Clear this bit by writing a 1 to it.

START_PIC_STAT

This bit indicates that the XGA display mechanism is starting to display a frame of information on the screen, and that the vertical blank period for the current frame is over. As with the other interrupt status bits, once set, this bit remains set until cleared by writing a 1 to it.

START_BLNK_STAT

This bit indicates that the XGA display mechanism is starting a vertical blanking/retrace period, and has just finished displaying a frame of display data. Just as with the other interrupt status bits, once set, this bit remains set until cleared by writing a 1 to it. This is perhaps the most useful bit in this register, since it can be used to synchronize software with a recurring, constant event. It can also be used by animation software to minimize the "tearing" that occurs when a part of display memory is being updated at the same time that data is being displayed on the screen. Proper use of this bit (when the START_BLNK_ENAB bit is cleared) is accomplished by clearing the bit, then waiting for it (in a tight loop) to become set again.

Comments

Writing a 0 to any of these bits has no effect on their setting, while a 1 will clear a bit. This is apparently designed to allow the read-back value of the register to be used as the clearing value.

Note that the status bits will reflect the state of the specified event, regardless of the setting of the interrupt enable bits in the Interrupt Enable register. If you are using an interrupt handler to deal with XGA interrupts, this register can be used to determine the source of the interrupt. Once the source has been determined, the related interrupt status bit should be cleared to prevent the interrupt from immediately recurring after return from the interrupt service routine. The reserved bits are undefined on a read, and must be set to 0 on writes to this register.

Mnemonic

INT_STATUS

I/O 21x6   Virtual Memory Control Register

Read/Write, 8 bits

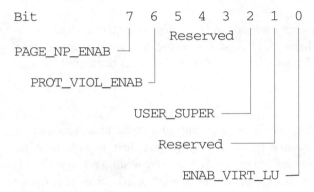

PAGE_NP_ENAB

This bit is used to enable the virtual memory (VM) Page Not Present CPU interrupt. This condition is triggered when a required virtual memory page in PC memory is not available. If this bit is cleared, the interrupt is disabled.

PROT_VIOL_ENAB

When this bit is set, the XGA device will issue a Protection Violation interrupt to the CPU when a VM memory protection violation occurs.

USER_SUPER

This bit controls the privilege level of the current task.

Bit	Function
0	The current task will have a supervisor privilege level, equivalent to 386/486 privilege levels 0, 1, and/or 2. When set at this level, the XGA will not perform any checking on page directory or page table protection bits.
1	The current task will have a user privilege level, equivalent to a 386/486 privilege 3. If set to this privilege level, the XGA device will check for violations, and issue a violation interrupt (if enabled). In addition to memory access violations, in this mode the XGA will also cause an I/O violation interrupt to be issued if this I/O register is accessed. This is a way for the XGA to provide write protection for this register.

ENAB_VIRT_LU

This bit, if set, enables the XGA's virtual memory feature. If the virtual memory feature is enabled, all XGA address references are translated through the 386/486 Memory Management Unit–compatible page directory mechanism. This allows the XGA to perform bus mastering operations even in a fragmented, protected mode environment. If virtual memory use is disabled (the default state), then all PC address references are physical PC memory addresses.

Comments

The interrupt caused by setting the PAGE_NP_ENAB or PROT_VIOL_ENAB bits comes into the PC as IRQ 2, and therefore as interrupt 0AH. The state of these two bits has no effect on the comparable status bits in the Virtual Memory Interrupt Status register (see next section). Reserved bits are undefined on reads, and must be written with 0s.

Mnemonic

VIRT_MEM_CTRL

I/O 21x7 Virtual Memory Interrupt Status Register

Read/Write, 8 bits

```
Bit            7  6  5  4  3  2  1  0
                     —— Reserved ——

PAGE_NP_STAT   ─┘

PROT_VIOL_STAT ─┘
```

PAGE_NP_STAT

This bit reflects the state of the VM Page Not Present interrupt. If set, such an interrupt, or at least condition, has occurred. This bit is cleared by writing a 1 to it. Note, however, that writing a 1 will cause a page retry. If the fault has not been handled properly, an infinite loop could result.

PROT_VIOL_STAT

This bit shows the status of the Protection Violation interrupt. If set, the interrupt has happened at some point in the past. Clear it by writing a 1 to it. Note, however, that writing a 1 will cause a page retry. If the fault has not been handled properly, an infinite loop could result.

Comments

Writing a 0 to any of these bits has no effect on their setting, while a 1 will clear a bit. This is apparently designed to allow the read-back value of the register to be used as the clearing value. All of these bits also behave as documented, whether or not the associated interrupt bits have been set in the Virtual Memory Control register. Reserved bits are undefined on reads, and must be written with 0s.

Mnemonic

VIRT_MEM_INT_STAT

I/O 21x8   Aperture Index Register

Read/Write, 8 bits

```
Bit        7  6  5  4  3  2  1  0
           Rsvd  ── MEMWIN_BANK ──
```

MEMWIN_BANK

This field controls which bank of display memory shows up in both the 64KB and 1MB memory windows. If the 64KB memory window is enabled, then this field defines which 64KB bank of the XGA's memory is available at the 0A0000H or 0B0000H locations.

If the 64KB memory window is disabled, then this field controls the contents of the 1MB memory window whose system address is specified in the 1MB Aperture Base Address register (in the POS). Note that in this case, bits 3–0 must be kept clear, since the 1MB memory window can view only display memory that is located on a 1MB boundary.

Comments

Reserved bits are not defined for reads, and must be written with 0s.

Mnemonic

MEMWIN_INDEX

I/O 21x9   Memory Access Mode

Read/Write, 8 bits

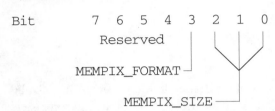

MEMPIX_FORMAT

This bit controls the byte ordering format for PC to XGA memory accesses only. If cleared, the format is Intel format, and if set, the format is Motorola (see the Operating Mode register for details on the difference between the two).

MEMPIX_SIZE

This field selects the pixel size for use by the system CPU when accessing XGA display memory. The field is defined as follows:

Bit 2	Bit 1	Bit 0	Pixel Size
0	0	0	1 bit
0	0	1	2 bits
0	1	0	4 bits
0	1	1	8 bits
1	0	0	16 bits
1	0	1	Reserved
1	1	0	Reserved
1	1	1	Reserved

Comments

It is important to set this field properly because it affects the interpretation of reads and writes from/to XGA display memory by the system CPU. This is because the XGA has an integrated pixel swapper that converts reads/writes from/to an internal storage format. This register has no impact on the way XGA sees memory. The reserved bits in the register must be cleared on writes.

Mnemonic

MEM_ACCESS_MODE

I/O 21xA   Index Register

Read/Write, 8 bits

```
Bit        7  6  5  4  3  2  1  0
           ── Register Index ──
```

Comments

This register should be loaded with the index of the desired Index register. A list of valid Index registers is listed earlier in this chapter, with the descriptions of the Index registers starting in the section after the next. The data for the Index registers can be written via the Data and Supplemental Data registers. Even better, you can load an Index register with a 16-bit I/O write to this register, where the index is located in the low byte, and the data is in the high byte of the word.

Mnemonic

IO_INDEX

I/O 21xB   Data Register

Read/Write, 8 bits

```
Bit        7  6  5  4  3  2  1  0
           ─Index Register Data ─
```

Comments

This register should be written with the data destined for the Index register whose index has been loaded into the Index register. For usage, see the description of the Index register in the previous section.

Mnemonic

IO_DATA

I/O 21xC-21xF   Supplemental Data Registers

Read/Write, 8 bits each

```
Bit        7  6  5  4  3  2  1  0
                 Index Register Data
Reserved ─┘
```

Comments

Each of these registers is individually identical in function to the Data register. They are just replicated in order to allow multiple-byte writes and reads.

Specifically, these four registers are designed to be used if more than 1 byte of data is to be written to a given Index register at once, as might be with the State A, State B, and Palette and Sprite Data registers (where a significant number of bytes can be written or read in rapid succession). Writing a word of data to 21xC will result in two bytes of data being sent to the current Index register, using Intel byte ordering. For a double-word (32-bit) I/O write to this register, four bytes of data are sent to the same Index register. The same mechanism may be used to read data as well.

Mnemonic

IO_MOREDATA

Index 00H   Memory Configuration 0

Read/Write, 8 bits

```
Bit        7  6  5  4  3  2  1  0
           ──── Reserved ────
           VRAM_SERDATA_WID ─┘
```

VRAM_SERDATA_WID

This field selects the serial data width for VRAM transfers:

Bit 1	Bit 0	Function
0	0	Reserved
0	1	16-bit serial data width
1	0	32-bit serial data width
1	1	Reserved

Comments

This register is board implementation-specific, and should not be used by application software. This register is initialized by the POST process. Reserved bits should be preserved when writing this register.

Mnemonic

MEM_CONFIG0

Index   01H   Memory Configuration 1

Read/Write, 8 bits

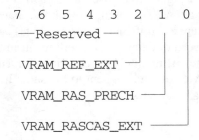

```
Bit        7  6  5  4  3  2  1  0
           ─── Reserved ───
                           VRAM_REF_EXT

                           VRAM_RAS_PRECH

                           VRAM_RASCAS_EXT
```

VRAM_REF_EXT

If set, this bit will extend the Column Address Select (CAS) and Row Address Select (RAS) signal active times for VRAM refresh cycles.

VRAM_RAS_PRECH

Setting this bit will extend the RAS precharge time between consecutive VRAM cycles.

VRAM_RASCAS_EXT

If set, this bit will extend Column Address Select (CAS) and Row Address Select (RAS) signal active times for all VRAM cycles except refresh.

Comments

This register is board implementation-specific, and should not be used by application software. This register is initialized by the POST process. Reserved bits should be preserved when writing this register.

Mnemonic

MEM_CONFIG1

Index   02H   Memory Configuration 2

Read/Write, 8 bits

```
Bit        7  6  5  4  3  2  1  0
           -Reserved-   ⌐Reserved
           VRAM_SER_LEN ⌐
```

VRAM_SER_LEN

This field selects the VRAM serializer length: $0 = 256$, and $1 = 512$.

Comments

This register is board implementation-specific, and should not be used by application software. This register is initialized by the POST process. Reserved bits should be preserved when writing this register.

Mnemonic

MEM_CONFIG2

Index   04H   Auto-Configuration

Read Only, 8 bits

```
Bit        7  6  5  4  3  2  1  0
           ——— Reserved ———  ⌐
                 BUS_SIZE ⌐
```

BUS_SIZE

This bit provides information on the type of bus interface/slot the XGA device is hooked up through. This information is useful to applications, because it indicates both address and data transfer limitations.

0   16-bit (16MB maximum address space)

1   32-bit (full 4GB address space)

Comments

Do not write to this register.

Mnemonic

AUTO_CONFIG

Index   0CH   State A Data

Read/Write, 8 bits

```
Bit        7  6  5  4  3  2  1  0
           ——— State A Data ———
```

State A Data

This register is designed for use during task switches when the state of the XGA device must be saved or restored. The amount of data to be read from or written to this register is specified in the State A Length Memory register. The length of the State A data is specified in double-word (32-bit) units. When doing a state restore, all state data must be restored in exactly the same sequence as they were read; otherwise the XGA will be left in an undefined state (that is, it may "hang" the XGA).

Comments

Using the State A Data and State B Data registers allows multitasking software to save the entire internal state of the XGA coprocessor, which is vital when a drawing operation is interrupted by a task switch. The task switcher must go and suspend the current operation via the Control register. Then the switcher needs to read the State A Length and State B Length registers in order to determine how much data to save. The data should be read from the State A Data and State B Data registers, and the XGA frame buffer should also be saved. To restore a state, the same procedure should be followed in reverse, with the switcher turning off the operation suspension in the Control register once everything has been fully restored. This will cause the previously suspended operation to be resumed.

Mnemonic

STATE_A_DATA

Index   0DH   State B Data

Read/Write, 8 bits

```
Bit        7  6  5  4  3  2  1  0
           ——— State B Data ———
```

State B Data

This register is designed for use during task switches when the state of the XGA device must be saved or restored. The amount of data to be read from or written to this register is specified in the State B Length Memory register. The length of the State B Data is specified in double-word (32-bit) units. When doing a state restore, all state data must be restored in exactly the same sequence as they were read; otherwise the XGA will be left in an undefined state.

Comments

Using the State A Data and State B Data registers allows multitasking software to save the entire internal state of the XGA coprocessor, which is vital when a drawing operation is interrupted by a task switch. The task switcher must go and suspend the current operation via the Control register. Then the switcher needs to read the State A and State B Length registers in order to determine how much data to save. The data should be read from the State A Data and State B Data registers, and the XGA frame buffer should also be saved. To restore a state, the same procedure should be followed in reverse, with the switcher turning off the operation suspension in the Control register once everything has been fully restored. This will cause the previously suspended operation to be resumed.

Mnemonic

STATE_B_DATA

Index   10H   Horizontal Total Low

Read/Write, 8 bits

```
Bit        7  6  5  4  3  2  1  0
           —Horizontal Total Low—
```

Horizontal Total Low

This register contains the low 8 bits of the 16 bits required for the Horizontal Total. The horizontal total is the size of one scan line, measured in 8 pixel units, including the sync times. The horizontal total, in pixels, is calculated as *(Horizontal Total + 1) * 8*.

Comments

Both this register and the Horizontal Total High register must be loaded in order to set a horizontal total value for the XGA.

Mnemonic

HTOTAL_LO

Index   11H   Horizontal Total High

Read/Write, 8 bits

```
Bit      7  6  5  4  3  2  1  0
         Horizontal Total High
```

Horizontal Total High

This register contains the high 8 bits of the 16 bits required for the Horizontal Total. The horizontal total is the size of one scan line, measured in 8 pixel units, including the sync times. The horizontal total, in pixels, is calculated as *(Horizontal Total + 1) * 8*.

Comments

Both this register and the Horizontal Total Low register must be loaded in order to set a horizontal total value for the XGA. This register generally will be loaded with a 00H, since horizontal totals for current XGA resolutions do not exceed 2048 (which is a Horizontal Total value of 00FFH).

Mnemonic

HTOTAL_HI

Index   12H   Horizontal Display End Low

Read/Write, 8 bits

```
Bit      7  6  5  4  3  2  1  0
         Horizontal Disp. End Low
```

Horizontal Display End Low

This register contains the low 8 bits of the 16 bits required for the Horizontal Display End. The horizontal display end is the position of the end of the active display area on a horizontal scan line, relative to the start of the active display on the line. The horizontal display end, in pixels, is calculated as *(Horizontal Display End + 1) * 8*.

Comments

Both this register and the Horizontal Display End High register must be loaded in order to set a horizontal display end value for the XGA.

Mnemonic

HDISP_END_LO

Index   13H   Horizontal Display End High

Read/Write, 8 bits

```
Bit      7  6  5  4  3  2  1  0
         Horizontal Disp. End High
```

Horizontal Display End High

This register contains the high 8 bits of the 16 bits required for the Horizontal Display End. The horizontal display end is the position of the end of the active display area on a horizontal scan line, relative to the start of the active display on the line. The horizontal display end, in pixels, is calculated as *(Horizontal Display End + 1) * 8.*

Comments

Both this register and the Horizontal Display End Low register must be loaded in order to set a horizontal display end value for the XGA. This register generally will be loaded with a 00H, since the horizontal display end for current XGA resolutions does not exceed 2048 (which is a Horizontal Display End value of 00FFH).

Mnemonic

HDISP_END_HI

Index   14H   Horizontal Blank Start Low

Read/Write, 8 bits

```
Bit      7  6  5  4  3  2  1  0
         Horizontal Blank Start Low
```

Horizontal Blank Start Low

This register contains the low 8 bits of the 16 bits required for the Horizontal Blank Start. The horizontal display end is the position of the start of the horizontal blanking period on a horizontal scan line, relative to the start of the active display on the line. The horizontal blank start, in pixels, is calculated as *(Horizontal Blank Start + 1) * 8.*

Comments

Both this register and the Horizontal Blank Start High register must be loaded in order to set a horizontal blank start value for the XGA.

Mnemonic

HBLANK_START_LO

Index 15H Horizontal Blank Start High

Read/Write, 8 bits

```
Bit       7  6  5  4  3  2  1  0
          Horizontal Blank Start High
```

Horizontal Blank Start High

This register contains the high 8 bits of the 16 bits required for the Horizontal Blank Start. The horizontal display end is the position of the start of the horizontal blanking period (and the end of right-hand display border area) on a horizontal scan line, relative to the start of the active display on the line. The horizontal blank start, in pixels, is calculated as *(Horizontal Blank Start + 1) * 8*.

Comments

Both this register and the Horizontal Blank Start Low register must be loaded to set a horizontal blank start value for the XGA. This register generally will be loaded with a 00H, since the horizontal blank start for current XGA resolutions does not exceed 2048 (a Horizontal Blank Start value of 00FFH).

Mnemonic

HBLANK_START_HI

Index 16H Horizontal Blank End Low

Read/Write, 8 bits

```
Bit       7  6  5  4  3  2  1  0
          Horizontal Blank End Low
```

Horizontal Blank End Low

This register contains the low 8 bits of the 16 bits required for the Horizontal Blank End. The horizontal display end is the position of the end of the horizontal blanking period on a horizontal scan line, relative to the start of the active display on the line. The horizontal blank end, in pixels, is calculated as *(Horizontal Blank End + 1) * 8*.

Comments

Both this register and the Horizontal Blank End High register must be loaded to set a horizontal blank end value for the XGA.

Mnemonic

HBLANK_END_LO

Index   17H   Horizontal Blank End High

Read/Write, 8 bits

```
Bit      7  6  5  4  3  2  1  0
         Horizontal Blank End High
```

Horizontal Blank End High

This register contains the high 8 bits of the 16 bits required for the Horizontal Blank End. The horizontal blank end is the position of the end of the horizontal blanking period (and the start of the left-hand display border area) on a horizontal scan line, relative to the start of the active display on the line. The horizontal blank end, in pixels, is calculated as *(Horizontal Blank End + 1) * 8.*

Comments

Both this register and the Horizontal Blank End Low register must be loaded in order to set a horizontal blank end value for the XGA. This register generally will be loaded with a 00H, since the horizontal blank end for current XGA resolutions does not exceed 2048 (which is a Horizontal Blank End value of 00FFH).

Mnemonic

HBLANK_END_HI

Index   18H   Horizontal Sync Pulse Start Low

Read/Write, 8 bits

```
Bit      7  6  5  4  3  2  1  0
         H-Sync Pulse Start Low
```

H-Sync Pulse Start Low

This register contains the low 8 bits of the 16 bits required for the Horizontal Sync Pulse Start. The horizontal display start is the position of the start of the horizontal sync on a horizontal scan line, relative to the start of the active display on the line. The horizontal sync pulse start, in pixels, is calculated as *(Horizontal Sync Pulse Start + 1) * 8.*

Comments

Both this register and the Horizontal Sync Pulse Start High register must be loaded in order to set a horizontal sync pulse start value for the XGA.

Mnemonic

HSYNC_START_LO

Index   19H   Horizontal Sync Pulse Start High

Read/Write, 8 bits

```
Bit        7  6  5  4  3  2  1  0
           H-Sync Pulse Start High
```

H-Sync Pulse Start High

This register contains the high 8 bits of the 16 bits required for the Horizontal Sync Pulse Start. The horizontal display start is the position of the start of the horizontal sync on a horizontal scan line, relative to the start of the active display on the line. The horizontal sync pulse start, in pixels, is calculated as *(Horizontal Sync Pulse Start + 1) * 8*.

Comments

Both this register and the Horizontal Sync Pulse Start Low register must be loaded in order to set a horizontal sync pulse start value for the XGA. This register generally will be loaded with a 00H, since the horizontal sync pulse start for current XGA resolutions does not exceed 2048 (which is a Horizontal Sync Pulse Start value of 00FFH).

Mnemonic
HSYNC_START_HI

Index   1AH   Horizontal Sync Pulse End Low

Read/Write, 8 bits

```
Bit        7  6  5  4  3  2  1  0
           H-Sync Pulse End Low
```

H-Sync Pulse End Low

This register contains the low 8 bits of the 16 bits required for the Horizontal Sync Pulse End. The horizontal display end is the position of the end of the horizontal sync on a horizontal scan line, relative to the start of the active display on the line. The horizontal sync pulse end, in pixels, is calculated as *(Horizontal Sync Pulse End + 1) * 8*.

Comments

Both this register and the Horizontal Sync Pulse End High register must be loaded in order to set a horizontal sync pulse end value for the XGA. The Horizontal Sync Pulse End registers are also used in the XGA's 132-column text mode in lieu of the VGA's Horizontal Retrace End register.

Mnemonic
HSYNC_END_LO

Index   1BH   Horizontal Sync Pulse End High

Read/Write, 8 bits

```
Bit      7  6  5  4  3  2  1  0
         H-Sync Pulse End High
```

H-Sync Pulse End High

This register contains the high 8 bits of the 16 bits required for the Horizontal Sync Pulse End. The horizontal display end is the position of the end of the horizontal sync on a horizontal scan line, relative to the start of the active display on the line. The horizontal sync pulse end, in pixels, is calculated as *(Horizontal Sync Pulse End + 1) * 8*.

Comments

Both this register and the Horizontal Sync Pulse End Low register must be loaded to set a horizontal sync pulse end value for the XGA. The Horizontal Sync Pulse End registers are also used in the XGA's 132-column text mode in lieu of the VGA's Horizontal Retrace End register. This register generally will be loaded with a 00H, since the horizontal sync pulse end for current XGA resolutions does not exceed 2048 (a Horizontal Sync Pulse End value of 00FFH).

Mnemonic

HSYNC_END_HI

Index   1CH   Horizontal Sync Pulse Position 1

Write Only, 8 bits

```
Bit      7  6  5  4  3  2  1  0
                     — Reserved —
Reserved ⌙  \  ⌐
SYNC_PULSE_DLY1 ⌙
```

SYNC_PULSE_DLY1

This field controls the sync pulse delay, which allows the XGA sync pulse to be shifted by up to half a horizontal unit (8 pixels):

Bit 6	Bit 5	Sync Pulse Delay (in pixels)
0	0	0
0	1	Reserved
1	0	4
1	1	Reserved

Comments

This register must be programmed with the same SYNC_PULSE_DLY as the Horizontal Sync Position 2 register. This register is also used in the 132-column text mode, in lieu of the Horizontal Retrace Delay field of the VGA's Horizontal Retrace End register. The reserved bits must be set to 0 when writing to this register.

Mnemonic

HSYNC_POS1

Index   1EH   Horizontal Sync Pulse Position 2

Write Only, 8 bits

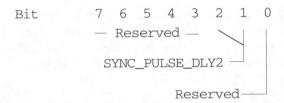

SYNC_PULSE_DLY2

This field controls the sync pulse delay, which allows the XGA sync pulse to be shifted by up to half a horizontal unit (8 pixels):

Bit 2	Bit 1	Sync Pulse Delay (in pixels)
0	0	0
0	1	Reserved
1	0	4
1	1	Reserved

Comments

This register must be programmed with the same SYNC_PULSE_DLY as the Horizontal Sync Position 1 register (see previous section). The reserved bits must be set to 0 when writing to this register, which is also used in the 132-column text mode, in lieu of the Horizontal Retrace Delay field of the VGA's Horizontal Retrace End register.

Mnemonic

HSYNC_POS2

Index   20H   Vertical Total Low

Read/Write, 8 bits

```
Bit        7  6  5  4  3  2  1  0
           —Vertical Total Low—
```

Vertical Total Low

This register contains the low 8 bits of the 11 bits required for the Vertical Total. The vertical total is the total length of a display frame, specified in units of scan lines, including the sync times. The vertical total, in scan lines, is calculated as *(Vertical Total + 1)*.

Comments

Both this register and the Vertical Total High register must be loaded in order to set a vertical total value for the XGA.

Mnemonic

VTOTAL_LO

Index   21H   Vertical Total High

Read/Write, 8 bits

```
Bit        7  6  5  4  3  2  1  0
           — Reserved —      \   /
                              \ /
           Vertical Total High ┘
```

Vertical Total High

This register contains the high 8 bits of the 11 bits required for the Vertical Total. The vertical total is the total length of a display frame, specified in units of scan lines, including the sync times. The vertical total, in scan lines, is calculated as *(Vertical Total + 1)*.

Comments

Both this register and the Vertical Total Low register must be loaded in order to set a vertical total value for the XGA. Reserved bits should be written with 0s.

Mnemonic

VTOTAL_HI

Index   22H   Vertical Display End Low

Read/Write, 8 bits

```
Bit        7  6  5  4  3  2  1  0
           Vertical Disp. End Low
```

Vertical Display End Low

This register contains the low 8 bits of the 11 bits required for the Vertical Display End. The vertical display end is the position of the end of the active display area, defined in scan lines, relative to the start of the active display area. The vertical display end, in scan lines, is calculated as *(Vertical Display End + 1)*.

Comments

Both this register and the Vertical Display End High register must be loaded in order to set a vertical display end value for the XGA.

Mnemonic

VDISPLAY_END_LO

Index   23H   Vertical Display End High

Read/Write, 8 bits

```
Bit        7  6  5  4  3  2  1  0
           — Reserved —        \  /
        Vertical Disp. End High ⌐
```

Vertical Display End High

This register contains the high 3 bits of the 11 bits required for the Vertical Display End. The vertical display end is the position of the end of the active display area, defined in scan lines, relative to the start of the active display area. The vertical display end, in scan lines, is calculated as *(Vertical Display End + 1)*.

Comments

Both this register and the Vertical Display End Low register must be loaded in order to set a vertical display end value for the XGA. Reserved bits should be written with 0s.

Mnemonic

VDISPLAY_END_HI

Index   24H   Vertical Blank Start Low

Read/Write, 8 bits

```
Bit      7  6  5  4  3  2  1  0
         Vertical Blank Start Low
```

Vertical Blank Start Low

This register contains the low 8 bits of the 11 bits required for the Vertical Blank Start, which is the position of the start of the vertical blanking signal (and the end of the lower display border area), defined in scan lines, relative to the start of the active display area. The vertical blank start, in scan lines, is calculated as *(Vertical Blank Start + 1)*.

Comments

Both this register and the Vertical Blank Start High register must be loaded in order to set a vertical blank start value for the XGA.

Mnemonic

VBLANK_START_LO

Index   25H   Vertical Blank Start High

Read/Write, 8 bits

```
Bit      7  6  5  4  3  2  1  0
         ─ Reserved ─        \    /
                              \  /
                               \/
   Vertical Blank Start High ──┘
```

Vertical Blank Start High

This register contains the high 8 bits of the 16 bits required for the Vertical Blank Start, which is the position of the start of the vertical blanking signal (and the end of the lower display border area), defined in scan lines, relative to the start of the active display area. The vertical blank start, in scan lines, is calculated as *(Vertical Blank Start + 1)*.

Comments

Both this register and the Vertical Blank Start Low register must be loaded in order to set a vertical blank start value for the XGA. Reserved bits should be written with 0s.

Mnemonic

VBLANK_START_HI

Index   26H   Vertical Blank End Low

Read/Write, 8 bits

```
Bit        7  6  5  4  3  2  1  0
           Vertical Blank End Low
```

Vertical Blank End Low

This register contains the low 8 bits of the 11 bits required for the Vertical Blank End, which is the position of the end of the vertical blanking signal (and the start of the upper display border area), defined in scan lines, relative to the start of the active display area. The vertical blank end, in scan lines, is calculated as *(Vertical Blank End + 1)*.

Comments

Both this register and the Vertical Blank End High register must be loaded in order to set a vertical blank end value for the XGA.

Mnemonic

VBLANK_END_LO

Index   27H   Vertical Blank End High

Read/Write, 8 bits

```
Bit        7  6  5  4  3  2  1  0
           — Reserved —        \ | /
     Vertical Blank End High  ─┘
```

Vertical Blank End High

This register contains the high 3 bits of the 11 bits required for the Vertical Blank End, which is the position of the end of the vertical blanking signal (and the start of the upper display border area), defined in scan lines, relative to the start of the active display area. The vertical blank end, in scan lines, is calculated as *(Vertical Blank End + 1)*.

Comments

Both this register and the Vertical Blank End Low register must be loaded in order to set a vertical blank end value for the XGA. Reserved bits should be written with 0s.

Mnemonic

VBLANK_END_HI

Index   28H   Vertical Sync Start Low

Read/Write, 8 bits

```
Bit        7  6  5  4  3  2  1  0
           Vertical Sync Start Low
```

Vertical Sync Start Low

This register contains the low 8 bits of the 11 bits required for the Vertical Sync Start. The vertical sync start is the position of the start of the vertical sync signal, defined in scan lines, relative to the start of the active display area. The vertical sync start, in scan lines, is calculated as *(Vertical Sync Start + 1)*.

Comments

Both this register and the Vertical Sync Start High register must be loaded in order to set a vertical sync start value for the XGA.

Mnemonic

VSYNC_START_LO

Index   29H   Vertical Sync Start High

Read/Write, 8 bits

```
Bit        7  6  5  4  3  2  1  0
           — Reserved —       \   /
                               \ /
     Vertical Sync Start High   
```

Vertical Sync Start High

This register contains the high 3 bits of the 11 bits required for the Vertical Sync Start. The vertical sync start is the position of the start of the vertical sync signal, defined in scan lines, scan lines, relative to the start of the active display area. The vertical sync start, in scan lines, is calculated as *(Vertical Sync Start + 1)*.

Comments

Both this register and the Vertical Sync Start Low register must be loaded in order to set a vertical sync start value for the XGA. Reserved bits should be written with 0s.

Mnemonic

VSYNC_START_HI

Index   2AH   Vertical Sync End

Read/Write, 8 bits

```
Bit       7  6  5  4  3  2  1  0
          — Vertical Sync End —
```

Vertical Sync End

This register contains the Vertical Sync End, which is the position of the end of the vertical sync signal, defined in scan lines, relative to the start of the active display area. The value placed in this register should be the low order byte of the 16-bit value that contains the actual Vertical Sync End, which must be no more than 31 scan lines greater than the Vertical Sync Start.

Comments

Before setting the XGA into either VGA or 132-column text mode (via the Operating Mode register), you should set bit 5 of this register to 1. Also, while a read of this register may not return the same value you wrote, the read value is valid for save and restore operations.

Mnemonic

VSYNC_END

Index   2CH   Vertical Line Compare Low

Read/Write, 8 bits

```
Bit       7  6  5  4  3  2  1  0
        Vertical Line Compare Low
```

Vertical Line Compare Low

This register contains the low 8 bits of the 11 bits required for the Vertical Line Compare. The vertical line compare is the position of the end of the scrollable display area, defined in scan lines, relative to the start of the active display area. The vertical line compare, in scan lines, is calculated as *(Vertical Line Compare + 1)*.

Comments

Both this register and the Vertical Line Compare High register must be loaded in order to set a vertical line compare value for the XGA. The vertical line compare alters the Display Start registers to prevent a horizontal strip at the bottom of the display from being scrolled.

Mnemonic

VLINE_COMP_LO

Index   2DH   Vertical Line Compare High

Read/Write, 8 bits

```
Bit       7  6  5  4  3  2  1  0
          — Reserved —    \   /
Vertical Line Compare High ┘
```

Vertical Line Compare High

This register contains the high 3 bits of the 11 bits required for the Vertical Line Compare. The vertical line compare is the position of the end of the scrollable display area, defined in scan lines, relative to the start of the active display area. The vertical line compare, in scan lines, is calculated as *(Vertical Line Compare + 1)*.

Comments

Both this register and the Vertical Line Compare Low register must be loaded in order to set a vertical line compare value for the XGA. The vertical line compare alters the Display Start registers to prevent a horizontal strip at the bottom of the display from being scrolled. Reserved bits should be written with 0s.

Mnemonic

VLINE_COMP_HI

Index   30H   Sprite Position X Low

Read/Write, 8 bits

```
Bit       7  6  5  4  3  2  1  0
          Sprite Position X Low
```

Sprite Position X Low

This register contains the low 8 bits of the 11 bits required to set the Sprite's horizontal position on the display, specified in pixels, relative to the left hand edge of the screen.

Comments

The X position specified in the 16-bit Sprite Position X register, positions the hotspot of the sprite, which is defined in the Sprite Hotspot registers. A diagram describing sprite positioning is shown in Figure 4.2. Both this register and the Sprite Position X High register must be loaded in order to set a Sprite Position X value.

Mnemonic

SPRITE_POSX_LO

Index   31H   Sprite Position X High

Read/Write, 8 bits

```
Bit       7  6  5  4  3  2  1  0
          — Reserved —    \    /
                           \  /
                            \/
          Sprite Position X High ┘
```

Sprite Position X High

This register contains the high 8 bits of the 16 bits required to set the Sprite's horizontal position on the display, specified in pixels, relative to the left hand edge of the screen.

Comments

The X position specified in the 16-bit Sprite Position X register, positions the hotspot of the sprite, which is defined in the Sprite Hotspot registers. A diagram describing sprite positioning is shown in Figure 4.2. Both this register and the Sprite Position X Low register must be loaded in order to set a Sprite Position X value. Reserved bits should be written with 0s.

Mnemonic

SPRITE_POSX_HI

Index   32H   Sprite Hotspot X

Read/Write, 8 bits

```
Bit       7  6  5  4  3  2  1  0
          Rsvd  Sprite Hotspot X
```

Sprite Hotspot X

This register contains the X hotspot position of the sprite. The hot spot is the point within the 64x64 sprite which is used by the Sprite Position X & Y registers to position the sprite on the screen. The hot spot is specified relative from the upper-right corner of the sprite, in pixels.

Comments

A diagram describing sprite positioning is shown in Figure 4.2. Reserved bits must be set to 0, and are undefined on reads.

Mnemonic

SPRITE_HOTX

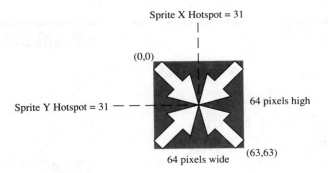

Figure 4-2a. This is a sample sprite. The dotted lines that bisect the sprite indicate the sample Sprite X and Y Hotspot position of (31,31), which happens to be pretty much the center of the sprite.

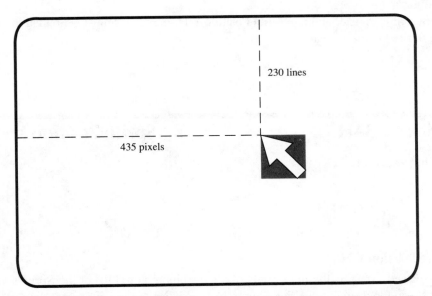

Figure 4.2. These diagrams show how the Sprite Hotspot X and Y affect the display of the sprite on the graphics screen. The hotspot is the point from which the sprite starts displaying. The Sprite X and Y Positions position the hotspot on the display. The top figure shows a sprite. The dotted lines that bisect the sprite indicate the sample Sprite X and Y Hotspot position (31, 31), which is the center of the sprite. The bottom figure is a not-to-scale representation of the sprite above, as it would appear on the display if you set the Sprite X Position to 435 and the Sprite Y Position to 230.

Index 33H   Sprite Position Y Low

Read/Write, 8 bits

```
Bit        7  6  5  4  3  2  1  0
           Sprite Position Y Low
```

Sprite Position Y Low

This register contains the low 8 bits of the 11 bits required to set the Sprite's vertical position on the display, specified in scan lines, relative to the top edge of the screen.

Comments

The Y position specified in the 16-bit Sprite Position Y register, positions the hotspot of the sprite, which is defined in the Sprite Hotspot registers. Figure 4.2 describes sprite positioning.

Both this register and the Sprite Position Y High register must be loaded in order to set a Sprite Position Y value.

Mnemonic

SPRITE_POSY_LO

Index 34H   Sprite Position Y High

Read/Write, 8 bits

```
Bit        7  6  5  4  3  2  1  0
           — Reserved —       \   /
                               \ /
           Sprite Position Y High ⏌
```

Sprite Position Y High

This register contains the high 3 bits of the 11 bits required to set the Sprite's vertical position on the display, specified in scan lines, relative to the top edge of the screen.

Comments

The Y position specified in the 16-bit Sprite Position Y register, positions the hotspot of the sprite, which is defined in the Sprite Hotspot registers. Figure 4.2 describes sprite positioning. Both this register and the Sprite Position Y Low register must be loaded in order to set a Sprite Position Y value. Reserved bits should be written with 0s.

Mnemonic

SPRITE_POSY_HI

Index   35H   Sprite Hotspot Y

Read/Write, 8 bits

```
Bit       7  6  5  4  3  2  1  0
          Rsvd   Sprite Hotspot Y
```

Sprite Hotspot Y

This register contains the Y hotspot position of the sprite. The hot spot is the point within the 64x64 sprite which is used by the Sprite Position X & Y registers to position the sprite on the screen. The hot spot is specified relative from the upper-right corner of the sprite, in pixels.

Comments

A diagram describing sprite positioning is shown in Figure 4.2. Reserved bits must be set to 0, and are undefined on reads.

Mnemonic

SPRITE_HOTY

Index   36H   Sprite Control

Read/Write, 8 bits

```
Bit       7  6  5  4  3  2  1  0
          ——  Reserved  ——
               SPRITE_ENAB ——
```

SPRITE_ENAB

This bit controls the display of the XGA sprite on the display. If the bit is set, the sprite is displayed at the position set via the Sprite Position and Hotspot registers. If cleared, the sprite display is disabled.

Comments

Sprite display must be disabled during sprite data modification in order to avoid corruption of the sprite data. Reserved bits must be set to 0, and are undefined on reads.

Mnemonic

SPRITE_CTRL

Index   38H   Sprite Color 0 Red

Read/Write, 8 bits

```
Bit        7  6  5  4  3  2  1  0
              —Sprite Color 0 Red—
```

Sprite Color 0 Red

This register sets the red color component for sprite color 0.

Comments

There are two possible sprite colors, which are defined in a similar fashion to regular color palette entries. The benefit of this approach is that the sprite color does not tie up 2 regular palette entries as happens in other graphics architectures. Each sprite color has its own 8-bit red, green, and blue color intensities. However, the least significant 2 bits of each 8-bit color component intensity are ignored in XGA implementations shipped between 1990 and mid-1992.

Mnemonic

SPRITE_COLOR0_RED

Index   39H   Sprite Color 0 Green

Read/Write, 8 bits

```
Bit        7  6  5  4  3  2  1  0
              -Sprite Color 0 Green-
```

Sprite Color 0 Green

This register sets the green color component for sprite color 0.

Comments

There are two possible sprite colors, which are defined in a similar fashion to regular color palette entries. The benefit of this approach is that the sprite color does not tie up 2 regular palette entries as happens in some other graphics architectures. Each sprite color has its own 8-bit red, green, and blue color intensities. However, the least significant 2 bits of each 8-bit color component intensity are ignored in XGA implementations shipped between 1990 and mid-1992.

Mnemonic

SPRITE_COLOR0_GREEN

Index 3AH   Sprite Color 0 Blue

Read/Write, 8 bits

```
Bit       7  6  5  4  3  2  1  0
          -Sprite Color 0 Blue-
```

Sprite Color 0 Blue

This register sets the blue color component for sprite color 0.

Comments

There are two possible sprite colors, which are defined in a similar fashion to regular color palette entries. The benefit of this approach is that the sprite color does not tie up two regular palette entries as happens in some other graphics architectures. Each sprite color has its own 8-bit red, blue, and blue color intensities. However, the least significant two bits of each 8-bit color component intensity are ignored in XGA implementations shipped between 1990 and mid-1992.

Mnemonic

SPRITE_COLOR0_BLUE

Index 3BH   Sprite Color 1 Red

Read/Write, 8 bits

```
Bit       7  6  5  4  3  2  1  0
          —Sprite Color 1 Red—
```

Sprite Color 1 Red

This register sets the red color component for sprite color 1.

Comments

There are two possible sprite colors, which are defined in a similar fashion to regular color palette entries. The benefit of this approach is that the sprite color does not tie up 2 regular palette entries as happens in some other graphics architectures. Each sprite color has its own 8-bit red, green, and blue color intensities. However, the least significant 2 bits of each 8-bit color component intensity are ignored in XGA implementations shipped between 1990 and mid-1992.

Mnemonic

SPRITE_COLOR1_RED

Index   3CH   Sprite Color 1 Green

Read/Write, 8 bits

```
Bit       7  6  5  4  3  2  1  0
          -Sprite Color 1 Green-
```

Sprite Color 1 Green

This register sets the green color component for sprite color 1.

Comments

There are two possible sprite colors; they are defined in a similar fashion to regular color palette entries. The benefit of this approach is that the sprite color does not tie up two regular palette entries, as happens in some other graphics architectures. Each sprite color has its own 8-bit red, green, and blue intensities. However, the least significant 2 bits of each 8-bit color component intensity are ignored in the XGA implementations shipped between 1990 and mid-1992.

Mnemonic

SPRITE_COLOR1_GREEN

Index   3DH   Sprite Color 1 Blue

Read/Write, 8 bits

```
Bit       7  6  5  4  3  2  1  0
          -Sprite Color 1 Blue-
```

Sprite Color 1 Blue

This register sets the blue color component for sprite color 1.

Comments

There are two possible sprite colors, which are defined in a similar fashion to regular color palette entries. The benefit of this approach is that the sprite color does not tie up 2 regular palette entries as happens in some other graphics architectures. Each sprite color has its own 8-bit red, blue, and blue color intensities. However, the least significant 2 bits of each 8-bit color component intensity are ignored in XGA implementations shipped between 1990 and mid-1992.

Mnemonic

SPRITE_COLOR1_BLUE

Index   40H   Display Start Low

Read/Write, 8 bits

```
Bit        7  6  5  4  3  2  1  0
              —Display Start Low—
```

Display Start Low

This register is the low byte of the 19-bit Display Start value. The Display Start specifies which part of XGA display memory will be shown on the XGA display.

Comments

The Display Start is specified in units of 8 bytes, and affects the entire display, except for whatever horizontal strip at the bottom of the screen is protected by the Vertical Line Compare registers. The pitch (the number of bytes between the start of one scan line and the start of the subsequent scan line) of the display buffer is set via the Display Buffer Pitch registers. All three Display Start registers should be set to guarantee proper results.

Mnemonic

DISP_ADDR_LO

Index   41H   Display Start Middle

Read/Write, 8 bits

```
Bit        7  6  5  4  3  2  1  0
              -Display Start Middle-
```

Display Start Middle

This register is the middle byte of the 19-bit Display Start value. The Display Start specifies which part of XGA display memory will be shown on the XGA display.

Comments

The Display Start is specified in units of 8 bytes, and affects the entire display, except for whatever horizontal strip at the bottom of the screen is protected by the Vertical Line Compare registers. The pitch (the number of bytes between the start of one scan line and the start of the subsequent scan line) of the display buffer is set via the Display Buffer Pitch registers. All three Display Start registers should be set to guarantee proper results.

Mnemonic

DISP_ADDR_MID

Index   42H   Display Start High

Read/Write, 8 bits

```
Bit        7  6  5  4  3  2  1  0
           — Reserved —      \   /
           Display Start High —⌐
```

Display Start High

This register is the high byte of the 19-bit Display Start value. The Display Start specifies which part of XGA display memory will be shown on the XGA display.

Comments

The Display Start is specified in units of 8 bytes, and affects the entire display, except for any horizontal strip at the bottom of the screen protected by the Vertical Line Compare registers. The pitch (the number of bytes between the start of one scan line and the start of the subsequent scan line) of the display buffer is set via the Display Buffer Pitch registers. A value of more than 1 in this register will cause unpredictable results in current XGA devices, since they only offer a maximum of 1MB of VRAM, and a Display Start of 20000H or greater goes beyond that. All three Display Start registers should be set for proper results. Reserved bits should be set to 0 on writes.

Mnemonic

DISP_ADDR_HIGH

Index   43H   Display Buffer Pitch Low

Read/Write, 8 bits

```
Bit        7  6  5  4  3  2  1  0
           Display Buffer Pitch Low
```

Display Buffer Pitch Low

This register is the low byte of the 11 bit Display Buffer Pitch value. The Display Buffer Pitch specifies the width of display memory for display purposes.

Comments

The Display Buffer Pitch is specified in units of 8 bytes, and affects the entire display. The pitch is the number of bytes between the start of one scan line and the start of the subsequent scan line.

Mnemonic

BUFFER_PITCH_LO

Index   44H

Display Buffer Pitch High

Read/Write, 8 bits

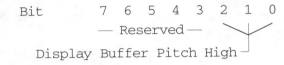

```
Bit        7  6  5  4  3  2  1  0
           — Reserved —
Display Buffer Pitch High
```

Display Buffer Pitch High

This register is the high byte of the 16-bit Display Buffer Pitch value. The Display Buffer Pitch specifies the width of display memory for display purposes.

Comments

The Display Buffer Pitch is specified in units of 8 bytes, and affects the entire display. The pitch is the number of bytes between the start of one scan line and the start of the subsequent scan line. This register should not be set higher than 7, which will provide a maximum pitch of 16,376 bytes (7FFH * 8). Reserved bits should be set to 0 when writing this register.

Mnemonic

BUFFER_PITCH_HI

Index   50H

Display Control 1

Read/Write, 8 bits

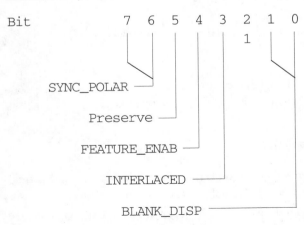

```
Bit            7  6  5  4  3  2  1  0
                             1

        SYNC_POLAR
        Preserve
        FEATURE_ENAB
        INTERLACED
        BLANK_DISP
```

SYNC_POLAR

This field controls sync polarity of the horizontal and vertical sync signals. IBM monitors, and some others, use the sync polarity signal to determine the number of scan lines displayed, and hence, the frequency of a given mode. The 2 bits define the vertical resolution in the follow manner:

Bit 7	Bit 6	V-SYNC	H-SYNC	# of Lines
0	0	Positive	Positive	768
0	1	Positive	Negative	400
1	0	Negative	Positive	350
1	1	Negative	Negative	480

FEATURE_ENAB

This bit enables the XGA feature connector (also known as the Video Extension), which carries all the video signals from the XGA before it enters the DAC. The feature connector can be used as a video source for devices like the IBM 8514/A which support a video pass-through feature. If cleared, the feature connector is disabled, the preferred setting while in 132-column text and XGA graphics mode. This bit should be set when in VGA mode. This bit also enables the plasma screen in the XGA graphics mode on the IBM PS/2 Model P75.

INTERLACED

This bit indicates whether or not the display output is interlaced (see glossary). If this bit is set, interlacing is enabled.

BLANK_DISP

This field controls the blanking of the display, per the following chart:

Bit 1	Bit 0	Function
0	0	Display blanked, CRT controller reset
0	1	Display blanked in preparation for CRTC reset
1	0	Reserved
1	1	Normal operation

In order to reset the CRT controller, you should first use a value of 01b in this field to prepare for the reset, and then perform the actual reset operation.

If you just want to blank the display, use the Palette Mask register, with palette entry 0 set to all 0s.

Comments

Bit 6 must be preserved on writes, which means that it should be read first, and masked in to the new write value for this register. Bit 2 should always be set to 1 on writes, and is undefined on reads.

Mnemonic

DISP_CTRL1

Index   51H   Display Control 2

Read/Write, 8 bits

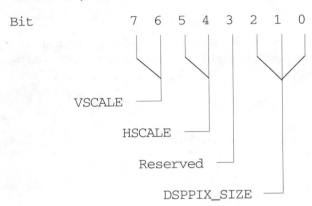

VSCALE

This field controls the vertical scale factor of pixels on the display. The vertical scale factor determines the number of times a given scan line of display data is duplicated on the screen:

Bit 7	Bit 6	Vertical Scale Factor
0	0	1 (normal display)
0	1	2 (each scan line is shown twice)
1	0	4
1	1	Reserved

HSCALE

This field controls the horizontal scale factor of pixels on the display. The horizontal scale factor determines the number of times a given pixel of display data is duplicated on the screen horizontally:

Bit 5	Bit 4	Horizontal Scale Factor
0	0	1 (normal display)
0	1	2 (each pixel doubled in width)
1	0	4
1	1	Reserved

DSPPIX_SIZE

This field selects the pixel size for use by the CRT controller in display graphical data on the screen. This pixel size helps determine how the CRT controller interprets the data for display purposes, such as palette and pixel scaling. The field is defined as follows:

Bit 2	Bit 1	Bit 0	Pixel Size
0	0	0	1 bit
0	0	1	2 bits
0	1	0	4 bits
0	1	1	8 bits
1	0	0	16 bits
1	0	1	Reserved (some XGA clones may use this combination to indicate 24 bits)
1	1	0	Reserved
1	1	1	Reserved

Comments

The reserved bit (bit 3) is undefined on reads, and must be set to 0 on writes.

Mnemonic

DISP_CTRL2

Index   52H   Monitor ID and Gun Output

Read Only, 8 bits

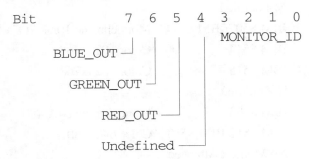

BLUE_OUT

This bit reflects the current state of the blue gun of the DAC. When the blue gun output is high, then this bit is 1, and when the output is low this bit is 0.

GREEN_OUT

This bit reflects the current state of the green gun of the DAC. When the green gun output is high, then this bit is 1, and when the output is low this bit is 0.

RED_OUT

This bit reflects the current state of the red gun of the DAC. When the red gun output is high, then this bit is 1, and when the output is low this bit is 0.

MONITOR_ID

This field reflects the monitor ID bits returned by the monitor attached to the XGA device. The following chart shows the monitor IDs for current IBM monitors:

Bit 3	Bit 2	Bit 1	Bit 0	Monitor Type	Maximum Resolution
0	0	0	0	Not defined	—
0	0	0	1	Not defined	—
0	0	1	0	Not defined	—
0	0	1	1	Not defined	—
0	1	0	0	Not defined	—
0	1	0	1	Not defined	—

continued...

...from previous page

0	1	1	0	Not defined	—
0	1	1	1	Not defined	—
1	0	0	0	Not defined	—
1	0	0	1	IBM 8507/IBM 8604	Monochrome 1024x768
1	0	1	0	IBM 8514	Color 1024x768
1	0	1	1	IBM 8515	Color 1024x768
1	1	0	0	Not defined	—
1	1	0	1	IBM 8503	Monochrome 640x480
1	1	1	0	IBM 8512/IBM 8513	Color 640x480
1	1	1	1	No Monitor Attached	—

Comments

The contents of bit 4 are not defined when reading this register. The primary use for the xxx_OUT bits is diagnostic. The MONITOR_ID field is useful for determining the type and maximum resolution capabilities of the attached monitor, although any software you write for the XGA should provide a manual override in case an older monitor without an ID is attached to the XGA.

Some programmers feel that this type of monitor sensing is useless since a sizeable number of non-IBM monitors do not support it. The suggested alternative is to have the user tell you what's attached.

Mnemonic

MON_ID_GUN_OUT

Index   54H   Clock Select 1

Read/Write, 8 bits

```
Bit        7  6  5  4  3  2  1  0
          - Reserved -
                       CLK_SEL1
                          CLK_SCALE
```

CLK_SEL1

This field, when used in conjunction with the CLK_SEL2 bit in the CLOCK_SEL2 register (index 70H), selects the video clock for use by the XGA to generate a given resolution. In the following table, the * bit refers to CLK_SEL2:

Bit *	Bit 3	Bit 2	Clock selected
0	0	0	VGA 8-pixel character text mode and 640x480 graphics mode
0	0	1	VGA 9-pixel character text mode
0	1	0	Clock from the feature connector
0	1	1	1024x768 interlaced graphics mode
1	0	0	132-column text mode
1	0	1	Reserved
1	1	0	Reserved
1	1	1	Reserved

CLK_SCALE

This field controls the clock scale factor via a hardware divider, and needs to be set in conjunction with the CLK_SEL1 field and CLK_SEL2 bit.

Bit 1	Bit 0	Video clock scale factor
0	0	1 (used in VGA text and 640x480 graphics modes)
0	1	2 (used in 132-column text and 1024x768 graphics modes)
1	0	Reserved
1	1	Reserved

Comments

Both the CLOCK_SEL1 and CLOCK_SEL2 registers need to be set in order for a video clock to properly set for a given mode.

Mnemonic

CLOCK_SEL1

Index   55H   Border Color

Read/Write, 8 bits

```
Bit          7  6  5  4  3  2  1  0
             ——— Border Color ———
```

Border Color

This register should be loaded with the 8-bit color palette index which is to be used when displaying the display border. This 8-bit value is translated by the color look-up table into the appropriate red, green, and blue display values.

Comments

The screen border area is the area between the active display region and the sync signals on the display. It is also known as the overscan area. This register is physically the same as the VGA's overscan register.

Mnemonic

BORDER_COLOR

Index   60H   Sprite Index Low/Palette Index Low

Read/Write, 8 bits

```
Bit          7  6  5  4  3  2  1  0
             Sprite/Palette Index Low
```

Sprite/Palette Index Low

This register is use to load the low byte of the 14-bit Sprite Data Index register, or the full 8 bits of the index for palette data operations. This applies primarily to write operations, but may be used for some read operations as well.

Comments

For sprite indexing, both this register and either the Sprite/Palette Index High or Sprite/Palette Prefetch Index High must be written in order to set an initial value for reading or writing sprite data. However, reading the palette or sprite data should be done in conjunction with the Sprite/Palette Index Low with Prefetch or the Sprite Index High with Prefetch register. See the description of these registers for more information.

Once data is read or written via the Sprite Data or Palette Data registers, the index value (16 bit for the sprite, 8 bit for the palette) will increment in proportion to the type of data being transferred. For sprite data, the index will increment on every byte transfer, while for palette data, the index will increment every three or four transfers, depending on the state of the Palette Sequence register. This allows consecutive accesses to the appropriate data register to access consecutive units of data.

This register should be saved and restored, as appropriate, during task switch operations.

Mnemonic

SPRITE_INDEX_LO, PALETTE_INDEX_LO

Index   61H   Sprite Index High

Read/Write, 8 bits

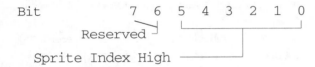

Sprite Index High

This register is used to load the high byte of the 14-bit Index register for sprite data operations. This applies to both read and write operations.

Comments

This register *and* either the Sprite/Palette Index Low or Sprite/Palette Index Low with Prefetch must be written to set an initial value for reading or writing sprite data. However, reading the palette or sprite data should be done in conjunction with the Sprite/Palette Index Low with Prefetch or the Sprite Index High with Prefetch register. See the sections on these registers for details.

Once data is read or written via the Sprite Data registers, the 16-bit index value will increment in proportion to the type of data being transferred. For sprite data, the index will increment on every byte transfer.

This register should be saved and restored, as appropriate, during task switch operations.

Mnemonic

SPRITE_INDEX_HI

Index 62H Sprite/Palette Index Low with Prefetch

Read/Write, 8 bits

```
Bit           7  6  5  4  3  2  1  0
              Sprite/Palette Index Low
```

Sprite/Palette Index Low

This register is used to load the low byte of the 14-bit Sprite Data Index register, or the full 8 bits of the index for palette operations. This applies only to read operations.

Comments

This register differs from the normal Sprite/Palette Index Low register in two ways. First, it is used exclusively for reading the sprite or palette data. Second, as soon as this register is written with a value, both the Sprite and Palette Prefetch registers are loaded with the data currently pointed to by this index for the palette, and by the combined High/Low index value for the sprite. As soon as the Prefetch registers are loaded, the index is incremented.

The data pointed to by the initially set index is available through the Prefetch register(s) and the appropriate Data register. If at least one of the Prefetch Index registers is not used, the read information from the Sprite Data registers will be 1 byte out of sync; that is, it will be delayed by 1 byte. The read information for Palette Data registers will be multiple bytes out of sync. Subsequent reads from the Sprite Data or Palette Data registers will cause the index to increment as well.

For reading sprite data, the regular Sprite/Palette Index Low register should be written first, then the Sprite Index High with Prefetch should be written with the desired 16-bit index value.

For palette read operations, load *this* register—not the normal Sprite/Palette Index Low register—with the desired index.

This register should be not saved or restored during task switch operations.

Mnemonic

SPRITE_INDEX_LO_PRE, PALETTE_INDEX_LO_PRE

Index   63H   Sprite Index High with Prefetch

Read/Write, 8 bits

```
Bit            7  6  5  4  3  2  1  0
               — Sprite Index High —
```

Sprite Index High

This register is used to load the high byte of the 14-bit Sprite Data Index register for read operations only.

Comments

This register differs from the normal Sprite/Palette Index High register in two ways. First, it is used exclusively for reading the sprite data. Second, as soon as this register is written with a value, the Sprite Prefetch register is loaded with the data currently pointed to by the combined High/Low index value for the sprite. As soon as the Prefetch register is loaded, the low byte of the index is incremented.

The data pointed to by the initially set index is available through both the Prefetch register and the Sprite Data register. If one of the Prefetch Index registers (High or Low) is not used, the read information from the Sprite Data registers will be 1 byte out of sync; the read information from the Palette Data registers will be multiple bytes out of sync. After this, subsequent reads from the Sprite Data register will cause the 14-bit index to increment as well.

For reading sprite data, the regular Sprite/Palette Index Low register should be written first, and this register written next with the desired 14-bit index value.

This register should be not saved and restored during task switch operations.

Mnemonic
SPRITE_INDEX_HI_PRE

Index   64H   Palette Mask

Read/Write, 8 bits

```
Bit            7  6  5  4  3  2  1  0
               —— Palette Mask ——
```

Palette Mask

This register should be loaded with a mask value that will be ANDed with each pixel as it comes out of memory and is about to be passed through the DAC.

Comments

This register should be programmed with a value of 0FFH for normal operations. The screen can be blanked by setting this register to 00H. If you do blank the display in this fashion, you should make sure that palette entry 0 is set to the color to which you want the screen blanked.

This register is physically the same as the VGA's DAC Mask register, located at I/O address 3C6H.

Mnemonic

PALETTE_MASK

Index   65H   Palette Data

Read/Write, 8 bits

```
Bit             7  6  5  4  3  2  1  0
                ——  Palette Data  ——
```

Palette Data

This register is used for reading and writing palette data.

Comments

For details on which part of the palette is accessed when this register is read or written, see the description of the Sprite/Palette Index Low registers a few pages back. The sequence of palette data is controlled by the Palette Sequence register (see next section).

Note that if a monochrome display is attached to the XGA device, the red and blue bytes of each palette entry should be cleared to 0.

Also, since the base IBM XGA supports only 6 bits per color gun, the low 2 bits of this register are ignored on writes, and return 0s if read. This will not necessarily be the case with forthcoming XGA clones.

The contents of this register should not be saved or restored during task switch operations, since that's actually handled by the Palette Prefetch registers. However, the full palette should be saved by *accessing* the palette via this register.

Mnemonic

PALETTE_DATA

Index 66H Palette Sequence

Read/Write, 8 bits

COLOR_FORMAT

This bit controls the format of the palette data as it is read or written. The following table shows the sequence of such data for each palette entry:

0   Red, Green, Blue

1   Red, Blue, Green, discard

The latter case is intended to allow double-word writes and reads, but for some reason IBM felt that an **RBG**x format, instead of the more traditional **RGB**x format, was the suitable way to do this.

COLOR_COMPNT

This field indicates which component of a palette entry is in the process of being read or written, according to the following table:

Bit 1	Bit 0	Color component
0	0	Red byte
0	1	Green byte
1	0	Blue byte
1	1	The discard byte

Comments

This register can be read or written at any time, and its contents should be saved and restored during task switch operations. The reserved bits are undefined on reads and should be written with 0s.

This register should be saved and restored during task switch operations.

Mnemonic

PALETTE_SEQUENCE

Index   67H   Palette Red Prefetch

Read/Write, 8 bits

```
Bit          7  6  5  4  3  2  1  0
            — Red Prefetch Data —
```

Red Prefetch Data

This register will contain the red prefetch data loaded when the Sprite/Palette Index Low with Prefetch register is written with an index value. The red prefetch data is the red component of the palette entry specified by the index value written to the Palette Index register.

Comments

This register will also contain the red component for the currently accessed palette entry for both read and write operation.

   This register should be saved and restored during task switch operations.

Mnemonic

PALETTE_RED_PRE

Index   69H   Palette Green Prefetch

Read/Write, 8 bits

```
Bit          7  6  5  4  3  2  1  0
            — Green Prefetch Data —
```

Green Prefetch Data

This register will contain the green prefetch data loaded when the Sprite/Palette Index Low with Prefetch register is written with an index value. The green prefetch data is the green component of the palette entry specified by the index value written to the Palette Index register.

Comments

This register will also contain the green component for the currently accessed palette entry for both read and write operations.

   This register should be saved and restored during task switch operations.

Mnemonic

PALETTE_GREEN_PRE

Index   68H   Palette Blue Prefetch

Read/Write, 8 bits

```
Bit           7  6  5  4  3  2  1  0
              — Blue Prefetch Data—
```

Blue Prefetch Data

This register will contain the blue prefetch data loaded when the Sprite/Palette Index Low with Prefetch register is written with an index value. The blue prefetch data is the blue component of the palette entry specified by the index value written to the Palette Index register.

Comments

This register will also contain the blue component for the currently accessed palette entry for both read and write operation.

This register should be saved and restored during task switch operations.

Mnemonic

PALETTE_BLUE_PRE

Index   6AH   Sprite Data

Read/Write, 8 bits

```
Bit           7  6  5  4  3  2  1  0
              ——— Sprite Data ———
```

Sprite Data

This register is used for reading and writing sprite data. Each sprite data byte defines four pixels of 2 bits each (bits 7 and 6; 5 and 4; 3 and 2; and 1 and 0). Each 2-bit pixel is defined as follows:

Bit 1	Bit 0	Definition
0	0	Sprite color 0
0	1	Sprite color 1
1	0	Transparent (allows underlying pixel data to show through)
1	1	Complement (1's complement of underlying pixel data)

Comments

More information on sprite programming is available at the beginning of this chapter and in the next chapter.

This register should not be saved or restored during task switch operations.

Mnemonic

SPRITE_DATA

Index　6BH　　　　　　　　　　　　　　　Sprite Data Prefetch

Read/Write, 8 bits

```
Bit         7  6  5  4  3  2  1  0
            ──────  Sprite Data ──────
```

Sprite Data

This register can be used for reading the prefetch sprite data, loaded by the XGA device when the Sprite/Data Index Lo with Prefetch register, or the Sprite Index High with Prefetch register is written with an index value.

Comments

More information on sprite prefetch is available under the descriptions of the Prefetch Index registers. I recommend you don't use this register. Instead, use the Sprite Data register to read sprite data, while still using the Sprite Index High with Prefetch register.

This register should be saved and restored during task switch operations.

Mnemonic

SPRITE_DATA_PRE

Index　70H　　　　　　　　　　　　　　　　　Clock Select 2

Read/Write, 8 bits

```
Bit         7  6  5  4  3  2  1  0
              ──────  Reserved ──────
       CLK_SEL2 ──┘
```

CLK_SEL2

This field, when used in conjunction with the CLK_SEL1 field in the CLOCK_SEL1 register (index 54H), selects the video clock for use by the XGA to generate a given resolution. In the table below, the 3 and 2 bits refer to CLK_SEL1, while the 7 bit refers to CLK_SEL2:

Bit 7	Bit 3	Bit 2	Clock selected
0	0	0	VGA 8-pixel character text mode and 640x480 graphics
0	0	1	VGA 9-pixel character text mode
0	0	1	VGA 9-pixel character text mode
0	1	0	Clock from the feature connector
0	1	1	1024x768 interlaced graphics mode
1	0	0	132-column text mode
1	0	1	Reserved
1	1	0	Reserved
1	1	1	Reserved

Comments

Both the CLOCK_SEL1 and CLOCK_SEL2 registers need to be set in order for a video clock to properly set for a given mode. Reserved bits are undefined on reads, and must be written with 0s.

Mnemonic

CLOCK_SEL2

Memory 00H — Page Directory Base Address

Write Only, 32 bits

Bit	31 30 29 28 27 26 25 24 23 22 21 20 19 18 17 16
	Page Directory Base Address; High 16 Bits

Bit	15 14 13 12 11 10 9 8 7 6 5 4 3 2 1 0
	Low 4 Bits —— These bits all set to 0 ——

Page Directory Base Address

This register should be loaded with the physical 32-bit PC address of the current x86 MMU Page Table (for the current task), which resides at the start of a 4KB page; hence the low 12 bits must all be set to 0.

Comments

This register is active only if the ENAB_VIRT_LU bit in the Virtual Memory Control register has been set. Also, you can set this register only if you have placed the XGA device into supervisor mode via the USER_SUPER bit in the VM Control register. Writing to this register clears the Table Look-aside Buffer (TLB) discussed in Chapter 8.

   This register should not be read.

Mnemonic

PAGE_DIR_BASE_ADDR

Memory   04H   Current Virtual Address

Read Only, 32 bits

```
Bit     31 30 29 28 27 26 25 24 23 22 21 20 19 18 17 16
                 Address of Page Fault; High 16 Bits

Bit     15 14 13 12 11 10 9  8  7  6  5  4  3  2  1  0
        Low 4 Bits ——— These bits all set to 0 ———
```

Address of Page Fault

Upon receiving a VM Hardware Not Present or Protection interrupt, this register will contain the physical 32 bit PC address of the page that caused the fault. Since an x86 page is 4KB in size, and starts on 4KB boundaries, the low 12 bits of the page address will all be set to 0.

Comments

This register is active only if the ENAB_VIRT_LU bit in the Virtual Memory Control register has been set.

   This register should not be written.

Mnemonic

CURR_VIRT_ADDR

Memory   0CH   State A Length

Read Only, 8 bits

```
Bit           7  6  5  4  3  2  1  0
              —— State A Length ——
```

State A Length

This register specifies the amount of data to be saved and restored via the State A Data register for a task switch. The length given in this register is specified as the number of double words to save/restore, and will not exceed 1KB in size.

Comments

Using the State A Length and State B Length registers allows multitasking software to save the entire internal state of the XGA coprocessor, which is vital when a drawing operation is interrupted by a task switch. The task switcher must suspend the current operation via the Control register, then read the State A Length and State B Length registers to determine how much data to save. The data should be read from the State A and State B Data registers, and the XGA frame buffer should also be saved. To restore a state, the same procedure should be followed in reverse, with the switcher turning off the operation suspension in the Control register once everything has been fully restored. This will cause the previously suspended operation to be resumed. It will probably be necessary to terminate the current operation after a state save and prior to a new state load.

Mnemonic

STATE_A_LEN

Memory   0DH   State B Length

Read Only, 8 bits

```
Bit           7  6  5  4  3  2  1  0
              —— State B Length ——
```

State B Length

This register specifies the amount of data to be saved and restored via the State B Data register for a task switch. The length given in this register is specified as the number of double words to save/restore, and will not exceed 1KB in size.

Comments

Using the State A Length and State B Length registers allows multitasking software to save the entire internal state of the XGA coprocessor, which is vital when a drawing operation is interrupted by a task switch. The task switcher must suspend the current operation via the Control register, then read the State A Length and State B Length registers to determine how much data to save. The data should be read from the State A and State B Data registers, and the XGA frame buffer should also be saved. To restore a state, the same procedure should be followed in reverse, with the switcher turning off the operation suspension in the Control register once everything has been fully restored. This will cause the previously suspended operation to be resumed. It will probably be necessary to terminate the current operation after a state save and prior to a new state load.

Mnemonic

STATE_B_LEN

Memory   11H   Control Register

Read/Write, 8 bits

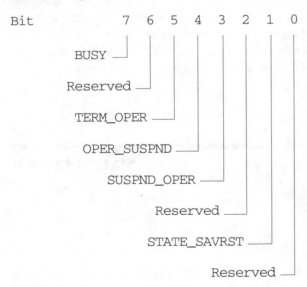

BUSY

If this bit is set during a read of this register, the XGA drawing engine is in the process of executing some type of drawing operation. While this bit is set, you should not write to any memory registers. If this bit is 0 on a read, then the XGA memory registers can be written to and an XGA operation can be initiated. This bit should be written as a 0 (if you need to write to this register).

Checking this bit in a tight loop will slow down the XGA's current drawing operation. This is a flaw in the original XGA silicon, and IBM has added a new register in the XGA-NI to minimize the impact of checking busy status on graphic operations. See Appendix C for details.

TERM_OPER

This bit should be set to 1 if you want to terminate a currently executing XGA operation. After terminating an operation in this fashion, you need to make sure it has really terminated before going on. This can be accomplished by either waiting for the BUSY bit to become 0, or by waiting for the CMD_DONE_STAT bit to be set in the Interrupt Status register (I/O 21x5). This latter scenario is the result of a "Command Done" interrupt being set by the XGA.

Once the operation has been terminated, this bit is automatically cleared, and the XGA coprocessor is reset to its original power-on state. This means that all XGA interrupts have been disabled, some other bits have been reset, and the contents of all memory registers are in an undetermined state and need to be reprogrammed for further use.

Writing a 0 to this bit has no effect on the operation of the XGA.

OPER_SUSPND

This bit is valid only during a read operation, and signifies (if set) that an XGA drawing operation is currently suspended.

SUSPND_OPER

Setting this bit to a 1 will suspend the XGA drawing engine's operation. Once the current operation (if any) is suspended, the XGA will set the OPER_SUSPND bit. The main purpose in suspending the XGA's drawing operations is to prepare for a task switch.

To restart a suspended operation, write a 0 to this bit. This is necessary after a state restore operation has been completed in order to get the XGA up and running in the new state. Once the operation is restarted, the OPER_SUSPND bit is cleared.

To start a new operation after suspending the current operation, you must set the TERM_OPER bit, and go through the motions necessary to terminate an operation, thereby terminating the suspended state.

Writing this bit clears the Table Look-aside Buffer (TLB).

STATE_SAVRST

This bit is used to signal the XGA for a state restore or save operation. When set to 0, the XGA's state may be restored. When set to 1, an XGA state save may be performed. Either way, when saving or restoring the XGA's state, it is necessary to set the SUSPND_OPER bit in order to suspend the current operation.

Comments

The reserved bits are undefined on reads, and must be written as 0s. The latter also applies to the BUSY and OPER_SUSPND bits.

Mnemonic

CTRL_REG

Memory   12H   Pixel Map Index

Write Only, 8 bits

```
Bit        7  6  5  4  3  2  1  0
           —— Reserved ——
                             MAP_INDEX
```

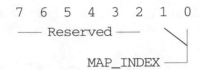

MAP_INDEX

This field is used to select which one of four pixel maps will have its definitions accessible to the host processor. The host CPU can modify these definitions via the four Pixel Map registers listed on the following pages. The field is defined as follows:

Bit 1	Bit 0	Pixel map specified (*n*)
0	0	Mask map
0	1	Pixel map A
1	0	Pixel map B
1	1	Pixel map C

Comments

Maps are discussed in some detail at the beginning of this chapter. The reserved bits must be set to 0 when writing to this register.

Mnemonic

MAP_INDEX

Memory 14H   Pixel Map *n* Base

Write Only, 32 bits

```
Bit     31 30 29 28 27 26 25 24 23 22 21 20 19 18 17 16
        —— Pixel Map n Base Address; High 16 bits ——

Bit     15 14 13 12 11 10 9  8  7  6  5  4  3  2  1  0
        —— Pixel Map n Base Address; Low 16 bits ——
```

Pixel Map *n* Base Address

This register should be loaded with the 32-bit physical PC address of the location of the pixel map. If the XGA is in VM mode (set via the ENAB_VIRT_LU bit in the Virtual Memory Control register), then the address needs to be a virtual address.

Comments

The map for this register is set via the Pixel Map Index register. Also, to specify a Pixel Map address within the XGA's display memory, remember that the 4MB aperture is always mapped as a PC 32-bit physical address, even when in a 16-bit slot. However, if pointing to system memory when the XGA is attached via a 16-bit path (determined by the Auto Configuration register), the physical address must be less than 00100000H (the 16MB mark). In order to safely use a map with BitBLT operations that are combined with mixes or color compare (that is, read/modify/write operations), it is important that you specify the base as a multiple of 4 bytes. Even if you will be using write operations only (mix is Src, and no color compare), use a base that starts on a double-word boundary, just to be safe.

Mnemonic

MAP_BASE

Memory   18H   Pixel Map *n* Width

Write Only, 16 bits

```
Bit       15 14 13 12 11 10 9  8  7  6  5  4  3  2  1  0
                     ──────── Pixel Map n Width ────────
```

Pixel Map *n* Width

This register specifies the width of the selected pixel map in units of pixels. The number placed in this register must be 1 less than the desired width (*desired width – 1*).

Comments

The purpose of this register is to tell the XGA about the width of a given pixel map so that it knows how to address each line of the map. In order to safely use a map with BitBLT operations that are combined with mixes or color compare (read-modify-write operations), it is important that you specify the width as a multiple of 4 bytes. For 1 bpp maps, the width should be divisible by 32; for 2 bpp maps, it should be divisible by 16; for 4 bit per pixel maps, it should be divisible by 8; and for 8 bit per pixel maps, it should be divisible by 4. If you will be using write operations only (mix is Src, and no color compare), any width will do.

Mnemonic

MAP_WIDTH

Memory   18H   Pixel Map *n* Height

Write Only, 16 bits

```
Bit       15 14 13 12 11 10 9  8  7  6  5  4  3  2  1  0
                     ──────── Pixel Map n Height ────────
```

Pixel Map *n* Height

This register specifies the height of the selected pixel map in units of lines. The number placed in this register must be 1 less than the desired height (*desired height – 1*).

Comments

The purpose of this register is to tell the XGA the height of a given pixel map so that it knows how to wrap source and pattern data.

Mnemonic

MAP_HEIGHT

Memory 1CH

Pixel Map *n* Format

Write Only, 8 bits

```
Bit          7  6  5  4  3  2  1  0
             - Reserved-
             PIX_FORMAT
                    PIXEL_SIZE
```

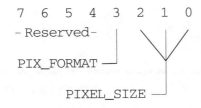

PIX_FORMAT

This bit sets the format for pixels:

0	Intel format
1	Motorola format

Intel format and Motorola format for pixels differ in both bit and byte order, as shown in Figure 4.3.

PIXEL_SIZE

These 3 bits select the pixel size of the selected map:

Bit 2	Bit 1	Bit 0	Pixel Size
0	0	0	1 bit
0	0	1	2 bits
0	1	0	4 bits
0	1	1	8 bits
1	0	0	Reserved (16 bits on XGA-NI and some clones)
1	0	1	Reserved (24 bits on some XGA clones)
1	1	0	Reserved
1	1	1	Reserved

This field is used to tell the XGA's drawing engine the size of a pixel for drawing operations. The original IBM XGA supports drawing operations only in 1, 2, 4, and 8 bit per pixel modes. Future XGA devices will most likely allow a setting of 100 to mean 16 bits, since they will probably support 16-bit drawing operations. Note that many 16-bit drawing operations on original IBM XGAs can be faked by using 8-bit operations.

Comments

For the mask map, only the PIX_FORMAT field may can be set. The PIXEL_SIZE field for the mask map should always be set for 1 bit per pixel. This rule also applies to whichever map (A, B, or C) you choose to use as a pattern map in drawing operations.

Mnemonic

MAP_FORMAT

Memory 20H   Bresenham Error Term

Read/Write, 16 bits

```
Bit      15 14 13 12 11 10 9  8  7  6  5  4  3  2  1  0
         ─────────────── Bresenham Error Term ───────────
```

Bresenham Error Term

This register specifies the Bresenham Error Term used in line drawing on the XGA. The Error Term is calculated as:

$$2 * (Delta\ Y) - (Delta\ X) - Fixup$$

The "Fixup" is a value of either 0 or 1, depending on the direction of the line (see Chapter 5), and is used to allow for retracing of lines even if coordinates are swapped. The contents of this register may be altered by execution of a line drawing command.

Comments

The error term value is a 2's complement number (i.e., a normal signed integer), and must be between –8192 and +8191. See the next chapter for details on drawing lines with the XGA.

Mnemonic

BRES_ERROR

Memory 24H   Bresenham Constant 1

Write Only, 16 bits

```
Bit      15 14 13 12 11 10 9  8  7  6  5  4  3  2  1  0
         ─────────────── Bresenham Constant 1 ───────────
```

Intel Format	Byte 0								Byte 1								Byte 2							
Bit Position In Byte	7	6	5	4	3	2	1	0	7	6	5	4	3	2	1	0	7	6	5	4	3	2	1	0
Bits Per Pixel:																								
1 BPP Pixel Order:	7	6	5	4	3	2	1	0	15	14	13	12	11	10	9	8	23	22	21	20	19	18	17	16
Bit significance	0	0	0	0	0	0	0	0	0	0	0	0	0	0	0	0	0	0	0	0	0	0	0	0
2 BPP Pixel Order:	3	3	2	2	1	1	0	0	7	7	6	6	5	5	4	4	11	11	10	10	9	9	8	8
Bit significance	1	0	1	0	1	0	1	0	1	0	1	0	1	0	1	0	1	0	1	0	1	0	1	0
4 BPP Pixel Order:	1	1	1	1	0	0	0	0	3	3	3	3	2	2	2	2	5	5	5	5	4	4	4	4
Bit significance	3	2	1	0	3	2	1	0	3	2	1	0	3	2	1	0	3	2	1	0	3	2	1	0
8 BPP Pixel Order:	0	0	0	0	0	0	0	0	1	1	1	1	1	1	1	1	2	2	2	2	2	2	2	2
Bit significance	7	6	5	4	3	2	1	0	7	6	5	4	3	2	1	0	7	6	5	4	3	2	1	0
16 BPP Pixel Order:	0	0	0	0	0	0	0	0	0	0	0	0	0	0	0	0	1	1	1	1	1	1	1	1
Bit significance	7	6	5	4	3	2	1	0	15	14	13	12	11	10	9	8	7	6	5	4	3	2	1	0

Motorola Format	Byte 0								Byte 1								Byte 2							
Bit Position In Byte	7	6	5	4	3	2	1	0	7	6	5	4	3	2	1	0	7	6	5	4	3	2	1	0
Bits Per Pixel:																								
1 BPP Pixel Order:	0	1	2	3	4	5	6	7	8	9	10	11	12	13	14	15	16	17	18	19	20	21	22	23
Bit significance	0	0	0	0	0	0	0	0	0	0	0	0	0	0	0	0	0	0	0	0	0	0	0	0
2 BPP Pixel Order:	0	0	1	1	2	2	3	3	4	4	5	5	6	6	7	7	8	8	9	9	10	10	11	11
Bit significance	1	0	1	0	1	0	1	0	1	0	1	0	1	0	1	0	1	0	1	0	1	0	1	0
4 BPP Pixel Order:	0	0	0	0	1	1	1	1	2	2	2	2	3	3	3	3	4	4	4	4	5	5	5	5
Bit significance	3	2	1	0	3	2	1	0	3	2	1	0	3	2	1	0	3	2	1	0	3	2	1	0
8 BPP Pixel Order:	0	0	0	0	0	0	0	0	1	1	1	1	1	1	1	1	2	2	2	2	2	2	2	2
Bit significance	7	6	5	4	3	2	1	0	7	6	5	4	3	2	1	0	7	6	5	4	3	2	1	0
16 BPP Pixel Order:	0	0	0	0	0	0	0	0	0	0	0	0	0	0	0	0	1	1	1	1	1	1	1	1
Bit significance	15	14	13	12	11	10	9	8	7	6	5	4	3	2	1	0	15	14	13	12	11	10	9	8

Figure 4.3. The top table shows the pixel order in the Intel format; the bottom table shows the pixel order in the Motorola format. Both tables use the first three bytes of a scan line to determine the pixel order. Only in 8 bpp mode are Intel and Motorola the same. Also, Motorola format should look familiar to you if you've ever done any CGA, EGA, or VGA programming, since its pixel order is similar to those architectures.

Bresenham Constant 1

This register specifies the Bresenham line drawing constant 1 (sometimes referred to as the **axial step constant**). It is calculated as:

```
2 * (Delta Y)
```

Comments

This constant is a 2's complement number, and must be between –8192 and +8191.

Mnemonic

BRES_K1

Memory   28H   Bresenham Constant 2

Write Only, 16 bits

```
Bit      15 14 13 12 11 10 9  8  7  6  5  4  3  2  1  0
         ─────────────────── Bresenham Constant 2 ───────────
```

Bresenham Constant 2

This register specifies the Bresenham line drawing constant 2 (sometimes referred to as the **diagonal step constant**). It is calculated as:

```
2 * (Delta Y) - 2 * (Delta X)
```

Comments

This constant is a 2's complement number, and must be between –8192 and +8191.

Mnemonic

BRES_K2

Memory   2CH   Short Stroke Register

Write Only, 32 bits

```
Bit      31 30 29 28 27 26 25 24 23 22 21 20 19 18 17 16
         ───── Stroke Code 4 ─────   ───── Stroke Code 3 ─────

Bit      15 14 13 12 11 10 9  8  7  6  5  4  3  2  1  0
         ───── Stroke Code 2 ─────   ───── Stroke Code 1 ─────
```

Stroke Code

Each short stroke code is composed of 8 bits, which are broken down as follows:

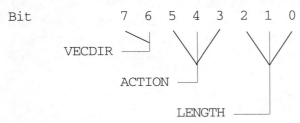

VECDIR

The direction of the short stroke vector in degrees, as measured counter-clockwise from the positive X axis. The values are defined as follows:

Bit 7	Bit 6	Bit 5	Direction in degrees (from positive X axis)
0	0	0	0
0	0	1	45
0	1	0	90
0	1	1	135
1	0	0	180
1	0	1	225
1	1	0	270
1	1	1	315

ACTION

Determines whether only the current position is moved or pixels are drawn as well.

0	Move current position
1	Draw the vector and move the current position

LENGTH

The length of the vector in pixels, and ranges from 0 to 15 in value.

Comments

Assigning a value of 0 to a stroke code is the equivalent of doing nothing. The whole contents of the 32-bit Short Stroke register are processed once Stroke Code 4 is written. This means that you can execute one short stroke drawing command by writing a single byte to Stroke Code 4, two commands by writing a word to Stroke Codes 4 and 3, and four commands by loading the whole 32-bit register at once. Many commands can be executed in sequence, just by writing successive data to this register. For this register to respond correctly, you must set up the Command register for the short stroke operation by loading the proper Short Stroke command (read or write), and by specifying all the proper source and destination maps and the start position in the Destination X and Y registers.

Mnemonic

SHORT_STROKE

Memory   48H   Foreground Mix

Write Only, 8 bits

```
Bit          7  6  5  4  3  2  1  0
           —  Foreground Mix  —
```

Foreground Mix

This register sets the foreground mix for subsequent graphics operations initiated via the Command register. The possible mix values are defined as follows:

Value	Mix
00H	0 (all bits cleared)
01H	Src AND Dst
02H	Src AND NOT Dst
03H	Src
04H	NOT Src AND Dst
05H	Dst
06H	Src XOR Dst
07H	Src OR Dst
08H	NOT Src AND NOT Dst
09H	Src XOR NOT Dst
0AH	NOT Dst

continued...

...from previous page

0BH	Src OR NOT Dst
0CH	NOT Src
0DH	NOT Src OR Dst
0EH	NOT Src OR NOT Dst
0FH	1 (all bits set)
10H	MAXIMUM (Src, Dst)
11H	MINIMUM (Src, Dst)
12H	Src + Dst [with saturate]
13H	Dst – Src [with saturate]
14H	Src – Dst [with saturate]
15H	(Src + Dst) / 2
16H–0FFH	Reserved

Src means the source pixel from the color registers or the source map. **Dst** means the destination pixel that already resides in the destination map. AND, OR, XOR, NOT are all bitwise binary operators. **Saturate** means that the operations are bounded at 0 in the case of subtractions, and at the maximum pixel value in the case of additions.

Comments

The selection of the foreground or background mixes is determined by the contents of the pattern map used (if selected) during the graphics operation. A 0 bit in the pattern map for the given pixel being operated on selects the background mix as an operator, and if no source map is defined, the background color is used. If the respective pattern map bit is 1 for the current pixel, then the selected operation is the foreground mix. In the latter case, if no source map is specified for the operation, then the source color value is used instead. Of course, if the mask map is in use, or the color compare is in effect, for a given operation, then it is possible that no pixel data whatsoever may be written, since these two items override the changing of destination pixel values.

Mnemonic

FORE_MIX

Memory   48H   Background Mix

Write Only, 8 bits

```
Bit          7  6  5  4  3  2  1  0
             ── Background Mix ──
```

Background Mix

This register sets the background mix for subsequent graphics operations initiated via the Command register. The possible mix values are defined as follows:

Value	Mix
00H	0 (all bits cleared)
01H	Src AND Dst
02H	Src AND NOT Dst
03H	Src
04H	NOT Src AND Dst
05H	Dst
06H	Src XOR Dst
07H	Src OR Dst
08H	NOT Src AND NOT Dst
09H	Src XOR NOT Dst
0AH	NOT Dst
0BH	Src OR NOT Dst
0CH	NOT Src
0DH	NOT Src OR Dst
0EH	NOT Src OR NOT Dst
0FH	1 (all bits set)
10H	MAXIMUM(Src, Dst)
11H	MINIMUM(Src, Dst)
12H	Src + Dst [with saturate]
13H	Dst − Src [with saturate]
14H	Src − Dst [with saturate]
15H	(Src + Dst) / 2
16H–0FFH	Reserved

   Src means the source pixel from the color registers or the source map. **Dst** means the destination pixel that already resides in the destination map. **AND, OR, XOR, NOT** are all bitwise binary operators. **Saturate** means that the operations are bounded at 0 in the case of subtractions, and at the maximum pixel value in the case of additions.

Comments

The selection of the foreground or background mixes is determined by the contents of the pattern map used (if selected) during the graphics operation. A 0 bit in the pattern map for the given pixel being operated on selects the background mix as an operator, and if no source map is defined, the background color is used. If the respective pattern map bit is 1 for the current pixel, then the selected operation is the foreground mix. In the latter case, if no source map is specified for the operation, then the source color value is used instead. Of course, if the mask map is in use, or the color compare is in effect, for a given operation, then it is possible that no pixel data whatsoever may be written, since these two items override the changing of destination pixel values.

Mnemonic

BACK_MIX

Memory   4AH   Color Compare Function

Write Only, 8 bits

```
Bit            7  6  5  4  3  2  1  0
               — Reserved —   CC_COND
```

CC_COND

This field is used to select the color compare condition to be used on all pixels drawing operations:

Bit 5	Bit 4	Bit 3	Description
0	0	0	Always TRUE
0	0	1	Dst > CC
0	1	0	Dst == CC
0	1	1	Dst < CC
1	0	0	Always FALSE
1	0	1	Dst >= CC
1	1	0	Dst != CC
1	1	1	Dst <= CC

Dst refers to the destination pixel, and **CC** refers to the color specified in the Color Compare Color register. If the result of the operation is FALSE, the destination pixel is updated by the result of the mix operation.

Comments

The default value of this register should be 4 (always FALSE) to enable the update of all pixels. If you choose to change the color compare condition, make sure to set the color compare color as well. The reserved bits in this register must be written with 0s. (For a flow diagram of how the XGA's various pixel processing modifiers interact, see Figure 4.4.)

Mnemonic

CC_FUNC

Memory   4CH   Color Compare Color

Write Only, 32 bits

```
Bit     31 30 29 28 27 26 25 24 23 22 21 20 19 18 17 16
        ——— Color Compare Color; High 16 bits ———

Bit     15 14 13 12 11 10 9  8  7  6  5  4  3  2  1  0
        ——— Color Compare Color; Low 16 bits ———
```

Color Compare Color

This register contains the color compare color used when the Color Compare Function register is loaded with a color compare condition requires a comparison between a destination pixel value and this register.

Comments

This register need only have the lowest order bits loaded, with the number of low order bits specified by the pixel bit depth of the destination map. For example, in an 8 bit per pixel mode, only bits 7–0 need to be loaded with the appropriate color compare color value.

Mnemonic

CC_COLOR

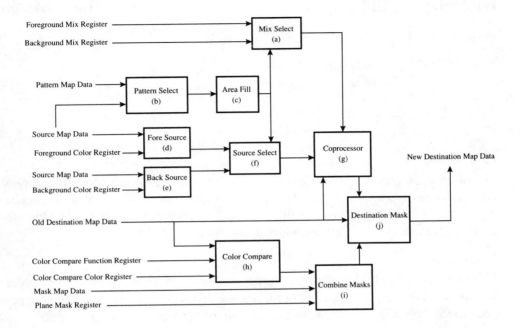

(a) Mix Select. This block selects which mix—foreground or background—to use, based on the output of blocks (b) and (c).

(b) Pattern Select. This block selects whether to use the pattern map or source map, based on the command sent via the Command register. The output of this block is fed into the Area Fill processor.

(c) Area Fill. If an area fill command is in process, this block performs the area fill operation. If area fill is not active, then pattern data is passed right through it.

(d) Foreground Source. This block selects either the foreground map data or the foreground color register data as the source for the operation, depending on the setting of the foreground source bits in the Command register.

(e) Background Source. Same as block (d), except that it deals with background source data.

(f) Source Select. This block sends out the data from either block (d) or block (e), depending on the input from blocks (b) and (c).

(g) Coprocessor. This is where the source and destination data are "mixed."

(h) Color Compare. This block generates mask information based on the old (but still current) destination map data combined with the color compare function.

(i) Combine Masks. This block combines the Plane Mask register contents with the current Mask Map data (if used for the operation) and with the result of block (h), in order to determine how much of the destination map pixel can be modified.

(j) Destination Mask. Using the combined mask from block (i), this block actually determines how much of the destination map pixel can be modified. Those portions that can be modified are taken from the output of block (g).

Figure 4.4. Block diagram of how the XGA's pixel processing functions.

Memory 50H   Plane Mask

Write Only, 32 bits

```
Bit   31 30 29 28 27 26 25 24 23 22 21 20 19 18 17 16
      ─────────────── Plane Mask, High 16 bits ───────────

Bit   15 14 13 12 11 10  9  8  7  6  5  4  3  2  1  0
      ─────────────── Plane Mask,  Low 16 bits ──────────
```

Plane Mask

The plane mask controls update access to each bit of a given destination pixel during XGA drawing operations. A 0 bit means that the respective bit is disabled, and hence will not be updated during a pixel write. A 1 enables updates to that bit. Masked bits are excluded from both color compare and mix operations.

Comments

This register need only have the lowest order bits loaded, with the number of low order bits specified by the pixel bit depth of the destination map. For example, in an 8 bit per pixel mode, only bits 7–0 need to be loaded with the appropriate plane mask value.

Mnemonic

PLANE_MASK

Memory 54H   Carry Chain Mask

Write Only, 32 bits

```
Bit    31 30 29 28 27 26 25 24 23 22 21 20 19 18 17 16
       ─────────── Carry Chain Mask; High 16 bits ───────

Bit    15 14 13 12 11 10 9  8  7  6  5  4  3  2  1  0
       ─────────── Carry Chain Mask;  Low 16 bits ───────
```

Carry Chain Mask

The carry chain mask controls bit-to-bit carries during the arithmetic mix and/or color compare operations. A 1 bit indicates that the carry state of the operation for that bit is propagated to the next bit to the left (the next more significant bit). A 0 bit means that the carry state is not propagated. This allows you to break a pixel into numerous "standalone" subpixels, as you may want to do, for instance, when treating an 8 bit per pixel map as two layered, independent 4 bit per pixel maps. In such a case, you would write a binary value of 01110111 to the lower 8 bits of this register.

Comments

This register need have only the lowest order bits loaded, with the number of low order bits specified by the pixel bit depth of the destination map less 1, since the upper bit of the carry chain mask will, by definition, not need to be set. For example, in an 8 bit per pixel mode, only bits 6–0 need to be loaded with the appropriate carry chain mask value.

Mnemonic

CARRY_CHAIN_MASK

Memory   58H   Foreground Color

Write Only, 32 bits

```
Bit     31 30 29 28 27 26 25 24 23 22 21 20 19 18 17 16
        ───────────  Foreground Color; High 16 bits ───────

Bit     15 14 13 12 11 10 9  8  7  6  5  4  3  2  1  0
        ───────────  Foreground Color; Low 16 bits ───────
```

Foreground Color

This register should be loaded with the foreground color to be used during drawing operations in which it is necessary.

Comments

This register need have only the lowest order bits loaded, with the number of low order bits specified by the pixel bit depth of the destination map. For example, in an 8 bit per pixel mode, only bits 7–0 need to be loaded with the appropriate foreground color value. For information on when the foreground color is used as a source, refer to both the Foreground Mix and Command register descriptions.

Mnemonic

FORE_COLOR

Memory 5CH   Background Color

Write Only, 32 bits

```
Bit     31 30 29 28 27 26 25 24 23 22 21 20 19 18 17 16
        ──────── Background Color; High 16 bits ────────

Bit     15 14 13 12 11 10 9  8  7  6  5  4  3  2  1  0
        ──────── Background Color;  Low 16 bits ────────
```

Background Color

This register should be loaded with the background color to be used during drawing operations in which a background color is utilized.

Comments

This register need have only the lowest order bits loaded, with the number of low order bits specified by the pixel bit depth of the destination map. For example, in an 8 bit per pixel mode, only bits 7–0 need to be loaded with the appropriate background color value. For information on when the background color is used as a source, refer to both the Background Mix and Command register descriptions.

Mnemonic

BACK_COLOR

Memory 60H   Operation Dimension 1

Write Only, 16 bits

```
Bit      15 14 13 12 11 10 9  8  7  6  5  4  3  2  1  0
         ──────── Operation Dimension 1 ────────
```

Operation Dimension 1

This register has two uses. The first is to specify the pixel width of BitBLT operations, and the second is to set the pixel length of a line draw operation. Either way, this register should be loaded with a number that is 1 less than the desired value. The line length can be calculated as being the greater of the absolute value of either the x delta or y delta— this automatically incorporates the "minus 1" rule.

Comments

The value placed in this register must be between 0 and 4095.

Mnemonic

DIM1

Memory 62H   Operation Dimension 2

Write Only, 16 bits

```
Bit      15 14 13 12 11 10 9  8  7  6  5  4  3  2  1  0
                    Operation Dimension 2
```

Operation Dimension 2

This register is used to specify the line height of BitBLT operations. It should be loaded with a number that is 1 less than the desired value.

Comments

The value placed in this register must be between 0 and 4095.

Mnemonic

DIM2

Memory 6CH   Mask Map Origin X Offset

Write Only, 16 bits

```
Bit      15 14 13 12 11 10 9  8  7  6  5  4  3  2  1  0
                    Mask Map Origin X Offset
```

Mask Map Origin X Offset

This register should be loaded with the X position within the destination map of the origin of the mask map.

Comments

The Mask Map Origin registers allow the map to be moved around the destination map so that a clipping rectangle can be defined. The Pixel Map 0 Width and Height registers are used to define the dimension of the mask map. See the Command register for information on how the mask map is utilized. The value placed in this register must be between 0 and 4095. (See Figure 4.5 for an example of how this register is used.)

Mnemonic

MASK_ORG_X

Memory   6EH   Mask Map Origin Y Offset

Write Only, 16 bits

```
Bit      15 14 13 12 11 10 9  8  7  6  5  4  3  2  1  0
         ──────────── Mask Map Origin Y Offset ────────
```

Mask Map Origin Y Offset

This register should be loaded with the Y position within the destination map of the origin of the mask map.

Comments

The Mask Map Origin registers allow the map to be moved around the destination map so that a clipping rectangle can be defined. The Pixel Map 0 Width and Height registers are used to define the dimension of the mask map. See the Command register for information on how the mask map is utilized. The value placed in this register must be between 0 and 4095.

Mnemonic

MASK_ORG_Y

Memory   70H   Source Map X

Read/Write, 16 bits

```
Bit      15 14 13 12 11 10 9  8  7  6  5  4  3  2  1  0
         ──────────────── Source Map X ─────────────
```

Source Map X

This register should be loaded with the X position within the source map of the first pixel to be used as source data.

Comments

The value placed in this register must be between 0 and 4095.

Mnemonic

SRC_X

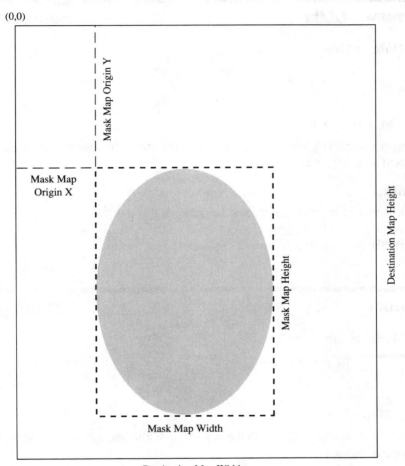

Figure 4.5. This figure demonstrates how the Mask Map Origin relates to the Destination Map coordinate space. In this example, the Mask Map Origin is offset from the Destination Map Origin. The Mask Map is also smaller than the destination map, and consists of an elliptical filled area that, when the Mask Map is enabled, will not allow any data outside of the dotted line to be drawn at all, and within the dotted line, the only pixels that will be updated are those that fall within the ellipsis. This is how the Mask Map's arbitrary clipping functions. In the less complex clipping rectangle mode, the Mask Map data need not be defined. The corners of the clipping rectangle are described by the combination of the Mask Map Origin and Mask Map Width and Height settings.

Memory   72H   Source Map Y

Read/Write, 16 bits

```
Bit       15 14 13 12 11 10 9  8  7  6  5  4  3  2  1  0
          ─────────────────── Source Map Y ───────────────
```

Source Map Y

This register should be loaded with the Y position within the source map of the first pixel to be used as source data.

Comments

The value placed in this register must be between 0 and 4095.

Mnemonic

SRC_Y

Memory   74H   Pattern Map X

Read/Write, 16 bits

```
Bit       15 14 13 12 11 10 9  8  7  6  5  4  3  2  1  0
          ─────────────────── Pattern Map X ───────────────
```

Pattern Map X

This register should be loaded with the X position within the pattern map of the first pixel to be used as pattern data.

Comments

The value placed in this register must be between 0 and 4095.

Mnemonic

PATT_X

Memory   76H   Pattern Map Y

Read/Write, 16 bits

```
Bit     15 14 13 12 11 10 9  8  7  6  5  4  3  2  1  0
                    ———————— Pattern Map Y ————————
```

Pattern Map Y

This register should be loaded with the Y position within the pattern map of the first pixel to be used as pattern data.

Comments

The value placed in this register must be between 0 and 4095.

Mnemonic

PATT_Y

Memory   78H   Destination Map X

Read/Write, 16 bits

```
Bit      15 14 13 12 11 10 9  8  7  6  5  4  3  2  1  0
                    ———————— Destination Map X ————————
```

Destination Map X

This register should be loaded with the X position within the destination map of the first pixel to be used as destination data.

Comments

The value placed in this register must be between –2048 and +6143 (using 2's complement notation).

Mnemonic

DEST_X

Memory   7AH   Destination Map Y

Read/Write, 16 bits

```
Bit      15 14 13 12 11 10 9  8  7  6  5  4  3  2  1  0
         ──────────────── Destination Map Y ────────────
```

Destination Map Y

This register should be loaded with the Y position within the destination map of the first pixel to be used as destination data.

Comments

The value placed in this register must be between –2048 and +6143, using 2's complement notation.

Mnemonic

DEST_Y

Memory   7CH   Command Register

Write Only, 32 bits

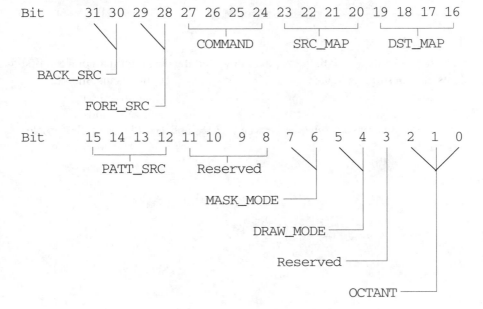

BACK_SRC

This field is used to select the source for background mix operations:

Bit 31	Bit 30	Function
0	0	Background color
0	1	Reserved
1	0	Source pixel map
1	1	Reserved

The background source becomes effective when a pattern map is used, and the corresponding bit in the pattern map is set to 0.

FORE_SRC

This field is used to select the source for foreground mix operations:

Bit 29	Bit 28	Function
0	0	Foreground color
0	1	Reserved
1	0	Source pixel map
1	1	Reserved

The foreground source becomes effective when a pattern map is used and the corresponding bit in the pattern map is set to 1, or when the pattern source is specified as Foreground.

COMMAND

This is the field used to tell the XGA to initiate a drawing operation, which starts as soon as this portion of the Command register is written. The only exception is the Short Stroke register, which must be loaded with short stroke data in order for actual drawing to occur after the Short Stroke command has been initiated here. The valid commands are as follows (all other bit combinations are reserved for future use):

Bit 27	Bit 26	Bit 25	Bit 24	Function
0	0	1	0	Short stroke read
0	0	1	1	Line draw read
0	1	0	0	Short stroke write
0	1	0	1	Line draw write
1	0	0	0	BitBLT
1	0	0	1	Inverting BitBLT
0	1	0	1	Area Fill

Short Stroke Read

This function will read each pixel from the source map that is supposed to be "drawn" as a short stroke vector, and put the data in the destination map, in a linear format. This way the data under a short stroke operation can be read and saved for later restoration. All short stroke drawing operations must be sent to the XGA via the Short Stroke register.

Line Draw Read

This function will read each pixel from the source map that is supposed to be "drawn" as a line, and put the data in the destination map, in a horizontal linear format. This way the data under a line operation can be read and saved for later restoration. The line direction and length are set via the various Bresenham registers and the Dimension 1 register.

Short Stroke Write

This function is used for putting the XGA into Short Stroke drawing mode, where drawing is performed into the destination map. All actual short stroke drawing commands must be sent to the Short Stroke register after this command has been sent.

Line Draw Write

This function is used for drawing lines into the destination map. The line direction and length are set via the various Bresenham registers and the Dimension 1 register.

BitBLT

This operation will initiate a bit block transfer operation that will copy a block of data from the X,Y position in the source map, with dimensions DIM1 by DIM2, to the X,Y position in the destination map. It is also possible to use this command to perform a Filled Rectangle command, by specifying a foreground source of the foreground color instead of the source map. Finally, you can tile the destination map by using a small source map or source map area, and as the BitBLT operation hits an edge of the source map, it will wrap, in both horizontal and vertical directions. If this function is used for an actual BitBLT operation specifying both the same source and destination map (a screen-to-screen BitBLT, for example), then it is important for your software to determine the exact order in which to perform the BitBLT in order to avoid data corruption that may occur if you are BitBLTing overlapping source and destination areas. The OCTANT field of this register can be used to set the BitBLT transfer directions.

Inverting BitBLT

This function is identical to the regular BitBLT operation with one major exception. It treats the destination map as having the Y = 0 line at the bottom of the destination map instead of at the top, as is the default case with all other XGA drawing functions. This means that data BitBLTed via this function will be vertically flipped in during the Inverting BitBLT process, and will be placed at a destination Y that is calculated as a line offset from the bottom of the map, not the top. All overlap rules still apply with this version.

This function scans each designated (via the PATT_X, PATT_Y, DIM1, and DIM2 registers) line of the pattern map for enabled bits. Every time it finds a set bit, it toggles an internal fill flag. During the scanning, if the fill flag is set, a pixel is written to the destination map at the point relative (from the destination map X & Y) to the one just scanned. This is a very quick way to fill objects. In the event that you want to do an area fill with a pattern, you must perform a two-step operation. The first is the one just described, except that destination must be a 1bpp map as well. Once the fill is complete, use the newly created fill map as the mask map for a normal BitBLT function. The specialized outline required by the area fill can be drawn by setting the DRAW_MODE field to the Area Boundary mode, and then drawing all the necessary area-fill outlines via the line drawing or short stroke commands. Additionally, lines should always be drawn in XOR mix mode (the 1 bpp map should be cleared prior to starting the outline).

SRC_MAP

This field controls the source map for the next drawing operation sent to the XGA via the COMMAND field:

Bit 23	Bit 22	Bit 21	Bit 20	Function
0	0	0	1	Pixel Map A
0	0	1	0	Pixel Map B
0	0	1	1	Pixel Map C

All undefined values for this field are reserved.

DST_MAP

This field controls the destination map for the next drawing operation sent to the XGA via the COMMAND field:

Bit 19	Bit 18	Bit 17	Bit 16	Function
0	0	0	1	Pixel Map A
0	0	1	0	Pixel Map B
0	0	1	1	Pixel Map C

All undefined values for this field are reserved.

PATT_SRC

This field controls the source of the pattern information for the next drawing operation sent to the XGA via the COMMAND field. The pattern data determines whether the background or foreground data are used as the source for the drawing operations. The background and foreground source contents are determined by the BACK_SRC and FORE_SRC fields, respectively. The valid values for this field are:

Bit 15	Bit 14	Bit 13	Bit 12	Function
0	0	0	1	Pixel Map A
0	0	1	0	Pixel Map B
0	0	1	1	Pixel Map C
1	0	0	0	Foreground source always selected
1	0	0	1	Generate pattern from source data

All undefined values for this field are reserved.

MASK_MODE

This field determines how the mask map comes into play during subsequent drawing operations:

Bit 7	Bit 6	Function
0	0	Mask map disabled. The mask map does not come into play at all with this setting.
0	1	Mask map boundary enabled. With this setting, the edges of the mask map (defined by the Mask Map Origin and Pixel Map 0 Width/Height registers) define a clipping rectangle, in which no pixel updates will occur outside the rectangle. No real data needs to actually be located at the Pixel Map 0 Base value in order to use this setting.
1	0	Mask map enabled. This setting enables the mask map. Each 0 bit in the map disables the update for the destination pixel tied to that bit, while a 1 bit allows the update to occur. This way arbitrary clipping can be performed. As with the prior setting, any pixel writes outside the mask map rectangle are disabled.
1	1	Reserved

DRAW_MODE

This field sets the drawing mode for line drawing and short stroke vector drawing operations:

Bit 5	Bit 4	Function
0	0	Draw all pixels of the line or vector
0	1	Draw all but the first pixel of the line or vector
1	0	Draw all but the last pixel of the line or vector (useful for polylines in XOR mode)
1	1	Draw area boundary; used for setting up for an area fill operation

OCTANT

This field is used to set the direction of line draws, as well as the scanning/copying direction for BitBLT operations, starting at the required X & Y parameters for the function to be used. For line drawing, the 3 bits have the following meaning:

Bit	Mnemonic/Meaning
0	**YMAJOR.** If set, this bit indicates that the line is longer in the Y dimension than in the X dimension. If clear, the X dimension is longer. If the X & Y dimensions are the same, it doesn't matter how this bit is set.
1	**DEC_Y.** If this bit is set, it means that the line has to be drawn in the negative Y direction (up if your origin is upper-left). If cleared, the line is drawn in the positive Y direction.
2	**DEC_X.** If set, this bit means that the line is to be drawn in the negative X direction (left if origin is at upper-left). If cleared, the line is drawn in the positive X direction.

For BitBLTs, the YMAJOR bit is ignored, but the DEC_Y and DEC_X bits still have the same meaning, in the sense that the copy operation may progress in any of the positive or negative X and Y directions.

Comments

Prior to writing a command to this register, it is necessary to make sure that all support registers, such as the X & Y start and destination, the dimension, and the color and mix registers, all have the desired values for the operation to be executed. All reserved bits must be set to 0 on writes.

Mnemonic

CMD_REG

Chapter 5

XGA Hardware Register Tutorial

This chapter provides a solid overview on programming the XGA registers, including XGA detection, initialization, maps, drawing, and special functions.

A quick note about how the code in this chapter is organized. Because we're programming directly at the hardware level, it doesn't make much sense to write a lot of tight code in C when it can be written more easily in assembly language. However, since not everyone is proficient in assembly language, I will provide C code wherever possible.

To facilitate use of both C and assembly language programming, I have provided two include files, XGA.H and XGA.INC, which can be found in Appendices E and F, respectively. All unfamiliar references in the code in this chapter can be resolved by referring to the appropriate appendix.

Finally, the tools used here are MASM 5.1 and Microsoft C v5.1. The assembly language code is also written with full 8088-compatibility in mind, even though the IBM XGA will function only in an i386 system. However, some clone XGAs should be able to run in at least 80286-based systems, and some may even work in original PCs. I thought it was best to play it safe and program to the lowest potential common denominator.

Now, on to the code....

Locating the XGA(s) in Your System

You can detect and initialize XGAs in your system using the new VESA XGA Extensions standard (see Appendix B), and IBM's DMQS interface (Appendix N).

It is likely, however, that neither of these mechanisms exists on your XGA hardware (as would be the case for all XGAs shipped prior to July 1992); therefore, you need to be able to detect XGAs in your system using a more low-level approach.

It is also possible to have several XGA devices in your system, and each can have any of a number of possible locations. Hence, it is necessary to either scan all devices in your system, or check all possible locations for an XGA.

Because the original IBM XGA sits on the Micro Channel bus, you can check all of the devices by selectively enabling the POS registers (located at I/O addresses 100H–104H) for each device, and checking to see whether the POS ID is a valid XGA ID. If the device is an XGA, you need to log its information, and then disable the POS registers.

Listing 5.1 shows XGAFIND.ASM, a series of assembly language routines that can be used to scan all Micro Channel slots, as well as the planar devices. Listing 5.2 shows SHOWXGAS.C, a small C program that uses the routines in XGAFIND.ASM, and displays the statistics for all XGAs in the system. Please note that it is recommended that you check for a VESA XGA BIOS first, then IBM's DMQS, and only if all that fails, use the code I've supplied here.

Listing 5.1. XGAFIND.ASM.

```
;************************************************************************
;
; XGAFIND.ASM - Contains XGA detection and selection routines.
;
;
; This file should be assembled via the following line:
;
;          MASM -ml XGAFIND;
;
; This will produce a file called XGAFIND.OBJ which can be linked
; with the calling program.
;
;************************************************************************
                 Include XGA.INC

XGA_INFO          struc
xiMonitor         db      ?              ; Monitor type
xiMode            db      ?              ; Native or VGA mode
xiBaseVRML        dw      ?              ; Base VRAM address (low)
```

```
xiBaseVRMH       dw      ?               ; Base VRAM address (high)
xiIOReg          dw      ?               ; I/O Reg address
xiMemReg         dw      ?               ; Mem Reg address
xiMemSize        dw      ?               ; Memory Size for board
XGA_INFO         ends

                 .MODEL  SMALL
                 .DATA

                 public  _xgaList, _xgaCount

_xgaCount        dw      ?               ; Count of XGAs in the system.
                                         ; Allocate space for up to 8 XGAs
_xgaList         db      8 * size XGA_INFO dup(?)

_ioRegBaseAddr   dw      ?
_memRegBaseAddr  dw      ?               ; Used by XGA code.

vramBaseAddr     label   dword;          Absolute base of VRAM in PC space
vramBaseAddrLo   dw      ?
vramBaseAddrHi   dw      ?

monitorSize      db      ?
xgaMode          db      ?
memorySize       dw      ?               ; # of 256K pages, either 2 or 4.
vgaState         dw      ?
;
; Monitor table stores sizes of monitor IDs:
;                0       = 640x480
;                1       = 1024x768
;                FFH     = No or Invalid monitor
;
monitorTable     db      0FFH            ; x000 - ?
                 db      001H            ; x001 - 8507/8604    (mono)
                 db      001H            ; x010 - 8514 (color)
                 db      001H            ; x011 - 8515 (color)
                 db      0FFH            ; x100 - ?
                 db      000H            ; x101 - 8503 (mono)
                 db      000H            ; x110 - 8512/13       (color)
                 db      0FFH            ; x111 - No Monitor

                 .CODE

                 public  _GetXGAList     ; Code entry point
```

continued...

...from previous page

```
;-------------------------------------------------------------------------
;
; GetPOSInfo
;
; Gets the XGA configuration information from the POS registers.
; This includes the register addresses, both I/O and memory, as well
; as the address of the XGA VRAM.
;
; Assumes that the POS registers have been activated and refer to a
; real XGA device.
;
;-------------------------------------------------------------------------

GetPOSInfo proc
            push    CX
            mov     DX, POS_CONFIG
            in      AL, DX          ; Load byte from XGA Config Reg.
            mov     CL, AL          ; Save It Away
;
; Get base address of I/O regs
;
            and     AL, INSTANCE    ; Mask unwanted bits
            shl     AL, 1
            shl     AL, 1
            shl     AL, 1           ; Shift instance to top nibble
            mov     AH, 21H         ; AX now has I/O base address (21x0H)
            mov     _ioRegBaseAddr, AX ; Save it temporarily
;
; Get base address of memory mapped registers.
;
```

```
        xor     AX, AX                  ; Build memory offset in AX
                                        ; AX is ls word of address

        mov     AL, CL                  ; Restore XGA Config Reg info
        and     AL, EXT_MEM_ADDR        ; Obtain ROM Address index
        shl     AX, 1
        shl     AX, 1
        shl     AX, 1                   ; Shift over three bits to align
                                        ; with register page
        and     CL, INSTANCE            ; Get the instance number
        or      AL, CL                  ; OR it into the address

        shl     AX, 1                   ; Shift over by 2 more bits
        shl     AX, 1

        or      AX, 0C1C0h              ; Add in the mem reg base
        mov     _memRegBaseAddr, AX     ; Save it
;
; Get the address of the VRAM in XGA address space.
;
        xor     BX, BX                  ; Clear BX
        mov     DX, POS_DISPMEMBASE
        in      AL, DX                  ; Read the Disp. Mem. Base
        mov     BL, AL
        and     BL, DISP_MEM_BASE       ; Kill DISP_MEM_ACCESS
        shl     BX, 1
        shl     BX, 1
        shl     BX, 1                   ; Make room for Instance
        mov     DX, POS_CONFIG
        in      AL, DX                  ; Read XGA Configuration
        and     AL, INSTANCE            ; Mask in Instance
        or      BL, AL                  ; Put together
        shl     BX, 1                   ; Make BX the msb word => shift left
        shl     BX, 1                   ; by 16 (lsb word is zero).
        shl     BX, 1
        shl     BX, 1
        shl     BX, 1                   ; Total shift now = 21 left
                                        ; Scales To 4 MegaByte Boundry
```

continued...

...from previous page

```
            mov    word ptr vramBaseAddr, 0
            mov    word ptr vramBaseAddr+2, BX
            pop    CX
            ret                         ; Done
GetPOSInfo endp

; ------------------------------------------------------------------------
; GetXGAConfig()
;
; Input: CX has MCA slot number
; Output: See below
;
; Gets XGA configuration information on the potential XGA in the
; slot specified by CX. If CX is 0, it refers to the Planar (or
; motherboard).
;
; If an XGA is found, the XGA specific information is stored at [SI],
; SI is incremented to point at the next XGA data, and _xgaCount is
; incremented.
;
; If an XGA is not found, _xgaCount and SI are not changed.
;
; NOTE: The section of code executed between the "cli" and "sti"
; statements should not be single stepped through, since your
; display may go away in the process, and/or your system may hang.
;
;
; ------------------------------------------------------------------------

GetXGAConfig proc
            cmp    CX, 0               ; Are we checking the planar?
            jne    GXC_SlotCheck

            cli                        ; Checking planar, Disable
                                       ; Interupts
            mov    DX, 94H             ; Planar setup register
            mov    AL, 0DFH            ; Enable the Planar Video check
            out    DX, AL              ; Tell The Hardware
```

```
          mov    DX, 101H           ; Check if XGA is present (via POS)
          in     AL, DX             ; Load POS ID MSB into AL
          mov    AH, AL
          mov    DX, 100H
          in     AL, DX             ; Load POS ID LSB into AL
          and    AL, 0FCH           ; Clear lower two bits
          cmp    AX, 08FD8H         ; Check POS ID
          jne    GXC_NoPlanar
          call   GetPOSInfo         ; Get I/O Base and Mem Addresses
          mov    DX, 94H            ; Planar setup register
          mov    AL, 0FFH           ; Disable the planar
          out    DX, AL             ; Tell The Hardware
          sti                       ; Enable Interupts
          jmp    GXC_XGAFound       ; Monitor found OK

GXC_NoPlanar:  ; Not on the planar, disable
          mov    DX, 94H            ; Planar setup register
          mov    AL, 0FFH           ; Disable the planar
          out    DX, AL             ; Tell The Hardware
          sti                       ; Re-Enable Interupts
          ret                       ; Return without doing anything.

GXC_SlotCheck:                      ; Not planar, must be slot.
          mov    BX, CX             ; Enable slot CX, Set the slot ID
          mov    AX, 0C401H         ; POS Request Enable
          int    15H                ; from Systems Services BIOS
          mov    DX, 101H           ; Check if XGA present
          in     AL, DX             ; Load POS ID MSB into AL
mov              AH, AL
          mov    DX, 100H
          in     AL, DX             ; Load POS ID LSB into AL
          and    AL, 0FCH           ; Clear lower two bits
          cmp    AX, 08FD8H         ; Check POS ID
          jne    GXC_NoSlot
          call   GetPOSInfo         ; Calculate Base Positions
          mov    BX, CX             ; Shut the slot down. Set the ID first
          mov    AX, 0C402H         ; POS  Request Disable
          int    15H                ; from Systems Services BIOS
          jmp    GXC_XGAFound       ; Yup.
```

continued...

...from previous page

GXC_NoSlot:

```
                mov     BX, CX                  ; Shut the slot down. Set the ID first
                mov     AX, 0C402h              ; POS  Request Disable
                int     15H                     ; from Systems Services BIOS
                ret
```

GXC_XGAFound:

```
                IOREGREADB OP_MODE              ; Read XGA mode (XGA or VGA)
                mov     xgaMode, AL             ; Set XGA Mode For Disable
                cmp     AL, DISP_VGA_MODE       ; Is XGA is in VGA mode?
                jne     GXC_SizeMemory
                mov     AX, 0F00H               ; Fetch VGA state from BIOS
                int     10H                     ; (Used when disabling XGA)
                mov     vgaState, AX            ; Save the state
```

GXC_SizeMemory: ; Enable XGA in native mode

```
                mov     AL, 0                   ; Switch Off XGA Interupts
                IOREGWRITEB INT_ENABLE, AL
                mov     AL, DISP_XGA_MODE       ; We're going native!
                IOREGWRITEB             OP_MODE, AL ; Set the new mode
                xor     AH, AH                  ; Blank screen until CRTC's set up
                mov     AL, PALETTE_MASK
                IOREGWRITEB             IO_INDEX, AX

                mov     AX, 0A000H              ; Set memory window segment
                mov     ES, AX
                mov     AL, 1                   ; Open memory window at A000H
                IOREGWRITEB MEMWIN_CTRL, AL
                mov     AL, 3                   ; First page to search (192KB)
                mov     CX, 8                   ; Search first 2MB (8 * 64 * 4)
                push    CX                      ; Save it for loop
```

GXC_BlitLoop:

```
                IOREGWRITEB MEMWIN_INDEX, AL    ; Select a 64K page of VRAM
                add     AL, 4                   ; Step up by 256KB
                mov     BH, byte ptr ES:[0FFFEH] ; Do a pattern read/write
                mov     byte ptr ES:[0FFFEH], 0A5H
                mov     byte ptr ES:[0], 0
```

```
            cmp     byte ptr ES:[0FFFEH], 0A5H
            jne     GXC_BlitEndLoop      ; If no match, end of RAM found
            mov     byte ptr ES:[0FFFEH], 05AH
            mov     byte ptr ES:[0], 0
            cmp     byte ptr ES:[0FFFEH], 05AH
            jne     GXC_BlitEndLoop      ; If no match, end of RAM found
            mov     byte ptr ES:[0FFFEH], BH
            loop    GXC_BlitLoop         ; Try looking at next 256KB

GXC_BlitEndLoop:
            pop     AX                   ; Restore the max # of 256KB pages
            sub     AX, CX               ; Calculate actual # of pages found
            mov     memorySize, AX       ; Save it
;
; Now that we have basically all the other information we need, let's
; get the current monitor info.
;
            mov     AL, MON_ID_GUN_OUT; Set the proper register
            IOREGWRITEB IO_INDEX, AL
            IOREGREADB  IO_DATA          ; Read its value
            and     AX, 07H              ; Mask off all but lower 3 bits
            mov     BX, AX               ; Put into indexable reg.
            mov     AL, monitorTable[BX] ; Get monitor size
            mov     monitorSize, AL
;
; Having got the information we need, we should fall back into
; the original mode (whatever it was) and disable the XGA native mode.
;
            mov     AL, 0                ; Close VRAM Window
            IOREGWRITEB MEMWIN_CTRL, AL
            IOREGWRITEB MEMWIN_INDEX, AL ; Clear memory window index
            cmp     xgaMode, DISP_VGA_MODE ; IF XGA was in VGA mode
            jne     GXC_DisableFinished  ; THEN
                                         ; Return to original status
            IOREGWRITEB INT_ENABLE, AL   ; Clear interrupt enables
            IOREGWRITEB INT_STATUS, AL   ; Clear interrupt status
            mov     AH, 0FFH             ; Set palette mask
```

continued..

...from previous page

```
            mov     AL, PALETTE_MASK    ; to VGA default
            IOREGWRITEB IO_INDEX, AX
            mov     AH, 15H             ; Prepare CRTC for reset
            mov     AL, DISP_CTRL1
            IOREGWRITEW IO_INDEX, AX
            mov     AH, 14H             ; Reset CRTC
            IOREGWRITEW IO_INDEX, AX
            mov     AH, 00H             ; Clear display mode 2
            mov     AL, DISP_CTRL2      ; for VGA mode
            IOREGWRITEW IO_INDEX, AX
            mov     AH, 04H             ; Set clock frequency
            mov     AL, CLOCK_SEL_1     ; for VGA mode
            IOREGWRITEW IO_INDEX, AX
            mov     AH, 20H             ; Load value BIOS expects
            mov     AL, VSYNC_END       ; to find in this register
            IOREGWRITEW IO_INDEX, AX    ; when used by the VGA
            mov     AL, DISP_VGA_MODE   ; Set into VGA mode
            IOREGWRITEB OP_MODE, AL
            mov     AL, 1               ; Enable as a VGA
            mov     DX, 03C3H
            out     DX, AL
            mov     AX, vgaState        ; Set mode through BIOS call
            xor     AH, AH              ; Clear AH for INT10, Func. 0
            int     10H                 ; Set XGA back to original state
GXC_DisableFinished:
            mov     AL, monitorSize     ; Copy monitor size
            mov     [SI].xiMonitor, AL
            mov     AL, xgaMode         ; Copy video mode, and everything
                                        ; else
            mov     [SI].xiMode, AL
            mov     AX, word ptr vramBaseAddr[0]
            mov     [SI].xiBaseVRML, AX
            mov     AX, word ptr vramBaseAddr[2]
            mov     [SI].xiBaseVRMH, AX
            mov     AX, _ioRegBaseAddr
            mov     [SI].xiIOReg, AX
            mov     AX, _memRegBaseAddr
```

```
              mov      [SI].xiMemReg, AX
              mov      AX, memorySize
              mov      [SI].xiMemSize, AX
              add      SI, size XGA_INFO    ; Bump pointer and board count
              inc      _xgaCount
              ret
GetXGAConfig endp
;-----------------------------------------------------------------------------
;
; _GetXGAList()
;
; Find all XGAs in the system, and store their information in
; "_xgaList".
;
; The structure of the data in the _xgaList data area is documented
; at the top of this file.
;
;-----------------------------------------------------------------------------
_GetXGAList proc
              push     SI
              mov      _xgaCount, 0         ; No XGAs yet
;
; Let's call our XGAConfig routine for each of 10 possible slots and
; the planar. The planar is slot 0, the others sequential from 1 to 10.
;
              lea      SI, _xgaList         ; Point to start of XGA list area
              mov      CX, 10
GXL_GetLoop:
              push     CX
              call     GetXGAConfig         ; Uses CX as index for request
              pop      CX
              loop     GXL_GetLoop
              call     GetXGAConfig         ; For slot 0 (i.e. Planar)
              pop      SI
              ret
_GetXGAList endp

              end
```

continued...

...from previous page

Listing 5.2. SHOWXGAS.C

```
/*------------------------------------------------------------------------

    SHOWXGAS.C - Shows how to locate all the XGAs in the system

    This program can be run by compiling it with the following lines:

            CL -c SHOWXGAS.C

            LINK SHOWXGAS XGAFIND;

-------------------------------------------------------------------------*/


/*------------------------------------------------------------------------

    Include file section
    (the fail safe approach, include everything you might need later)

-------------------------------------------------------------------------*/

#include    <stdio.h>
#include    <stdlib.h>
#include    <string.h>
#include    <errno.h>
#include    <fcntl.h>
#include    <dos.h>
#include    <conio.h>
#include    <io.h>
#include    <malloc.h>
#include    <sys\types.h>
#include    <sys\stat.h>
#include    "xga.h"

/*------------------------------------------------------------------------

    Structures

-------------------------------------------------------------------------*/
```

```
typedef struct XGA_Info
    {
    BYTE        xiMonitor;          /* Monitor type */
    UBYTE       xiMode;             /* Native or VGA mode */
    UWORD       xiBaseVRML;         /* Base VRAM address (low) */
    UWORD       xiBaseVRMH;         /* Base VRAM address (high) */
    UWORD       xiIOReg;            /* I/O Reg address */
    UWORD       xiMemReg;           /* Mem Reg address */
    UWORD       xiMemSize;          /* Memory Size for board (in 256Ks) */
    } XGA_INFO;

/*-------------------------------------------------------------------

Externals

--------------------------------------------------------------------
                                   */
extern  XGA_INFO  xgaList[];        /* In XGAFIND.ASM, contains XGA info
                                       */
extern  UWORD     xgaCount;         /* Number of XGAs found */
extern  VOID      GetBoardConfig(); /* Function to find XGAs */

/*-------------------------------------------------------------------

    Locally Defined Variables

--------------------------------------------------------------------
                                   */

UBYTE   *monSizeStr[3] =            /* Message strings for Resolution */
            {
            "None",
            "Low Resolution (640x480)",
            "High Resolution (1024x768)"
            };
UBYTE   *modeString[5] =            /* Message strings for mode */
            {
            "VGA (No XGA Decode)",
            "VGA (with XGA Decode)",
            "132 Column (No XGA Decode)",
```

continued...

...from previous page

```
          "132 Column (with XGA Decode)",
          "XGA Graphics"
          };

/*-------------------------------------------------------------------

   Code

-------------------------------------------------------------------*/

main(argc, argv)
WORD  argc;
BYTE  **argv;
{
  UWORD         i;                    /* Loop counter */
  GetXGAList();                       /* Are any XGAs present? */
  if (!xgaCount)                      /* Check the count */
    {
    printf("No XGAs found in system!\n");
    return(1);                        /* Abort with an error code */
    }
  /*
     If we get this far, at least one XGA has been found.
     Let's list them all.
  */
  for (i = 0; i < xgaCount; i++)
    {
    printf("\nXGA Board Number %d\n", i+1);
    printf("=======================================\n");
    printf("Monitor Type:              %s\n",
      monSizeStr[xgaList[i].xiMonitor + 1]);
    printf("Current Mode:              %s\n",
      modeString[xgaList[i].xiMode]);
    printf("Base VRAM address:         %0.8lXH\n",
      ((UDWORD) xgaList[i].xiBaseVRMH << 16) |
    xgaList[i].xiBaseVRML);
    printf("Base I/O register address:      %0.4XH\n",
      xgaList[i].xiIOReg);
    printf("Base Memory reg. address:       %0.4XH\n",
```

```
        xgaList[i].xiMemReg);
    printf("Amount of VRAM:          %d\n\n",
        xgaList[i].xiMemSize * 256);
    }
  return(0);                         /* Return with no error */
}
```

You may have noticed that in SHOWXGAS.C, we make a call to GetXGAList() (located in XGAFIND.ASM) in order to create a list of the XGA boards in the system. The information for each board is stored in the structure defined at the start of both listings (XGA_INFO is the name of the structure).

GetXGAList(), in turn, makes calls to GetXGAConfig() for each possible slot in the system, including the motherboard. If GetXGAConfig() locates an XGA device in the specified slot (by checking the POS ID registers for a valid XGA Micro Channel ID), the code then proceeds to obtain all of the information it needs about the XGA, including the mode it is currently in, the amount of memory it has on board, the type of monitor attached, and its I/O and memory addresses. This information is then stuffed into the structure. (Note that the memory check requires a switch into XGA graphics mode in order to access the necessary memory.) Once all slots and the motherboard have been checked, control is returned to the calling routine, which, in this case, just dumps all the XGA information found, providing that at least one XGA has been located.

Where to Find the XGA's Memory Address

To understand where an XGA resides in memory, you must know how the ROM and memory register addresses are obtained in XGAFIND.ASM, in the GetPOSInfo() routine.

XGA ROM addresses start at physical address 0C0000H. The memory registers start in the last 1KB of the 8KB allocated to the XGA ROM space, which is an offset of 01C00H (7172 decimal) bytes into the ROM. The 128 byte page within that 1KB is determined by the Instance number of the XGA. Therefore, using C notation, the calculation can be broken down as follows (with EXT_MEM_ADDR and INSTANCE assumed to be right aligned):

```
    0C1C00H + (EXT_MEM_ADDR * 2000H) + (INSTANCE * 80H)
```

which equals:

```
    0C1C00H + (EXT_MEM_ADDR << 13) + (INSTANCE << 7)
```

Since we can will use the memory base address as a segment, we can strip off a nibble (4 bits):

```
0C1C0H + (EXT_MEM_ADDR << 9) + (INSTANCE << 3)
```

Finally, since EXT_MEM_ADDR is already shifted over by 4 bits, and INSTANCE is shifted over by 1 bit:

```
0C1C0H + (EXT_MEM_ADDR << 5) + (INSTANCE << 2)
```

This equation is implemented about half-way through GetPOSInfo().

Initializing the XGA

Now that we know how to locate an XGA in the system, we need to determine how to initialize it. First, however, we need to figure out which XGA we want to use in the event of multiple XGAs in the system with monitors attached. There are basically three ways to do this:

1. Just use the first XGA you find. This is certainly the easiest method to use, but it has certain drawbacks. First, if you have more than one XGA in the system, chances are that one of them is currently in VGA mode, and that it may be expedient to use another one instead in order to provide a dual (or multiple) screen-display environment with one of those screens being VGA. The other drawback is that you may not necessarily want the first XGA because of its monitor/memory configuration—it may not support a desired resolution.

2. Another way to locate the XGA you want to use is to select the first one you find that is not currently in VGA mode, assuming there is more than one XGA in the system. This approach suffers from one of the same drawbacks as the first approach_namely, that it might not be the ideal XGA to use. However, if you know that you should make your non-VGA XGA the one with the larger monitor and best memory configuration, this approach can work quite well. This is how the AutoCAD driver supplied by IBM for the XGA functions.

3. The final way to determine which XGA to use is to scan the XGA information to determine the ideal configuration of memory and monitor, regardless of whether an XGA is in VGA mode. The XGA's Windows driver does this.

Once it locates all XGAs, it determines which one can achieve the highest resolution, and uses it. The minor drawback here is that an XGA in VGA may be the one selected, leaving other monitors unused.

Listing 5.3 shows a C program for initializing an XGA. This program— INITXGA.C—will be used as the basis for most of the subsequent listings in this chapter. This listing uses method #2 (above) to select an XGA, and then initializes it for the highest possible spatial resolution it can support.

Listing 5.3. Initializing an XGA

```
/*--------------------------------------------------------------------

   INITXGA.C - Shows how to initialize an XGA

   This program can be run by compiling it with the following lines:

      CL -c -Zp INITXGA.C
      LINK INITXGA XGAFIND;

   ----------------------------------------------------------------*/


/*--------------------------------------------------------------

   Include file section
   (the fail safe approach, include everything you might need later)

   ----------------------------------------------------------------*/

#include  <stdio.h>
#include  <stdlib.h>
#include  <string.h>
#include  <errno.h>
#include  <fcntl.h>
#include  <dos.h>
#include  <conio.h>
#include  <io.h>
#include  <malloc.h>
#include  <sys\types.h>
#include  <sys\stat.h>
#include  "xga.h"
```

continued...

...from previous page

```c
/*-----------------------------------------------------------------

   Structures

-------------------------------------------------------------*/

typedef struct XGA_Info
   {
   BYTE     xiMonitor;                /* Monitor type */
   UBYTE    xiMode;                   /* Native or VGA mode */
   UWORD    xiBaseVRML;               /* Base VRAM address (low) */
   UWORD    xiBaseVRMH;               /* Base VRAM address (high) */
   UWORD    xiIOReg;                  /* I/O Reg address */
   UWORD    xiMemReg;                 /* Mem Reg address */
   UWORD    xiMemSize;                /* Memory Size for board (in 256Ks)
*/
   } XGA_INFO;

typedef struct PalEntry             /* A palette entry */
   {
   UBYTE    r;                       /* The Red component */
   UBYTE    g;                       /* The Green component */
   UBYTE    b;                       /* The Blue component */
   } PALENTRY;

/*-----------------------------------------------------------------

      Externals (all in XGAFIND.ASM)

-------------------------------------------------------------
*/

extern XGA_INFO xgaList[];           /* Contains XGA information */
extern UWORD    xgaCount;            /* Number of XGAs found */
extern VOID     GetBoardConfig();    /* Function to find XGAs */

/*-----------------------------------------------------------------

      Locally Defined Variables

-------------------------------------------------------------
*/

static UBYTE    initRegs[] =
```

```
                {
                DISP_CTRL1, DISP_CTRL1, HTOTAL_LO, HDISP_END_LO,
                HBLANK_START_LO, HBLANK_END_LO, HSYNC_START_LO,
                HSYNC_END_LO, HSYNC_POS1, HSYNC_POS2, VTOTAL_LO,
                VTOTAL_HI, VDISPLAY_END_LO, VDISPLAY_END_HI,
                VBLANK_START_LO, VBLANK_START_HI, VBLANK_END_LO,
                VBLANK_END_HI, VSYNC_START_LO, VSYNC_START_HI,
                VSYNC_END, VLINE_COMP_LO, VLINE_COMP_HI,
                CLOCK_SEL_1, DISP_CTRL2, DISP_CTRL1, 0
                };
/*
```

The above table contains a list of registers to set when
initializing the XGA into a given graphics mode.

The two tables below contain the values necessary to initialize
the XGA into a 640x480 mode and 1024x768 mode, respectively.
The init values assume an 8 bpp mode.

To change to a different pixel depth, all we need to do is modify
the content of DISP_CTRL2 and MEM_ACCESS_MODE registers, as well
as the buffer width registers. None of the CRTC registers needs
to be modified.

```
*/
static UBYTE    mode640[] =
                {
                1, 0, 99, 79, 79, 99, 85, 97, 0, 0, 0x0C, 2, 0xDF,
                1, 0xDF, 1, 0x0C, 2, 0xEA, 1, 0xEC, 0xFF, 0xFF, 0,
                3, 0xC7
                };
static UBYTE    mode1024[] =
                {
                1, 0, 157, 127, 127, 157, 135, 156, 0x40, 4, 0x30,
                3, 0xFF, 2, 0xFF, 2, 0x30, 3, 0, 3, 8, 0xFF, 0xFF,
                0x0D, 3, 0x0F
                };
/*
```

The following table is a conversion table between a bit per pixel
value and the value to be set in various registers for the bit
per pixel size (such as the Memory Access Mode, Display Control 2,
and Pixel Map n Format registers). Note that all of our pixel
mappings are going to be Intel oriented, not Motorola.

continued...

...from previous page

```c
*/
static UBYTE    bppMapInfo[] =
                { 0, 0, 1, 0, 2, 0, 0, 0, 3, 0, 0, 0, 0, 0, 0, 0, 4 };
/*
   The following is the palette for the first 16 entries. The
   remaining palette can be derived from this one.
*/
static PALENTRY  paletteData[16] =
                {
                        { 0x00, 0x00, 0x00 },    /* Black */
                        { 0x00, 0x00, 0x80 },    /* Blue */
                        { 0x00, 0x80, 0x00 },    /* Green */
                        { 0x00, 0x80, 0x80 },    /* Cyan */
                        { 0x80, 0x00, 0x00 },    /* Red */
                        { 0x80, 0x00, 0x80 },    /* Magenta */
                        { 0x80, 0x80, 0x00 },    /* Yellow */
                        { 0x80, 0x80, 0x80 },    /* Gray */
                        { 0x40, 0x40, 0x40 },    /* Dark Grey */
                        { 0x00, 0x00, 0xFF },    /* Bright Blue */
                        { 0x00, 0xFF, 0x00 },    /* Bright Green */
                        { 0x00, 0xFF, 0xFF },    /* Bright Cyan */
                        { 0xFF, 0x00, 0x00 },    /* Bright Red */
                        { 0xFF, 0x00, 0xFF },    /* Bright Magenta */
                        { 0xFF, 0xFF, 0x00 },    /* Bright Yellow */
                        { 0xFF, 0xFF, 0xFF }     /* White */
                };
union REGS    inRegs, outRegs;        /* Used for reinit'ing video mode */

UWORD         xRes, yRes;             /* The XGA mode dimensions */
UWORD         bpp;                    /* The bits per pixel for the XGA mode */
UWORD         oldVGAmode = 0;         /* Save area for current VGA mode */
UBYTE FAR     *memRegBaseAddr;        /* The memory register base address */
UWORD         ioRegBaseAddr;          /* The I/O register base address */
UDWORD        vramBaseAddr;           /* The VRAM base address */
WORD          selectXGA = -1;         /* Index to selected XGA in xgaList */

/*-----------------------------------------------------------------------
```

Code

```
---------------------------------------------------------------------------*/

/*------------------------------

VOID    InitializeXGA()
```

This function uses the globally defined variables xRes, bpp, and selectXGA to set additional global variables and initialize the specified XGA into the mode selected by the globally defined variables.

The variables set in this routine are:

        ioRegBaseAddr   - The I/O base address of the selected XGA
        memRegBaseAddr - The XGA's memory register base address

These two variables are used by the macros defined in XGA.H
Also defined is the following for use in other Map operations:

        vramBaseAddr   - The XGA's VRAM base address

```
----------------------------------------*/

VOID    InitializeXGA()
{
   UBYTE *modeData = mode1024; /* Assume a 1024x768 res. */
   UBYTE *modeRegs = initRegs; /* Pointer to reg. #s */
   UWORD i, j;  /* Scratch variables */
   /*

      If the XGA is in VGA mode, we need to save the mode it's
      in, so we can restore it later. We're not going to worry
      about the XGA being in 132 column mode, because that's
      something that will generally only be implemented in
      applications, and run something that one will run in
      under DOS.

   */
   if (xgaList[selectXGA].xiMode == DISP_VGA_MODE)
      {
      inRegs.x.ax = 0x0F00;               /* Read current video mode */
      int86(0x10, &inRegs, &outRegs);
      oldVGAmode = outRegs.x.ax;          /* Save the mode for later */
      }
   /*

      Next, let's set the necessary variables for accessing
      the XGA device.
```

continued...

...from previous page

> memRegBaseAddr is a byte far pointer to a segment in the upper
> end of the PC's lower 1MB of address space. Since the value
> in the structure we created is actually a segment, we need
> to place it in the upper 16 bits of our far pointer address.
>
> ioRegBaseAddr is a word I/O address.
>
> vramBaseAddr is a dword value containing the linear base address
> of the XGA's VRAM in PC address space.

```
*/
memRegBaseAddr = (UBYTE FAR *)
                        ((DWORD)xgaList[selectXGA].xiMemReg << 16);
ioRegBaseAddr = xgaList[selectXGA].xiIOReg;
vramBaseAddr = ((UDWORD)xgaList[selectXGA].xiBaseVRMH << 16)
                    | xgaList[selectXGA].xiBaseVRML;

/*
    Now we're ready to start the actual initialization.
    First, we need to switch the XGA into XGA graphics mode
    by disabling any XGA interrupts that may have been hanging
    around enabled, and then switching the XGA's operating mode.
*/
IOREGWRITEB(INT_ENABLE, 0);
IOREGWRITEB(OP_MODE, DISP_XGA_MODE);
IOREGWRITEB(PALETTE_MASK, 0);  /* Also blank the display for now */

/*
    This is where we need to load the CRTC registers, which help
    define how the XGA should arrange the display (i.e. syncs).
    The register info list is null terminated, by the way.
*/
if (xRes == 640)
    modeData = mode640;         /* Set if not 1024x768 */

while (*modeRegs)               /* Because of null termination */
    {                           /* First, set index, next, write data */
    IOREGWRITEB(IO_INDEX, *modeRegs++);
    IOREGWRITEB(IO_DATA, *modeData++);
    }
/*
    At this point, the XGA's CRTC registers have been loaded.
    Now we need to set the proper bit per pixel operation.
*/
```

```
IOREGWRITEB(IO_INDEX, DISP_CTRL2);
IOREGWRITEB(IO_DATA, bppMapInfo[bpp]);
IOREGWRITEB(MEM_ACCESS_MODE, bppMapInfo[bpp]);
/*

  Next, we need to set some other registers, including the
  Virtual Memory Control and Display Start Address register.
*/
IOREGWRITEB(VIRT_MEM_CTRL, 0);
IOREGWRITEB(IO_INDEX, DISP_ADDR_LO);
IOREGWRITEB(IO_DATA, 0);
IOREGWRITEB(IO_INDEX, DISP_ADDR_MID);
IOREGWRITEB(IO_DATA, 0);
IOREGWRITEB(IO_INDEX, DISP_ADDR_HI);
IOREGWRITEB(IO_DATA, 0);
IOREGWRITEB(IO_INDEX, PALETTE_MASK);
IOREGWRITEB(IO_DATA, 0xFF);    /* Enable viewing of all planes */
IOREGWRITEB(IO_INDEX, PALETTE_SEQUENCE);
IOREGWRITEB(IO_DATA, 0);         /* RGB access to palette */
/*

  Now we set the buffer pitch for the proper resolution.
  Since the granularity of the XGA Horizontal CRTC regs is
  8 bytes, we need to provide the pitch in units of 8 bytes.
  This means that we need to convert from pixels to bytes.
*/
i = (xRes >> 6) << bppMapInfo[bpp]; /* Divide by 64, mult. by bpp */
IOREGWRITEB(IO_INDEX, BUFFER_PITCH_LO);
IOREGWRITEB(IO_DATA, (UBYTE)(i & 0xFF));   /* Low byte first */
IOREGWRITEB(IO_INDEX, BUFFER_PITCH_HI);
IOREGWRITEB(IO_DATA, (UBYTE)((i >> 8) & 0xFF)); /* High byte next */

/*

  All the display initialization is complete at this point.
  Now we need to initialize the graphics engine.

  First step is to create a map which references the whole
  screen and starts at the beginning of the XGA's display
  memory (the address of which is located in xgaList under the
  xiBaseVRML & H fields).
*/
XGAWAIT;      /* Wait for the XGA to be ready */
SENDB(MAP_INDEX, MAP_INDEX_A);      /* Create Map A */
SENDW(MAP_BASE, xgaList[selectXGA].xiBaseVRML);
SENDW(MAP_BASE+2, xgaList[selectXGA].xiBaseVRMH);
SENDW(MAP_WIDTH, xRes - 1);
SENDW(MAP_HEIGHT, yRes - 1);
SENDW(MAP_FORMAT, bppMapInfo[bpp]);
```

continued...

...from previous page

```
/*

   Initialize the graphics operator functions.
*/
SENDB(FORE_MIX, MIX_SRC);   /* Set dest=source mix */
SENDB(BACK_MIX, MIX_SRC);   /* Set dest=source mix */
SENDB(CC_FUNC, CC_COND_FALSE);      /* Disable Color Compare */
SENDW(PLANE_MASK, 0xFFFF); /* Allow writes to all planes */
SENDW(BACK_COLOR, 0);        /* Set all background color bits off */
SENDW(CARRY_CHAIN_MASK, (0x7FFF >> (16 - bpp)));  /* Carry Chain */
/*

   Now we will load the palette.
*/
IOREGWRITEB(IO_INDEX, PALETTE_INDEX);
IOREGWRITEB(IO_DATA, 0);    /* Start at index 0 */
IOREGWRITEB(IO_INDEX, PALETTE_DATA);

for (i = 0; i < 16; i++)    /* Set first 16 entries */
    {
    IOREGWRITEB(IO_DATA, paletteData[i].r);
    IOREGWRITEB(IO_DATA, paletteData[i].g);
    IOREGWRITEB(IO_DATA, paletteData[i].b);
    }
for (i = 16; i < 256; i++)  /* Set next 15 sets of 16 */
    {
    IOREGWRITEB(IO_DATA, paletteData[i >> 4].r);
    IOREGWRITEB(IO_DATA, paletteData[i >> 4].g);
    IOREGWRITEB(IO_DATA, paletteData[i >> 4].b);
    }
/*

Finally, let's clear the screen to color 0.
*/
XGAWAIT;                          /* Again, wait for XGA ready */
SENDW(FORE_COLOR, 0);             /* Set all foreground color bits off */
SENDW(DEST_X, 0);                 /* At 0,0, full screen size */
SENDW(DEST_Y, 0);
SENDW(DIM1, xRes - 1);
SENDW(DIM2, yRes - 1);
SENDW(CMD_REG, PATT_SRC_FORESRC);
SENDW(CMD_REG+2, CMD_BITBLT | SRC_MAP_A | DST_MAP_A);
XGAWAIT;                          /* Again, wait for XGA ready */
SENDW(FORE_COLOR, 0xFFFF);        /* Set all foreground color bits on */
return;                           /* Initialization is all done! */
}
```

```
/*------------------------------------

VOID    CloseXGA()

This routine shuts down the XGA and returns it to whatever
VGA mode it was previously in (if it was in one). If it was
previously in XGA graphics mode, then that's how we leave it.

----------------------------------*/

VOID    CloseXGA()
{
  /*

    We need to check if we were previously in VGA mode, because
    if we were, we need to return the XGA to this mode.

  */
  IOREGWRITEB(MEMWIN_CTRL, 0);        /* Disable MemWin access */
  IOREGWRITEB(MEMWIN_INDEX, 0);       /* Reset the index for future use */

  if (xgaList[selectXGA].xiMode == DISP_VGA_MODE)
    {
    IOREGWRITEB(INT_ENABLE, 0);       /* Turn off all interrupts */
    IOREGWRITEB(INT_STATUS, 0);       /* Clear status */
    IOREGWRITEB(IO_INDEX, PALETTE_MASK);
    IOREGWRITEB(IO_DATA, 0xFF);       /* Enable palette mask */
    IOREGWRITEB(IO_INDEX, DISP_CTRL1);
    IOREGWRITEB(IO_DATA, 0x15);       /* Prepare CRTC for Reset */
    IOREGWRITEB(IO_DATA, 0x14);       /* Reset CRTC */
    IOREGWRITEB(IO_INDEX, DISP_CTRL2);
    IOREGWRITEB(IO_DATA, 0);          /* Prepare for VGA mode */
    IOREGWRITEB(IO_INDEX, CLOCK_SEL_1);
    IOREGWRITEB(IO_DATA, 4);          /* Select VGA Clock */
    IOREGWRITEB(IO_INDEX, VSYNC_END);
    IOREGWRITEB(IO_DATA, 0x20);       /* Load expected value */
    IOREGWRITEB(OP_MODE, DISP_VGA_MODE);   /* Set it! */
    outp(0x3C3, 1);                   /* Enable as VGA */
    inRegs.x.ax = oldVGAmode & 0xFF;
    int86(0x10, &inRegs, &outRegs); /* Restore previous mode */
    }

  return;

}

/*--------------------------------

WORD    main(argc, argv)

This is the main entry point into the program.

------------------------------*/
```

continued...

...from previous page

```
WORD    main(argc, argv)
WORD    argc;
BYTE    **argv;
{
  UWORD    i;                        /* Loop counter */

  GetXGAList();                      /* Are any XGAs present? */
  if (!xgaCount)                     /* Check the count */
    {
    printf("No XGAs found in system!\n");
    return(1);                       /* Abort with an error code */
    }
  /*
     If we get this far, at least one XGA has been found.
     Let's use method #2, and select the first XGA we find which
     is in XGA graphics mode (i.e. not in VGA or 132 column mode,
     and which has a monitor attached. First check if there is
     only one XGA, since that's the most likely thing to happen.
  */
  if ((xgaCount == 1) && (xgaList[0].xiMonitor != -1))
    selectXGA = 0;                   /* Only 1 XGA, with monitor */
  else
    for (i = 0; i < xgaCount; i++)
      {
      if (xgaList[i].xiMonitor < 0)
        continue;                    /* Ignore XGAs with no monitor */
      if (xgaList[i].xiMode != DISP_XGA_MODE)
        continue;                    /* Ignore XGAs in VGA mode */
      selectXGA = i;
      break;
      }

  if (selectXGA == -1)
    {
    /*
       If we get here, one of two things has happened:

       1) We have at least two XGAs in the system, but the only
          one with a monitor attached is also in VGA mode.
       2) There is in fact no usable XGA in the system (i.e.
          no monitor attached).

       Let's check for case #1 first, and then drop to #2 if
       that didn't pan out.
    */
    for (i = 0; i < xgaCount; i++)
```

```
{
        if (xgaList[i].xiMonitor < 0)
        continue;        /* Ignore XGAs with no monitor */
        selectXGA = i;
        break;
        }
        if (selectXGA == -1)   /* If still none found... */
        {
        printf("None of the XGAs in the system have valid monitors!\n");
        return(2);       /* Return with an error */
        }
    }
/*

    Once we get here, it means we have found a valid XGA to use.
    Now we need to determine what the highest resolution we can use
    is. We'll do that by first determining the monitor type, and then
    by the amount of memory on board. The chart below indicates the
    maximum resolution we can achieve based on monitor and memory
    configuration:

                              512KB          1MB
                              ==========     ==========
    Low-Res Monitor           640x480x8      640x480x8 (or 16bpp too)
    High-Res Monitor          1024x768x4     1024x768x8
*/
if (xgaList[selectXGA].xiMonitor == 1)
    {
    xRes = 1024;
    yRes = 768;
    if (xgaList[selectXGA].xiMemSize > 2)
      bpp = 8;
    else
      bpp = 4;
    }
    else
        {
        xRes = 640;
        yRes = 480;
        bpp = 8;
        }
    InitializeXGA();                 /* Let's initialize the XGA */

    DoSomething();                   /* Plugging in all of our examples */

    CloseXGA();                      /* Restore things back to normal */

    return(0);                       /* Return with no error */

}
```

The XGA initialization code in Listing 5.3 uses the monitor configuration of the selected XGA device to determine which spatial resolution to initialize for using the InitializeXGA() function (whose parameters are global variables, not stack passed). Then, the amount of memory on the XGA is used to determine the pixel depth of the display mode (we'll stick to 4 or 8 bpp for now). This is an important change from the way the 8514/A and the VGA work, since on the XGA you program the CRTC for a given spatial resolution and a given display frequency (i.e. 640x480x60Hz), and then set the display depth separately. The only registers that change for the display of various pixel depths are the Display Control 2, Memory Access Mode, and Buffer Pitch registers.

Continuing on with InitializeXGA(), the palette is initialized to be identical to the default AI palette defined in Figure 7.1, all the graphics coprocessor registers are initialized, and the display is cleared to color 0 (black, in this case). Also during this function, two global variables, used by the XGA access macros in XGA.H, are initialized: ioRegBaseAddr, which is set to the XGA's base I/O address (21x0H, where x is the XGA's instance), and memRegBaseAddr, which is a far pointer to the XGA's memory registers.

Once the device is fully initialized, we call a routine called DoSomething(), which will be defined in subsequent listings (it's the routine in which we demonstrate how to access other XGA features). Please note that you should first try to find and initialize any XGA in your system via the VESA defined methods in Appendix B; if you can't, try to use DMQS, as defined in Appendix N.

Some of the code in Listing 5.3 requires additional discussion, since it really applies no matter what initialization mechanism you use.

Using Maps

First is the creation of a "map" in order allow the XGA's graphics engine access to graphics memory. As you'll notice, halfway through InitializeXGA(), we use the XGAWAIT macro to wait for the XGA's graphics engine to become ready for access. Using IBM's XGA silicon shipped prior to mid-1992, if you try to write to any of the memory registers while a graphics operation is in progress, you may hang the graphics engine. That's why it is important to check the engine's state before writing any data. Once it's safe, as in our sample code, you may proceed to program the XGA. In our case, we are defining Map A as the map that allows drawing in the memory displayed on the screen. The first step in this process is indicating which map's information you want to alter by setting the MAP_INDEX register. There are four maps: A, B, C, and Mask. Maps A, B, and C, are for general-purpose drawing, while the mask map is used primarily for arbitrary clipping.

Once you have selected which map's information to modify, you should specify where in memory it points to. Specifying a physical PC address forces the XGA to bus master whenever it wants to access the defined map. In order to have the XGA access its own graphics memory (that is, the VRAM attached to the XGA silicon), you must specify a 32-bit address that reflects the mapping of the XGA's memory in the PC's address space. The base location of the memory is derived by using the display memory base (DISP_MEM_BASE) value from the Display Memory Base Address POS register, shifting it over, masking it with the XGA's instance number, and then shifting the whole amount over 21 bits to end up with a physical 32-bit linear address. From what I've seen so far, the display memory base ends up being 0FC000000H, with instance 1 mapping in at 0FC400000H, instance 2 at 0FC800000H, and so on, and instances 7 and 0 never used due to potential addressing conflicts.

Loading the Palette

Almost directly after initializing Map A in InitializeXGA(), the palette is loaded. This is a complete palette load of all 256 entries, so I initialize the Palette Index to 0, since I have to start loading with the first palette entry. Then, I set up the IO_INDEX register to point at the Palette Data register. Because I'm simulating the AI palette, I need to load the first sixteen entries with the contents of a table I defined that most closely approximates the sixteen basic IBM colors, and then load the remaining 240 according to the value of the high nibble of the color index.

If you want to set a single palette entry, all you need to do is load the palette index with the index number you wanted to use, and then write the three (or four) bytes of data desired to set the contents of that palette location.

Note that the palette must also be loaded in a special way to accomodate the display of the XGA's 16 bpp mode. This is documented in an example later in this chapter.

Using XGAWAIT

In three cases, I used the macro *XGAWAIT* in InitializeXGA(). This macro checks the BUSY bit in the memory-based Control register to make sure the XGA is ready to accept another command, and is defined as follows:

```
#define XGAWAIT  while (memRegBaseAddr[CTRL_REG] & BUSY)
```

Now, as pointed out in Chapter 4, polling the BUSY bit causes the XGA to temporarily suspend its current drawing operation to service the PC's request for a BUSY status, and though the new XGA-NI extension discussed in Appendix C helps solve this problem, if you have a normal IBM XGA, the problem still exists. As such, there are a couple of ways to work around the problem. The first, recommended by IBM, is to not bang on the BUSY bit. Instead, read the BUSY bit, and if it's set, wait a while before going back to check again, as in the following revision of the XGAWAIT macro (make sure your C compiler doesn't optimize the delay out of the code):

```
#define XGAWAIT  {while (memRegBaseAddr[CTRL_REG] & BUSY) \
                 {  int xgaDelayLoop = 100;\
                 while (xgaDelayLoop—); }}
```

and in XGA.INC, it would look something like this:

```
XGAWAIT      macro
             local        mainLoop, delayLoop, doneWait
mainLoop:
             test         byte ptr ES:[CTRL_REG], BUSY
             jz           short doneDelay
             push         CX
             mov          CX, 100
delayLoop:
             loop         delayLoop
             jmp          short mainLoop
doneWait:
             endm
```

As I see it, there are three problems with this approach. First, it ties up the system CPU in needless delay loops while it could be doing other things. Second, it generates more code for every invocation of the macro, thereby increasing your end code size. Third, when clone XGAs come out, they will be based on the original IBM XGA, not the NI, and hence, if they did things correctly, reading their BUSY bits will not suspend drawing operations temporarily. In the latter case, then, your code would simply be spinning its wheels.

To use the XGAWAIT macros supplied in the include files, don't wait for a drawing operation to finish via an XGAWAIT; let it run in parallel with your PC code, and check for XGA availability only before you're about to draw something else. This way, you tend to get the optimal parallel processing advantage, since most XGA operations will tend to complete faster than it might take normal application code to get in a request for another drawing operation. You'll see what I mean later in this chapter.

Drawing

Now that we've taken care of all the background material, it's time to start putting things up on your screen. In the following examples, all that is supplied is a C program with the entry function DoSomething(), which, as you may recall, is called from INITXGA.C. These new examples also use globals that have been defined in INITXGA.C—namely xRes, yRes, memRegBaseAddr, and ioRegBaseAddr.

Drawing Rectangles

The best place to start is drawing with filled rectangles, since you've seen how this is done in INITXGA.C's screen clearing code (at the end of the InitializeXGA() routine). Listing 5.4 shows FILLRECT.C, which draws rectangles filled with different colors on the display.

Listing 5.4. FILLRECT.C.

```
/*------------------------------------------------------------------

   FILLRECT.C - Shows how to draw filled rectangles on an XGA

   This program can be run by compiling it with the following lines:

        CL -c -Zp FILLRECT.C
        LINK FILLRECT INITXGA XGAFIND;

   ---------------------------------------------------------------*/
/*------------------------------------------------------------------

        Include file section
        (the fail safe approach, include everything you might need later)
   ---------------------------------------------------------------*/

#include <stdio.h>
#include <stdlib.h>
#include <string.h>
#include <errno.h>
#include <fcntl.h>
#include <dos.h>
#include <conio.h>
#include <io.h>
#include <malloc.h>
#include <sys\types.h>
#include <sys\stat.h>
#include "xga.h"
```

continued...

...from previous page

```
/*---------------------------------------------------------------------

    Externals (all in INITXGA.C)
-----------------------------------------------------------------------*/

extern  UWORD         xRes, yRes;       /* The XGA mode dimensions */
extern  UWORD         bpp;              /* Bits per pixel for the mode */
extern  UBYTE FAR    *memRegBaseAddr;   /* Memory Register address */
extern  UWORD         ioRegBaseAddr;    /* I/O Register address */

/*---------------------------------------------------------------------

    Code
-----------------------------------------------------------------------*/

/*----------------------------------
```

```
VOID    FillRectangle( UWORD x, UWORD y,
        UWORD width, UWORD height, UWORD color)
```

This function draws a filled rectangle at (x,y) with the specified dimensions, in Map A.

The dimensions are assumed to be positive, non-zero values, while the color is assumed to be valid for the pixel depth. The current foreground mix is used (which is set to DST=SRC, i.e. replace, in INITXGA.C).

The Foreground color is left set to the passed color, and is not restored.

```
----------------------------------*/
VOID  FillRectangle( UWORD x, UWORD y,
                     UWORD width, UWORD height, UWORD color)
{
  /*
     First, let's make sure the XGA is ready to draw a rectangle.
  */
  XGAWAIT;       /* Wait for XGA ready */
  SENDW(FORE_COLOR, color);   /* Set the foreground color */
  SENDW(DEST_X, x);    /* Set position */
  SENDW(DEST_Y, y);
  SENDW(DIM1, width - 1);
  SENDW(DIM2, height - 1);     /* Set dimensions of the rectangle */
  /*
     Now we need to actually program the proper command into
     the XGA's Command Register. The command is initiated with
     the loading of the high word of the 32-bit Command register.
  */
  SENDW(CMD_REG, PATT_SRC_FORESRC);
  SENDW(CMD_REG+2, CMD_BITBLT | SRC_MAP_A | DST_MAP_A);
```

```
    return;      /* Done with filling rectangles! */
}
/*-------------------------------------

VOID    DoSomething()

This routine is called from main(), located in INITXGA.C.
Here this routine makes repetitive calls to FillRectangle()
to draw a sequence of rectangles on the display.

-------------------------------------*/
VOID    DoSomething()
{
    UWORD i, j;

    /*
       Let's draw a whole bunch of 16x16 rectangles in different
       colors to fill the screen.

       A couple of notes:

       1) We are using the xRes and yRes set in INITXGA.C
       2) Since we may be running either 16 or 256 colors,
          we'll just assume the least common denominator of
          a max of 16 colors.
    */
    for (i = 0; i < xRes; i +=16)
      for (j = 0; j < yRes; j += 16)
        FillRectangle(i, j, 16, 16, (i / 16 + j / 16) & 0x0F);

    /*
       Now, let's wait until a key is struck to exit.
       The reason for putting the getch() in an "if" statement
       is because it's possible that the hit key might be an
       enhanced key (if the result is 0) such as the function
       or arrow keys, requiring a second keyboard read to empty
       the buffer so strange character don't appear at the DOS
       command line upon exit.
    */
    if (!getch())
      getch();

    return;
}
```

Seems pretty simple once you get the initialization taken care of, doesn't it?

In the routine FillRectangle(), the procedure is pretty straightforward. First, we wait for the XGA drawing engine to be ready for access. Next, we set the color, the drawing position, and the dimensions of the rectangle.

The really interesting part, though, is programming the Command register. Since the Command register is 32 bits, we need to write 4 bytes to it. The simplest way to do this while maintaining compatibility with an 8088 architecture is to write two 16-bit words; this also makes the programming easier to interpret. The actual execution of the data in the Command register is triggered by a write to the most significant byte (byte 3 of the register, regardless of whether the registers are in Intel or Motorola addressing mode). So, when we write two words, we need to write the low order word first, then the high order word to trigger the command (the high byte of the high word is the last one written by the CPU).

For a filled rectangle operation, you actually use the BitBLT function of the XGA, but specify the source for foreground data as the foreground color, and the pattern source for the information as the foreground source (which effectively disables the pattern). Note that I didn't OR in any parameters that are known to be equal to 0 (such as FORE_SRC_COLOR) for the sake of space conservation. Otherwise, you'd end up with 5 lines of ORs.

Drawing Modifiers

Now that you know how to get some graphics on the screen, it's time to talk about drawing modifiers. There are three basic modifiers that affect just about all graphics operations: Mixes, Color Compare, and Plane Mask.

None of these drawing modifiers are map-specific. In other words, they apply to all applicable XGA graphics operations. Demonstration of how these modifiers change the result of a graphics operation is left as an exercise (but some different mixes are used in subsequent examples). The following information should minimize the agony of playing with these modifiers.

Mixes

Mixes, also known as raster operations, are boolean or arithmetic functions that combine the source data—usually the foreground color—and the destination data, which is always a pixel in the destination map. The default mix set by INITXGA.C is MIX_SRC, which basically means that the destination pixel will be set to the source data. Another common mix is MIX_XOR, which performs an XOR using the source data and destination pixel as its operands, and places the result in the destination. An XOR is immensely useful for things like cursors and highlights, because a secondary application of the XOR removes the first application, thereby acting like a pixel value toggle.

Below is a complete list of mixes available on the XGA (this is an excerpt from XGA.H). The number in the middle column is used to program the XGA's mix registers:

```
MIX_ZEROS                       0x00 /* 0 (all bits cleared) */
MIX_0                           0x00 /* 0 (all bits cleared) */

MIX_AND                         0x01 /* Src AND Dst */

MIX_SRC_AND_NOT_DST             0x02 /* Src AND NOT Dst */

MIX_SRC                         0x03 /* Src */
MIX_PAINT                       0x03 /* Src */

MIX_NOT_SRC_AND_DST             0x04 /* NOT Src AND Dst */

MIX_DST                         0x05 /* Dst */
MIX_LEAVE_ALONE                 0x05 /* Dst */

MIX_SRC_XOR_DST                 0x06 /* Src XOR Dst */
MIX_XOR                         0x06 /* Src XOR Dst */

MIX_SRC_OR_DST                  0x07 /* Src OR Dst */
MIX_OR                          0x07 /* Src OR Dst */

MIX_NOT_SRC_AND_NOT_DST         0x08 /* NOT Src AND NOT Dst */
MIX_NOR                         0x08 /* NOT Src AND NOT Dst */

MIX_SRC_XOR_NOT_DST             0x09 /* Src XOR NOT Dst */

MIX_NOT_DST                     0x0A /* NOT Dst */

MIX_SRC_OR_NOT_DST              0x0B /* Src OR NOT Dst */

MIX_NOT_SRC                     0x0C /* NOT Src */

MIX_NOT_SRC_OR_DST              0x0D /* NOT Src OR Dst */

MIX_NOT_SRC_OR_NOT_DST          0x0E /* NOT Src OR NOT Dst */
MIX_NAND                        0x0E /* NOT Src OR NOT Dst */

MIX_ONES                        0x0F /* 1 (all bits set) */
MIX_1                           0x0F /* 1 (all bits set) */

MIX_MAX                         0x10 /* MAXIMUM(Src, Dst) */

MIX_MIN                         0x11 /* MINIMUM(Src, Dst) */

MIX_PLUS_SAT                    0x12 /* Src + Dst [with saturate] */

MIX_DST_MINUS_SRC_SAT           0x13 /* Dst - Src [with saturate] */

MIX_SRC_MINUS_DST_SAT           0x14 /* Src - Dst [with saturate] */

MIX_AVERAGE                     0x15 /* (Src + Dst) / 2 */
```

In some cases, several names have been assigned to the same mix. This is so you can use conventions you're familiar with. The first sixteen mixes are all bitwise boolean, meaning they operate on the binary representation of the source and destination data. The remaining six mixes are arithmetic and provide some image-processing capabilities. These latter six functions are also affected by the setting of the Carry Chain Mask register.

Mix registers are only 8 bits wide, so always make sure you're not writing more than a byte to them (that is, always use the SENDB, not SENDW).

Color Compare

The color compare is a feature IBM introduced with the 8514/A, and it allows selective alteration of destination map data based on the value of that data. Using the XGA's color compare feature, you can write-protect a range of pixel values. The color compare has two components: a compare color, and a compare operation. There are eight color compare operations:

- Always TRUE (Disable all updates)
- Destination Pixel > Compare Color
- Destination Pixel == Compare Color
- Destination Pixel < Compare Color
- Always FALSE (Enable all updates)
- Destination Pixel >= Compare Color
- Destination Pixel != Compare Color
- Destination Pixel <= Compare Color

The destination pixel is updated only when the result of the color compare operation is false. As you can see, the various color compare operations let you write-protect pixels of an individual value, all but one value pixel, and just about any other numerical comparison possible. Color compares have limited use, and require a certain amount of ingenuity to use properly. The biggest reason not to use the color compare is that it exists only on the XGA, the 8514/A, and the Image Adapter/A (via the AI), so that if you write a code to support it, your application isn't all that portable to other graphics platforms.

Plane Mask

The plane mask resides in a 32-bit register, called, appropriately enough, the Plane Mask register. Each bit in the register controls access to 1 bit of graphical data in a pixel. So, for example, bit 0 of the plane mask controls access to all bit 0 bits for all pixel-write operations. When a plane mask bit is set to 1, all corresponding pixel bits can be written. A 0 in a plane mask bit disables writes to that bit.

The plane mask is something I've seen in just about every advanced graphics architecture there is, and have yet to find a real use for. You can use it to take a colorful mode, such as an 8bpp mode, and use it as two separate 4bpp planes. In such a situation, the plane mask allows BitBLTs to affect only the desired bits. Of course, since the XGA supports all pixel depths that such a scheme would buy you, the plane mask's usefulness is questionable.

Lines

Drawing lines isn't much more difficult than drawing filled rectangles, except that there is a little bit more set-up involved.

Instead of specifying the two end point pairs when drawing a line, the XGA requires that you precalculate three drawing parameters. These, combined with a single coordinate pair and the number of pixels to draw, allow the XGA to properly draw the line. This mechanism is virtually identical to the one used by the 8514/A. The unfortunate aspect of this setup operation is that it hinders better performance for short lines, since the setup burns some processor cycles.

My line drawing example is shown in Listing 5.5.

Listing 5.5. DRAWLINE.C

```
/*-------------------------------------------------------------------

   DRAWLINE.C - Shows how to draw lines on an XGA

   This program can be run by compiling it with the following lines:

      CL -c -Zp DRAWLINE.C
      LINK DRAWLINE INITXGA XGAFIND;

   ------------------------------------------------------------------*/


/*-------------------------------------------------------------------

   Include file section
   (the fail safe approach, include everything you might need later)

   ------------------------------------------------------------------*/

#include <stdio.h>
#include <stdlib.h>
#include <string.h>
#include <errno.h>
#include <fcntl.h>
#include <dos.h>
#include <conio.h>
#include <io.h>
#include <malloc.h>
#include <sys\types.h>
#include <sys\stat.h>
#include "xga.h"
```

continued...

...from previous page

```
/*-------------------------------------------------------------------

   Externals (all in INITXGA.C)

-----------------------------------------------------------------*/

extern    UWORD       xRes, yRes;        /* The XGA mode dimensions */
extern    UWORD       bpp;               /* Bits per pixel for the mode */
extern    UBYTE FAR   *memRegBaseAddr;   /* Memory Register address */
extern    UWORD       ioRegBaseAddr;     /* I/O Register address */

/*-------------------------------------------------------------------

        Code

-----------------------------------------------------------------*/

/*----------------------------------
```

```
VOID    DrawLine( UWORD x1, UWORD y1, UWORD x2, UWORD y2, UWORD color)
```

This function draws a line from (x1, y1) to (x2, y2), in Map A.

The color is assumed to be valid for the pixel depth. The current foreground mix is used (which is set to DST=SRC, i.e. replace, in INITXGA.C).

The Foreground color is left set to the passed color, and is not restored.

```
------------------------------------*/

VOID    DrawLine( UWORD x1, UWORD y1, UWORD x2, UWORD y2, UWORD color)
{
  UWORD octant = 0;    /* The line octant */
  WORD deltaX, deltaY;        /* The deltas for calculations */
  WORD fixUp = -1;     /* Fix up for drawing direction */
  WORD lineLength;     /* The longer line dimension */
  WORD smallerDelta;   /* The smaller line dimension */
  WORD twiceSmaller;   /* 2 * the smaller dimension */

  /*

     Calculate the distance between points for each axis

  */

  deltaX = x2 - x1;
  deltaY = y2 - y1;

  /*

     If X1 > X2, make delta positive, set the DEC_X bit
     in the octant field, and eliminate the fix up.

  */
```

```
if (deltaX < 0)
   {
   deltaX = -deltaX;
   octant |= DEC_X;
   fixUp = 0;
   }
/*
   If Y1 > Y2, make delta positive and set the DEC_Y
   bit in the octant field.
*/
if (deltaY < 0)
   {
   deltaY = -deltaY;
   octant |= DEC_Y;
   }

/*
   If Y delta is bigger, indicate that in the octant
   field. Also, set the long and short axis delta values.
*/
if (deltaX < deltaY)
   {
   octant |= YMAJOR;
   lineLength = deltaY;
   smallerDelta = deltaX;
   }
else
   {
   lineLength = deltaX;
   smallerDelta = deltaY;
   }

/*
   Precalculate the smaller delta * 2, as this is used
   repeatedly below.
*/
twiceSmaller = smallerDelta * 2;

/*
   Let's make sure the XGA is ready to draw a line.
*/
XGAWAIT;                             /* Wait for XGA ready */
SENDW(FORE_COLOR, color);            /* Set the foreground color */
SENDW(DEST_X, x1);                   /* Set start position */
```

continued...

...from previous page

```
    SENDW(DEST_Y, y1);
    SENDW(DIM1, lineLength);              /* No need to decrement deltas */
    SENDW(BRES_ERROR, twiceSmaller - lineLength + fixUp);
    SENDW(BRES_K1, twiceSmaller);
    SENDW(BRES_K2, twiceSmaller - 2 * lineLength);
    /*
       Now we need to actually program the proper command into
       the XGA's Command Register. The command is initiated with
       the loading of the high word of the 32-bit Command register.
    */
    SENDW(CMD_REG, PATT_SRC_FORESRC | octant);
    SENDW(CMD_REG+2, CMD_LINE | SRC_MAP_A | DST_MAP_A);

    return;       /* Done with drawing the line! */
}


/*------------------------------------

VOID DoSomething()

This routine is called from main(), located in INITXGA.C.
Here this routine makes repetitive calls to DrawLine()
to draw a line sweep on the display.

------------------------------------*/
VOID  DoSomething()
{
    UWORD i, j;  /* Scrap variables */

    for (i = 1; i < 16; i++)     /* Outer loop sets color, skip 0 */
       {
       /*
         Sweep horizontally
       */
       for (j = 0; j < xRes; j++)
         DrawLine(j, 0, xRes - j - 1, yRes - 1, i);

       /*
         Sweep vertically
       */
       for (j = 0; j < yRes; j++)
         DrawLine(0, j, xRes - 1, yRes - j - 1, i);
       }

    if (!getch())
       getch();

    return;
}
```

If you happen to look at the descriptions of the Bresenham Error Term, Bresenham Constant 1, and Bresenham Constant 2, in Chapter 4, you'll notice that the equations are slightly different from those presented here. The equations in Chapter 4 assume a Y and X delta normalized to the octant, meaning that in some octant situations, the X and Y deltas are actually swapped. To simplify matters I just call one delta the longer one, and the other the smaller one, in the code above.

DRAWLINE.C is a perfect example of how inefficient (albeit easy to read) C code can be. Listing 5.6 offers DRAWLINE.ASM, an optimized version of its C counterpart, designed to show why register-level programming should really be performed in assembly language instead of C, even though C is easier to read (and port).

Listing 5.6. DRAWLINE.ASM

```
;*********************************************************************
;
; DRAWLINE.ASM - Contains the ASM version of DRAWLINE.C
;
;
; This file should be assembled via the following line:
;
;       MASM -ml DRAWLINE;
;
; Then link it via:
;
;       LINK DRAWLINE XGAFIND INITXGA;
;
; This will produce a file called DRAWLINE.EXE which can be run.
;
;*********************************************************************

          include  XGA.INC

          .MODEL   SMALL
          .DATA

          extrn    _xRes:WORD
          extrn    _yRes:WORD
          extrn    _bpp:WORD
          extrn    _memRegBaseAddr:DWORD
          extrn    _ioRegBaseAddr:WORD

          .CODE
```

continued...

...from previous page

```
;------------------------------------------------------------------------
;
; VOID DrawLine(x1, y1, x2, y2, color)
;
; This is the assembly language version of the C DrawLine routine.
;
; This function draws a line from (x1, y1) to (x2, y2), in Map A.
;
; The color is assumed to be valid for the pixel depth. The current
; foreground mix is used (which is set to DST=SRC, i.e. replace, in
; INITXGA.C).
;
; The Foreground color is left set to the passed color, and is not
; restored.
;
;------------------------------------------------------------------------
;
; The following is a stack parameter definition, designed to make
; the code easier to read.
;
ARG_X1      equ     word ptr [BP+4]   ; Assume SMALL model as base
ARG_Y1      equ     word ptr [BP+6]
ARG_X2      equ     word ptr [BP+8]
ARG_Y2      equ     word ptr [BP+10]
ARG_COLOR   equ     word ptr [BP+12]
FIXUP       equ     word ptr [BP-2]

            public  _DrawLine           ; So C can call it sometime
_DrawLine   proc
            push    BP
            mov     BP, SP              ; Set up stack frame
            sub     SP, 2               ; Make room for FIXUP
            push    ES                  ; Trashed by MEMREGBASE
            push    DI
            push    SI                  ; Save regs C wants saved
            MEMREGBASE                  ; Load ES
            mov     SI, PATT_SRC_FORESRC ;  Set up low word of command
            mov     AX, ARG_Y2          ; Get the Y2 coordinate
            mov     CX, ARG_Y1          ; Get Y1
            sub     AX, CX              ; Compute dy = Y2 - Y1
            jge     DrawLine_10         ; IF dy < 0 THEN
            or      SI, DEC_Y           ;     tell XGA to y- instead of y++
            neg     AX                  ;     dy = -dy
```

```
DrawLine_10:                               ; END IF
        mov     DI, AX                     ; Minor axis count is dy into DI
        mov     DX, ARG_X2
        mov     FIXUP, -1                  ; Compute for Bresenham algorithm
        sub     DX, ARG_X1                 ; Compute dx = X2 - X1
        jge     DrawLine_20                ; IF dx < 0 THEN
        or      SI, DEC_X                  ;       tell XGA to x— instead of x++
        neg     DX                         ;       dx = -dx
        mov     FIXUP, 0                   ;       Update fixup
DrawLine_20:                               ; END IF
        cmp     DX, DI                     ; Set longer and smaller deltas
        jg      DrawLine_30                ; IF minor >= major THEN
        xchg    DX, DI                     ;       Swap them
        or      SI, YMAJOR                 ;       Tell XGA: y is major, not x
DrawLine_30:                               ; END IF
        XGAWAIT                            ; Wait for current operation to
                                           ; finish.

        mov     AX, ARG_COLOR
        SENDW   FORE_COLOR, AX             ; Set the foreground color.
        mov     AX, ARG_X1
        SENDW   DEST_X, AX                 ; Set the line start as X1, Y1
        SENDW   DEST_Y, CX
        shl     DI, 1                      ; 2 * smaller delta
        mov     AX, DI                     ; Get smaller delta
        SENDW   BRES_K1, AX                ; K1 = 2 * smaller delta
        sub     AX, DX                     ; Error = (longer * 2) - smaller
        add     AX, FIXUP                  ;         + fixup
        SENDW   BRES_ERROR, AX             ; Output Error term
        mov     AX, DI                     ; K2 = (smaller * 2) - (longer * 2)
        sub     AX, DX
        sub     AX, DX
        SENDW   BRES_K2, AX                ; Output K2
        SENDW   DIM1, DX                   ; Output longer length
                                           ; Regs are all set. Draw the line!
        SENDD   CMD_REG, <CMD_LINE OR SRC_MAP_A OR DST_MAP_A>, SI
        pop     SI
        pop     DI
        pop     ES
        mov     SP, BP                     ; Restore stack pointer
        pop     BP
        ret
_DrawLine  endp
;-----------------------------------------------------------------
;
; VOID DoSomething()
;
; This is the assembly language version of the C DoSomething
```

continued...

...from previous page

```
;
; This routine is called from main(), located in INITXGA.C.
; Here this routine makes repetitive calls to DrawLine()
; to draw a line sweep on the display.
;
;-----------------------------------------------------------------------
            public   _DoSomething
_DoSomething proc
            push    DI
            push    SI              ; Save because C wants it
            mov     DI, 1           ; Outer loop count, start at 1
DoSome_Outer:
            xor     SI, SI          ; Inner loop cnt for horizontal
            push    DI              ; Save Color as parm on stack
DoSome_HorSwp:
            mov     AX, _yRes
            dec     AX
            push    AX              ; Save Y2 = yRes - 1
            mov     AX, _xRes
            sub     AX, SI
            dec     AX
            push    AX              ; Save X2 = xRes - cnt - 1
            xor     AX, AX
            push    AX              ; Save Y1 = 0
            push    SI              ; Save X1 = count
            call    _DrawLine       ; Draw the line
            add     SP, 8           ; Keep color on the stack
            inc     SI
            cmp     SI, _xRes       ; One line per x position
            jl      DoSome_HorSwp
            xor     SI, SI          ; Inner loop cnt for vertical
DoSome_VerSwp:
            mov     AX, _yRes
            sub     AX, SI
            dec     AX
            push    AX              ; Save Y2 = yRes - cnt - 1
            mov     AX, _xRes
            dec     AX
            push    AX              ; Save X2 = xRes - 1
            xor     AX, AX
            push    SI              ; Save Y1 = count
            push    AX              ; Save X1 = 0
            call    _DrawLine       ; Draw the line
            add     SP, 8           ; Keep color on the stack
            inc     SI
```

```
        cmp     SI, _yRes           ; One line per y position
        jl      DoSome_VerSwp
        add     SP, 2               ; Get rid of color on stack
        inc     DI
        cmp     DI, 16              ; Only 15 times (16 - 1)
        jl      DoSome_Outer
        pop     SI
        pop     DI                  ; Restore stack.

        extrn   _getch:near         ; Declaration for _getch
        call    _getch              ; Wait for keystroke.
        or      AX, AX
        jnz     DoSome_Done
        call    _getch
DoSome_Done:
        ret
_DoSomething endp

        end
```

Short Stroke Vectors

As we saw in the previous examples, setting up the XGA to draw lines is far from simple. For a limited application—specifically one in which small vectors (15 pixels or less) are to be drawn—you may want to consider using the XGA's short stroke vector capability.

Short stroke vectors are limited to 15 pixels in length, and can be drawn at any angle that is a multiple of 45 degrees, meaning horizontal, vertical, and 45 degree diagonal lines (rise = run = +/–1). Another feature of the short stroke vectors is that you can indicate whether a given command is a move or draw command, meaning that instead of drawing a vector, you can just force the current drawing position to be shifted in any allowable direction by up to 15 pixels.

Short stroke vectors are particularly good for drawing characters on the display. The IBM XGA ships with three short stroke fonts: FONT0715.DLD, FONT0814.DLD, and FONT1220.DLD (all located in the directory with Panacea's DLD-XGA AutoCAD driver). All three are on the disk accompanying this book (their file extension is .SSV). These fonts are copyrighted, but can be used with your software thanks to an arrangement between IBM and Panacea. If you choose to use these fonts in your software, the only requirement is that you credit both companies in your documentation and software copyright notices as follows:

XGA fonts are Copyright (C) 1987-1992 IBM Corporation, and Copyright (C) 1992 Panacea Inc.—All Rights Reserved.

The complete documentation on the format of the short stroke vector font files can be found in Appendix K.

Listing 5.7 shows SHRTSTRK.C, which includes sample code to load an IBM AI short stroke vector file, as well as code to display short stroke characters on the display.

Listing 5.7. SHRTSTRK.C

```
/*-----------------------------------------------------------------------

   SHRTSTRK.C - Shows how to draw short stroke lines on an XGA

   This program can be run by compiling it with the following lines:

      CL -c -Zp DRAWLINE.C
      LINK DRAWLINE INITXGA XGAFIND;
-----------------------------------------------------------------------*/

/*-----------------------------------------------------------------------

   Include file section
   (the fail safe approach, include everything you might need later)
-----------------------------------------------------------------------*/
#include <stdio.h>
#include <stdlib.h>
#include <string.h>
#include <errno.h>
#include <fcntl.h>
#include <dos.h>
#include <conio.h>
#include <io.h>
#include <malloc.h>
#include <sys\types.h>
#include <sys\stat.h>
#include "xga.h"

/*-----------------------------------------------------------------------

      Structures

-----------------------------------------------------------------------*/
/*
   Font file header
*/
typedef struct CharSetDef      /* Character Set Definition block */
   {
   UBYTE        reserve1;
   UBYTE        type;
   DWORD        reserve2;
```

```
    UBYTE          reserve3;
    UBYTE          cellwidth
    UBYTE          cellheight;
    UBYTE          reserve4;
    WORD           cellnbytes;
    WORD           flags;
    WORD FAR       *indextbl;
    UBYTE FAR      *enveltbl;
    UBYTE          cdpt1st;
    UBYTE          cdptlast;
    UBYTE FAR      *chardef1;
    WORD           reserve5;
    UBYTE FAR      *chardef2
    WORD           reserve6
    UBYTE FAR      *chardef3;
    }  CHARSETDEF;
typedef struct FontFileDefn
    {
    WORD           no_pages; /* # of code pages in the file (size of page_array) */
    WORD           def_page; /* default page index (into page_array) */
    WORD           alt_page; /* alternate default page index (into page_array) */
    struct
      {
      BYTE         code_page_id[4];
      WORD         csd_offset;
      } page_array[1];
    } FFDEF;

/*-------------------------------------------------------------------

   Externals (all in INITXGA.C)

-------------------------------------------------------------------*/

extern   UWORD       xRes, yRes;        /* The XGA mode dimensions */
extern   UWORD       bpp;               /* Bits per pixel for the mode */
extern   UBYTE FAR   *memRegBaseAddr;   /* Memory Register address */
extern   UWORD       ioRegBaseAddr;     /* I/O Register address */

/*-------------------------------------------------------------------

   Statics

-------------------------------------------------------------------*/

static FFDEF   *ioAddr;       /* Address to load font to */

/*-------------------------------------------------------------------
```

continued...

...from previous page

Code

```
------------------------------------------------------------------------*/
/*-------------------------------------

    LoadFont(name)

    This routine loads fonts from IBM AI format short stroke font
    files. These files are supplied with the IBM XGA as FONTxxxx.SSV,
    and/or with the disk accompanying "Power Programming the IBM XGA".

    This function requires the file name of the AI compatible font
    file, and if the font is successfully loaded, returns a pointer
    to the character set definition, as required by the code. If the
    return value is 0, an error occurred while trying to load the
    file. Also, if you really want to be neat about things, the
    memory allocated for the font should be freed prior to exiting
    to DOS. Refer to Appendix K for more information on font file
    formats.

------------------------------------------------------------------------*/
CHARSETDEF      *LoadFont(BYTE *name)
{
    UWORD         fontLen;                  /* Size of font to load */
    WORD          fontHdl;                  /* Font file handle */
    CHARSETDEF    *pCSD;                    /* Pointer to Char Set Def. */
                                            /* Open the Font file */
    if ((fontHdl = open(name, O_RDONLY|O_BINARY)) == -1)
        {
        printf("Could not open font file '%s'!!!\n", name);
        return(0);
        }
                                      /* Get size of font file */
    fontLen = (UWORD) lseek(fontHdl, 0L, SEEK_END);

                                      /* Allocate enough space for file */
    ioAddr = (FFDEF *) malloc(fontLen);
    if (!ioAddr)
        {
        printf("Not enough memory to load font!\n");
        return(0);
        }

    lseek(fontHdl, 0L, SEEK_SET);        /* Return to start of file */

                                      /* Load the whole file into mem. */
    read(fontHdl, (BYTE *)ioAddr, fontLen);

                                      /* Point to start of def. font */
    pCSD = (CHARSETDEF *) (((BYTE *) ioAddr) +
            ioAddr->page_array[ioAddr->def_page].csd_offset);
```

```
                  /* Update all address fields with load address */
   pCSD->chardef1 = ((UBYTE FAR *) ioAddr) + ((DWORD) pCSD->chardef1);
   pCSD->chardef2 = ((UBYTE FAR *) ioAddr) + ((DWORD) pCSD->chardef2);
   pCSD->chardef3 = ((UBYTE FAR *) ioAddr) + ((DWORD) pCSD->chardef3);
   pCSD->indextbl = (WORD FAR *)
               (((UBYTE FAR *) ioAddr) + ((DWORD) pCSD->indextbl));
   pCSD->enveltbl = ((UBYTE FAR *) ioAddr) + ((DWORD) pCSD->enveltbl);

   close(fontHdl);                      /* Close the font handle */

   return(pCSD);                        /* Return pointer to the font */
}

/*------------------------------------

   DrawCharacter(x, y, character, color, fontPtr)

   Draws a short stroke vector character from the font defined by
   "fontPtr". Returns without doing anything if font type isn't
   short stroke. Remember that with the IBM version of the font,
   x,y specify the lower left corner of the font cell. In a really
   well-behaved program, you should also check to see if the
   character being passed is a valid one for the current font
   definition. Current mixes, clipping rectangle, etc. are observed.
   Drawing is done in Map A, which is assumed to be the full
   display.

------------------------------------*/
VOID DrawCharacter(WORD x, WORD y, UBYTE character,
                  UWORD color, CHARSETDEF *fontPtr)
{
   UWORD                         vecs;
   UWORD FAR                     *charPtr;

   if (fontPtr->type != 3)
      return;                       /* Return if not SSV font */

                                    /* Point to the char definition */
   charPtr = (WORD FAR *)(fontPtr->chardef1 + fontPtr-
>indextbl[character]);

   XGAWAIT;                         /* Wait for existing command to clear
*/
   SENDW(FORE_COLOR, color);        /* Set the foreground color */
   SENDW(DEST_X, x);
   SENDW(DEST_Y, y);                /* Starting point */

                                    /* Set the command register for SSV op.
*/
```

continued...

...from previous page

```
SENDW(CMD_REG, PATT_SRC_FORESRC | DRAW_MODE_NOT_LAST);
SENDW(CMD_REG+2, CMD_SSV | SRC_MAP_A | DST_MAP_A);

do
    {
    XGAWAIT;                        /* Play it safe and wait */
    vecs = *charPtr++;              /* Get a SSV word */
    if (!(vecs & 0x00FF))           /* If first vec is nul, we're done */
        break;
    SENDW(SHORT_STROKE+2, vecs);    /* Send it out to the XGA */
    } while (vecs & 0xFF00);        /* Quit if 2nd vec is nul */

return;
}

/*------------------------------------

    DoSomething()

    Print a string of characters using LoadFont and DrawCharacter.

------------------------------------*/
VOID DoSomething()
{
    static      UBYTE   string[] = "Hello World!";
                UBYTE   *strPtr = string;
                WORD    x = 100, y = 100;
                CHARSETDEF  *fontPtr;

    /*
        Load the font - makes an assumption about file name.
    */
    fontPtr = LoadFont("FONT1220.SSV");
    if (!fontPtr)                   /* Return if no font loaded */
        return;

    /*
        NOTE: Short stroke fonts, which the FONT????.SSV files happen
        to contain, do not clear the background when displayed. This
        means that you need to do a filled rectangle to clear an area
        before displaying short stroke font characters. This can have
        some positive uses as well, especially if you don't want to
        alter the background of the character cell.
    */
    while (*strPtr)                 /* Print the string */
        { /* Draw each character in white */
        DrawCharacter(x, y, *strPtr++, 15, fontPtr);
        x += fontPtr->cellwidth;/* Update position */
        }
```

```
    free(ioAddr);                    /* Free up the font buffer */

    if (!getch())                    /* Wait for key stroke */
       getch();

    return;
}
```

SHRTSTRK.C shows a few strange things. In the LoadFont() function, we load the font specified by the incoming string. In the case of this program, the font name is FONT1220.SSV, a 12x20 cell short stroke font, located in the current directory. First, the size of the font file is determined by a seek to the end of the file. Next, the entire font file is loaded. In the case of the font files here, none is much larger than about 9KB, so you should be able to allocate space for them in local RAM. Once the font file is loaded, the header is used to get a pointer to the start of the character set definition header. The character set definition header is then updated to reflect the position of the font data in local memory by adding the start address of the font file in RAM to the character data definition pointers. Once this is done, the pointer to the character set definition table is returned to the calling function. Note that all font-related structures are defined at the beginning of SHRTSTRK.C.

The next step is to actually draw characters, as shown by the routine DrawCharacter(). In this function, a pointer is calculated to the short stroke data defining the character that is to be drawn on the display; in this case, Map A.

Then, the XGA is set for the desired drawing color and the starting X, Y position for the character. Finally, the XGA is told that it should enter the short stroke vector (SSV) drawing mode via a command placed in the Command register. This command setting is necessary to enable the Short Stroke register on the XGA. Once the register is enabled, SSV commands can be passed to it.

As described in Chapter 4, the Short Stroke register is actually 32 bits (4 bytes) wide, and execution of the SSV data is initiated when the high byte of the register (byte offset 3 in both Intel and Motorola modes) is loaded with data. The SSV font data is set up so that 16 bits (2 bytes or SSV commands) can be written to the SSV registers at once. A 00H in either command byte (high or low) terminates the SSV sequence for the character. Note that I wrote the SSV word to the high order 16 bits of the Short Stroke register. This is required to execute the SSV command word, since this way the high byte of the register is written as well. Another important thing about loading the Short Stroke register is that you *must* make sure the XGA is ready for access. If you just dump data into the Short Stroke register without waiting to see if the XGA is done processing what you gave it during the last write, you end up with illegible squiggles, at the least.

One final note about SSV fonts is that since you can only draw short stroke vectors in one color, the background of the font cell is never cleared by the SSV action. This means that if you don't want text transparently laid over the existing screen information, you must clear the character cell via a filled rectangle prior to drawing the SSV character on it.

BitBLTs

BitBLTs are the work horse of GUI environments because they move blocks of graphics data all over the place. This is required when popping up windows, moving windows, saving portions of the display, and even displaying icons and fonts.

We've already seen BitBLTs in action in the DrawRectangle() routine, but there, instead of copying from one place in memory to another, we used the foreground color as our source.

In Listing 5.8, you'll see how color BitBLTs work, and also a couple of variants.

Listing 5.8. BITBLTS.C

```
/*------------------------------------------------------------------------

   BITBLTS.C - Shows how BitBLTs work on an XGA

   This program can be run by compiling it with the following lines:

       CL -c -Zp BITBLTS.C
       LINK BITBLTS INITXGA XGAFIND;

   ------------------------------------------------------------------------*/
/*------------------------------------------------------------------------

   Include file section

   (the fail safe approach, include everything you might need later)

   ------------------------------------------------------------------------*/
#include <stdio.h>
#include <stdlib.h>
#include <string.h>
#include <errno.h>
#include <fcntl.h>
#include <dos.h>
#include <conio.h>
#include <io.h>
#include <malloc.h>
```

```
#include <sys\types.h>
#include <sys\stat.h>
#include "xga.h"

/*-------------------------------------------------------------------

   Externals (all in INITXGA.C)

--------------------------------------------------------------------*/

extern   UWORD       xRes, yRes;        /* The XGA mode dimensions */
extern   UWORD       bpp;               /* Bits per pixel for the mode */
extern   UBYTE FAR   *memRegBaseAddr;   /* Memory Register address */
extern   UWORD       ioRegBaseAddr;     /* I/O Register address */

/*-------------------------------------------------------------------

   Code

--------------------------------------------------------------------*/

/*-----------------------------------

VOID  FillRectangle( UWORD x, UWORD y,
                     UWORD width, UWORD height, UWORD color)
Same as the function in FILLRECT.C, less most of the comments.

-----------------------------------*/

VOID  FillRectangle( UWORD x, UWORD y,
                     UWORD width, UWORD height, UWORD color)
{
  XGAWAIT;                              /* Wait for XGA ready */
  SENDW(FORE_COLOR, color);            /* Set the foreground color */
  SENDW(DEST_X, x);                    /* Set position */
  SENDW(DEST_Y, y);
  SENDW(DIM1, width - 1);
  SENDW(DIM2, height - 1);             /* Set dimensions of the rectangle */
  SENDW(CMD_REG, PATT_SRC_FORESRC);
  SENDW(CMD_REG+2, CMD_BITBLT | SRC_MAP_A | DST_MAP_A);

  return;                              /* Done with filling rectangles! */
}

/*-----------------------------------
VOID  BitBLT( UWORD srcX, UWORD srcY,
              UWORD dstX, UWORD dstY,
              UWORD width, UWORD height, UWORD invert)
```

This function performs a BitBLT within Map A. The position of
the source block of data is specified by (srcX, srcY), while
the destination of the block is specified by (dstX, dstY).

continued...

...from previous page

The type of BLT (normal or inverted) is specified by the "invert"
parameter. If 0, it's a normal BLT. If non-zero, the BLT should
be inverted.

The dimensions are assumed to be positive, non-zero values, while
the color is assumed to be valid for the pixel depth. The current
foreground mix is used (which is set to DST=SRC, i.e. replace, in
INITXGA.C).

Note: This function does NOT take overlapping source and
destination blocks into account. All BLTting is performed
with data copies in the positive X and Y directions.

```
---------------------------------------*/
VOID  BitBLT( UWORD srcX, UWORD srcY,
              UWORD dstX, UWORD dstY,
              UWORD width, UWORD height, UWORD invert)
{
   UWORD cmdHi;

                                    /* Set the command high word */
   cmdHi = BACK_SRC_SRCMAP | FORE_SRC_SRCMAP | SRC_MAP_A | DST_MAP_A;
   /*
      Let's set the function to perform in the upper
      command word based on the state of the invert flag.
   */
   if (invert)
      cmdHi |= CMD_INVERT_BITBLT;
   else
      cmdHi |= CMD_BITBLT;

   /*
      Next, let's make sure the XGA is ready to BitBLT
   */
   XGAWAIT;                         /* Wait for XGA ready */
   SENDW(SRC_X, srcX);              /* Set pattern start */
   SENDW(SRC_Y, srcY);
   SENDW(DEST_X, dstX);             /* Set destination */
   SENDW(DEST_Y, (invert ? (dstY + height - 1) : dstY));
   SENDW(DIM1, width - 1);
   SENDW(DIM2, height - 1);         /* Set dimensions of the BLT */
                                    /* Send whole 32 bits of command */
   SENDD(CMD_REG, cmdHi, PATT_SRC_FORESRC);

   return;                          /* Done with filling areas! */
}
```

```
/*-------------------------------------

VOID DoSomething()

This routine is called from main(), located in INITXGA.C.

This version of DoSomething() will perform a series of color
intra-map BitBLTs - both normal and inverted.

-------------------------------------*/
VOID DoSomething()
{
    UWORD       i, j, k;                /* Scrap variables */

    /*
        For our example, we're going to need something visible and
        bright. Let's construct a 64x64 pixel block consisting of
        a bunch of smaller rectangles. A black box is in the upper
        left, and a bright white will be in the lower right.

        Note that we will wait for a keystroke after every operation.
    */
    for (i = 0; i < 16; i++)
        FillRectangle((i % 4) * 16, (i / 4) * 16, 16, 16, i);

    if (!getch())
        getch();

    /*
        Let's show a BitBLT by taking our newly created graphic,
        and BLTting it in a row across the bottom of the display.
    */
    for (i = 0; i < xRes; i += 128)
        BitBLT(0, 0, i, yRes - 64, 64, 64, FALSE);

    if (!getch())
        getch();

    /*
        Now, let's use an Inverted BitBLT to do the same thing.
    */
    for (i = 64; i < xRes; i += 128)
        BitBLT(0, 0, i, yRes - 64, 64, 64, TRUE);

    if (!getch())
        getch();

    /*
        For the finale, BitBLT that bottom row of graphics
        across the rest of the display, alternating regular and
        inverted BitBLTs.
    */
```

continued...

...from previous page

```
for (i = 0; i < (yRes - 64) / 64; i++)
  BitBLT(0, yRes - 64, 0, i * 64, xRes, 64, i & 1);

if (!getch())
  getch();

return;
}
```

BITBLT.C basically shows the two types of XGA BitBLT functions: normal and inverted. Normal BitBLTs are exactly what they imply—normal. They just BLT data from one place to another.

Inverted BitBLTs are something of an oddity, left over from the days when graphics devices and environments had origins in the lower-left corner of the display, as opposed to the upper-left. When you specify an inverted BitBLT, each scan line of the source block is copied to the reverse end of the destination block. In other words, if the BLT is copying top-down, the top line of the source would end up at the bottom of the destination, and so on. With an inverted BitBLT, you need to modify the Y destination for the BLT to account for the BLT being processed backward. Ultimately, the end result of an inverted BLT would be that the destination block would look like you flipped the source block vertically around an imaginary line halfway down the source block. The only general use this type of BLT might have is in flipping objects, such as fonts or icons, when a user desires a mirrored 180 degree rotation. But, since it's there, you might as well see it in action.

The first routine in BITBLT.C is just a condensed version of FillRectangle(), used to create a sample image to BLT around. The next routine is BitBLT(). The parameters taken by this routine include the source and destination block positions, as well as the dimensions of the block. I've also added a flag that lets you select whether you want a normal or inverted BLT. One very important thing to note is that BitBLT() does not check for block overlap.

Overlap of the source and destination areas is important, since you may end up overwriting your source data as part of your BLT operation before the BLT is actually complete. To avoid this, the XGA BitBLT commands allow you to specify the direction of the actual copy process via the DEC_X and DEC_Y bits in the Command register (the YMAJOR bit has no impact on BLTs). So, for example, if your source area overlaps the upper-left corner of your destination area, you will want to set your starting source and destination positions to the lower-right corner of the respective blocks, and set both the DEC_X and DEC_Y bits in the BLT command. This way, the BLT starts in the lower-right corner and works its way up and left, so that once the BLT starts corrupting the source block, the BLT has already used that source region and is processing uncorrupted data further up and left in the source (see Figure 7.2) for a visual represenation). Determining how to set the DEC_X and DEC_Y bits is a matter of a handful of coordinate comparisons, which, for the sake of brevity and a challenge, I've left out.

Another thing that might be apparent in BitBLT() is that we're specifying the source map data as the source for both the background and foreground data. In this case, since we're not using a pattern map, the background source doesn't really matter, but I like to keep things well-rounded. This is basically what differentiates a BitBLT from a filled rectangle. Next, we also need to set the SRC_X and SRC_Y registers with the source start position. The DEST_X and DEST_Y are set as you might suspect—to the destination coordinates of the BLT operation.

The remainder of the program is designed to demonstrate BLT performance and use. Once you run the program, you'll also notice the visual difference between the normal and inverted BLTs. While the example deals only with BitBLTs within the same map, keep in mind that BLTing to an off-screen map and back is an excellent way to save and restore portions of the display.

Area Fills

You can do area fills with the XGA, but not in what I would consider a normal fashion. A classic area fill works by giving the area fill function a start position, a boundary color, and a fill color, and then the function uses a search mechanism to fill an area within the specified boundary.

On the XGA, the boundary is defined as part of the area fill process, as opposed to beforehand. The benefit is that this is an extremely efficient implementation in terms of performance. The drawback is that it doesn't respond in quite the way that a typical area fill does.

For the XGA area fill, you must draw your boundary onto a monochrome map (preferably cleared to 0), using a special line drawing mode and the XOR mix. You then use the XGA's area fill command to perform the operation, using the boundary definition map as a pattern source. The XGA then starts processing the monochrome map, one bit at a time.

At the start of each scan line, the XGA's fill mechanism is disabled. As it scans in the increasing X direction, each set monochrome pixel (that is, those with a pixel value of 1) toggles the XGA's filling mode.

For example:

Pixel #	0	1	2	3	4	5	6	7	8	9

Source Scan Line:

	0	1	0	0	0	1	0	1	1	0

Destination Fill Line:

	B	F	F	F	F	B	B	F	B	B

The source scan line reflects the monochrome source data for a given scan line of map after boundary information has been drawn on it. The destination fill line reflects the destination map the fill was performed into; B means that the background mix was used, and F means that the foreground mix was used to set the pixel in question. As the example demonstrates, the area fill engine hits a set pixel in position 1, and turns on the fill mode until it hits the next set pixel (in position 5), and so on.

The resulting fill and its relation to mixes is very important, as it is the key to how monochrome patterns work on the XGA. We'll discuss this in greater detail shortly.

Listing 5.9 shows AREAFILL.C, a sample program that shows how an XGA area fill is set up and executed.

Listing 5.9. AREAFILL.C

```
/*--------------------------------------------------------------------

   AREAFILL.C - Shows how to fill areas on an XGA

   This program can be run by compiling it with the following lines:

       CL -c -Zp AREAFILL.C
       LINK AREAFILL INITXGA XGAFIND;

   --------------------------------------------------------------------*/

/*--------------------------------------------------------------------

   Include file section
   (the fail safe approach, include everything you might need later)

   --------------------------------------------------------------------*/
#include <stdio.h>
#include <stdlib.h>
#include <string.h>
#include <errno.h>
#include <fcntl.h>
#include <dos.h>
#include <conio.h>
```

```
#include <io.h>
#include <malloc.h>
#include <sys\types.h>
#include <sys\stat.h>
#include "xga.h"
/*--------------------------------------------------------------------

   Externals (all in INITXGA.C)

--------------------------------------------------------------------*/

extern   UWORD       xRes, yRes;        /* The XGA mode dimensions */
extern   UWORD       bpp;               /* Bits per pixel for the mode */
extern   UBYTE FAR   *memRegBaseAddr;   /* Memory Register address */
extern   UWORD       ioRegBaseAddr;     /* I/O Register address */
extern   UDWORD      vramBaseAddr;      /* The start of the XGA's VRAM */

/*--------------------------------------------------------------------

   Code

--------------------------------------------------------------------*/

/*-----------------------------------

VOID    DrawBound( UWORD x1, UWORD y1, UWORD x2, UWORD y2)

This function draws a line from (x1, y1) to (x2, y2), in Map B,
which is assumed to be a monochrome Map.

The line drawn is set to be an area fill boundary line, and drawn
in XOR mode to avoid problems during line crossings.

The Foreground color is set to 1, and is not restored. The
Background Mix is reset to replace mode.

-----------------------------------*/

VOID DrawBound( UWORD x1, UWORD y1, UWORD x2, UWORD y2)
{
   UWORD   octant = 0;              /* The line octant */
   WORD    deltaX, deltaY;          /* The deltas for calculations */
   WORD    fixUp = -1;              /* Fix up for drawing direction */
   WORD    lineLength;              /* The longer line dimension */
   WORD    smallerDelta;            /* The smaller line dimension */
   WORD    twiceSmaller;            /* 2 * the smaller dimension */

   /*
      Do standard line drawing stuff. For details see DRAWLINE.C
   */
   deltaX = x2 - x1;
   deltaY = y2 - y1;
   if (deltaX < 0)
```

continued...

...from previous page

```
      {
      deltaX = -deltaX;
      octant |= DEC_X;
      fixUp = 0;
      }
  if (deltaY < 0)
      {
      deltaY = -deltaY;
      octant |= DEC_Y;
      }
  if (deltaX < deltaY)
      {
      octant |= YMAJOR;
      lineLength = deltaY;
      smallerDelta = deltaX;
      }
  else
      {
      lineLength = deltaX;
      smallerDelta = deltaY;
      }
  twiceSmaller = smallerDelta * 2;

  /*
      Let's make sure the XGA is ready to draw a line.
  */
  XGAWAIT;                            /* Wait for XGA ready */
  SENDB(FORE_MIX, MIX_XOR);          /* Need to be in XOR mode */
  SENDW(FORE_COLOR, 1);              /* Set the foreground color */
  SENDW(DEST_X, x1);                 /* Set start position */
  SENDW(DEST_Y, y1);
  SENDW(DIM1, lineLength);           /* No need to decrement deltas */
  SENDW(BRES_ERROR, twiceSmaller - lineLength + fixUp);
  SENDW(BRES_K1, twiceSmaller);
  SENDW(BRES_K2, twiceSmaller - 2 * lineLength);
  /*

      Load the Command register with a draw line command, but
      with Map B as the destination and the boundary draw mode
      enabled.
  */
  SENDW(CMD_REG, PATT_SRC_FORESRC | DRAW_MODE_BOUNDARY | octant);
  SENDW(CMD_REG+2, CMD_LINE | SRC_MAP_B | DST_MAP_B);

  XGAWAIT;                            /* Wait for XGA ready again */
  SENDB(FORE_MIX, MIX_SRC);          /* Restore to replace mix */

  return;                            /* Done with drawing the line! */
}
```

```
/*------------------------------------

VOID ClearMapB()

This routine clears Map B to a color of 0.

The foreground color is left at 0 upon return. The current
mix and other drawing modifiers are left in effect. This
function is basically a fixed function version of FillRectangle.

------------------------------------*/
VOID ClearMapB()
{
   XGAWAIT;                              /* Wait for XGA to be ready */
   SENDW(FORE_COLOR, 0);                 /* Set all foreground color bits off */
   SENDW(DEST_X, 0);                     /* At 0,0, full screen size */
   SENDW(DEST_Y, 0);
   SENDW(DIM1, xRes - 1);
   SENDW(DIM2, yRes - 1);
   SENDW(CMD_REG, PATT_SRC_FORESRC);
   SENDW(CMD_REG+2, CMD_BITBLT | SRC_MAP_B | DST_MAP_B);

   return;
}

/*------------------------------------

VOID AreaFill( UWORD x, UWORD y,
               UWORD width, UWORD height, UWORD color)
```

This function fills the area specified by Map B onto the
display (Map A) using the passed color as the color for
the fill.

"x" & "y" are the destination of the area fill in Map A, and width
and height are the dimensions of the fill (and pattern). The
area fill source pattern is assumed to start at the origin in
the pattern map.

The dimensions are assumed to be positive, non-zero values, while
the color is assumed to be valid for the pixel depth. The current
foreground mix is used (which is set to DST=SRC, i.e. replace, in
INITXGA.C).

The Foreground color is left set to the passed color, and is not
restored. The Background Mix is reset to replace.

```
------------------------------------*/
VOID AreaFill( UWORD x, UWORD y,
               UWORD width, UWORD height, UWORD color)
{
```

continued...

...from previous page

```
    /*
        First, let's make sure the XGA is ready to area fill
    */
    XGAWAIT;                                /* Wait for XGA ready */
    SENDW(FORE_COLOR, color);               /* Set the foreground color */
    SENDB(BACK_MIX, MIX_DST);               /* Don't disturb the background */
    SENDW(PATT_X, 0);                       /* Set pattern start */
    SENDW(PATT_Y, 0);
    SENDW(DEST_X, x);                       /* Set destination */
    SENDW(DEST_Y, y);
    SENDW(DIM1, width - 1);
    SENDW(DIM2, height - 1);                /* Set dimensions of the fill */
    /*
        In this case, we'll use Map B as the pattern source, and
        specify the area fill function when we load the Command
        register.
    */
    SENDW(CMD_REG, PATT_SRC_B);
    SENDW(CMD_REG+2, CMD_AREA_FILL | SRC_MAP_A | DST_MAP_A);
    XGAWAIT;
    SENDB(BACK_MIX, MIX_SRC);               /* Reset the background mix */

    return;                                 /* Done with filling areas! */
}
/*------------------------------------

VOID    DoSomething()

This routine is called from main(), located in INITXGA.C.
Here we set up Map B as a monochrome source map, and
then perform an area fill example.

--------------------------------------*/
VOID    DoSomething()
{
  UWORD         i, j, k;          /* Scrap variables */
  UDWORD        screenSize;
  /*
      First step is to initialize Map B as a monochrome bitmap the
      size of the display. However, we need to specify a base
      address for Map B which does not interfere with the display,
      which is mapped as Map A. So, we can place Map B directly
      after the end of Map A. This address can be calculated by
      determining the amount of memory Map A consumes and adding
      it to the VRAM base address.

      One thing to be aware of in an application is that you only
      a limited amount of VRAM on the XGA. In this case here, we
      know that even in the worst case scenario (1024x768x4bpp
```

with 512KB of VRAM) we still have enough memory for the
monochrome map (which would take up 96KB).
```c
*/
                                    /* Size of display in bytes */
screenSize = ((UDWORD)yRes * xRes * bpp) / 8;
                                    /* Round up to next DWORD for address */
screenSize = (screenSize + 3) & 0xFFFFFFFC;
                                    /* Add base address of VRAM */
screenSize += vramBaseAddr;

XGAWAIT;                            /* Wait for the XGA to be ready */
SENDB(MAP_INDEX, MAP_INDEX_B);     /* Create Map B */
                                    /* Send low and high word of address */
SENDW(MAP_BASE, (UWORD)(screenSize & 0xFFFF));
SENDW(MAP_BASE+2, (UWORD)((screenSize >> 16) & 0xFFFF));
SENDW(MAP_WIDTH, xRes - 1);        /* Same dimensions as screen */
SENDW(MAP_HEIGHT, yRes - 1);
SENDW(MAP_FORMAT, PIXEL_SIZE_1);   /* 1 bit per pixel */

/*
    Next, we need to clear Map B to all 0s in order to start
    drawing on it.
*/
ClearMapB();

/*
    Let's do a simple area fill object: an "hour glass"
    (basically an "X" with the top and bottom edges connected).
    Since our AreaFill function assumes a pattern start of 0,0,
    that's where we should start drawing.
*/
i = xRes / 4;                   /* Quarter of screen width */
j = yRes / 2;                   /* Half of screen height */

DrawBound(0, 0, i, 0);          /* Top line */
DrawBound(i, 0, 0, j);          /* Upper right to lower left */
DrawBound(0, j, i, j);          /* Botton line */
DrawBound(i, j, 0, 0);          /* Lower right back to start */

/*
    Now let's put a whole bunch of differently colored hour
    glasses on the screen (8 to be exact - 2 lines of 4 each)
    in bright colors.
*/
for (k = 0; k < 8; k++)
    AreaFill(i * (k / 2), j * (k % 2), i, j, k + 8);

if (!getch())
    getch();

return;

}
```

Looking through AREAFILL.C, the first routine you hit is DrawBound(), which is an adaptation of the DrawLine() routine presented earlier in the chapter. The difference is that DrawBound() draws in Map B, with an XOR mix, and has the DRAW_MODE_BOUNDARY field set when the line is drawn via the Command register. The purpose of this is to make sure that only 1 pixel is drawn per scan line for a given line boundary. The reason this is important can best be seen in the scan line fill example provided just before the listings above, in pixels 7 and 8. For example, if you were drawing a horizontal line the normal way and then used it for an area fill, the fill would end up with an alternating foreground/background pattern, since each set pixel would be toggling the fill state. Since any line that is less than 45 percent of horizontal will have at least occasional multiple pixel per scan line runs, this boundary drawing mode avoids this problem. The boundary line draw also doesn't draw the last pixel of each line, so that a polygon outline won't have vertices that are drawn twice. This is because if you draw a pixel twice in an XOR mix in the same color, a background color pixel (0 in a monochrome map) will be drawn, leaving a hole in the outline where the area fill might "leak" out.

The XOR mix used when drawing the boundary line is also important, since it prevents "inverse" leaks during the area fill. In the AREAFILL.C program, if you were to disable the setting of the XOR mix, you would find that a pixel would be drawn at the intersection of the two diagonal lines. The area fill would treat this as an indication that filling should be turned on, and you would have a horizontal fill on that scan line, extending from the intersection of the two lines to the edge of the fill area. Using the XOR mix, however, produces a minor drawback, which is that single-point intersections in a complex polygon are not drawn at all in the final object. Also, since the area fill turns off when it hits a second set pixel (instead of *after* it hits that pixel), you will miss 1 pixel off of each right-hand edge of a fill.

To solve this XOR/missing pixel fill problem, once the area fill is complete, draw the outline of the area on the destination map (Map A in this case) in a MIX_SRC mix. This will fill in all the gaps created by the unusual fill process. If you need to fill to perform a raster operation, you may need an intermediate step that involves filling the map the boundary is in, drawing a real outline, and then doing a monochrome-color expansion BitBLT to the destination map with the correct mix set.

The Area Fill Routine

The next item of interest in AREAFILL.C is the AreaFill() routine. First, notice that we set the background mix to MIX_DST, which leaves destination map pixels unchanged when used. The foreground mix is still set to MIX_SRC, meaning that all destination pixels are set to the foreground color when the foreground mix is in effect. All of this ties into the destination fill scan line and monochrome pattern described earlier. When a pattern map is used (and the intermediary result of the area fill could be considered a pattern map), each 0 bit in the pattern is treated as an application of the background source to the destination, and each 1 bit in the pattern uses the foreground source on the respective destination pixel. For all the graphics operations we've used so far, the background source has been the background mix and color, and the foreground source has been the foreground mix and color. To get back to the start of this particular discussion, it means that for the area fill, those areas that are filled use the foreground mix, and all others use the background mix. Thus, if the background mix is MIX_DST, only the fill areas are actually written to the destination. This is also how a monochrome-to-color BitBLT (also known as an **expansion BitBLT**) works. Additional tricks can be played by manipulating the sources to use source map data instead of the current mixes.

Setting the starting position within the pattern for the operation is also important when using both area fills and patterns. This is set in the PATT_X and PATT_Y registers. This tells the XGA how to align the pattern with the destination (and source, if used). So, in AreaFill(), position (0,0) in the pattern is tied to (x,y) in the destination, and as the operation progresses in both the positive X and Y direction, so does the position pointer within the pattern. Thus, points in various maps are always kept relative to one another. For area fills in particular, it is very important that you never have the DEC_X bit set in the Command register, because the fill scans only in the positive X direction.

Patterns

We've already discussed patterns quite a bit, but primarily in the context of area fills. Patterns can be applied to other operations as well, including lines, short stroke vectors, and filled rectangles. And patterns need not be only monochrome data. You can use color patterns as well, as Listings 5.10 and 5.11 show.

Listing 5.10. PATTERNS.C

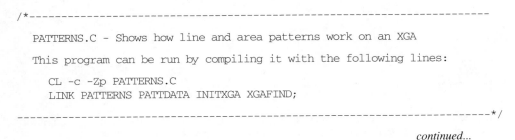

```
/*------------------------------------------------------------------

   PATTERNS.C - Shows how line and area patterns work on an XGA

   This program can be run by compiling it with the following lines:

      CL -c -Zp PATTERNS.C
      LINK PATTERNS PATTDATA INITXGA XGAFIND;

   -----------------------------------------------------------------*/
```

continued...

...from previous page

```
/*-------------------------------------------------------------------

   Include file section
   (the fail safe approach, include everything you might need later)

-----------------------------------------------------------------*/
#include <stdio.h>
#include <stdlib.h>
#include <string.h>
#include <errno.h>
#include <fcntl.h>
#include <dos.h>
#include <conio.h>
#include <io.h>
#include <malloc.h>
#include <sys\types.h>
#include <sys\stat.h>
#include "xga.h"

/*-------------------------------------------------------------------
Externals (first five in INITXGA.C, last three in PATTDATA.ASM)

-----------------------------------------------------------------*/

extern   UWORD        xRes, yRes;         /* The XGA mode dimensions */
extern   UWORD        bpp;                /* Bits per pixel for the mode */
extern   UBYTE FAR    *memRegBaseAddr;    /* Memory Register address */
extern   UWORD        ioRegBaseAddr;      /* I/O Register address */
extern   UDWORD       vramBaseAddr;       /* The start of the XGA's VRAM */

extern   UBYTE        monoLinePattern[];  /* The monochrome line pattern */
extern   UBYTE        monoAreaPattern[];  /* The monochrome area pattern */
extern   UBYTE        colorLinePattern4[];   /* The color line pattern */
extern   UBYTE        colorLinePattern8[];   /* The color line pattern */
extern   UBYTE        colorAreaPattern4[];   /* The color area pattern */
extern   UBYTE        colorAreaPattern8[];   /* The color area pattern */

/*-------------------------------------------------------------------

   Code

-----------------------------------------------------------------*/

/*-----------------------------------

VOID  SetMapB( UBYTE FAR *address,
               UWORD width, UWORD height, UWORD bppMask)
```

This function sets up Map B using the specified parameters.
Note that the passed address is in segment offset format, while
the MAP_BASE requires a linear address, so we must do a conversion.

```
-------------------------------------*/
VOID  SetMapB( UBYTE FAR *address,
              UWORD width, UWORD height, UWORD bppMask)
{
   UDWORD       linearAddr;    /* Our conversion variable */

   /*
      To convert a segment:offset address to linear, we need to
      take the 16-bit segment, and shift it left a nibble, and
      then add the offset. Since our segment address is located
      in the upper 16 bits of a 32 bit word, instead of shifting
      16 bits right, and then 4 bits left, we'll mask the upper
      16 bits, and shift right 12 bits (16R - 4L).
   */
      linearAddr = (((UDWORD)address & 0xFFFF0000L) >> 12)
                             + ((UDWORD)address & 0xFFFF);

   XGAWAIT;                            /* Wait for the XGA to be ready */
   SENDB(MAP_INDEX, MAP_INDEX_B);   /* Create Map B */
                                      /* Send low and high word of address */
   SENDW(MAP_BASE, (UWORD)(linearAddr & 0xFFFF));
   SENDW(MAP_BASE+2, (UWORD)((linearAddr >> 16) & 0xFFFF));
   SENDW(MAP_WIDTH, width - 1);
   SENDW(MAP_HEIGHT, height - 1);
   SENDW(MAP_FORMAT, bppMask);

   return;
}

/*-----------------------------------

VOID PattLine( UWORD x1, UWORD y1, UWORD x2, UWORD y2, UWORD mono)
```

This function draws a line from (x1, y1) to (x2, y2) in Map A, using
either a monochrome or color pattern, located in Map B. The type of
pattern is specified via the "mono" parameter, which if 0 indicates
a color pattern, and if non-zero indicates a monochrome pattern.

The line is drawn using the current mixes, and if a monochrome
pattern is specified, the foreground and background colors are
used for expansion.

The pattern start is reset to 0,0 prior to each line drawn.

```
                      -*/
VOID PattLine( UWORD x1, UWORD y1, UWORD x2, UWORD y2, UWORD mono)
{
   UWORD   octant = 0;            /* The line octant */
   WORD    deltaX, deltaY;        /* The deltas for calculations */
   WORD    fixUp = -1;            /* Fix up for drawing direction */
   WORD    lineLength;            /* The longer line dimension */
```

continued...

...from previous page

```
WORD  smallerDelta;              /* The smaller line dimension */
WORD    twiceSmaller;            /* 2 * the smaller dimension */

/*
    Do standard line drawing stuff. For details see DRAWLINE.C
*/
deltaX = x2 - x1;
deltaY = y2 - y1;
if (deltaX < 0)
    {
    deltaX = -deltaX;
    octant |= DEC_X;
    fixUp = 0;
    }
if (deltaY < 0)
    {
    deltaY = -deltaY;
    octant |= DEC_Y;
    }
if (deltaX < deltaY)
    {
    octant |= YMAJOR;
    lineLength = deltaY;
    smallerDelta = deltaX;
    }
else
    {
    lineLength = deltaX;
    smallerDelta = deltaY;
    }
twiceSmaller = smallerDelta * 2;

/*
    Let's make sure the XGA is ready to draw a line.
*/
XGAWAIT;                          /* Wait for XGA ready */
if (mono)                         /* If monochrome, set pattern start */
    {
    SENDW(PATT_X, 0);
    SENDW(PATT_Y, 0);
    }
else
    {                             /* Otherwise, set color source start */
    SENDW(SRC_X, 0);
    SENDW(SRC_Y, 0);
    }
SENDW(DEST_X, x1);                /* Set line start position */
SENDW(DEST_Y, y1);
```

```
   SENDW(DIM1, lineLength);              /* No need to decrement deltas */
   SENDW(BRES_ERROR, twiceSmaller - lineLength + fixUp);
   SENDW(BRES_K1, twiceSmaller);
   SENDW(BRES_K2, twiceSmaller - 2 * lineLength);
   /*
      Load the Command register with a draw line command, but
      with Map B as the pattern. If it's a monochrome pattern,
      you need to set the pattern source, and if it's a color
      pattern, you need to specify it as a source map, and change
      the foreground source.
   */
   if (mono)
      {
      SENDW(CMD_REG, PATT_SRC_B | octant);
      SENDW(CMD_REG+2, CMD_LINE | SRC_MAP_A | DST_MAP_A);
      }
   else
      {
      SENDW(CMD_REG, PATT_SRC_FORESRC | octant);
      SENDW(CMD_REG+2, BACK_SRC_SRCMAP | FORE_SRC_SRCMAP
                           | CMD_LINE | SRC_MAP_B | DST_MAP_A);

      }
   return;                               /* Done with drawing the line! */
}

/*-----------------------------------

VOID  PattRectangle( UWORD x, UWORD y,
                     UWORD width, UWORD height, UWORD mono)
```

This function draws a filled rectangle at (x,y) with the specified
dimensions, in Map A, using either a monochrome or color pattern,
located in Map B. The type of pattern is specified via the "mono"
parameter, which if 0 indicates a color pattern, and if non-zero
indicates a monochrome pattern.

The pattern start is reset to 0,0 prior to each line drawn.

The dimensions are assumed to be positive, non-zero values, while
the color is assumed to be valid for the pixel depth. The current
foreground mix is used, and if a monochrome
pattern is specified, the foreground and background colors are
used for expansion.

```
--------------------------------------*/
VOID  PattRectangle( UWORD x, UWORD y,
                     UWORD width, UWORD height, UWORD mono)
{
```

continued...

...from previous page

```
XGAWAIT;                                /* Wait for XGA ready */
  if (mono)                             /* Do the mono/color start stuff */
    {
    SENDW(PATT_X, 0);
    SENDW(PATT_Y, 0);
    }
  else
    {
    SENDW(SRC_X, 0);
    SENDW(SRC_Y, 0);
    }
  SENDW(DEST_X, x);                     /* Set start position for rect. */
  SENDW(DEST_Y, y);
  SENDW(DIM1, width - 1);
  SENDW(DIM2, height - 1);              /* Set dimensions of the rectangle */
  /*
    Use the same process here as for the patterned line, with
    respect to how to get monochrome and color patterns up on
    the screen.
  */
  if (mono)
    {
    SENDW(CMD_REG, PATT_SRC_B);
    SENDW(CMD_REG+2, CMD_BITBLT | SRC_MAP_A | DST_MAP_A);
    }
  else
    {
    SENDW(CMD_REG, PATT_SRC_FORESRC);
    SENDW(CMD_REG+2, BACK_SRC_SRCMAP | FORE_SRC_SRCMAP
                     | CMD_BITBLT | SRC_MAP_B | DST_MAP_A);
    }

  return;                               /* Done with filling rectangles! */
}

/*-------------------------------------

VOID DoSomething()

This routine is called from main(), located in INITXGA.C.
In this version, we'll be going through a series of pattern
examples.

-------------------------------------*/
VOID DoSomething()
{
  UWORD   i, j;                         /* Scrap variables */
```

```
/*
   For our first experiment, let's do a monochrome line pattern
   using a derivative of our sweep example from DRAWLINE.C.
   First, we need to set up Map B with the line pattern.
   While we're drawing the lines, we'll also be changing
   the foreground and background colors to add some pizazz
   to the display.
*/
SetMapB((UBYTE FAR *)monoLinePattern, 16, 1, PIXEL_SIZE_1);

for (j = 0; j < xRes; j++) /* Horizontal Sweep */
   {
   XGAWAIT;                         /* Wait for the XGA to be ready */
   SENDW(FORE_COLOR, (j / 16) & 0x0F);
   SENDW(BACK_COLOR, (j % 16) & 0x0F);
   PattLine(j, 0, xRes - j - 1, yRes - 1, TRUE);
   }

for (j = 0; j < yRes; j++) /* Vertical Sweep */
   {
   XGAWAIT;                         /* Wait for the XGA to be ready */
   SENDW(FORE_COLOR, (j % 16) & 0x0F);
   SENDW(BACK_COLOR, (j / 16) & 0x0F);
   PattLine(0, j, xRes - 1, yRes - j - 1, TRUE);
   }

if (!getch())
   getch();
/*
   For our second experiment, let's do a color line using
   a similar sweep example. Note that the color pattern map
   must be the same pixel depth as the destination map. We
   know we're either in 4 or 8 bpp mode, so let's try for
   4 bpp first.
*/
if (bpp == 4)
   SetMapB((UBYTE FAR *)colorLinePattern4, 16, 1, PIXEL_SIZE_4);
else
   SetMapB((UBYTE FAR *)colorLinePattern8, 16, 1, PIXEL_SIZE_8);

for (j = 0; j < xRes; j++) /* Horizontal Sweep */
   PattLine(j, 0, xRes - j - 1, yRes - 1, FALSE);

for (j = 0; j < yRes; j++) /* Vertical Sweep */
   PattLine(0, j, xRes - 1, yRes - j - 1, FALSE);

if (!getch())
   getch();
```

continued...

...from previous page

```
    /*
        Now let's do some monochrome and color patterns with
        rectangles, using some of the code from FILLRECT.C
    */
    SetMapB((UBYTE FAR *)monoAreaPattern, 16, 16, PIXEL_SIZE_1);

    for (i = 0; i < xRes; i +=16)
        for (j = 0; j < yRes; j += 16)
            {
            XGAWAIT;                        /* Wait for the XGA to be ready */
            SENDW(FORE_COLOR, (i / 16) & 0x0F);
            SENDW(BACK_COLOR, (j / 16) & 0x0F);
            PattRectangle(i, j, 16, 16, TRUE);
            }

    if (!getch())
        getch();
    /*
        Now that we've done the mono, let's play with a color map,
        and providing a tiling example.
    */
    if (bpp == 4)
        SetMapB((UBYTE FAR *)colorAreaPattern4, 16, 16, PIXEL_SIZE_4);
    else
        SetMapB((UBYTE FAR *)colorAreaPattern8, 16, 16, PIXEL_SIZE_8);

    PattRectangle(0, 0, xRes, yRes, FALSE);

    if (!getch())
        getch();

    return;
}
```

Listing 5.11. PATTDATA.ASM

```
;**********************************************************************
;
; PATTDATA.ASM - Contains the Pattern Data for PATTERNS.C
;
;
; This file should be assembled via the following line:
;
;       MASM -ml PATTDATA;
;
; Then link it via:
;
;       LINK PATTERNS PATTDATA XGAFIND INITXGA;
```

```
;
; This will produce a file called PATTERNS.EXE which can be run.
;
;************************************************************************

        include XGA.INC

        .MODEL  SMALL

        .DATA
;
; The reason for defining the patterns here instead of PATTERNS.C
; because an XGA bus-mastering operation requires that you define
; a map on a 32 bit boundary, and I haven't found a simple way to
; do that with MS-C v5.1.
;
        align   4        ; DWORD Boundary

        public _monoLinePattern      ; Monochrome line pattern
_monoLinePattern label byte          ; 3 off,3 on,2 off,2 on,3 off,3 on
        db      00111000B, 11100011B

        align   4                    ; DWORD Boundary

        public _monoAreaPattern      ; Monochrome area pattern
_monoAreaPattern label byte          ; Basically a mosaic design
        db      10000000B, 00000001B
        db      10001000B, 00010001B
        db      00010100B, 00101000B
        db      00010010B, 01001000B
        db      11111100B, 00111111B
        db      00010000B, 00001000B
        db      11010000B, 00001011B
        db      11010011B, 11001011B
        db      11010011B, 11001011B
        db      11010000B, 00001011B
        db      00010000B, 00001000B
        db      11111100B, 00111111B
        db      00010010B, 01001000B
        db      00010100B, 00101000B
        db      10001000B, 00010001B
        db      10000000B, 00000001B

        align   4                    ; DWORD Boundary

        public _colorLinePattern4    ; 4bpp Color line pattern
_colorLinePattern4 label byte        ; 4 pix ea.: white,blue,red,green
        db      0FFH, 0FFH, 099H, 099H, 0CCH, 0CCH, 0AAH, 0AAH
```

continued...

...from previous page

```
        align   4                       ; DWORD Boundary

        public  _colorLinePattern8; 8bpp Color line pattern
_colorLinePattern8 label byte           ; 4 pix ea.: white,blue,red,green
        db      0FH, 0FH, 0FH, 0FH, 09H, 09H, 09H, 09H
        db      0CH, 0CH, 0CH, 0CH, 0AH, 0AH, 0AH, 0AH

        align   4                       ; DWORD Boundary

        public  _colorAreaPattern4      ; 4bpp Color area pattern
_colorAreaPattern4 label byte           ; Color shift from corners
        db      010H, 032H, 054H, 076H, 098H, 0BAH, 0DCH, 0FEH
        db      021H, 043H, 065H, 087H, 0A9H, 0CBH, 0EDH, 0EFH
        db      032H, 054H, 076H, 098H, 0BAH, 0DCH, 0FEH, 0DEH
        db      043H, 065H, 087H, 0A9H, 0CBH, 0EDH, 0EFH, 0CDH
        db      054H, 076H, 098H, 0BAH, 0DCH, 0FEH, 0DEH, 0BCH
        db      065H, 087H, 0A9H, 0CBH, 0EDH, 0EFH, 0CDH, 0ABH
        db      076H, 098H, 0BAH, 0DCH, 0FEH, 0DEH, 0BCH, 09AH
        db      087H, 0A9H, 0CBH, 0EDH, 0EFH, 0CDH, 0ABH, 089H
        db      098H, 0BAH, 0DCH, 0FEH, 0DEH, 0BCH, 09AH, 078H
        db      0A9H, 0CBH, 0EDH, 0EFH, 0CDH, 0ABH, 089H, 067H
        db      0BAH, 0DCH, 0FEH, 0DEH, 0BCH, 09AH, 078H, 056H
        db      0CBH, 0EDH, 0EFH, 0CDH, 0ABH, 089H, 067H, 045H
        db      0DCH, 0FEH, 0DEH, 0BCH, 09AH, 078H, 056H, 034H
        db      0EDH, 0EFH, 0CDH, 0ABH, 089H, 067H, 045H, 023H
        db      0FEH, 0DEH, 0BCH, 09AH, 078H, 056H, 034H, 022H
        db      0EFH, 0CDH, 0ABH, 089H, 067H, 045H, 023H, 002H

        align   4                       ; DWORD Boundary

        public  _colorAreaPattern8      ; 8bpp Color area pattern
_colorAreaPattern8 label byte           ; Color shift from corners
        db      00H, 01H, 02H, 03H, 04H, 05H, 06H, 07H
        db      08H, 09H, 0AH, 0BH, 0CH, 0DH, 0EH, 0FH
        db      01H, 02H, 03H, 04H, 05H, 06H, 07H, 08H
        db      09H, 0AH, 0BH, 0CH, 0DH, 0EH, 0FH, 0EH
        db      02H, 03H, 04H, 05H, 06H, 07H, 08H, 09H
        db      0AH, 0BH, 0CH, 0DH, 0EH, 0FH, 0EH, 0DH
        db      03H, 04H, 05H, 06H, 07H, 08H, 09H, 0AH
        db      0BH, 0CH, 0DH, 0EH, 0FH, 0EH, 0DH, 0CH
        db      04H, 05H, 06H, 07H, 08H, 09H, 0AH, 0BH
        db      0CH, 0DH, 0EH, 0FH, 0EH, 0DH, 0CH, 0BH
        db      05H, 06H, 07H, 08H, 09H, 0AH, 0BH, 0CH
        db      0DH, 0EH, 0FH, 0EH, 0DH, 0CH, 0BH, 0AH
        db      06H, 07H, 08H, 09H, 0AH, 0BH, 0CH, 0DH
        db      0EH, 0FH, 0EH, 0DH, 0CH, 0BH, 0AH, 09H
```

```
db          07H, 08H, 09H, 0AH, 0BH, 0CH, 0DH, 0EH
db              0FH, 0EH, 0DH, 0CH, 0BH, 0AH, 09H, 08H
db          08H, 09H, 0AH, 0BH, 0CH, 0DH, 0EH, 0FH
db              0EH, 0DH, 0CH, 0BH, 0AH, 09H, 08H, 07H
db          09H, 0AH, 0BH, 0CH, 0DH, 0EH, 0FH, 0EH
db              0DH, 0CH, 0BH, 0AH, 09H, 08H, 07H, 06H
db          0AH, 0BH, 0CH, 0DH, 0EH, 0FH, 0EH, 0DH
db              0CH, 0BH, 0AH, 09H, 08H, 07H, 06H, 05H
db          0BH, 0CH, 0DH, 0EH, 0FH, 0EH, 0DH, 0CH
db              0BH, 0AH, 09H, 08H, 07H, 06H, 05H, 04H
db          0CH, 0DH, 0EH, 0FH, 0EH, 0DH, 0CH, 0BH
db              0AH, 09H, 08H, 07H, 06H, 05H, 04H, 03H
db          0DH, 0EH, 0FH, 0EH, 0DH, 0CH, 0BH, 0AH
db              09H, 08H, 07H, 06H, 05H, 04H, 03H, 02H
db          0EH, 0FH, 0EH, 0DH, 0CH, 0BH, 0AH, 09H
db              08H, 07H, 06H, 05H, 04H, 03H, 02H, 02H
db          0FH, 0EH, 0DH, 0CH, 0BH, 0AH, 09H, 08H
db              07H, 06H, 05H, 04H, 03H, 02H, 02H, 00H

end
```

By now you're probably pretty proficient at reading the XGA drawing code, so I won't bore you with a detailed review of the examples.

Looking at PATTERNS.C, especially at the PattLine() and PattRect() routines, you should be able to see that patterns are quite simple to draw with. The most difficult part of using patterns is getting the pattern where the XGA can use it. For the best possible performance and reliability, you really want to put the pattern in the XGA's VRAM, but since we haven't covered memory mapping the XGA into the first megabyte of PC memory space, you can't copy the pattern directly into the XGA's VRAM.

The alternative is bus-mastering, which is how I have implemented the patterns for this example.

PATTERNS.C contains four pattern examples: two line pattern examples, and two rectangle pattern examples; one of each uses monochrome patterns, and one uses color patterns.

The monochrome patterns are quite straightforward; all you need to do is specify the right pattern source in the low word of the Command register. As mentioned earlier, each 0 in the pattern expands to use the background source, and each 1 in the pattern expands to use the foreground source. Color patterns, instead of being specifed via the pattern source process, are set as the source map for a graphics operation. Additionally, the foreground source needs to be set to FORE_SRC_SRCMAP, indicating that data is being read from the source map for the destination. To complicate things, a Color Pattern command can also incorporate a monochrome pattern, which chooses between the foreground source and background source settings, and is useful for transparency and other operations.

Patterned line examples use a pattern that is significantly shorter than the line being drawn. This shows how the pattern wraps. In our examples, the line pattern is 16 pixels long, and at the start of each line draw, the pattern or source map start X position is reset to 0 (I also reset the Y position, just to be safe). Once the line drawing starts, each pixel drawn bumps up the pattern X position by one. When the sixteenth pixel has been drawn, and the seventeenth pixel is about to be drawn, the XGA determines that it has hit the edge of the pattern map, and resets the X position back to 0. This process continues until all pixels are drawn.

It works the same way for area pattern maps. As each pixel is drawn horizontally, the pattern X position is incremented as well, until the edge of the pattern map is hit, at which point the X position is reset. The same thing happens to the Y pattern position in a vertical direction. The net result (as seen when running the last pattern example) is that you can tile a rectangle with a repeating pattern block.

The final issue surrounding patterns is pixel order. PATTDATA.ASM is not quite in left-to-right reading order (especially for _colorAreaPattern4). This is because the XGA's pixel ordering at less than 8bpp depends on whether the XGA is treating the pixel data as Intel or Motorola format. Refer back to Figure 4.3 for a chart showing the difference between the two formats at various pixel depths.

Using Read Line and Read SSV

In addition to using color source data for drawing, the XGA can read such data during an operation and save it. The Read Line and Read SSV functions perform this task. When doing a Read Line function, for example, you end up reading all of the pixels that the line would have obscured had it been drawn. The potential use of these two functions is that the data that will be overwritten by a line draw or SSV operation can be saved for later retrieval. Otherwise, you have to save a rectangular block of data, which eats up significantly more space than just the pixels obscured by a diagonal line.

The Mask Map

The mask map is monochrome, and serves two purposes. The first is as a traditional clipping rectangle; that is, it inhibits drawing outside of the rectangle. In order to take advantage of this feature, you have to do three things. First, you must define the mask map via the Pixel Mask creation mechanism. The width and height of the mask map determine the width and height of the clipping rectangle. Second, you must set the Mask Map Origin X and Y registers to the X and Y position in the destination map where you want the clipping rectangle to start. Finally, when loading a new command, you must use the MASK_MODE_CLIP setting in the Command register to specify that you want to use the rectangular clip mode of the mask map. For this use, the mask map does not need to point (via the Map Base register) to any valid data.

The other purpose of the mask map is to act as an arbitrary clipping region, on a pixel-by-pixel basis. In this case, the mask map must point to a meaningful monochrome pattern of some sort. In this mode, the mask map still acts like a clipping rectangle in that it inhibits drawing outside of the boundary it has defined. But within the clipping rectangle things are a little different. As you operate on each pixel of a graphics function that has MASK_MODE_ENAB set in its Command register setting, the mask map is checked to see if the resultant data may actually be written to the destination map. A 0 bit in the mask map disables writes to that pixel in the destination map, while a 1 bit allows the update of the destination pixel. So, by creating a specific filled shape in the mask map, you can also clip to it.

The mask map can be used in addition to a pattern map, in the same command.

Bus-Mastering

Now we're ready to discuss this sticky topic. You may have wondered why I didn't just include the pattern data in PATTERNS.C instead of putting it into its own file—and an assembly language file, at that. The reason is simple: MS-C v5.1 does not allow you to easily align a variable or array on a 32-bit DWORD boundary, while MASM v5.1 does (using the align 4 command). This alignment is necessary to satisfy the requirements of map positioning, since maps should start on a 32-bit boundary.

The next item with my particular use of bus-mastering regards the map definition, seen in the SetMapB() function of PATTERNS.C. The map base address must be a 32-bit linear PC address, and not segment:offset, as real mode software deals with addresses. The conversion is quite simple.

When a map with a PC memory base address (as opposed to the XGA's VRAM address), is accessed, the XGA board performs bus-mastering operations; that is, it takes control of the system's bus (Micro Channel in the case of the original IBM XGA) and starts issuing its own memory cycles to access the desired system memory. In fact, in a system with multiple XGAs, under certain conditions, an XGA can use bus-mastering to access another XGA's memory.

Up to this point, bus-mastering sounds pretty wonderful. Unfortunately, it has a number of drawbacks, most of which have to do with the accessibility of specific memory. You must know the physical address of the area you want the XGA to bus-master. This may not seem problematic, but it's really a nightmare.

The first potential problem area comes with the use of Expanded Memory Managers (EMMs), such as Microsoft's HIMEM.SYS, Quarterdeck's QEMM, and Qualitas' 386MAX. On 386 and 486 systems, EMMs use the CPU's Memory Management Unit (MMU) to remap extended memory into the first megabyte of PC address space (used by normal DOS applications). EMMs, under software control, page memory in and out of this first megabyte, usually concentrating on the area above the 640KB mark (known as **high memory**). This swapping allows applications to use more memory than would normally be available in real mode. The problem from a bus-mastering perspective is that while this mapped memory is accessible to applications at linear addresses like 0D0000H, the actual memory is located somewhere above the 1MB mark. The CPU's MMU takes care of this type of translation for software running on it, but a bus-mastering device has no access to the MMU, since it resides on the bus. Hence, the bus-mastering device must know the true location of the data in order to access it. There are ways to determine the correct address, but it's a hassle. On the bright side, EMMs tend not to muck with memory below the 640KB mark, so you might be able to get away with bus-mastering in that region.

The second problem is not bad now, but will grow as decent DOS multitaskers, such as OS/2 2.0, Windows, and DesqView, gain popularity. These multitaskers simulate a DOS box using this **Virtual-86 mode**, which is built into 386 and 486 chips, and utilized by operating environments that want to control the DOS application's access to the rest of the machine. The V86 mode actually runs in a megabyte of memory that can be located anywhere, but tricks real mode applications to thinking they're in the first megabyte of memory (as they expect to be). This means that even the PATTERNS.C example would potentially fail since the address the software thought it had might not be valid, resulting in the XGA reading garbage data from the wrong location. IBM's OS/2 2.0 drivers handle this situation fairly well, but other environments certainly don't have the XGA expertise necessary. And, it is not easy to detect whether you're in V86 mode and mapped properly into the first megabyte.

The final bus-mastering problem has to do with an ever-increasing subset of PC applications—those that run in protected mode. In protected mode, you have the MMU problem, but magnified. Software running in protected mode has no concept of where it is actually located in physical memory, due to the architecture of the protected mode environment. Instead of segments, protected mode applications use selectors, which are pointers into a memory translation table not accessible to normal protected mode applications. A protected mode application must ask its operating environment to provide it with the physical address of a given piece of data, but because the MMU deals with 4KB chunks of memory at a time, memory that appears contiguous from an application standpoint may not be contiguous in physical memory, and 4KB holds only a little graphical data. As if that weren't enough, if you're running within a multitasking environment, it is possible for these 4KB blocks to be swapped out to disk without your application knowing about it, meaning that you need to lock the blocks in memory to avoid having them swapped out when trying to bus-master. The recommended way of dealing with the whole problem of bus-mastering in protected mode is to have your protected mode application allocate a contiguous block of memory, 64KB in size, lock it in place, and use it as a transfer buffer. This means you copy data from you application into this buffer and then tell the XGA to access it for reading, or vice versa.

The XGA can support protected mode directly, and can handle discontiguous blocks of memory. This support also parallels the MMU tables in the 386 and 486 CPUs. Unfortunately, this support is extremely complicated to use, and so far only the driver in OS/2 2.0 uses it. All other XGA bus mastering software I know of avoids these advanced features.

Bus-mastering can double or even quadruple performance achieved by just having the CPU copy the data to the XGA via the XGA's memory mapped interface (to be discussed shortly). This performance benefit drops a little if you implement the 64KB fixed buffer concept in your protected mode application, since the CPU has to copy memory to and from this buffer before or after the XGA uses it; but if you're willing to sweat a bit, it might pay off. It's how IBM has managed to squeeze more performance out of its latest Windows drivers.

I recommend avoiding bus-mastering in real mode applications unless you can be 100 percent sure about your environment, and using it in protected mode applications if it makes sense. (Note that bus-mastering in ISA bus systems is also quite unreliable.)

The Sprite

While you're digesting the whole bus-mastering issue, let's take a look at the display side of the XGA for a while—specifically, the hardware cursor, or sprite. The sprite is completely independent of the XGA's graphics memory, and as such, does not affect the contents of display memory.

There are four components to the sprite: the sprite shape/data, the sprite colors, the sprite hotspot and position, and whether or not the sprite is actively displayed.

The sprite shape is defined by data passed through index I/O registered. It is 64 by 64 pixels in size, and each sprite pixel is 2 bits deep, thereby supporting four possible definitions:

Bit 1	Bit 0	Definition
0	0	Sprite color 0
0	1	Sprite color 1
1	0	Transparent (allows underlying pixel data to show through)
1	1	Complement (1's complement of underlying pixel data)

The two sprite colors are independent of the palette colors, and each sport separate red, green, and blue definitions. One benefit of this is that the sprite does not require an application to reserve two slots in the palette for it, unlike other hardware sprite implementations I've seen. The other benefit is that you can set the sprite colors to anything you choose. The complete definition is quite handy, as it allows easy conversion from a dual XOR and AND mask cursor, such as that used by Microsoft Windows and AutoCAD.

The hotspot selects which pixel in the sprite is considered its starting display position. Then, setting the sprite position (which is always relative to the display, and never to a map) positions this hotspot. Any part of the sprite above and to the left of this point will not be displayed. This allows you to shrink the size of the sprite.

Finally, the state of the sprite is controlled by a single bit that determines whether the sprite is currently displayed. Please note that you cannot correctly update the sprite shape when the sprite is enabled; you must disable it first in order to load a new shape.

Listing 5.12 shows a program that creates and then propels a sprite across the display.

Listing 5.12. SPRITE.C

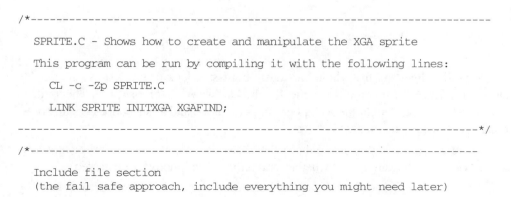

```
/*--------------------------------------------------------------------

   SPRITE.C - Shows how to create and manipulate the XGA sprite

   This program can be run by compiling it with the following lines:

      CL -c -Zp SPRITE.C

      LINK SPRITE INITXGA XGAFIND;

--------------------------------------------------------------------*/

/*--------------------------------------------------------------------

   Include file section
   (the fail safe approach, include everything you might need later)
```

```
-------------------------------------------------------------------*/

#include <stdio.h>
#include <stdlib.h>
#include <string.h>
#include <errno.h>
#include <fcntl.h>
#include <dos.h>
#include <conio.h>
#include <io.h>
#include <malloc.h>
#include <sys\types.h>
#include <sys\stat.h>
#include "xga.h"

/*-------------------------------------------------------------------

   Externals (all in INITXGA.C)

-------------------------------------------------------------------*/

extern   UWORD       xRes, yRes;        /* The XGA mode dimensions */
extern   UWORD       bpp;               /* Bits per pixel for the mode */
extern   UBYTE FAR   *memRegBaseAddr;   /* Memory Register address */
extern   UWORD       ioRegBaseAddr;     /* I/O Register address */

/*-------------------------------------------------------------------

   Local Data
```

This is where we define our sprite. To demonstrate how AND/XOR cursor masks can be converted to an XGA sprite format, I have chosen to provide the sprite data in that format.

The sprite will look as follows (one character = 4x4 pixels):

```
                    1111111111111111
                    1111111111111111
                    11TTTTTTNNNNNN11
                    11TTTTTTNNNNNN11
                    11TTTTTTNNNNNN11
                    11TTTTTTNNNNNN11
                    11TTT000000NNN11
                    11TTT000000NNN11
                    11TTT000000NNN11
                    11TTT000000NNN11
                    11TTTTTTNNNNNN11
                    11TTTTTTNNNNNN11
                    11TTTTTTNNNNNN11
                    11TTTTTTNNNNNN11
                    1111111111111111
                    1111111111111111
```

continued...

...from previous page

Where the characters are defined as follows:

        0 - Sprite Color 0
        1 - Sprite Color 1
        T - Transparent sprite pixel
        N - Bitwise NOT of displayed pixel

```
------------------------------------------------------------------------*/

UBYTE  spriteANDData[] =
        {
        0x00, 0x00, 0x00, 0x00, 0x00, 0x00, 0x00, 0x00,
        0x00, 0x00, 0x00, 0x00, 0x00, 0x00, 0x00, 0x00,
        0x00, 0x00, 0x00, 0x00, 0x00, 0x00, 0x00, 0x00,
        0x00, 0x00, 0x00, 0x00, 0x00, 0x00, 0x00, 0x00,
        0x00, 0x00, 0x00, 0x00, 0x00, 0x00, 0x00, 0x00,
        0x00, 0x00, 0x00, 0x00, 0x00, 0x00, 0x00, 0x00,
        0x00, 0x00, 0x00, 0x00, 0x00, 0x00, 0x00, 0x00,
        0x00, 0x00, 0x00, 0x00, 0x00, 0x00, 0x00, 0x00,
        0x00, 0xFF, 0xFF, 0xFF, 0xFF, 0xFF, 0xFF, 0x00,
        0x00, 0xFF, 0xFF, 0xFF, 0xFF, 0xFF, 0xFF, 0x00,
        0x00, 0xFF, 0xFF, 0xFF, 0xFF, 0xFF, 0xFF, 0x00,
        0x00, 0xFF, 0xFF, 0xFF, 0xFF, 0xFF, 0xFF, 0x00,
        0x00, 0xFF, 0xFF, 0xFF, 0xFF, 0xFF, 0xFF, 0x00,
        0x00, 0xFF, 0xFF, 0xFF, 0xFF, 0xFF, 0xFF, 0x00,
        0x00, 0xFF, 0xFF, 0xFF, 0xFF, 0xFF, 0xFF, 0x00,
        0x00, 0xFF, 0xFF, 0xFF, 0xFF, 0xFF, 0xFF, 0x00,
        0x00, 0xFF, 0xFF, 0xFF, 0xFF, 0xFF, 0xFF, 0x00,
        0x00, 0xFF, 0xFF, 0xFF, 0xFF, 0xFF, 0xFF, 0x00,
        0x00, 0xFF, 0xFF, 0xFF, 0xFF, 0xFF, 0xFF, 0x00,
        0x00, 0xFF, 0xFF, 0xFF, 0xFF, 0xFF, 0xFF, 0x00,
        0x00, 0xFF, 0xFF, 0xFF, 0xFF, 0xFF, 0xFF, 0x00,
        0x00, 0xFF, 0xFF, 0xFF, 0xFF, 0xFF, 0xFF, 0x00,
        0x00, 0xFF, 0xFF, 0xFF, 0xFF, 0xFF, 0xFF, 0x00,
        0x00, 0xFF, 0xFF, 0xFF, 0xFF, 0xFF, 0xFF, 0x00,
        0x00, 0xFF, 0xF0, 0x00, 0x00, 0x0F, 0xFF, 0x00,
        0x00, 0xFF, 0xF0, 0x00, 0x00, 0x0F, 0xFF, 0x00,
        0x00, 0xFF, 0xF0, 0x00, 0x00, 0x0F, 0xFF, 0x00,
        0x00, 0xFF, 0xF0, 0x00, 0x00, 0x0F, 0xFF, 0x00,
        0x00, 0xFF, 0xF0, 0x00, 0x00, 0x0F, 0xFF, 0x00,
        0x00, 0xFF, 0xF0, 0x00, 0x00, 0x0F, 0xFF, 0x00,
        0x00, 0xFF, 0xF0, 0x00, 0x00, 0x0F, 0xFF, 0x00,
        0x00, 0xFF, 0xF0, 0x00, 0x00, 0x0F, 0xFF, 0x00,
        0x00, 0xFF, 0xF0, 0x00, 0x00, 0x0F, 0xFF, 0x00,
        0x00, 0xFF, 0xF0, 0x00, 0x00, 0x0F, 0xFF, 0x00,
        0x00, 0xFF, 0xF0, 0x00, 0x00, 0x0F, 0xFF, 0x00,
        0x00, 0xFF, 0xF0, 0x00, 0x00, 0x0F, 0xFF, 0x00,
```

```
        0x00, 0xFF, 0xF0, 0x00, 0x00, 0x0F, 0xFF, 0x00,
        0x00, 0xFF, 0xF0, 0x00, 0x00, 0x0F, 0xFF, 0x00,
        0x00, 0xFF, 0xF0, 0x00, 0x00, 0x0F, 0xFF, 0x00,
        0x00, 0xFF, 0xF0, 0x00, 0x00, 0x0F, 0xFF, 0x00,
        0x00, 0xFF, 0xFF, 0xFF, 0xFF, 0xFF, 0xFF, 0x00,
        0x00, 0xFF, 0xFF, 0xFF, 0xFF, 0xFF, 0xFF, 0x00,
        0x00, 0xFF, 0xFF, 0xFF, 0xFF, 0xFF, 0xFF, 0x00,
        0x00, 0xFF, 0xFF, 0xFF, 0xFF, 0xFF, 0xFF, 0x00,
        0x00, 0xFF, 0xFF, 0xFF, 0xFF, 0xFF, 0xFF, 0x00,
        0x00, 0xFF, 0xFF, 0xFF, 0xFF, 0xFF, 0xFF, 0x00,
        0x00, 0xFF, 0xFF, 0xFF, 0xFF, 0xFF, 0xFF, 0x00,
        0x00, 0xFF, 0xFF, 0xFF, 0xFF, 0xFF, 0xFF, 0x00,
        0x00, 0xFF, 0xFF, 0xFF, 0xFF, 0xFF, 0xFF, 0x00,
        0x00, 0xFF, 0xFF, 0xFF, 0xFF, 0xFF, 0xFF, 0x00,
        0x00, 0xFF, 0xFF, 0xFF, 0xFF, 0xFF, 0xFF, 0x00,
        0x00, 0xFF, 0xFF, 0xFF, 0xFF, 0xFF, 0xFF, 0x00,
        0x00, 0xFF, 0xFF, 0xFF, 0xFF, 0xFF, 0xFF, 0x00,
        0x00, 0xFF, 0xFF, 0xFF, 0xFF, 0xFF, 0xFF, 0x00,
        0x00, 0xFF, 0xFF, 0xFF, 0xFF, 0xFF, 0xFF, 0x00,
        0x00, 0x00, 0x00, 0x00, 0x00, 0x00, 0x00, 0x00,
        0x00, 0x00, 0x00, 0x00, 0x00, 0x00, 0x00, 0x00,
        0x00, 0x00, 0x00, 0x00, 0x00, 0x00, 0x00, 0x00,
        0x00, 0x00, 0x00, 0x00, 0x00, 0x00, 0x00, 0x00,
        0x00, 0x00, 0x00, 0x00, 0x00, 0x00, 0x00, 0x00,
        0x00, 0x00, 0x00, 0x00, 0x00, 0x00, 0x00, 0x00,
        0x00, 0x00, 0x00, 0x00, 0x00, 0x00, 0x00, 0x00,
        0x00, 0x00, 0x00, 0x00, 0x00, 0x00, 0x00, 0x00
        };
UBYTE   spriteXORData[] =
        {
        0xFF, 0xFF, 0xFF, 0xFF, 0xFF, 0xFF, 0xFF, 0xFF,
        0xFF, 0xFF, 0xFF, 0xFF, 0xFF, 0xFF, 0xFF, 0xFF,
        0xFF, 0xFF, 0xFF, 0xFF, 0xFF, 0xFF, 0xFF, 0xFF,
        0xFF, 0xFF, 0xFF, 0xFF, 0xFF, 0xFF, 0xFF, 0xFF,
        0xFF, 0xFF, 0xFF, 0xFF, 0xFF, 0xFF, 0xFF, 0xFF,
        0xFF, 0xFF, 0xFF, 0xFF, 0xFF, 0xFF, 0xFF, 0xFF,
        0xFF, 0xFF, 0xFF, 0xFF, 0xFF, 0xFF, 0xFF, 0xFF,
        0xFF, 0xFF, 0xFF, 0xFF, 0xFF, 0xFF, 0xFF, 0xFF,
        0xFF, 0x00, 0x00, 0x00, 0xFF, 0xFF, 0xFF, 0xFF,
        0xFF, 0x00, 0x00, 0x00, 0xFF, 0xFF, 0xFF, 0xFF,
        0xFF, 0x00, 0x00, 0x00, 0xFF, 0xFF, 0xFF, 0xFF,
        0xFF, 0x00, 0x00, 0x00, 0xFF, 0xFF, 0xFF, 0xFF,
        0xFF, 0x00, 0x00, 0x00, 0xFF, 0xFF, 0xFF, 0xFF,
        0xFF, 0x00, 0x00, 0x00, 0xFF, 0xFF, 0xFF, 0xFF,
        0xFF, 0x00, 0x00, 0x00, 0xFF, 0xFF, 0xFF, 0xFF,
```

continued...

...from previous page

```
0xFF,  0x00,  0x00,  0x00,  0xFF,  0xFF,  0xFF,  0xFF,
0xFF,  0x00,  0x00,  0x00,  0xFF,  0xFF,  0xFF,  0xFF,
0xFF,  0x00,  0x00,  0x00,  0xFF,  0xFF,  0xFF,  0xFF,
0xFF,  0x00,  0x00,  0x00,  0xFF,  0xFF,  0xFF,  0xFF,
0xFF,  0x00,  0x00,  0x00,  0xFF,  0xFF,  0xFF,  0xFF,
0xFF,  0x00,  0x00,  0x00,  0xFF,  0xFF,  0xFF,  0xFF,
0xFF,  0x00,  0x00,  0x00,  0xFF,  0xFF,  0xFF,  0xFF,
0xFF,  0x00,  0x00,  0x00,  0xFF,  0xFF,  0xFF,  0xFF,
0xFF,  0x00,  0x00,  0x00,  0xFF,  0xFF,  0xFF,  0xFF,
0xFF,  0x00,  0x00,  0x00,  0x00,  0x0F,  0xFF,  0xFF,
0xFF,  0x00,  0x00,  0x00,  0x00,  0x0F,  0xFF,  0xFF,
0xFF,  0x00,  0x00,  0x00,  0x00,  0x0F,  0xFF,  0xFF,
0xFF,  0x00,  0x00,  0x00,  0x00,  0x0F,  0xFF,  0xFF,
0xFF,  0x00,  0x00,  0x00,  0x00,  0x0F,  0xFF,  0xFF,
0xFF,  0x00,  0x00,  0x00,  0x00,  0x0F,  0xFF,  0xFF,
0xFF,  0x00,  0x00,  0x00,  0x00,  0x0F,  0xFF,  0xFF,
0xFF,  0x00,  0x00,  0x00,  0x00,  0x0F,  0xFF,  0xFF,
0xFF,  0x00,  0x00,  0x00,  0x00,  0x0F,  0xFF,  0xFF,
0xFF,  0x00,  0x00,  0x00,  0x00,  0x0F,  0xFF,  0xFF,
0xFF,  0x00,  0x00,  0x00,  0x00,  0x0F,  0xFF,  0xFF,
0xFF,  0x00,  0x00,  0x00,  0x00,  0x0F,  0xFF,  0xFF,
0xFF,  0x00,  0x00,  0x00,  0x00,  0x0F,  0xFF,  0xFF,
0xFF,  0x00,  0x00,  0x00,  0x00,  0x0F,  0xFF,  0xFF,
0xFF,  0x00,  0x00,  0x00,  0x00,  0x0F,  0xFF,  0xFF,
0xFF,  0x00,  0x00,  0x00,  0x00,  0x0F,  0xFF,  0xFF,
0xFF,  0x00,  0x00,  0x00,  0xFF,  0xFF,  0xFF,  0xFF,
0xFF,  0x00,  0x00,  0x00,  0xFF,  0xFF,  0xFF,  0xFF,
0xFF,  0x00,  0x00,  0x00,  0xFF,  0xFF,  0xFF,  0xFF,
0xFF,  0x00,  0x00,  0x00,  0xFF,  0xFF,  0xFF,  0xFF,
0xFF,  0x00,  0x00,  0x00,  0xFF,  0xFF,  0xFF,  0xFF,
0xFF,  0x00,  0x00,  0x00,  0xFF,  0xFF,  0xFF,  0xFF,
0xFF,  0x00,  0x00,  0x00,  0xFF,  0xFF,  0xFF,  0xFF,
0xFF,  0x00,  0x00,  0x00,  0xFF,  0xFF,  0xFF,  0xFF,
0xFF,  0x00,  0x00,  0x00,  0xFF,  0xFF,  0xFF,  0xFF,
0xFF,  0x00,  0x00,  0x00,  0xFF,  0xFF,  0xFF,  0xFF,
0xFF,  0x00,  0x00,  0x00,  0xFF,  0xFF,  0xFF,  0xFF,
0xFF,  0x00,  0x00,  0x00,  0xFF,  0xFF,  0xFF,  0xFF,
0xFF,  0x00,  0x00,  0x00,  0xFF,  0xFF,  0xFF,  0xFF,
0xFF,  0x00,  0x00,  0x00,  0xFF,  0xFF,  0xFF,  0xFF,
0xFF,  0xFF,  0xFF,  0xFF,  0xFF,  0xFF,  0xFF,  0xFF,
0xFF,  0xFF,  0xFF,  0xFF,  0xFF,  0xFF,  0xFF,  0xFF,
0xFF,  0xFF,  0xFF,  0xFF,  0xFF,  0xFF,  0xFF,  0xFF,
0xFF,  0xFF,  0xFF,  0xFF,  0xFF,  0xFF,  0xFF,  0xFF,
0xFF,  0xFF,  0xFF,  0xFF,  0xFF,  0xFF,  0xFF,  0xFF,
0xFF,  0xFF,  0xFF,  0xFF,  0xFF,  0xFF,  0xFF,  0xFF,
```

```
        0xFF, 0xFF, 0xFF, 0xFF, 0xFF, 0xFF, 0xFF, 0xFF,
        0xFF, 0xFF, 0xFF, 0xFF, 0xFF, 0xFF, 0xFF, 0xFF
        };
/*-------------------------------------------------------------------

   Code

-------------------------------------------------------------------*/

/*-------------------------------------

VOID    LoadSpriteData(UBYTE *andMask, UBYTE *xorMask)
```

This function takes the passed AND and XOR masks and combines them
to create the actual XGA sprite. The masks are assumed to be 64 bits
wide and 64 lines high.

```
-------------------------------------*/
VOID    LoadSpriteData(UBYTE *andMask, UBYTE *xorMask)
{
    UWORD      i, j;
    UWORD      combo;
    UWORD      testMask;
    UWORD      setMask;
    UBYTE      *andPtr = andMask;
    UBYTE      *xorPtr = xorMask;

    /*
        Let's set up the all the sprite index pointers first.
        Since we're loading the complete sprite, let's just start
        at zero. Leave the I/O register index pointing to the
        data port. First, we must disable the sprite so we can
        modify its shape.
    */
    IOREGWRITEB(IO_INDEX, SPRITE_CTRL);
    IOREGWRITEB(IO_DATA, 0);

    IOREGWRITEB(IO_INDEX, SPRITE_INDEX_LO);
    IOREGWRITEB(IO_DATA, 0);

    IOREGWRITEB(IO_INDEX, SPRITE_INDEX_HI);
    IOREGWRITEB(IO_DATA, 0);

    IOREGWRITEB(IO_INDEX, SPRITE_DATA);

    /*
        Next, let's actually start loading the sprite data.
        What this means is that we need want to construct a word
        (two bytes) of data at a time and send it to the XGA.
        This needs to be done for all 64 lines (of 8 bytes each)
        of the masks.
```

continued...

...from previous page

```
        The way to combine the AND and XOR masks is to place the AND
        bit for a given sprite pixel in as bit 1 of the pixel, and
        the XOR bit as bit 0 of the sprite pixel. In C, bit
        test and set operations like this are painful, but here goes:
    */
    for (i = 0; i < 8*64; i++)
        { /* For each AND/XOR byte pair... */
        combo = 0;                       /* Clear the combo word */
        testMask = 0x80;                 /* Test mask for getting bits */
        setMask = 0x8000;                /* Set mask for setting bits */
        while (testMask)                 /* While we have a test mask... */
            {                            /* Test the AND mask and set in combo
*/
            if (testMask & *andPtr)
               combo |= setMask;

            setMask >>= 1;               /* Shift set mask, and then do XOR byte */
            if (testMask & *xorPtr)
               combo |= setMask;
            setMask >>= 1;               /* Shift set mask again, and test mask */
            testMask >>= 1;
            }
        andPtr++;                        /* Next byte */
        xorPtr++;

        /*
            We need to write as two bytes since the byte order in
            an Intel word is reversed from what the XGA needs
            right now. Output the high byte first, then the low
            byte.
        */
        IOREGWRITEB(IO_DATA, (UBYTE)(combo >> 8));
        IOREGWRITEB(IO_DATA, (UBYTE)(combo & 0xFF));
        }
    return;                              /* All done */
}

/*------------------------------------

VOID PositionSprite( UWORD x, UWORD y)

Sets the Sprite position registers to specified values.
Does not enable the sprite - that must be done external to
this routine.

--------------------------------------*/
VOID PositionSprite( UWORD x, UWORD y)
{
```

```
   /*
      Since the Sprite positioning registers are only
      a byte wide, we need to split both the X and the Y
      positions into two separate byte writes each.
   */
   IOREGWRITEB(IO_INDEX, SPRITE_POSX_LO);
   IOREGWRITEB(IO_DATA, (UBYTE)(x & 0xFF));
   IOREGWRITEB(IO_INDEX, SPRITE_POSX_HI);
   IOREGWRITEB(IO_DATA, (UBYTE)(x >> 8));

   IOREGWRITEB(IO_INDEX, SPRITE_POSY_LO);
   IOREGWRITEB(IO_DATA, (UBYTE)(y & 0xFF));
   IOREGWRITEB(IO_INDEX, SPRITE_POSY_HI);
   IOREGWRITEB(IO_DATA, (UBYTE)(y >> 8));
   return;
}
/*-----------------------------------

VOID FillRectangle( UWORD x, UWORD y,
                    UWORD width, UWORD height, UWORD color)

Same as example in FILLRECT.C less the comments.

-----------------------------------*/
VOID FillRectangle( UWORD x, UWORD y,
                    UWORD width, UWORD height, UWORD color)
{
   XGAWAIT;                           /* Wait for XGA ready */
   SENDW(FORE_COLOR, color);          /* Set the foreground color */
   SENDW(DEST_X, x);                  /* Set position */
   SENDW(DEST_Y, y);
   SENDW(DIM1, width - 1);
   SENDW(DIM2, height - 1);           /* Set dimensions of the rectangle */
   SENDW(CMD_REG, PATT_SRC_FORESRC);
   SENDW(CMD_REG+2, CMD_BITBLT | SRC_MAP_A | DST_MAP_A);
   return;                            /* Done with filling rectangles! */
}

/*-----------------------------------

VOID DoSomething()

Shows how to use the XGA sprite.

-----------------------------------*/
VOID DoSomething()
{
   WORD i, j, k;
   WORD speedX, speedY;
```

continued...

...from previous page

```
/*
    Let's draw a whole bunch of 16x16 rectangles in different
    colors to fill the screen, and then run the sprite over
    them so you can see the various sprite pixel options.
*/
for (i = 0; i < xRes; i +=16)
    for (j = 0; j < yRes; j += 16)
        FillRectangle(i, j, 16, 16, (i / 16 + j / 16) & 0x0F);

/*
    Now, let's initialize the sprite, starting with
    loading the sprite data, and then setting the sprite
    colors, sprite hotspot, initial position, and finally
    enabling it. We'll be boring and set sprite color 0 to
    black and sprite color 1 to white. The hot spot will be
    set to the origin (0,0) of the Sprite, and the sprite will
    be positioned at the display origin. Then, the sprite will
    be enabled for display.
*/
LoadSpriteData(spriteANDData, spriteXORData);

IOREGWRITEB(IO_INDEX, SPRITE_COLOR0_RED);
IOREGWRITEB(IO_DATA, 0);
IOREGWRITEB(IO_INDEX, SPRITE_COLOR0_GREEN);
IOREGWRITEB(IO_DATA, 0);
IOREGWRITEB(IO_INDEX, SPRITE_COLOR0_BLUE);
IOREGWRITEB(IO_DATA, 0);

IOREGWRITEB(IO_INDEX, SPRITE_COLOR1_RED);
IOREGWRITEB(IO_DATA, 0xFF);
IOREGWRITEB(IO_INDEX, SPRITE_COLOR1_GREEN);
IOREGWRITEB(IO_DATA, 0xFF);
IOREGWRITEB(IO_INDEX, SPRITE_COLOR1_BLUE);
IOREGWRITEB(IO_DATA, 0xFF);

IOREGWRITEB(IO_INDEX, SPRITE_HOTX);
IOREGWRITEB(IO_DATA, 0);
IOREGWRITEB(IO_INDEX, SPRITE_HOTY);
IOREGWRITEB(IO_DATA, 0);

PositionSprite(0, 0);

IOREGWRITEB(IO_INDEX, SPRITE_CTRL);
IOREGWRITEB(IO_DATA, SPRITE_ENAB);

i = j = 0;                      /* Position of the sprite (i,j) */
speedX = speedY = 1;            /* Speed of the sprite */

/*
```

In this loop, we animate the sprite for as long as a key isn't pressed on the keyboard.

Part of the sprite animation is a "bounce" effect off of edge of the display. In order to keep the sprite moving at a reasonable pace, we'll use the vertical blank start status bit to synchronize each move of the sprite with a vertical sync. This means about 60 moves per second for the 640x480 mode, and about 86 moves per second for 1024x768.

```
*/
while (!kbhit())                    /* Let this run until a key is hit */
    {
    /*
      Clear the START_BLNK_STAT bit and then wait for
      it to be set again.
    */
    IOREGWRITEB(INT_STATUS, START_BLNK_STAT);
    while (!(IOREGREADB(INT_STATUS) & START_BLNK_STAT)) ;
    i += speedX;                    /* Handle X direction motion */
    if (i >= (WORD)(xRes - 64))
        {
        i--;
        speedX = -1;
        }
    else
        if (i < 0)
            {
            i++;
            speedX = 1;
            }

    j += speedY;                    /* Handle Y direction motion */
    if (j >= (WORD)(yRes - 64))
        {
        j--;
        speedY = -1;
        }
    else
        if (j < 0)
            {
            j++;
            speedY = 1;
            }

    PositionSprite(i, j);          /* Set the new position */
    }
```

continued...

...from previous page

```
IOREGWRITEB(IO_INDEX, SPRITE_CTRL); /* Disable the sprite */
IOREGWRITEB(IO_DATA, 0);

if (!getch())
  getch();

return;
}
```

With respect to SPRITE.C, there are a few things to point out. First, the bit splicing code in LoadSpriteData() is decent for C, but it could be done much better in assembly language. In the following assembly language code snippet, the AND byte for the splice is in AL, and the XOR byte is in AH:

```
              mov     CX, 8               ; # of bits/byte
              xor     DX, DX              ; Receptor of sprite data.
CombineLoop:
              shl     AL, 1               ; Shift AND bit into carry.
              rcl     DX, 1               ; Move carry into DX.
              shl     AH, 1               ; Now shift XOR bit into carry.
              rcl     DX, 1               ; And put it in DX as well.
              loop    CombineLoop
              mov     AX, DX              ; Save new sprite value.
              xchg    AL, AH              ; Swap for proper order
              out     DX, AX              ; Write a word to sprite
```

This is significantly more efficient than its C counterpart, plus you don't have to go through hoops to write a full word of data to the Sprite Data register.

The only other thing worth pointing out in SPRITE.C is the vertical retrace check at the start of the animation loop in DoSomething(). At some point you may want to perform a task in synch with a regular event. One such task might be making a graphical cursor blink. Using the wait for vertical blank allows you to do this.

Other than that, the code and comments in SPRITE.C should be pretty self-explanatory.

Memory Mapping the XGA

The last thing to discuss about programming the XGA is how to get into its memory from the PC without bus-mastering. There are three ways to do this, all three of which allow you to treat XGA memory as if it were regular PC memory, meaning that you can read and write it and do block transfers.

The most obvious way is to access the XGA memory through its base VRAM address. Of course, this approach has a few pitfalls. First, the XGA must be in a 32-bit Micro Channel slot in your PS/2 (or in an EISA slot for upcoming EISA XGAs) in order for you to even have a chance to address the XGA's 4MB memory window located at the VRAM base address. The second pitfall is that this memory is difficult to access and utilize properly unless you are in protected mode or are willing to tackle programming the CPU's MMU yourself. However, if your software is running in protected mode, and you're in a 32-bit slot, then go for it—this is the best way to access the XGA's VRAM if you meet the requirements. Note that for access to the memory from your protected mode software, you'll have to ask your operating environment to create a selector that points to the XGA memory for you.

The second path to the XGA's memory, the 1MB memory window, is fraught with potential conflicts. This 1MB map is placed somewhere in the first 16MB of your system's address space, if there's room. Because of definite conflicts, this block is never placed in the first MB (this would trash your entire DOS environ), and because of potential ROM conflicts, it is not generally placed in the last megabyte (the sixteenth, starting at 00F00000H). That leaves fourteen potential slots. With the price of memory these days and the fact that most 486 systems are shipping with at least 8MB of RAM, it's unlikely that that 1MB window will remain accessible for long. Again, as with the VRAM base address above, the best way to access this window is from protected mode. The bright side is that you can have your XGA in a 16-bit slot and still maintain access to this window. The base address for the 1MB window is determined by reading the 1MB Aperture Base Address register (POS 105H). The low 4 bits of this register are bits 23-20 of the starting address of the 1MB aperture. If they are set to 0, then no place was found to put the 1MB aperture.

The last path to the XGA's memory is probably going to seem familiar if you've ever programmed SuperVGAs. This method uses a 64KB memory window to access the XGA's memory. In order to gain access to all of the XGA's memory, the 64KB memory window is paged (or bank switched) to point to the desired XGA memory location. The 64KB memory window can be mapped in at PC address space 0A0000H or 0B0000H. The latter will definitely conflict if you have another VGA or VGA-compatible device in the system, while the former will do so only if you're running that VGA in graphics mode (less likely if you already have an XGA in your system, right?). My personal preference is the 0A0000H mapping—I've found it to cause the fewest problems.

TGAXGA.C in Listing 5.13, and a companion file, XGA16BPP.ASM, in Listing 5.14 will give you an idea of how to use the 64KB memory window. TGAXGA.C is a TARGA file format loader that uses the 64KB memory window to load a TARGA image onto the display. An added bonus is that this is done in the XGA's 16bpp mode, so you can see some really nice colors, assuming you have an XGA board with 1MB of VRAM, which is what the 640x480 16bpp requires to operate.

Listing 5.13. TGAXGA.C

```
/*-----------------------------------

   TGAXGA.C - Loads Targa 16, 24 and 32 files into the XGA 16bpp mode

      Copyright (c) 1991,1992 Panacea Inc. - All Rights Reserved
      Written by Jake Richter

   This program can be run by compiling it with the following lines:

         CL -c -Zp TGAXGA.C
         LINK TGAXGA XGA16BPP XGAFIND;

   A few notes about this program:
   First, it supports TARGA 16, TARGA 24, and TARGA 32 file formats,
   both compressed and uncompressed.

   Second, 32KB of data is loaded into a local storage buffer at a
   pop. Everytime the TGA file decoder needs data, it calls GetByte()
   or GetLine(), which copy a byte or a image scan line into an
   intermediary translation buffer. If either one of these functions
   runs of out data in the main 32KB buffer, the buffer is reloaded
   with new data, and the copy to the intermediary buffer continues.

   Third, this program was written to be distributed as FreeWare. It
   is copyrighted material, but as long as you give Panacea credit,
   you may freely incorporate any or all of this code within your
   programs.

------------------------------------------------------------------------*/
/*----------------------------------------------------------------------

   Include file section
   (the fail safe approach, include everything you might need later)
------------------------------------------------------------------------*/
#include <stdio.h>
#include <stdlib.h>
#include <string.h>
#include <errno.h>
#include <fcntl.h>
#include <dos.h>
#include <conio.h>
#include <io.h>
#include <malloc.h>
#include <sys\types.h>
```

```
#include  <sys\stat.h>
#include  "xga.h"

/*--------------------------------------------------------------------

   Structures

--------------------------------------------------------------------*/
typedef struct XGA_Info
   {
   BYTE       xiMonitor;          /* Monitor type */
   UBYTE      xiMode;             /* Native or VGA mode */
   UWORD      xiBaseVRML;         /* Base VRAM address (low) */
   UWORD      xiBaseVRMH;         /* Base VRAM address (high) */
   UWORD      xiIOReg;            /* I/O Reg address */
   UWORD      xiMemReg;           /* Mem Reg address */
   UWORD      xiMemSize;          /* Memory Size for board (in 256Ks) */
   } XGA_INFO;

typedef struct
   {
   UBYTE      idLength;           /* length of id field */
   UBYTE      mapType;            /* color map type */
   UBYTE      imgType;            /* image storage type */
   UWORD      mapOrg;             /* index of first map entry in LUT */
   UWORD      mapLen;             /* num of elements to be loaded */
   UBYTE      mapBits;            /* number of bits in each element */
   UWORD      xOrg;               /* x position of lower left corner of image
*/
   UWORD      yOrg;               /* y position of lower left corner of image
*/
   UWORD      width;              /* width of image in pixels */
   UWORD      height;             /* height of image in pixels */
   UBYTE      pixSiz;             /* num of bits per pixel */
   UBYTE      imgDesc;            /* contains bit fields of descriptor info
*/
   } TARGA_HDR;

/*--------------------------------------------------------------------

   Defines

--------------------------------------------------------------------*/

#define   SCREEN_X     640       /* This is a fixed size for 16bpp mode */
#define   SCREEN_Y     480

#define   BUFF_SIZE    8192      /* The translation buffer size */
#define   MAX_MAIN     32767     /* The disk load buffer size */

/*--------------------------------------------------------------------
```

continued...

...from previous page

```
Externals (all in XGAFIND.ASM)

----------------------------------------------------------------------*/
extern    XGA_INFO    xgaList[];         /* Contains XGA information */
extern    UWORD       xgaCount;          /* Number of XGAs found */
extern    VOID        GetBoardConfig();  /* Function to find XGAs */

/*——————————————————————————————————————

   Local Data

——————————————————————————————————————*/
static UBYTE    initRegs[] =
                {
                DISP_CTRL1, DISP_CTRL1, HTOTAL_LO, HDISP_END_LO,
                HBLANK_START_LO, HBLANK_END_LO, HSYNC_START_LO,
                HSYNC_END_LO, HSYNC_POS1, HSYNC_POS2, VTOTAL_LO,
                VTOTAL_HI, VDISPLAY_END_LO, VDISPLAY_END_HI,
                VBLANK_START_LO, VBLANK_START_HI, VBLANK_END_LO,
                VBLANK_END_HI, VSYNC_START_LO, VSYNC_START_HI,
                VSYNC_END, VLINE_COMP_LO, VLINE_COMP_HI,
                CLOCK_SEL_1, DISP_CTRL2, DISP_CTRL1, 0
                };

static UBYTE    mode640[] =          /* Only interested in 640x480 */
                {
                1, 0, 99, 79, 79, 99, 85, 97, 0, 0, 0x0C, 2, 0xDF,
                1, 0xDF, 1, 0x0C, 2, 0xEA, 1, 0xEC, 0xFF, 0xFF, 0,
                3, 0xC7
                };

union REGS  inRegs, outRegs;       /* Used for reinit'ing video mode */
UWORD       oldVGAmode = 0;        /* Save area for current VGA mode */
UBYTE FAR   *memRegBaseAddr;       /* The memory register base address */
UWORD       ioRegBaseAddr;         /* The I/O register base address */
UDWORD      vramBaseAddr;          /* The VRAM base address */
WORD        selectXGA = -1;        /* Index to selected XGA in xgaList */

TARGA_HDR   hdr;                   /* The TGA header block */

UWORD       width;                 /* The width and height of the image */
UWORD       height;

UWORD       bmX = 0;               /* Offset into display for smaller TGAs
*/
UWORD       bmY = 0;
UWORD       bmPitch = SCREEN_X;    /* Pitch of the display buffer (pixels)
*/
UWORD       bmHeight = SCREEN_Y;   /* Height of the buffer */

UWORD       bytesPerPixel;         /* 2, 3, or 4, depending on image */
UWORD       bytesPerLine;          /* Depends on image */
```

```
UBYTE       fileName[81];           /* Place to store TGA file name */
UWORD       fileHandle;             /* Handle returned by open() */
UBYTE       buffer[BUFF_SIZE];      /* The source translation buffer */
UBYTE       dstBuffer[BUFF_SIZE];   /* The destination translation buffer */
                                    /* The disk I/O buffer */
UBYTE       mainBuffer[MAX_MAIN + 1];
                                    /* The index into the disk I/O buffer */
UBYTE       *mainBuffPtr = (mainBuffer + MAX_MAIN + 1);

/*-----------------------------------------------------------------------

   Code

------------------------------------------------------------------------*/

/*-----------------------------------

VOID DispUsage(BYTE *progName)

Displays information about how to use this program.

-----------------------------------*/
VOID DispUsage(BYTE *progName)
{
   printf("Usage:\n\n\t%s filename[.TGA]\n\n", progName);
   return;
}

/*-----------------------------------

   GetByte(UBYTE *dest)

   Returns a byte from our disk I/O buffer. If buffer becomes empty,
   then it gets reloaded. Function returns TRUE if no data left.
   The data is returned in *dest.

-----------------------------------*/
UWORD GetByte(UBYTE *dest)
{
   UWORD       readCnt;

      /* If past end of buffer, reload */
   if ((UWORD)(mainBuffPtr - mainBuffer) > MAX_MAIN)
      {
      readCnt = read(fileHandle, mainBuffer, MAX_MAIN + 1);
      if (readCnt)                   /* Was anything read? */
         mainBuffPtr = mainBuffer;
      else
         return (TRUE);
      }

   *dest = *mainBuffPtr++;           /* Return the data */
   return(FALSE);
}
```

continued...

...from previous page

```
/*-----------------------------------

   GetLine

   Copies a scan line from our disk I/O buffer. If buffer becomes
   empty, then it gets reloaded. Returns the amount of data read.

   What we need to do is copy as much as is currently available,
   and then reload, if necessary.

-----------------------------------*/
UWORD GetLine(UBYTE *dstBuff, UWORD byteCount)
{
   UWORD   readCnt, remCnt = byteCount, bytesLeft;
   bytesLeft = (UWORD)(MAX_MAIN + 1) - (UWORD)(mainBuffPtr - mainBuffer);
   if (bytesLeft > byteCount)
      {                              /* Have enough left for a line */
      memcpy(dstBuff, mainBuffPtr, byteCount);
      mainBuffPtr += byteCount;
      return(FALSE);
      }
   else
      {                              /* Copy what we can, reload, do rest */
      memcpy(dstBuff, mainBuffPtr, bytesLeft);
      dstBuff += byteCount;
      remCnt -= bytesLeft;
      readCnt = read(fileHandle, mainBuffer, MAX_MAIN + 1);
      if (readCnt)
         mainBuffPtr = mainBuffer;
      else
         return (TRUE);
      }

   memcpy(dstBuff, mainBuffPtr, remCnt);
   mainBuffPtr += remCnt;
   return(FALSE);
}

/*-----------------------------------

VOID    CloseXGA()

This routine shuts down the XGA and returns it to whatever
VGA mode it was previously in (if it was in one). If it was
previously in XGA graphics mode, then that's how we leave it.

-----------------------------------*/
VOID    CloseXGA()
```

```
{
  /*
     We need to check if we were previously in VGA mode, because
     if we were, we need to return the XGA to this mode.
  */
  IOREGWRITEB(MEMWIN_CTRL, 0);  /* Disable MemWin access */
  IOREGWRITEB(MEMWIN_INDEX, 0); /* Reset the index for future use */

  if (xgaList[selectXGA].xiMode == DISP_VGA_MODE)
    {
    IOREGWRITEB(INT_ENABLE, 0);   /* Turn off all interrupts */
    IOREGWRITEB(INT_STATUS, 0);   /* Clear status */
    IOREGWRITEB(IO_INDEX, PALETTE_MASK);
    IOREGWRITEB(IO_DATA, 0xFF);   /* Enable palette mask */
    IOREGWRITEB(IO_INDEX, DISP_CTRL1);
    IOREGWRITEB(IO_DATA, 0x15);   /* Prepare CRTC for Reset */
    IOREGWRITEB(IO_DATA, 0x14);   /* Reset CRTC */
    IOREGWRITEB(IO_INDEX, DISP_CTRL2);
    IOREGWRITEB(IO_DATA, 0);      /* Prepare for VGA mode */
    IOREGWRITEB(IO_INDEX, CLOCK_SEL_1);
    IOREGWRITEB(IO_DATA, 4);      /* Select VGA Clock */
    IOREGWRITEB(IO_INDEX, VSYNC_END);
    IOREGWRITEB(IO_DATA, 0x20);   /* Load expected value */
    IOREGWRITEB(OP_MODE, DISP_VGA_MODE);   /* Set it! */
    outp(0x3C3, 1);               /* Enable as VGA */
    inRegs.x.ax = oldVGAmode & 0xFF;
    int86(0x10, &inRegs, &outRegs); /* Restore previous mode */
    }

    return;
}

/*----------------------------------

  WORD InitXGA16()

  This routine tries to locate an XGA in the system which
  is capable of running at 640x480x16bpp.

  If it finds one, it initializes it and returns a zero.
  If it doesn't it returns a non-zero value.

----------------------------------*/
WORD InitXGA16()
{
  UBYTE *modeData = mode640;    /* 640x480 res. */
  UBYTE *modeRegs = initRegs;   /* Pointer to reg. #s */
  UWORD i, j;                   /* Scratch variables */
  GetXGAList();                 /* Are any XGAs present? */
  if (!xgaCount)                /* Check the count */
```

continued...

...from previous page

```
    {
    printf("No XGAs found in system!\n");
    return(1);                        /* Abort with an error code */
    }

/*
    Let's just find the first XGA with 1MB of RAM and a
    monitor attached.
*/
selectXGA = -1;

for (i = 0; i < xgaCount; i++)

    {
    if (xgaList[i].xiMemSize < 4)
        continue;                     /* Ignore XGAs w/o 1MB VRAM */
    if (xgaList[i].xiMonitor < 0)
        continue;                     /* Ignore XGAs with no monitor */
    selectXGA = i;
    break;
    }

if (selectXGA == -1)                  /* No suitable XGA found, abort */
    {
    printf("Could not locate a 1MB XGA with a monitor in your
system!\n");
    return(1);
    }

if (xgaList[selectXGA].xiMode == DISP_VGA_MODE)
    {
    inRegs.x.ax = 0x0F00;             /* Read current video mode */
    int86(0x10, &inRegs, &outRegs);
    oldVGAmode = outRegs.x.ax;        /* Save the mode for later */
    }

memRegBaseAddr = (UBYTE FAR *)
                                ((DWORD)xgaList[selectXGA].xiMemReg <<
16);

ioRegBaseAddr = xgaList[selectXGA].xiIOReg;

IOREGWRITEB(INT_ENABLE, 0);
IOREGWRITEB(OP_MODE, DISP_XGA_MODE);
IOREGWRITEB(PALETTE_MASK, 0); /* Also blank the display for now */

while (*modeRegs)                     /* Because of null termination */
    {                                 /* First, set index, next, write data
*/
```

```
    IOREGWRITEB(IO_INDEX, *modeRegs++);
    IOREGWRITEB(IO_DATA, *modeData++);
    }
/*
  At this point, the XGA's CRTC registers have been loaded.
  Now we need to set the proper bit per pixel operation.
*/
IOREGWRITEB(IO_INDEX, DISP_CTRL2);
IOREGWRITEB(IO_DATA, DSPPIX_SIZE_16);
IOREGWRITEB(MEM_ACCESS_MODE, MEMPIX_SIZE_16);
/*
  Next, we need to set some other registers, including the
  Virtual Memory Control and Display Start Address register.
/*
IOREGWRITEB(VIRT_MEM_CTRL, 0);
IOREGWRITEB(IO_INDEX, DISP_ADDR_LO);
IOREGWRITEB(IO_DATA, 0);
IOREGWRITEB(IO_INDEX, DISP_ADDR_MID);
IOREGWRITEB(IO_DATA, 0);
IOREGWRITEB(IO_INDEX, DISP_ADDR_HI);
IOREGWRITEB(IO_DATA, 0);
IOREGWRITEB(IO_INDEX, PALETTE_MASK);
IOREGWRITEB(IO_DATA, 0xFF);       /* Enable viewing of all planes */
IOREGWRITEB(IO_INDEX, PALETTE_SEQUENCE);
IOREGWRITEB(IO_DATA, 0);          /* RGB access to palette */

/*
  Now we set the buffer pitch.
*/
i = 160;               /* 1280 / 8 (1280 is 640 across * 2 bytes/pix) */
IOREGWRITEB(IO_INDEX, BUFFER_PITCH_LO);
IOREGWRITEB(IO_DATA, (UBYTE)(i & 0xFF));   /* Low byte first */
IOREGWRITEB(IO_INDEX, BUFFER_PITCH_HI);
IOREGWRITEB(IO_DATA, (UBYTE)((i >> 8) & 0xFF));   /* High byte next */

/*
  All the display initialization is complete at this point.
  Now we need to initialize the graphics engine.
*/
XGAWAIT;                          /* Wait for the XGA to be ready */
SENDB(MAP_INDEX, MAP_INDEX_A);    /* Create Map A */
SENDW(MAP_BASE, xgaList[selectXGA].xiBaseVRML);
SENDW(MAP_BASE+2, xgaList[selectXGA].xiBaseVRMH);
SENDW(MAP_WIDTH, 1279);           /* 640 * 2 to account for 16bpp */
SENDW(MAP_HEIGHT, 479);
SENDW(MAP_FORMAT, PIXEL_SIZE_8);
```

continued...

...from previous page

```
    /*
        Initialize the graphics operator functions.
    */
    SENDB(FORE_MIX, MIX_SRC);          /* Set dest=source mix */
    SENDB(BACK_MIX, MIX_SRC);          /* Set dest=source mix */
    SENDB(CC_FUNC, CC_COND_FALSE);     /* Disable Color Compare */
    SENDW(PLANE_MASK, 0xFFFF);         /* Allow writes to all planes */
    SENDW(BACK_COLOR, 0);              /* Set all background color bits off */
    SENDW(CARRY_CHAIN_MASK, 0x7FFF);   /* Carry Chain */

    /*
        Now we will load the palette.
    */
    IOREGWRITEB(IO_INDEX, PALETTE_INDEX);
    IOREGWRITEB(IO_DATA, 0);           /* Start at index 0 */
    IOREGWRITEB(IO_INDEX, PALETTE_DATA);
for (i = 0; i < 128; i++)              /* Set first 128 entries to 0 */
    {
    IOREGWRITEB(IO_DATA, 0);
    IOREGWRITEB(IO_DATA, 0);
    IOREGWRITEB(IO_DATA, 0);
    }
    for (i = 0; i < 128; i++)          /* Set last 128 for 16bpp mode */
    {
    IOREGWRITEB(IO_DATA, 0);
    IOREGWRITEB(IO_DATA, 0);
    IOREGWRITEB(IO_DATA, i * 8);  /* This is the key! */
    }

    /*
        Finally, let's clear the screen to color 0.
    */
    XGAWAIT;                           /* Again, wait for XGA ready */
    SENDW(FORE_COLOR, 0);              /* Set all foreground color bits off */
    SENDW(DEST_X, 0);                  /* At 0,0, full screen size */
    SENDW(DEST_Y, 0);
    SENDW(DIM1, 1279);                 /* XGA doesn't support 16bpp, fake it */
    SENDW(DIM2, 479);
    SENDW(CMD_REG, PATT_SRC_FORESRC);
    SENDW(CMD_REG+2, CMD_BITBLT | SRC_MAP_A | DST_MAP_A);
    XGAWAIT;                           /* Again, wait for XGA ready */
    SENDW(FORE_COLOR, 0xFFFF);         /* Set all foreground color bits on */

    return(0);
}

/*------------------------------------
```

```
WORD main(argc, argv)
```

This is the main entry point into the program.

```
------------------------------------*/
WORD main(WORD argc, BYTE *argv[])
{
   WORD      i, j, k;            /* Loop variables */
   WORD      readCnt;           /* Amount of data read */
   UWORD     x, y;              /* Destination position */
   UWORD     opType;           /* Used during decompression */
   UBYTE     count;             /* Ditto */
   UBYTE     *ptr;              /* Ditto */

   printf("TARGA File Viewer for XGA - TGAXGA v1.1\n");
   printf("Copyright (c) 1991,1992 Panacea Inc. - All Rights
Reserved\n\n");
   if (argc != 2)                /* Make sure a file name was spec'd */
      {
      printf("Incorrect number of parameters!\n\n");
      DispUsage(argv[0]);
      exit(1);
      }

   strcpy(fileName, argv[1]);    /* Append a ".TGA" if necessary. */
   if (!strchr(fileName, '.'))
      strcat(fileName, ".TGA");
                                 /* Try to open image file */
   fileHandle = open(fileName, O_RDWR|O_BINARY);
   if (fileHandle == -1)
      {
      printf("Error opening file: %s!\n", argv[1]);
      exit(2);
      }
                                 /* Load TARGA header */
   read(fileHandle, (UBYTE *)&hdr, sizeof (hdr));
   if (hdr.imgType != 2 && hdr.imgType != 10)
      {
      printf("Unsupported TGA file type: %d!\n", hdr.imgType);
      exit(3);
      }

                                 /* We don't support 8bpp TGA files */
   if (hdr.pixSiz < 16)
      {
      printf("This program supports only 16 bits per pixel or higher!\n");
      exit(4);
      }
```

continued...

...from previous page

```
width = hdr.width;                 /* Set the image width and height */
height = hdr.height;

                                   /* Choke if image is too large */
if (((UDWORD)width * height) > 1024L * 1024)
   {
   printf("The Image file is too large to process!\n");
   exit(6);
   }

if (width != SCREEN_X)             /* Center the image in screen */
   {
   if (width < SCREEN_X)
      bmX = (SCREEN_X - width) / 2;
      else                         /* Choke if too wide also */
      {
      printf("The Image file is too wide to process!\n");
      exit(6);
      }
   }

if (height != SCREEN_Y)
   {
   if (height < SCREEN_Y)
      bmY = (SCREEN_Y - height) / 2;
else
      bmHeight = height;
}
                                   /* Calculate bytesPerPix and Line */
bytesPerPixel = hdr.pixSiz / 8;
bytesPerLine = bytesPerPixel * width;
bmPitch *= 2;                       /* Account for 2 bytes per pixel */

if (InitXGA16())                    /* Try to find and use XGA */
   {
   close(fileHandle);
   exit(5);
   }

x = bmX;                            /* Set starting X position */
if (hdr.imgDesc & 0x20)             /* Determine if bottom-up load */
   y = bmY;                         /* Nope. */
else
   y = bmHeight - bmY;              /* Yup. */
ptr = dstBuffer;                    /* Point to dest. trans. buffer */
k = 0;                              /* Pixel count */
```

```
do
   {
   if (hdr.imgType == 2)
      {                              /* Non-Compressed, get scan line */
      if (GetLine(buffer, bytesPerLine))
         {
         y = -1;
         break;                      /* We're done! */
         }

      switch (bytesPerPixel)
         {                           /* Translate the scan line */
         case 2:                     /* into display */
           TGAtoXGA16(x, y, buffer, width);
           break;
         case 3:
           TGAtoXGA24(x, y, buffer, width);
           break;
         case 4:
           TGAtoXGA32(x, y, buffer, width);
           break;
         } /* Head in the proper direction */
      if (hdr.imgDesc & 0x20)
         y++;
      else
         y--;
      }
   else
      { /* Compressed TGA file */
      while (k < width)
         { /* Get OP type */
         if (GetByte((UBYTE *)&opType))
            {
            y = -1;
            break;                   /* We're done! */
            }
         count = (opType & 0x7F) + 1;
         if (opType & 0x80)
            {                        /* Run Length Packet */
            if (GetLine(buffer, bytesPerPixel))
               {
               y = -2;
               break;
               }                     /* Replicate the pixel */
            DupePixel(ptr, buffer, count, bytesPerPixel);
            ptr += count * bytesPerPixel;
            k += count;              /* Update the count of pixels    */
            }
```

continued...

...from previous page

```
        else
          {  /* Copy Packet */
          if (GetLine(ptr, count * bytesPerPixel))
            {
            y = -2;
            break;
            }
          k += count;                /* Update the count of pixels */
                                     /* Update destination ptr. */
          ptr += (count * bytesPerPixel);
          }
        }

      switch (bytesPerPixel)
        { /* Now that we've expanded, translate */
        case 2:                      /*  and put in XGA RAM */
          TGAtoXGA16(x, y, dstBuffer, width);
          break;
        case 3:
          TGAtoXGA24(x, y, dstBuffer, width);
          break;
        case 4:
          TGAtoXGA32(x, y, dstBuffer, width);
          break;
        }

      k = k - width;               /* Update the pixel count */
      ptr = dstBuffer;
      j = bytesPerLine;            /* Copy left over compressed data */
      for (i = 0; i < k * bytesPerPixel; i++)
        *ptr++ = dstBuffer[j++];

      if (hdr.imgDesc & 0x20)
        y++;
      else
        y--;
      }
    } while (y < bmHeight && y > bmY);

  if (!getch())                    /* Wait for keystroke */
    getch();

  close(fileHandle);

  CloseXGA();  /* Done */

  return(0);
}
```

Listing 5.14. XGA16BPP.ASM

```
;************************************************************************
;
; XGA16BPP.ASM - XGA Subroutines for 16 bpp use
;
; Copyright (C) 1990-1992  Panacea Inc. - All Rights Reserved
;
;
; This file should be assembled via the following line:
;
;       MASM -ml XGA16BPP;
;
; This will produce a file called XGA16BPP.OBJ which should be
; linked with TGAXGA.OBJ and XGAFIND.OBJ
;
;************************************************************************
            include    XGA.INC
P_ARG1      equ        [BP+4]              ; Used to grab parameters off
P_ARG2      equ        [BP+6]              ;  the stack.
P_ARG3      equ        [BP+8]
P_ARG4      equ        [BP+10]
P_ARG5      equ        [BP+12]
P_ARG6      equ        [BP+14]
P_ARG7      equ        [BP+16]
P_ARG8      equ        [BP+18]

            .MODEL     SMALL
            .DATA

            extrn      _bmPitch:word
            extrn      _bmHeight:word
            extrn      _ioRegBaseAddr:word
            extrn      _memRegBaseAddr:dword

curBank     db         ?                   ; Has current XGA bank #.

            .CODE

            public     _TGAtoXGA16
            public     _TGAtoXGA24
            public     _TGAtoXGA32
            public     _DupePixel
;-----------------------------------------------------------------
;
; DupePixel(ptr, buffer, count, bytesPerPixel);
;
; Duplicates "count" pixels (stored in "buffer") of length
; "bytesPerPixel" into "ptr".
;
```

continued...

...from previous page

```
;----------------------------------------------------------------------
_DupePixel proc
          push      BP
          mov       BP, SP             ; Stack frame
          push      ES
          push      SI
          push      DI
          push      DS
          pop       ES
          mov       DI, P_ARG1         ; Get Destination
          mov       SI, P_ARG2         ; Get source
          mov       DX, SI             ; Save for later restoration
          mov       CX, P_ARG3         ; Get pixel count
          mov       BX, P_ARG4         ; Get pixel size
DupPix_Loop:
          push      CX
          mov       CX, BX             ; Set rep counter to pixel size
          rep       movsb              ; Copy a pixel.
          pop       CX
          mov       SI, DX             ; Restore source address
          loop      DupPix_Loop        ; For however many pixels we need
          pop       DI
          pop       SI
          pop       ES
          pop       BP
          ret
_DupePixel endp
;----------------------------------------------------------------------
-
;
; TGAtoXGA16(x, y, buffer, width)
;
; Translates one scan line of information from a TGA 16bpp buffer to the
; x,y position in the XGA buffer. Note that TGA 16bpp format is
; Direct Color 1:5:5:5, while XGA is DC 5:6:5.
;
;----------------------------------------------------------------------
_TGAtoXGA16 proc
          push      BP
          mov       BP, SP             ; Stack frame
          push      ES
          push      SI
          push      DI
          mov       AL, 1
          IOREGWRITEB MEMWIN_CTRL, AL ; Set 64KB window to 0xA000.
```

```
            mov         SI, P_ARG3              ; Get buffer pointer
            mov         AX, _bmPitch
            mov         BX, P_ARG2              ; Calculate address.
            mul         BX
            mov         CX, P_ARG1
            shl         CX, 1                   ; Get byte count
            add         AX, CX
            adc         DX, 0                   ; Destination Address
            mov         DI, AX
            mov         AX, 0A000H              ; Point to XGA memory.
            mov         ES, AX
            mov         CX, P_ARG4              ; Width of image
            mov         AL, DL                  ; Page for pattern.
            mov         curBank, AL             ; Set bank for scan line write.
            IOREGWRITEB MEMWIN_INDEX, AL ; Point the window to correct VRAM.
TGA16_Loop:
            lodsw       ; Load a pixel
            mov         BX, AX                  ; Do the conversion to DC 5:6:5
            and         AX, 0FFE0H
            shl         AX, 1
            and         BX, 0001FH
            or          AX, BX
            mov         ES:[DI], AX
            add         DI, 2
            jz          TGA16_NextBank          ; If wrapped 64KB bound, next bank.
            loop        TGA16_Loop
            jmp         short TGA16_Done
TGA16_NextBank:
            inc         curBank                 ; Set next bank.
            mov         AL, curBank
            IOREGWRITEB MEMWIN_INDEX, AL ; Point the window to correct VRAM.
            loop        TGA16_Loop
TGA16_Done:
            xor         AL, AL
            IOREGWRITEB MEMWIN_CTRL, AL  ; Close window.
            pop         DI
            pop         SI
            pop         ES
            pop         BP
            ret
_TGAtoXGA16 endp
```

continued...

...from previous page

```
;------------------------------------------------------------------------
;
; TGAtoXGA24(x, y, buffer, width)
;
; Translates one scan line of information from a TGA 24bpp buffer to the
; x,y position in the XGA buffer.
;
;------------------------------------------------------------------------
_TGAtoXGA24 proc
            push    BP
            mov     BP, SP
            push    ES
            push    SI
            push    DI
            mov     AL, 1
            IOREGWRITEB MEMWIN_CTRL, AL  ; Set window to 0xA000.
            mov     SI, P_ARG3          ; Get buffer pointer
            mov     AX, _bmPitch
            mov     BX, P_ARG2          ; Calculate address.
            mul     BX
            mov     CX, P_ARG1
            shl     CX, 1               ; Get byte count
            add     AX, CX
            adc     DX, 0               ; Destination Address
            mov     DI, AX
            mov     AX, 0A000H
            mov     ES, AX
            mov     CX, P_ARG4
            mov     AL, DL              ; Page for pattern.
            mov     curBank, AL
            IOREGWRITEB MEMWIN_INDEX, AL ; Point the window to correct VRAM.
TGA24_Loop: ; DC 8:8:8 to DC 5:6:5
            xor     DX, DX
            lodsb                       ; Get Blue byte
            shr     AL, 1
            shr     AL, 1
            shr     AL, 1
            or      DL, AL
            lodsb                       ; Get Green byte
            and     AX, 00FCH
            shl     AX, 1
            shl     AX, 1
            shl     AX, 1
            or      DX, AX
            lodsb                       ; Get Red byte
            and     AL, 0F8H            ; Strip lower three bits
            or      DH, AL
```

```
          mov       ES:[DI], DX
          add       DI, 2
          jz        TGA24_NextBank
          loop      TGA24_Loop
          jmp       short TGA24_Done
TGA24_NextBank:
          inc       curBank
          mov       AL, curBank
          IOREGWRITEB MEMWIN_INDEX, AL ; Point the window to correct VRAM.
          loop      TGA24_Loop
TGA24_Done:
          xor       AL, AL
          IOREGWRITEB MEMWIN_CTRL, AL  ; Close window.
          pop       DI
          pop       SI
          pop       ES
          pop       BP
          ret
_TGAtoXGA24 endp
;-------------------------------------------------------------------------
;
;
; TGAtoXGA32(x, y, buffer, width)
;
; Translates one scan line of information from a TGA 24bpp buffer to the
; x,y position in the XGA buffer.
;
;-------------------------------------------------------------------------
_TGAtoXGA32 proc
          push      BP
          mov       BP, SP
          push      ES
          push      SI
          push      DI
          mov       AL, 1
          IOREGWRITEB MEMWIN_CTRL, AL  ; Set window to 0xA000.
          mov       SI, P_ARG3         ; Get buffer pointer
          mov       AX, _bmPitch
          mov       BX, P_ARG2         ; Calculate address.
          mul       BX
          mov       CX, P_ARG1
          shl       CX, 1              ; Get byte count
          add       AX, CX
          adc       DX, 0              ; Destination Address
          mov       DI, AX
          mov       AX, 0A000H
```

continued...

...from previous page

```
            mov        ES, AX
            mov        CX, P_ARG4
            mov        AL, DL                  ; Page for pattern.
            mov        curBank, AL
            IOREGWRITEB MEMWIN_INDEX, AL ; Point the window to correct
VRAM.
TGA32_Loop:
            xor        DX, DX                  ; DC 8:8:8:8 to DC 5:6:5
            lodsb                              ; Get Blue byte
            shr        AL, 1
            shr        AL, 1
            shr        AL, 1
            or         DL, AL
            lodsb                              ; Get Green byte
            and        AX, 00FCH
            shl        AX, 1
            shl        AX, 1
            shl        AX, 1
            or         DX, AX
            lodsb                              ; Get Red byte
            and        AL, 0F8H                ; Strip lower three bits
            or         DH, AL
            mov        ES:[DI], DX
            lodsb                              ; Get rid of Alpha
            add        DI, 2
            jz         TGA32_NextBank
            loop       TGA32_Loop
            jmp        short TGA32_Done
TGA32_NextBank:
            inc        curBank
            mov        AL, curBank
            IOREGWRITEB MEMWIN_INDEX, AL ; Point the window to correct
VRAM.
            loop       TGA32_Loop
TGA32_Done:
            xor        AL, AL
            IOREGWRITEB MEMWIN_CTRL, AL  ; Close window.
            pop        DI
            pop        SI
            pop        ES
            pop        BP
            ret
_TGAtoXGA32 endp
            end
```

The memory map access to the XGA is all performed in XGA16BPP.ASM, in the three _TGAtoXGAxx() routines. The first step is to enable the memory window at 0A0000H by writing a 1 (or MEMWIN_ENABLE_A) to the Aperture Control register.

Then, select which of the 16 64KB chunks of XGA memory you want to see at 0A0000H. This is controlled by the Aperture Index register. The bank number is written to this register, and poof, the proper bank appears at 0A0000H.

Calculating the bank you want to access is simple. Assuming that you are displaying from the start of the XGA's memory, all you need to do is multiply your desired Y position by your display buffer pitch (in bytes), and add X (also converted to a byte count) to the result of the multiplication. The bank you want will be in bits 19 to 16 of the combined result. This makes sense, since the memory window is 64KB, which is the amount of data you can reference with 16 bits of address. This process is used in all three of the routines.

You may notice that I enable the memory window upon entry to the routine and disable it upon exit. This is just a quirk of how I originally wrote this code. I could have just as easily enabled the memory window during initialization, and shut it down when exiting the program.

You must set the Memory Access Mode register to reflect the type of pixel information you plan to access via the various XGA memory windows. This is because the XGA stores different pixel depths in different ways, so if you forget to set the Memory Access Mode register, you may end up with unexpected results.

16 Bits Per Pixel

As mentioned earlier, TGAXGA.C and XGA16BPP.ASM work exclusively in the XGA's 16bpp mode. This mode is a bit of an oddity on the original IBM XGA, since the drawing engine doesn't support drawing in 16 bits per pixel (this is remedied in the newer XGA-NI; see Appendix C). This means that on an original XGA, you have to play some games if you want acceleration in this mode. One such "game" was used in InitXGA16(), where I used an 8bpp map to clear the display. Since 16 is 8 times 2, you can perform many of the graphics engine functions simply by doubling both your X position and your width. This applies primarily to filled rectangles and BitBLTs. For a filled rectangle, you just use a source map that is 16 bits (two 8-bit pixels) wide, containing the color you want to fill with. BitBLTs are even simpler, since all you're doing is copying data that should already be in the right format. Trying to use the line drawing or SSV functions in this mode is pretty hopeless.

The 16bpp mode uses a Direct Color 5:6:5 format, which is odd, because the PC industry standard is the Direct Color 1:5:5:5 format, originated by Truevision's TARGA 16 graphics board. IBM's reason for the DC 5:6:5 was twofold. First, it's an IBM internal standard, and second, the human eye is more sensitive to variations in green than in red or blue. Either way, it still looks good.

Initialization of the 16bpp mode is simple. You just perform a regular 640x480 initialization, then update the Display Control 2 register for the proper depth. However, you need to load the palette in a certain way. The first 128 palette entries must be cleared to 0, while the last 128 must have the red and green entries cleared, but the blue entry loaded with a repeating ramp. The blue starts at 0 in entry 128, and then goes up by 8 for each successive blue entry in the palette. After 32 entries it wraps back to 0 to start all over again until all of the last 128 palette entries are loaded. If you don't load the palette this way for the 16bpp mode, you get some very odd looking colors on your display.

Once the palette is loaded, and you've set the Display Control 2 and Memory Access Mode registers for 16 bpp operation, you're ready to go and look at near-photorealistic color. And, if you bought this book with the disk, you'll find a TGA file with a picture of me attempting to type on a typewriter.

In Conclusion

We've covered everything from initializing the XGA to dealing with bus-mastering on the XGA in this chapter. If you've managed to follow all of the examples and text in this chapter, then you have the information you need to do some serious register-level XGA programming. Enjoy!

Chapter 6

Programming the AI

This chapter is a reference for use of the IBM Adapter Interface (AI) under MS-DOS. The Adapter Interface (AI), as we have seen, is a reasonably well-rounded software interface. Though there is a definite speed advantage in going to the XGA registers, the AI does provide portability across non–XGA compatible hardware. The IBM 8514/A, its clones, and many TI 340 graphics boards have shipped or are shipping with an AI for their boards, and IBM's Image Adapter/A high-end imaging board also supports the AI.

Besides its portability to other platforms, including whatever IBM will come out with, the AI has another benefit: It's cheap. To get documentation for the AI requires a call to the IBM Technical Books ordering department (800-IBM-PCTB) and a major credit card. The base technical reference should cost you about $12 (P/N 68X2248, *IBM Personal System/2 Display Adapter 8514/A Technical Reference*), and a programmer's guide is also available for approximately $30 (P/N 68X2279, *IBM Personal System/2 Display Adapter 8514/A Adapter Interface Application Developer's Guide*). The technical reference has a number of typos and omissions, but still provides the basic information necessary to understand the AI. The programmer's guide is really handy because it comes shipped with a diskette that contains C language bindings and miscellaneous utility programs that make using the XGA easier to understand. The C language binding and a selection of fonts are also shipped with each IBM XGA board.

For XGA-specific AI information, you may want to order *IBM Personal System/2 XGA Adapter Interface Technical Reference,* part number S15F2154. A similar document exists for the IBM Image Adapter/A, part number S15F2162. Appendix H documents the major differences between the 8514/AAI and the XGA AI.

Accessing the AI

From a programming perspective, the AI is modeled to an extent after existing graphical interfaces with which you may be familiar. The XGA AI is loaded as a device driver (via your CONFIG.SYS file). With the IBM version of the AI, the device driver is called XGAAIDOS.SYS, and is loaded by adding the line

```
*DEVICE=\XGAPCDOS\XGAAIDOS.SYS
```

to your CONFIG.SYS file. (The XGAAIDOS>SYS file is typically installed on the boot drive in your XGAPCDOS directory.) There are no command line options available for XGAAIDOS.SYS. Once the AI is installed in memory, you can run an AI application. The internal steps involved in running an AI-based application are generally something like:

1. The application needs to check for the existence of the AI.
2. If the AI is installed, open the AI for use.
3. Initialize the graphics state of the AI and board.
4. Perform all of the drawing and other graphical operations necessary for the application.
5. Close the AI.

You may notice that this sequence is also similar to one that might be used for operating on a data file.

Since the AI is RAM-resident, applications need some way to communicate with it, so that it can issue the appropriate commands to the graphics board. When the AI is installed, it grabs interrupt vector 7FH. The various AI functions are actually addressed to a jump table located in the AI device driver. The address of this table can be obtained using the following assembly language code fragment:

```
;
; Check to see if the AI is loaded by checking the address
; at interrupt vector 7FH. If the address is 0:0, AI is not
; loaded.
;
. xor       AX, AX
  mov       ES, AX
```

```
        mov        AX, ES:[7FH * 4]
        or         AX, ES:[7FH * 4 + 2]
        jz         AI_Not_Installed
;
; AI might be loaded, call whatever function is at interrupt
; 7FH with a request for the jump table address. This
; requires calling INT 7FH with a value of 0105H in AX.
;
        xor        CX, CX
        mov        DX, LX
        mov        AX, 0105H
        int        7FH
        jc         AI_Not_Installed
        mov        AX, CX
        or         AX, DX
        jz         AI_Not_Installed
;
; If we make it this far, the pointer to the jump table is
; returned in CX:DX.
;
```

If you are using the C binding, the routine "getafi()" does this for you:

```
/*
    Sample C code to determine if AI is loaded, and if so,
    get the pointer to the jump table. The jump table pointer
    is stored internal to the C binding.
*/
if (!getafi())
        {
        printf("AI not loaded!\n");
        exit(1);
        }
```

NOTE: The source code to getafi() and other C-callable AI functions can be found in CALLAFI.ASM, which comes shipped with the IBM XGA or the AI *programmer's guide* referred to earlier. Also necessary are the include files IBMAFI.H and AFIDATA.H, which contain definitions necessary to use the AI with the C programming language. My implementation of IBMAFI.H, AFIDATA.H, and CALLAFI.ASM can be found in Appendices K, L, and M, respectively.

Once the jump table pointer has been obtained, calls can be made to the AI. In order to pass a command to the AI, you need to push the 32-bit segment:offset address of an AI function parameter block onto the stack and make a far call to the proper entry in the jump table.

With the ImageAdapter/A and the XGA versions of the AI comes the ability to support multiple AI-compatible devices, a feature not supported by existing versions of the AI. Refer to the source code for my GETAFI.ASM in Appendix M to see how this might be used.

Function Parameter Block

The AI function parameter block is a data structure whose actual contents and form vary between the different AI functions. So that the AI knows how large this block is, the first word of the block always contains the number of bytes remaining in the block after the count (similar to a string definition in Pascal). For example, when drawing a line from coordinate 0,42 to 511,13, the parameter block (for the HLINE function) would be set up as follows:

Parameter Block	Byte offset	Description
8	0	Number of bytes left in block
0	2	X1
42	4	Y1
511	6	X2
13	7	Y2

Some AI functions, like HOPEN, return information to the caller. Since the block is really still in the caller's memory, the AI needs to modify only the block's contents in order to "return" information. Other functions, such as HCLOSE, do not even require a parameter block, since no information other than the call itself needs to be transferred.

Coordinates

As with many PC-based graphics boards, the drawing origin on the XGA is the upper-left corner of the display. For example, in the XGA's 640x480 mode, this would mean that the upper-left corner is referenced by coordinate (0,0), and the lower-right by (639,479). The AI, through the capabilities of the XGA, also allows the use of coordinates outside of the display area. This can be very useful when interactively moving large blocks of data or even cursors around, since the edges of the object can go beyond the display area without requiring the application to do any clipping. The following table shows the extent of the coordinate values for the various modes.

8514/A and Compatible AIs

	Coordinates		Display		Drawable	
	Min.	Max.[1]	Min.	Max.[2]	Min.	Max.[3]
640x480	−512,−256	1536,767	0,0	639,479	0,0	1023,511[4]
1024x768	−512,−512	1536,1536	0,0	1023,767	0,0	1023,1023

XGA

	Coordinates		Display		Drawable	
	Min.	Max.[1]	Min.	Max.[2]	Min.	Max.[3]
640x480	−2048,−2048	6143,6143[5]	0,0	639,479	0,0	1023,1023
1024x768	−2048,−2048	6143,6143[5]	0,0	1023,767	0,0	1023,1023

1. These are the minimum and maximum coordinates that can be processed by the AI.

2. Minimum and maximum display are the coordinate ranges for displayable information.

3. There is off-screen memory available in both display modes. These values reflect the extent of all drawable memory for the given mode. The off-screen memory can be used for bitmap or font storage, or any other valid drawing function.

4. In the 640x480 256 color mode, the maximum addressable Y resolution is 1,024.

5. In no event can either delta (the difference between coordinates) X or Y, of a line be greater than 4096.

Combining the AI and XGA Registers

One way to gain the benefit of both the AI and the registers is to combine their operations. The AI is handy for initializing the board and environment, while the registers can be accessed for better graphics performance once the initialization is complete. This is simple to accomplish, as long as you realize that the AI may have some internal variable that reflects the state of the hardware, and that if you change that state, the AI may act oddly. Generally, this shouldn't be a problem. For example, you may want the AI to initialize the board, but do most of the drawing through the register mechanism. This would save the hassle of setting all the CRTC registers to their correct values, especially if you are running on XGA hardware that is not identical to the original IBM product.

This combined AI/register approach does have some drawbacks, however. One is that you have to have the AI loaded in memory, which may take valuable RAM from your application. The second drawback, much more important, is that you can't be guaranteed that you are running on an XGA register–compatible board. The AI is supported on a number of TI 340 boards, as well as IBM's 8514/A and ImageAdapter/A. But if you know your application will be running only on a specific hardware configuration, this may be a good compromise.

AI Speed

While our experiments on the IBM XGA have shown its AI to be half as fast as direct register access, the clone companies may have a different story to tell.

The IBM AI definitely has some inefficiencies, which many clone companies claim to have eliminated. The other thing to note is that the clone AIs take advantage of the special extensions that their particular version of the AI incorporates. This includes things like fast line drawing, which requires a substantial bit of setup on a regular XGA, but might be very quick on a clone. Since the AI masks that capability of the clone hardware, your AI programs on the clone will run faster than on the IBM board, and, conceivably, faster than a register-based version of the program on the IBM board as well.

This means that neglecting the AI may not be a good idea. For optimum results, try to support both the AI and the register set.

The AI Functions

What follows is a summary of each AI command, including its parameter block and any special information that is pertinent to the use of the function. This list uses only the AI C–binding function names; the function numbers are available in Appendix I.

Each summary starts with the name of the function, followed by a brief overview of what it does and a description of the parameter block used by the function.

The parameter information consists of three fields:

- **Byte offset** is the index into the parameter block;
- **Parameter type and value** indicates the type of parameter (BYTE = 1 Byte, WORD = 2 Bytes, DWORD = 4 bytes, and FARPTR = 4 Bytes in Segment:Offset notation), and its value if constant; and
- **Description** describes the parameter briefly.

Finally, there is a detailed function description and a reference to other pertinent instructions.

Please note that all reserved parameters and bit fields should be explicitly set to 0 so as to avoid incompatibility with future versions of the AI.

The AI commands are listed in this section alphabetically; the section at the end of this chapter sorts them by function.

If you're interested in seeing what an AI program looks like, refer to the sample programs offered in the following chapter.

ABLOCKCGA

Writes a rectangular block of characters to the display using CGA-type attributes. The parameter information is as follows:

Byte offset	Type and value	Description
0	WORD = 10	Size of the remaining parameter block
2	BYTE	Initial column
3	BYTE	Initial row
4	BYTE	Width of block (in characters)
5	BYTE	Height of block (in characters)
6	FARPTR	Pointer to block in PC memory
10	BYTE	Pitch of block in PC memory (in characters)
11	BYTE	AI highlight attribute for block

This function can be used to display a block of characters, each with its own foreground and background color, on the XGA display.

The initial row and column are based on the character cell height as defined by a previous call to HSMODE or ASCELL, and refer to the position at which the block of characters is placed. The row and column number start with 0,0 as the upper-left corner of the display (or the position defined by the ASGO command), with the row and column increasing as you go right and down, respectively.

The width and height of the block are used to tell the AI the dimensions of the block, both for purposes of display and for reading the character information out of PC memory.

The pointer to the block refers to a PC address that contains the information for the first character to be displayed.

The pitch of the block is the number of characters between the first character of one row and the first character of the subsequent row. For example, the pitch of a regular 80x25 text display is 80. This allows for the display of a block of text that is a subset of a larger configuration.

The highlight attribute byte is used to modify the display of the characters in the block in a global fashion, and is defined as follows:

Bit 7	Underline
Bit 6	Reverse video
Bit 5	Overstrike
Bit 4	1 = Set background transparent
	0 = Set background opaque (use background color)
Bit 3	Reserved
Bit 2	Reserved
Bit 1	Font selection bit 1
Bit 0	Font selection bit 0

The character block information is similar to what a normal CGA-type (color) text screen might use, which is one byte to indicate the ASCII value of the character and one byte for the attribute. The attribute byte is defined as:

Bits 7–4	Background color
Bits 3–0	Foreground color

To see how these color values relate to the normal color values, refer to the AXLATE function.

Related functions are ABLOCKMFI, ASCELL, ASGO, ASFONT, AXLATE, and HSMODE.

ABLOCKMFI

Writes a rectangular block of characters to the display using an AI-specific format. The parameter information is as follows:

Byte offset	Type and value	Description
0	WORD = 10	Size of the remaining parameter block
2	BYTE	Initial column
3	BYTE	Initial row
4	BYTE	Width of block (in characters)
5	BYTE	Height of block (in characters)
6	FARPTR	Pointer to block in PC memory
10	BYTE	Pitch of block in PC memory (in characters)
11	BYTE	Reserved (must be 0)

This function can be used to display a block of characters, each with its own foreground and background color and highlight attribute.

The initial row and column are based on the character cell height as defined by a previous call to HSMODE or ASCELL, and refer to the position at which the block of characters is placed. The row and column number start with 0,0 as the upper-left corner of the display (or the position defined by the ASGO command), with the column and row increasing as you go right and down, respectively.

The width and height of the block are used to tell the AI the dimensions of the block, both for purposes of display and for reading the character information out of PC memory.

The pointer to the block refers to a PC address that contains the information for the first character to be displayed.

The pitch of the block is the number of characters between the first character of one row and the first character of the subsequent row. For example, the pitch of a regular 80x25 text display is 80. This allows for the display of a block of text that is a subset of a larger configuration.

The character block information consists of four bytes of data for each character. The four bytes are defined as follows:

Byte 0	The ASCII character code
Byte 1	The color attribute
	Bits 7–4 = Background color
	Bits 3–0 = Foreground color
Byte 2	The highlight attribute (See ABLOCKCGA for definition)
Byte 3	Reserved

Related functions are ABLOCKCGA, ASCELL, ASGO, ASFONT, AXLATE, and HSMODE.

ACURSOR

Positions the alphanumeric text cursor. The parameter information is as follows:

Byte offset	Type and value	Description
0	WORD = 2	Size of the remaining parameter block
2	BYTE	Column of new cursor position
3	BYTE	Row of new cursor position

This function is used to position a cursor on the display. The cursor positioning is based on the character cell size defined by HSMODE or ASCELL. The cursor is drawn in the XOR mode so that it will always be visible.

Related functions are ASCELL, ASCUR, ASGO, and HSMODE.

AERASE

Erases a block of characters. The parameter information is as follows:

Byte offset	Type and value	Description
0	WORD = 5	Size of the remaining parameter block
2	BYTE	Initial column
3	BYTE	Initial row
4	BYTE	Width of block (in characters)
5	BYTE	Height of block (in characters)
6	BYTE	Color

This function is used to clear a rectangular region of the display to a specific color. It is meant to be used in conjunction with the alphanumeric text functions.

The initial row and column are based on the character cell height as defined by a previous call to HSMODE, and refer to the position at which the block of characters is placed. The row and column number start with 0,0 as the upper-left corner of the display (or the position defined by the ASGO command), with the column and row increasing as you go right and down, respectively.

The width and height of the block tell the AI how much space to clear.

The color byte is defined as follows:

Bits 7–4   Background color

Bits 3–0   Reserved (set to 0)

Related functions are ASCELL, ASGO, AXLATE, HRECT, and HSMODE.

ASCELL

Sets the cell size for alphanumeric text. The parameter information is as follows:

Byte offset	Type and value	Description
0	WORD = 2	Size of the remaining parameter block
2	BYTE	New cell width
3	BYTE	New cell height

This function resizes the alphanumeric cell size defined by an earlier call to HSMODE or ASCELL. The horizontal and vertical character dimensions, in units of character cells, of the display can be calculated by dividing the screen resolution by the appropriate font cell dimension.

Specifying a value of 0 for the height or width will cause the current default value to be used for that dimension instead.

If you do change the default cell size for the current mode, you must also load a new font that matches the newly defined cell size prior to doing any other alphanumeric calls, or you may get strange results.

Related functions are ASFONT and HSMODE.

ASCROLL

Copies a rectangular block of characters on the display to another position on the display. The parameter information is as follows:

Byte offset	Type and value	Description
0	WORD = 6	Size of the remaining parameter block
2	BYTE	Initial column
3	BYTE	Initial row
4	BYTE	Width of block (in characters)
5	BYTE	Height of block (in characters)
6	BYTE	Destination column
7	BYTE	Destination row

This function copies a block of characters from the initial column and row to the destination column and row. Block dimensions are defined by the width and height fields.

The row and column positions are based on the character cell height as defined by a previous call to HSMODE. The positions start with 0,0 at the upper-left corner of the display (or the position defined using the ASGO command), with the column and row increasing as you go right and down, respectively.

The coordinates and dimension must be specified to insure that all the copying occurs entirely on the screen; that is, both the original and destination blocks must be within the bitmap. The blocks can overlap.

Related functions are ASCELL, ASGO, and HSMODE.

ASCUR

Defines the alphanumeric cursor's shape and attributes. The parameter information is as follows:

Byte offset	Type and value	Description
0	WORD = 3	Size of the remaining parameter block
2	BYTE	Cursor start line
3	BYTE	Cursor stop line
4	BYTE	Cursor attribute

This function sets the cursor position and size within the cursor cell, as well as its attribute. The cursor cell size is the height of the current font as selected by HSMODE or ASCELL.

The cursor start line defines the line within the cursor cell at which the block cursor should start. The top of the cursor cell is 0. The cursor stop line specifies the last line of the block cursor relative to the cursor cell. The cursor is drawn using an XOR mix.

NOTE: If the cursor stop line is less than the cursor start line, no cursor is displayed, unless the start line is defined to be 255 (0xFF), in which case the previous cursor start and end line information is retained.

The cursor attribute specifies the type of cursor or the cursor state:

Attribute 0   Normal block cursor

Attribute 1   Hidden; this supercedes the start/stop values

Attribute 2   Left arrow

Attribute 3   Right arrow

Related functions are ACURSOR, ASCELL, and HSMODE.

ASFONT

Defines a character set for use with the alphanumeric functions. The parameter information is as follows:

Byte offset	Type and value	Description
0	WORD = 6	Size of the remaining parameter block
2	BYTE	Font number to use (0-3)
3	BYTE	Reserved
4	FARPTR	Address of the font definition

This function is used to define font numbers for use with the alphanumeric text functions ABLOCKCGA and ABLOCKMFI.

The font number can range in value from 0 to 3, and is used primarily as the font handle for the text operations.

The font definition, whose address is required by this function, can be one of two different font types: monochrome bitmapped and short stroke vector. For an example of how to use the latter with the regular text functions, refer to the tutorial section. For more detailed information about the font structure and definitions, refer to Appendix J.

Related functions are ABLOCKCGA, ASCELL, ASFONT, HSCS, and HSMODE.

ASGO

Sets the alphanumeric character grid origin for certain alphanumeric functions. The parameter information is as follows:

Byte offset	Type and value	Description
0	WORD = 4	Size of remaining parameter block
2	WORD	New X position of grid origin (in pixels)
4	WORD	New Y position of grid origin (in pixels)

This function can be used to set a new origin for AI alphanumeric character-based functions.

Normally, when HOPEN and/or HSMODE are used to initialize a given display mode, the character grid origin is set to 0,0, which is generally the upper-left corner of the display. Using this function, you can move that origin to any valid pixel position (negative or positive), so that an alphanumeric character drawn at character cell position 0,0 will actually be drawn at the new position specified via this function. This is especially useful if you want to use functions like ABLOCKCGA at any pixel position, not just those that are multiples of the cell width and height. The position set by this command refers to the upper-left corner of the first character cell.

Any subsequent calls to HSMODE will reset the character grid origin to 0,0, as will a call to this function with a position of 0,0.

This function is available only in Image Adapter/A and XGA implementations of the AI.

Related functions are ABLOCKCGA, ABLOCKMFI, AERASE, HOPEN, and HSMODE.

AXLATE

Defines alphanumeric color translation tables. The parameter information is as follows:

Byte offset	Type and value	Description
0	WORD = 128	Size of the remaining parameter block
2	DWORD	16 Foreground colors
66	DWORD	16 Background colors

This function sets up a table used to translate to AI-specific colors the foreground and background colors used by the ABLOCKCGA, ABLOCKMFI, and AERASE functions. Note that each entry is defined as a 32-bit entry. This is to maintain compatibility with future versions of the AI that might be able to support 32 bits of color.

The translation mechanism uses the 4 bit foreground or background color as an index into the foreground or background color table defined by this function, and the color from the table is the one actually used to display the text.

Related functions are ABLOCKCGA, ABLOCKMFI, AERASE, and HLDPAL.

HBAR

Begins area definition. No parameters are required.

Byte offset	Type and value	Description
0	WORD = 0	Size of the remaining parameter block

This function tells the AI to start using subsequent drawing commands to define an area on the display that can be used as a boundary for an area fill. This is the way you draw filled polygons with the AI if you don't want to implement your own polygon rendering algorithm. The definition process is completed or suspended by using the HEAR function.

A number of things have to observed when using this function. First, the boundary definition can consist of one or more closed graphical objects.

A closed object consists of a contiguous series of lines. The definition of the first closed object starts with the first drawing command subsequent to the HBAR command. The definition of the first closed object is finished when an HEAR command or move command (that is, a non-drawing command that moves the current drawing position) is received. The AI ensures that the object is closed by drawing a line from the last point defined to the first one. This process can go on ad infinitum with the same HBAR. Area definitions cannot be nested.

Once the HEAR command is received, the AI fills the designated areas using the odd/even technique: Imagine the whole area definition to be bounded by a rectangle. When the XGA scans each line of the rectangle, the filling is initially turned off, but as the scan process moves right, every time a set pixel is encountered, the fill state is changed. Thus, after each odd set pixel found, filling is enabled; after each even set pixel, it is disabled. In a definition consisting of a rectangle outline within an outline, for instance, only the space between the inner and the outer rectangles would be filled.

The following functions are not to be used during an area definition because they will cause unpredictable results: HCCHST, HCHST, HCLOSE, HOPEN, HSBP, HSCMP, HSHS, and HSMODE.

Other primitives that interfere with the current position might also cause problems if the current position is not properly restored prior to continuing with other drawing commands.

Also important is that the area definition will potentially use off-screen workspace; that is, the area of the XGA memory that resides beyond the display portion.

The related functions are HEAR and HSAFP.

HBBC

BitBLTs a rectangular region from one location to another on the board. The parameter information is as follows:

Byte offset	Type and value	Description
0	WORD = 16	Size of the remaining parameter block
2	WORD	The type of BitBLT
4	WORD	Width of the block (in pixels)
6	WORD	Height of the block (in lines)
8	BYTE	Source plane for bit expansion
9	BYTE	Reserved
10	WORD	Source X
12	WORD	Source Y
14	WORD	Destination X
16	WORD	Destination Y

This function will copy a block of image data on the XGA from one place to another using the current foreground mix (see HSMX).

The type of BitBLT indicates whether this is a straight copy of all planes (that is all 1, 2, 4, or 8 bits per pixel, depending on the current mode), or if in fact this is a monochrome to color expansion (or single-plane source) BitBLT. The expansion BitBLT is useful for quickly displaying bitmapped fonts, since most of these font definitions have bits turned on or off. When this type of operation has been selected, the foreground color and mix are used for all bits in the source plane rectangle that are set to one; for all bits set to 0, the background color and mix are used. The type is specified by a value:

Value	Operation
0	Expand a single plane
1 or 8	Copy all planes

The source plane for the bit expansion specifies which plane to use in the case of an expansion BitBLT. This parameter has no meaning in the all-plane BitBLT.

The width and height are used to tell the AI the dimensions of the block to be copied.

The source and destination coordinates refer to the upper-left pixel of the blocks to be manipulated. Overlapping blocks are handled correctly—the AI will always put the source information in the specified destination block area.

Related functions are HSCOL, HSBCOL, HSHS, and HSMX.

HBBCHN

Chains BitBLT data for board/PC transfer. The parameter information is as follows:

Byte offset	Type and value	Description
0	WORD = 6	Size of the remaining parameter block
2	FARPTR	Pointer to data buffer for transfer
6	WORD	Size of buffer

This function specifies a data buffer to be used for transferring data to or from the XGA, as specified by a prior HBBR, HBBW, or HCBBW command.

Multiple HBBCHN commands generally are used to effect the transfer of a whole image. If used in conjunction with rectangular PC data instead of linear data (defined by

HBBR, HBBW, and HCBBW), then the data pointed by this function must be in the rectangular format, with an appropriate size.

The current position is not affected by this function.

Related functions are HBBR, HBBW, and HCBBW.

HBBR

Reads image data from XGA (BitBLT from board). The parameter information is as follows:

Byte offset	Type and value	Description
0	WORD = 12 or 20	Size of the remaining parameter block
2	WORD	The type of BitBLT
4	WORD	Width of the block (in pixels)
6	WORD	Height of the block (in lines)
8	BYTE	Source plane for read
9	BYTE	Reserved
10	WORD	Source X
12	WORD	Source Y
14	WORD	X Offset
16	WORD	Y Offset
18	WORD	Destination Pitch
20	WORD	Destination Height

This function initiates a BitBLT on the XGA that results in image data being transferred to the PC via the HBBCHN function.

The type of BitBLT indicates whether this is a straight read of all planes (that is, all 1, 2, 4, or 8 bits per pixel, depending on current mode) or a single-plane read. The type is specified by a value:

Value	Operation
0	Read a single plane
1	Read all planes, packed pixel format*
8	Read all planes, one pixel per byte

* Not available in 8514/A AI.

The source plane for read specifies which plane to use in the case of a single-plane read. This parameter has no meaning in the all-plane read.

The width and height are used to tell the AI the dimensions of the block to be read.

The source X and Y specify the upper-left corner of the block to be read on the XGA.

In the all-plane read, each pixel gets a byte of its own, even if you're only dealing with a four bit per pixel XGA mode (unless you have selected the packed pixel read, in which case this function will pack as many pixels per byte as will fit). In the single-plane read, the bits are packed eight to a byte, and the first bit of each line read starts on a byte boundary. The end of the line is padded with 0 bits if the line width is not a multiple of eight.

If the parameter size field is twenty, the AI will copy the image data into a rectangular region in PC memory, instead of just a linear region. The X offset specifies, in pixels, the X offset into a rectangular region in memory, and the Y offset does the same for the Y, but in lines. The destination pitch specifies the width of the rectangle into which the data is being imported. The destination height specifies the height of the block in memory.

The current position is set to the source X and Y position.

The related function is HBBCHN.

HBBW

Writes image data from PC to XGA (BitBLT to board). The parameter information is as follows:

Byte offset	Type and value	Description
0	WORD = 10 or 18	Size of the remaining parameter block
2	WORD	The type of BitBLT
4	WORD	Width of the block (in pixels)
6	WORD	Height of the block (in lines)
8	WORD	Destination X
10	WORD	Destination Y
12	WORD	X Offset
14	WORD	Y Offset
16	WORD	Source Pitch
18	WORD	Source Height

This function initiates a BitBLT on the XGA that results in image data being transferred from the PC via the HBBCHN function.

The type of BitBLT indicates whether this is a straight write of all planes (that is, all 1, 2, 4, or 8 bits per pixel, depending on current mode) or a single-plane write. The type is specified by a value:

Value	Operation
0	Monochrome to color expansion write
1	Write all planes, packed pixel format*
8	Write all planes, one pixel per byte

* Not available in 8514/A AI.

The width and height tell the AI the dimensions of the block to be written.

The destination X and Y specify the upper-left corner of the block to be written on the XGA.

In the all-plane write, each source pixel must be in a byte of its own (unless you have selected the packed pixel write, in which case this function will pack as many pixels per byte as will fit). The foreground mix is used for this operation.

In the expansion write, the source bits are packed 8 to a byte, and the first bit of each line read starts on a byte boundary. Each source bit that is set to one is expanded into the foreground color using the foreground mix, and each 0 bit is expanded into the background color using the background mix.

If the parameter size field is 18, the AI will copy the image data from a rectangular region in PC memory, instead of just a linear region. The X offset specifies, in pixels, the X offset into a rectangular region in memory, and the Y offset does the same for the Y, but in lines. The destination pitch specifies the width of the rectangle into which the data is being imported. The destination height specifies the height of the block in memory.

The current position is set to destination X and Y.

Related functions are HBBCHN, HSCOL, HSBCOL, HSHS, and HSMX.

HBMC

Copies bitmap block data (via a BitBLT), either within a bitmap or between bitmaps. The parameter information is as follows:

Byte offset	Type and value	Description
0	WORD = 48	Size of remaining parameter block
2	WORD	Flags
4	WORD	Width of block to be copied (in pixels)
6	WORD	Height of block to be copied (in pixels)
8	BYTE	Destination bitmap depth
9	BYTE	Reserved
10	DWORD	Address of destination bitmap
14	WORD	Pitch of destination bitmap (in pixels)
16	WORD	Height of destination bitmap (in lines)
18	WORD	Destination X position
20	WORD	Destination Y position
22	BYTE	Source bitmap depth
23	BYTE	Reserved
24	DWORD	Address of source bitmap
28	WORD	Pitch of source bitmap
30	WORD	Height of source bitmap
32	WORD	Source X position
34	WORD	Source Y position
36	BYTE	Pattern bitmap depth
37	BYTE	Reserved
38	DWORD	Address of pattern bitmap
42	WORD	Pitch of pattern bitmap
44	WORD	Height of pattern bitmap
46	WORD	X position of pattern within pattern bitmap
48	WORD	Y position of pattern within pattern bitmap

This function is used to BitBLT data between bitmaps. The source and destination bitmap can be the same bitmap or different ones. Additionally, a pattern bitmap can be used to control which pixels in the destination map are updated, and how they are updated. You can also use the pattern map as a source of data for a BitBLT to the destination without using a source bitmap. All these types of operations are specified via the bits in the flags word.

The flags word has the following bit definitions:

Bits	Function
15,14	Selects the location of the destination bitmap. At this time only one valid value exists for this field:
	10b Device's VRAM
13,12	Selects the location of the source bitmap. At this time only two valid values exists for this field:
	00b Source bitmap not present (used when pattern map is meant to be source)
	10b Device's VRAM
11,10	Selects the location of the pattern bitmap. At this time only two valid values exists for this field:
	00b Pattern bitmap not present
	10b Device's VRAM
9	If set, source bitmap is inverted (that is, the bottom-left corner of the bitmap is treated as the origin instead of the upper-left).
8-0	Reserved (must be set to 0).

The depth of a bitmap is its number of bits per pixel. Values of 1, 2, 4, or 8 are valid for the source and destination bitmaps, while the pattern map can have a depth only of 1. The bitmap depth for the source and destination bitmaps must be the same, however.

The map pointers/addresses contain the byte offset of the start of the map relative to the beginning of the device's base display memory. Such an offset must begin on a 32-bit boundary (that is, it must be divisible by 4).

Source and pattern maps may have nonbyte widths, but the destination map must have a width that is a multiple of 32-bits (that is, it must be a multiple of 4 pixels in 8bpp mode, 8 pixels in 4bpp mode, and so on).

This function is only available in the XGA and Image Adapter/A AIs.

Related functions are HQBMAP, HSBMAP, HSCMP, HSHS, and HSMX.

HCBBW

Writes image data from PC to XGA (BitBLT to board) at current position. The parameter information is as follows:

Byte offset	Type and value	Description
0	WORD = 6 or 14	Size of the remaining parameter block
2	WORD	The type of BitBLT
4	WORD	Width of the block (in pixels)
6	WORD	Height of the block (in lines)
8	WORD	X Offset
10	WORD	Y Offset
12	WORD	Source Pitch
14	WORD	Source Height

This function initiates a BitBLT on the XGA that results in image data being transferred from the PC via the HBBCHN function. The only difference between this function and HBBW is that the current position is used as the destination of the block write.

The type of BitBLT indicates whether this is a straight write of all planes (that is, all 1, 2, 4 or 8 bits per pixel, depending on current mode) or a single-plane write. The type is specified by a value:

Value	Operation
0	Write a single plane
1	Write all planes, packed pixel format*
8	Write all planes, one pixel per byte

* Not available in 8514/A AI.

The width and height are used to tell the AI the dimensions of the block to be written.

The destination X and Y (current position) specify the upper-left corner of the block to be written on the XGA.

In the all-plane write, each source pixel must be in a byte of its own (unless you have selected the packed pixel write, in which case this function will pack as many pixels per byte as will fit). The foreground mix is used for this operation.

In the expansion write, the source bits are packed eight to a byte, and the first bit of each line read starts on a byte boundary. Each source bit that is set to 1 is expanded into the foreground color using the foreground mix, and each 0 bit is expanded into the background color using the background mix.

If the parameter size field is 14, the AI will copy the image data from a rectangular region in PC memory, instead of just a linear region. The X offset specifies, in pixels, the X offset into a rectangular region in memory, and the Y offset does the same for the Y, but in lines. The destination pitch specifies the width of the rectangle into which the data is being imported. The destination height specifies the height of the block in memory.

Related functions are HBBCHN, HSCOL, HSBCOL, HSHS, and HSMX.

HCCHST

Writes a text string at the current position. The parameter information is as follows:

Byte offset	Type and value	Description
0	WORD 0	Size of the remaining parameter block
2	BYTE	Character string

This function displays a text string in the current font (selected by HSCS) at the current drawing position. The length of the text string is determined by the parameter block size. The current position references the lower-left corner of the first character in the string. The current position is not altered by this function.

Related functions are HCHST, HSBCOL, HSCS, HSCOL, HSHS, and HSMX.

HCHST

Writes a text string at the given position. The parameter information is as follows:

Byte offset	Type and value	Description
0	WORD 4	Size of the remaining parameter block
2	WORD	X position
4	WORD	Y position
6	BYTE	Character string

This function displays a text string in the current font (selected by HSCS) at the given drawing position. The length of the text string is determined by the parameter block size minus 4 (the size of the position parameters). The given position references the lower-left corner of the first character in the string.

The current position is set to the given position.

Related functions are HCCHST, HSBCOL, HSCS, HSCOL, HSHS, and HSMX.

HCLINE

Draws a polyline starting at current position. The parameter information is as follows:

Byte offset	Type and value	Description
0	WORD 0	Size of the remaining parameter block
2	WORD	X0
4	WORD	Y0
6	WORD	X1
8	WORD	Y1
.		
.		
.		
n*4+2	WORD	Xn
n*4+4	WORD	Yn

This function will draw a polyline, starting at the current drawing position, to X0,Y0, from X0,Y0 to X1,Y1, and so forth. The number of points is determined by the size of the parameter block.

The current position is set to the last point in the polyline. This function does not reset the line pattern.

Related functions are HCRLINE, HLINE, HRLINE, HSBCOL, HSCOL, HSHS, HSLT, HSLW, and HSMX.

HCLOSE

Closes down the XGA AI.

Byte offset	Type and value	Description
0	WORD = 1	Size of the remaining parameter block
2	BYTE	Reserved (must be 0)

This function will disable the display of the XGA graphics mode on the monitor attached to it, and will reenable the default adapter mode (VGA in a single-XGA system with no other type of display controller).

The related function is HOPEN.

HCMRK

Draws a marker at current position, and all others specified. The parameter information is as follows:

Byte offset	Type and value	Description
0	WORD 0	Size of the remaining parameter block
2	WORD	X0
4	WORD	Y0
6	WORD	X1
8	WORD	Y1
.		
.		
.		
n*4+2	WORD	Xn
n*4+4	WORD	Yn

This function will draw a marker (as defined by the HSMARK command) at the current position. If additional points are present (determined by the size of the parameter block), markers are drawn at the additional points as well.

The marker is drawn so that it is centered about the point specified. Note that there may be a small (one pixel) discrepancy in positioning due to the integerized math being used. The formula for the positioning of the upper-left corner of the marker is:

```
ULX = X - (markWidth / 2), ULY = Y - (markHeight / 2).
```

The current position is set to the last point in the parameter block.

Related functions are HMRK, HSCOL, HSHS, HSLT, HSLW, and HSMX.

HCPSTEP

Draws short stroke-style at current position. The parameter information is as follows:

Byte offset	Type and value	Description
0	WORD = 4 or 8	Size of remaining parameter block
2	FARPTR	Address of short stroke-style data
6	FARPTR	Address of source pixel data buffer

This function will draw a sequence of short stroke-style vectors at the current position, using coding information identical to the short stroke vector requirements of the 8514/A and XGA subsystems.

The short stroke data is contained in the first specified buffer, and each byte in the buffer has the following format:

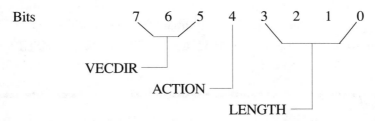

VECDIR is the direction of the short stroke vector in degrees, as measured counter-clockwise from the positive X axis. The values are defined as follows:

Bit 7	Bit 6	Bit 5	Direction in degrees (counter-clockwise from positive X axis)
0	0	0	0
0	0	1	45
0	1	0	90
0	1	1	135
1	0	0	180
1	0	1	225
1	1	0	270
1	1	1	315

ACTION determines whether only the current position is moved or pixels are drawn as well.

Value	Operation
0	Move current position.
1	Draw the vector and move the current position.

LENGTH is the length of the vector in pixels, and ranges from 0 to 15 in value.

The data in the buffer is terminated by a byte of 0.

If the parameter block size is set to 4, then the current foreground color and mix will be used to draw the vectors. However, if the parameter block size is set to 8, then a secondary buffer is used to contain the selected color information for each pixel drawn by this function. The data in the buffer is in a packed pixel format, with the number of pixels in this buffer matching the number to be drawn (or passed over in the event of a "move" operation) by the function, up to a maximum of 4095 bytes.

The last pixel is never drawn with this function.

This function is only available in the XGA and Image Adapter/A AIs.

Related functions are HPSTEP, HRSTEP, HSCMP, HSCOL, HSHS, HSLT, and HSMX.

HCRLINE

Draws a polyline starting at current position with relative coordinates. The parameter information is as follows:

Byte offset	Type and value	Description
0	WORD 0	Size of the remaining parameter block
2	BYTE	dX0
3	BYTE	dY0
4	BYTE	dX1
5	BYTE	dY1
.		
.		
.		
n*2+2	BYTE	dXn
n*2+3	BYTE	dYn

This function will draw a polyline, starting at the current drawing position (CPX, CPY), to CPX+dX0,CPY+dY0, from there to CPX+dX0+dX1,CPY+dY0+dY1, and so forth. The number of points is determined by the size of the parameter block. Note that each delta value is only a byte, which limits the range for each new point to between –128 and +127.

The current position is set to the last point calculated in the polyline. This function does reset the line pattern prior to executing.

Related functions are HCLINE, HLINE, HRLINE, HSBCOL, HSCOL, HSHS, HSLT, HSLW, and HSMX.

HDLINE

Draw disjoint line(s) at specified position, using absolute coordinates. The parameter information is as follows:

Byte offset	Type and value	Description
0	WORD 0	Size of remaining parameter block
2	WORD	X0
4	WORD	Y0
6	WORD	X1
8	WORD	Y1
.		
.		
.		
n*4 + 2	WORD	Xn
n*4 + 4	WORD	Yn

This function will potentially draw a series of disjoint lines; for example, from X0,Y0 to X1,Y1, and from X2,Y2 to X3,Y3, and so forth. The number of points is determined by the size of the parameter block, and this function does require an even number of coordinate pairs.

The current position is set to the last point in the last line drawn. This function resets the line pattern for each line.

This function is available only in the XGA and Image Adapter/A AIs.

Related functions are HSBCOL, HSCMP, HSCOL, HSGQ, HSHS, HSLT, HSLW, and HSMX.

HEAR

Begins area definition. The parameter information is as follows:

Byte offset	Type and value	Description
0	WORD = 1	Size of the remaining parameter block
2	BYTE	End area flags

This function ends an area definition initiated by HBAR. The flags are defined as follows:

Flag byte	Description
00H	Fill the defined area. This will perform an area fill as described in the HBAR function.
40H	Suspend the definition. Selecting this option will suspend the area definition until the next HBAR command, leaving the definition work area untouched. The definition should continue from where it left off after the HBAR command.
80H	Abort the definition. This aborts the definition and clears the buffer used to store the definition information.

If an area fill is selected, the current color, pattern, and mix are used.

Related functions are HBAR, HSAFP, HSCOL, HSHS, HSPATT, HSPATTO, and HSMX.

HEGS

Clears the graphics display. No parameters are required.

Byte offset	Type and value	Description
0	WORD = 0	Size of the remaining parameter block

This function erases the display by setting all pixels to 0. The erase is affected by the setting of the clipping rectangle, as well as by the plane enable.

Related functions are HSBP and HSHS.

HESC

Escape/abort current operation. No parameters are required:

Byte offset	Type and value	Description
0	WORD = 0	Size of the remaining parameter block

This function does not apply to the XGA. Apparently it has been defined for future use on other AI compatible adapters. If HESC is called, the AI just returns.

HINIT

Initializes the task data area. The parameter information is as follows:

Byte offset	Type and value	Description
0	WORD = 2	Size of the remaining parameter block
2	WORD	Segment of the task buffer

This function initializes the task data structure located at offset 0000 in the segment passed to the function.

The purpose of the task buffer is to ease multitasking by allowing for swapping of these task buffers. In the DOS environment, there really isn't a whole lot of use in doing this, except in customized applications. But, this function is a necessary step in using the AI. There are actually two types of task information: task dependent and task independent. The task-independent data consists of things like the color palette contents and the adapter mode. The task-dependent data refers to more application-specific attributes like the current position, color, and so on.

When HINIT is called, the task-dependent data, and therefore the current task's environment, is initialized with the following information:

Current position:	0,0
Foreground color:	All bits set
Background color:	All bits cleared
Foreground mix:	Dst = Src (replace mode)
Background mix:	Not initialized

Comparison color:	Not initialized
Compare function:	FALSE (everything is drawn)
Line type:	Solid
Line width:	1 pixel
Line pattern info:	Not initialized
Area pattern:	Solid
Area pattern origin:	0,0
Text and marker info:	Not initialized
Clipping rectangle:	Full screen
Graphics quality:	High precision, last pixel null
Plane mask:	All planes enabled
Color index translate table:	The 8 entries are set linearly, 0–7
Alphanumeric cursor:	At 0,0 and hidden
Alphanumeric color translate:	Two sets of 16 linear values, 0–15 each for foreground and background.
Alphanumeric character grid origin:	0,0*
Default font:	Not initialized

* Does not apply to 8514/A AI.

Related functions are HSYNC and HQDPS.

HINT

Waits for event or interrupt. The parameter information is as follows:

Byte offset	Type and value	Description
0	WORD = 4	Size of the remaining parameter block
2	DWORD	Event identifier

This function will wait until the requested event occurs. The event is specified by setting the appropriate bit in the event identifier parameter. All other non-pertinent bits should be cleared:

Bit	Event
31	Wait for vertical blank. This is useful for applications that need to time certain graphics operations; for example, to cut down on flicker during animations.
30	Wait for hardware to become free (i.e. not busy with a drawing operation).*
29–0	Reserved

*Does not apply to 8514/A AI.

Upon return to the calling program, the event identifier field will contain only the single bit set that caused the function to terminate the wait.

HLDPAL

Loads a palette into the color look-up table. The parameter information is as follows:

Byte offset	Type and value	Description
0	WORD = 1 or 10	Size of the remaining parameter block
2	BYTE	Palette type
3	BYTE	Reserved
4	WORD	Index of first entry
6	WORD	Number of entries
8	FARPTR	Address of data

This function will load either the default palette or an application-specific palette into the color look-up table located on the XGA.

The palette-type parameter indicates whether the default or application palette is to be used:

Value	Type
0	Application-specific. Use rest of parameters.
1	Default. The remaining parameters are ignored and the entire default palette is used. The default AI palette is the same as that used by a CGA (see HQDFPAL) for the first sixteen entries, and is the value of the index right-shifted four bit positions (one nibble) for the remaining 240 entries.

The index of the first entry specifies what part of the palette to start loading. This means that you can set only a small part of the palette if you choose to.

The number of entries allows you to specify how many entries in the color look-up table you would like to modify.

The look-up table data should contain four bytes for every entry you want to update:

Byte	Description
0	Red component
1	Green component
2	Blue component
3	Reserved

The values for the red, green, and blue bytes range from 0 to 255, with 255 being the highest intensity. On the IBM XGA the two low order bits are ignored because the IBM XGA only supports 6 bits of intensity per gun.

NOTE: Mode changes might corrupt the palette. You may want to use HRPAL and HSPAL to save and restore the palette while attempting a mode change.

Related functions are HRPAL and HSPAL.

HLINE

Draws a polyline starting at specified position. The parameter information is as follows:

Byte offset	Type and value	Description
0	WORD 0	Size of the remaining parameter block
2	WORD	X0
4	WORD	Y0
6	WORD	X1
8	WORD	Y1
.		
.		
.		
n*4+2	WORD	Xn
n*4+4	WORD	Yn

This function will draw a polyline, starting at X0,Y0, to X1,Y1, from X1,Y1 to X2,Y2, and so forth. The number of points is determined by the size of the parameter block.

The current position is set to the last point in the polyline. This function does not reset the line pattern.

Related functions are HCLINE, HCRLINE, HRLINE, HSBCOL, HSCOL, HSHS, HSLT, HSLW, and HSMX.

HMRK

Draws a marker at the specified positions. The parameter information is as follows:

Byte offset	Type and value	Description
0	WORD 0	Size of the remaining parameter block
2	WORD	X0
4	WORD	Y0
6	WORD	X1
8	WORD	Y1
.		
.		
.		
n*4+2	WORD	Xn
n*4+4	WORD	Yn

This function will draw a marker (as defined by the HSMARK command) at the specified points. The number of points is determined by the size of the parameter block.

The marker is drawn around a specified center point. Note that there may be a small (one pixel) discrepancy in positioning due to the integerized math being used. The formula for the positioning of the upper-left corner of the marker is:

```
ULX = X - (markWidth / 2), ULY = Y - (markHeight / 2).
```

The current position is set to the last point in parameter block.

Related functions are HSCOL, HSHS, HSLT, HSLW, HCMRK, and HSMX.

HOPEN

Enables the adapter the adapter for use. The parameter information is as follows:

Byte offset	Type and value	Description
0	WORD = 3	Size of the remaining parameter block
2	BYTE	Initialization flags
3	BYTE	Mode
4	BYTE	Return status

This function initializes the task-independent state (see HINIT).

The initialization flags tell the AI what should be initialized and what shouldn't:

Bit(s)	Meaning
7	Don't clear board memory if bit is set
6	Don't load default palette if bit is set
5–0	Reserved—set to 0

The mode specifies into which mode to initialize the adapter. The existing mode numbers are:

Mode	Screen size	Alpha text size	Text resolution
0	1024x768	12x20	85x38
1	640x480	8x14	80x34
2	1024x768	8x14	128x54
3	1024x768	7x15	146x52

All other modes are reserved for future use.

The return status is used to indicate whether or not the initialization was successful. If a nonzero status is returned, the initialization failed. (In post-8514/A versions of the AI, Bit 7 of the status signifies a driver/HW mismatch if set, and Bit 6 signifies a control program reject if set upon return.)

Related functions are HCLOSE, HINIT, and HSMODE.

HPEL

Draws strings of pixels at specified positions. The parameter information is as follows:

Byte offset	Type and value	Description
0	WORD 0	Size of remaining parameter block
2	WORD	X0
4	WORD	Y0
6	WORD	Pixel Count 0
8	WORD	X1
10	WORD	Y1
12	WORD	Pixel Count 1
.		
.		
.		
n*6+2	WORD	Xn
n*6+4	WORD	Yn
n*6+6	WORD	Pixel Count n

This function will draw a series of pixel strings. Each pixel string has a starting point (specified in the parameter block), and a pixel count (the number of pixels at the specified point to set using the current color and mix). Such pixels are written in the direction of an increasing X.

Multiple pixel strings can be specified. The number of pixel strings is determined by the size of the parameter block.

This function is also useful for setting individual pixels.

The current position is not affected by this function.

This function is available only in the XGA and Image Adapter/A AIs.

Related functions are HRPEL, HSBCOL, HSCOL, HSHS, and HSMX.

HPSTEP

Draws short stroke-style data at given position. The parameter information is as follows:

Byte offset	Type and value	Description
0	WORD = 8 or 12	Size of remaining parameter block
2	WORD	X
4	WORD	Y
6	FARPTR	Address of short stroke-style data
10	FARPTR	Address of source pixel data buffer

This function will draw a sequence of short stroke-style vectors at the specified position, using coding information identical to the short stroke vector requirements of the 8514/A and XGA subsystems.

The short stroke data is contained in the first specified buffer, and each byte in the buffer has the following format:

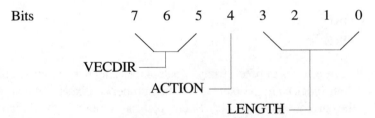

VECDIR is the direction of the short stroke vector in degrees, as measured counter clockwise from the positive X axis. The values are defined as follows:

Bit7	Bit 6	Bit 5	Direction in degrees (counter-clockwise from positive X axis)
0	0	0	0
0	0	1	45
0	1	0	90
0	1	1	135
1	0	0	180
1	0	1	225
1	1	0	270
1	1	1	315

ACTION determines whether only the current position is moved or pixels are drawn as well.

0	Move current position.
1	Draw the vector and move the current position.

LENGTH is the length of the vector in pixels, and ranges from 0 to 15 in value.

The data in the buffer is terminated by a byte of 0.

If the parameter block size is set to 8, then the current foreground color and mix will be used to draw the vectors. However, if the parameter block size is set to 12, then a secondary buffer is used to contain the selected color information for each pixel drawn by this function. The data in the buffer is in a packed pixel format, with the number of pixels in this buffer matching the number to be drawn (or passed over in the event of a "move" operation) by the function, up to a maximum of 4095 bytes.

The last pixel is never drawn with this function.

This function is available only in the XGA and Image Adapter/A AIs.

Related functions are HCPSTEP, HRSTEP, HSCMP, HSCOL, HSHS, HSLT, and HSMX.

HQBMAP

Queries current bitmap attributes. The parameter information is as follows:

Byte offset	Type and value	Description
0	WORD = 10 or 18	Size of remaining parameter block
2	BYTE	Flags
3	BYTE	Bitmap depth
4	DWORD	Address of bitmap
8	WORD	Width of bitmap (in pixels)
10	WORD	Height of bitmap (in lines)
12	WORD	Display window X origin
14	WORD	Display window Y origin
16	WORD	Display window width (in pixels)
18	WORD	Display window height (in lines)

This function returns information about the current bitmap, previously set via the HSBMAP function.

The Flag byte has the following meaning:

Bit	Description
7	Reserved (must be 1)
6	0 = Non-screen bitmap; 1 = Screen bitmap
5-0	Reserved (must be 0)

Valid bitmap depths will be 1, 2, 4, and 8.

The address of the bitmap is the linear byte offset of the beginning of the bitmap from the beginning of the display memory of the graphics device.

If the parameter block size is set to 18, then the returned parameter block also will contain display window information.

This function is available only in the XGA and Image Adapter/A AIs.

Related functions are HSBMAP and HSDW.

HQCOORD

Queries coordinate types. The parameter information is as follows:

Byte offset	Type and value	Description
0	WORD = 4	Size of the remaining parameter block
2	BYTE	Absolute coordinate format
3	BYTE	Relative coordinate format
4	BYTE	Number of dimensions
5	BYTE	Result

This function is used to determine the validity of a HSCOORD call before making it. While it is anticipated that this call will serve some real function in future implementations of the AI, in the IBM XGA version, there is only one viable setting for each parameter, as noted below.

The absolute coordinate formats specify the amount of space consumed by absolute coordinates:

Bits	Definition
7–4	Number of bytes in each coordinate. Default = 2.
3–0	Number of fractional bytes per coordinate. Default = 0.

The relative coordinate formats specify the space consumed by relative coordinates:

Bits	Definition
7–4	Number of bytes in each coordinate. Default = 1.
3–0	Number of fractional bytes per coordinate. Default = 0.

The number of dimensions can be two, three, or four. The XGA AI supports only two dimensions at present.

The result field is set based on the interpretation of the other parameters by the AI:

Bit	Definition
7	If set, the absolute coordinate format is not supported (and hence, the format information above is meaningless).
6	If set, the relative coordinate format requested is not supported.
5	If set, the number of dimensions requested is not supported.
4–0	Reserved

The related function is HSCOORD.

HQCP

Queries current position. The parameter information is as follows:

Byte offset	Type and value	Description
0	WORD = 4	Size of the remaining parameter block
2	WORD	Current X
4	WORD	Current Y

After this function is called, the current position is returned in the appropriate field in the parameter block.

Many of the drawing functions alter the current position, and are so documented.

The related function is HSCP.

HQDEVICE

Queries device-specific information.

This function is not available in the 8514/A AI, and is not used in the XGA AI. Its only function is specific to the Image Adapter/A, so it will not be documented here.

HQDFPAL

Queries default palette. The parameter information is as follows:

Byte offset	Type and value	Description
0	WORD = 64	Size of the remaining parameter block
2	DWORD	Color index values (16 of them)

This function returns sixteen color index values. When the default palette is used, these are:

Index	Color	Index	Color
0	Black	8	Grey
1	Blue	9	Light Blue
2	Green	10	Light Green
3	Cyan	11	Light Cyan
4	Red	12	Light Red
5	Magenta	13	Light Magenta
6	Brown	14	Yellow
7	White	15	Bright White

This function could be useful in modes in which direct color support is provided (although currently, there are none), where an application needs to display the basic sixteen colors used by most IBM-compatible display subsystems but does not know which color index/value to use to represent the desired colors.

Related functions are HLDPAL, HRPAL, and HSPAL.

HQDPS

Queries task state and driver stack usage sizes. The parameter information is as follows:

Byte offset	Type and value	Description
0	WORD = 6 or 14	Size of the remaining parameter block
2	WORD	Task buffer size
4	WORD	Stack usage
6	WORD	Palette save area size
8	DWORD	Amount of VRAM (in bytes)*
12	DWORD	Amount of VRAM space required for area fill plane (in bytes)*

* Does not apply to 8514/A AI.

The AI returns the size, in bytes, of several AI-related data areas. This function is called prior to HINIT so that the application can properly allocate memory for the task-dependent information, stack, and palette.

The task buffer size reflects how much memory the task-dependent information will occupy.

The stack usage value indicates the maximum amount of stack used by the AI driver.

The palette save area size is used to inform the application of how much memory it should allocate in order to use the HSPAL and HRPAL functions.

The VRAM size and area fill size, combined with the information returned by the HQBMAP function can provide you with the total amount of spare VRAM, and its position/address in the XGA.

Related functions are HINIT, HQBMAP, HRPAL, and HSPAL.

HQMODE

Queries the current mode and configuration. The parameter information is as follows:

Byte offset	Type and value	Description
0	WORD = 18	Size of the remaining parameter block
2	BYTE	Mode number
3	WORD	Drive code value
5	BYTE	Adapter type
6	BYTE	Display type (Reserved)
7	BYTE	Alphanumeric cell width (in pixels)
8	BYTE	Alphanumeric cell height (in pixels)
9	BYTE	Number of planes
10	WORD	Screen width (in pixels)
12	WORD	Screen height (in pixels or lines)
14	WORD	Pixels/inch—horizontal
16	WORD	Pixels/inch—vertical
18	BYTE	Monochrome or color
19	BYTE	Intensity levels
20	BYTE	Software area fill plane required (set to 1)*
21	BYTE	VGA mode support*

*Available only if Adapter Type is XGA (4) or Image Adapter/A (5).

This function returns information about the current mode and configuration of the XGA.

The mode number is one of the following (see HOPEN for more information):

Mode	Screen size
0	1024x768
1	640x480
2	1024x768
3	1024x768

The driver code level reflects the AI release number, planar configuration of the board, and whether or not the driver is running in protected mode:

Bits	Definition
15–12	Operating system (MS-DOS/PC-DOS is 0000B)
11-8	Specification level: 0000B—level 1.0 0001B—level 1.1 0010B—level 2.0
7-6	Minimum CPU level: 00—80286 01—8086 10—80386
5	0 = 4-plane board, 1 = 8-plane board
4–0	Release number (starts at 0)

The adapter type for an XGA is always 4 (the adapter type for the 8514/A is 3; for the Image Adapter/A it's 5). The display type is reserved and set to 0.

The alphanumeric cell width and height are dependent on the last HSMODE or ASCELL command.

The number of bit planes depends on the board's current configuration.

The screen width and height are specified in pixels and depend on the latest HOPEN or HSMODE call.

The pixels per inch depends on the monitor attached to the XGA and the resolution currently being displayed (the pixels per inch in all three cases apply to both horizontal and vertical dimensions):

Pixels/Inch	Monitor	Resolution
59	IBM 8514	640x480
79	IBM 8512 or 8513	640x480
92	IBM 8514	1024x768

The monochrome or color field is set to 0 for a monochrome display or 255 (0xFF) for a color display.

The intensity levels field reflects the number of intensity bits per gun in the palette. A value of 0 indicates nonloadable palettes. The normal value for an IBM XGA is 6 (with an XGA-NI, the returned intensity should be 8).

The VGA Mode Support byte specifies whether or not the device supports a VGA-compatible mode. If set to 1 it does; if set to 0, it does not.

Related functions are ASCELL, HOPEN, and HSMODE.

HQMODES

Queries available modes. The parameter information is as follows:

Byte offset	Type and value	Description
0	WORD = 33	Size of the remaining parameter block
2	BYTE	Adapter type
3	BYTE	First mode number
4	BYTE	Second mode number
.		
.		
.		
34	BYTE	Thirty-second mode number

This function returns information about the available modes for the current adapter. The adapter type returned is 3 for the XGA.

The mode numbers are returned in a list containing up to thirty-two mode numbers. If there are fewer than thirty-two valid modes for the current adapter/monitor configuration, the list is terminated by mode number with a value of 255 (0xFF). For example, with an IBM 8514 monitor attached, all four mode numbers that the board supports are listed: 0, 1, 2, and 3. A fifth mode entry is set to 255, indicating that no more real entries are available. For the IBM 8512 and 8513 monitors, only one real mode is listed: 1. Again, the second entry mode is 255. The resolutions of the modes are listed under HSMODE or HOPEN.

Related functions are HOPEN and HSMODE.

HRECT

Draws a filled rectangle. The parameter information is as follows:

Byte offset	Type and value	Description
0	WORD 8	Size of the remaining parameter block
2	WORD	X (top-left corner of first rectangle)
4	WORD	Y (top-left corner of first rectangle)
6	WORD	Width of the first rectangle (in pixels)
8	WORD	Height of the first rectangle (in lines)
10	WORD	X (top-left corner of second rectangle)
12	WORD	Y (top-left corner of second rectangle)
14	WORD	Width of the second rectangle (in pixels)
16	WORD	Height of the second rectangle (in lines)

.

.

.

This function will draw a rectangle filled with the current area pattern. Only monochrome patterns are supported.

The X and Y coordinates specify the upper-left corner of the rectangle, and the width and height specify the dimensions. The current position is set to X,Y.

The XGA and Image Adapter/A versions of the AI are the only ones to support multiple rectangle definitions. The 8514/A AI supports only a single rectangle parameter block.

Related functions are HSCOL, HSHS, HSMX, HSPATT, and HSPATTO.

HRFPAL

Restores full palette. The parameter information is as follows:

Byte offset	Type and value	Description
0	WORD = Special	Size of remaining parameter block
2	WORD	Format (set to 8)
4	BYTE	The palette data

This function restores the full palette and display mask to the board from the parameter block. The size of the palette-restore area is determined by a call to HQDPS. The palette is restored in the same format saved by the HSFPAL command.

This function should be used over the HRPAL and HSPAL functions, since it restores the full palette, not just the most significant 6 bits of each entry.

This function is available only on XGA and Image Adapter/A versions of the AI.

Related functions are HRPAL, HSPAL, and HSFPAL.

HRLINE

Draws a polyline, starting at the specified position, with relative coordinates. The parameter information is as follows:

Byte offset	Type and value	Description
0	WORD 0	Size of the remaining parameter block
2	WORD	X
4	WORD	Y
6	BYTE	dX0
7	BYTE	dY0
8	BYTE	dX1
9	BYTE	dY1
.		
.		
.		
n*2+6	BYTE	dXn
n*2+7	BYTE	dYn

This function will draw a polyline, starting at X,Y, to X+dX0,Y+dY0, from there to X+dX0+dX1,Y+dY0+dY1, and so on. The number of points is determined by the size of the parameter block. Note that each delta value is only a byte, which limits the range for each new point to between −128 and +127.

The current position is set to the last point calculated in the polyline. This function resets the line pattern prior to executing.

Related functions are HCLINE, HLINE, HRLINE, HSBCOL, HSCOL, HSHS, HSLT, HSLW, and HSMX.

HRLPC

Restores a previously saved line pattern count. No parameters are required:

Byte offset	Type and value	Description
0	WORD = 0 or 2	Size of the remaining parameter block
2	WORD	Optional line pattern count value to use for the restore*

*This field is available only in the Image Adapter/A and XGA versions of the AI.

This function restores the line pattern count that was previously saved by the HSLPC command.

The line pattern count is a pointer into the line bit pattern. As pixels in a line are drawn, the index is incremented until the end of the pattern is reached; then it is reset to the beginning of the pattern.

If the size of the parameter block is 2, then the additional word is used to supply the count for the pattern. This value must be greater than or equal to 0, and less than the pattern size.

If this function is called without a prior HSLPC, the default device value is used.

The related function is HSLPC.

HRPAL

Restores a previously saved palette. The parameter information is as follows:

Byte offset	Type and value	Description
0	WORD = Special	Size of the remaining parameter block
2	BYTE	The palette data

This function restores to the board the palette located in the parameter block. The size of the palette save area is determined by a call to HQDPS. The palette is saved in the save area by the HSPAL call.

The related function is HSPAL.

HRPEL

Reads a string of pixels at a specified position. The parameter information is as follows:

Byte offset	Type and value	Description
0	WORD = 10	Size of remaining parameter block
2	FARPTR	Address of buffer for read pixel data
2	WORD	X
4	WORD	Y
6	WORD	Pixel Count

This function will read the pixel data from display memory specified by the given position and the count of pixels. The pixel data is placed, in a packed pixel format, into the buffer indicated in the parameter block. Pixels are read in the direction of an increasing X.

The maximum number of bytes that can be read is 16,384.

This function is available only in the XGA and Image Adapter/A AIs.

The related function is HPEL.

HRSTEP

Reads short stroke-style data starting at given position. The parameter information is as follows:

Byte offset	Type and value	Description
0	WORD = 12	Size of remaining parameter block
2	WORD	X
4	WORD	Y
6	FARPTR	Address of short stroke-style data
10	FARPTR	Address of read pixel data buffer

This function will read the pixel data specified by a sequence of short stroke-style vectors, starting at the given position, using coding information identical to the short-stroke vector requirements of the 8514/A and XGA subsystems.

The short stroke data is contained in the first specified buffer, and each byte in the buffer has the following format:

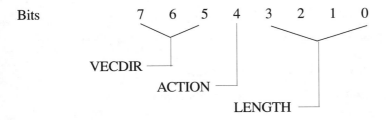

VECDIR is the direction of the short stroke vector in degrees, as measured counter-clockwise from the positive X axis. The values are defined as follows:

Bit 7	Bit 6	Bit 5	Direction in degrees (counter-clockwise from positive X axis)
0	0	0	0
0	0	1	45
0	1	0	90
0	1	1	135
1	0	0	180
1	0	1	225
1	1	0	270
1	1	1	315

ACTION determines whether only the current position is moved or pixels are drawn as well.

0	Move current position without reading data.
1	Read the pixel data under the vector and move the current position.

LENGTH is the length of the vector in pixels, and ranges from 0 to 15 in value.

The data in the buffer is terminated by a byte of 0.

The secondary buffer is used to contain the read color information for each pixel selected by this function. The data that is stored in the buffer is in a packed pixel format, with the number of pixels in this buffer matching the number selected (and passed over in the event of a "move" operation) by the function, to a maximum of 4095 bytes.

This function, when combined with the HPSTEP or HCSTEP functions, can be used to save and restore arbitrary portions of the display memory of the graphics device.

This function is available only in the XGA and Image Adapter/A AIs.

Related functions are HCPSTEP, HSCMP, HSCOL, HSHS, HSLT, and HSMX.

HRWVEC

Reads/writes polyline vector draw data. The parameter information is as follows:

Byte offset	Type and value	Description
0	WORD 0	Size of remaining parameter block
2	BYTE	Flags
3	BYTE	Reserved (set to 0)
4	FARPTR	Address of data buffer
8	WORD	X0
10	WORD	Y0
12	WORD	X1
14	WORD	Y1
.		
.		
.		
n*4+8	WORD	Xn
n*4+10	WORD	Yn

This function can be used to read or write the individual pixel data for the supplied polyline.

The flag byte determines whether this is a read or write operation:

Bit	Description
7	0 = Read data; 1 = Write Data
6-0	Reserved (set to zero)

For read operations, each pixel that the polyline-drawing algorithm would normally draw is instead read into the specified data buffer, in a packed pixel format.

For write operations, the specified data buffer contains the pixel data for each individual pixel drawn via the device's line-drawing algorithm. A source pixel data value of 0 indicates that the background mix should be used, while all other pixel values imply foreground mix.

The maximum amount of data to be read or written is 4095 bytes. For write operations, the last pixel of each vector in the polyline is not drawn, and the current position is set to the last position specified by the parameter block.

This function is available only in the XGA and Image Adapter/A AIs.

Related functions are HCLINE, HLINE, HSBCOL, HSCMP, HSCOL, HSHS, and HSMX.

HSAFP

Sets area fill plane. The parameter information is as follows:

Byte offset	Type and value	Description
0	WORD = 5	Size of remaining parameter block
2	DWORD	Address of the area fill plane
6	BYTE	Reserved (must be 080H)

This function sets the area fill plane buffer address for use with area fill, raster text, and marker operations. This call needs to be made only if the default bitmap has been altered via the HSBMAP function.

The address is a linear byte offset from the start of display memory, and must be on a 32-bit boundary (that is, it must be a multiple of 4 bytes).

Whether or not an area fill plane needs to be defined can be determined via the HQMODE function, while the amount of space required by the area fill plane can be determined by calling HQDPS.

This function is available only in the XGA and Image Adapter/A versions of the AI.

Related functions are HQDPS, HQMODES, and HSBMAP.

HSBCOL

Sets the background color. The parameter information is as follows:

Byte offset	Type and value	Description
0	WORD = 4	Size of the remaining parameter block
2	DWORD	The color

This function sets the background color on the XGA. Currently, only the *x* least significant bits (where *x* is the number of bits per pixel for the current mode) of the color value are used. Note that color 0FFFFFFFFH is a reserved value, used for color fonts.

The related function is HSCOL.

HSBMAP

Sets current bitmap and its attributes. The parameter information is as follows:

Byte offset	Type and value	Description
0	WORD = 10	Size of remaining parameter block
2	BYTE	Flags
3	BYTE	Bitmap depth
4	DWORD	Address of bitmap
8	WORD	Width of bitmap (in pixels)
10	WORD	Height of bitmap (in lines)

This function sets the current bitmap to be used for all subsequent drawing operations. In the 8514/A AI, you could access display memory only as a fixed entity. With the Image Adapter/A and XGA devices, the display and display memory are no longer tied together, so it's possible to draw in off-screen memory, as well as in a bitmap that does not necessarily have the same depth as the displayed bitmap. To encompass this new hardware capability, this function has been added to post-8514/A versions of the AI.

The flag byte has the following meaning:

Bit	Description
7	Reserved (must be 1)
6	0 = Non-screen bitmap; 1 = Screen bitmap
5-0	Reserved (must be 0)

Valid bitmap depths are 1, 2, 4, and 8.

The address of the bitmap is the linear byte offset of the beginning of the bitmap from the beginning of the graphics device's display memory, and must be a multiple of 8 bytes for screen bitmaps, and a multiple of 4 bytes for non-screen bitmaps. The same applies to the bitmap width; that is, it must be a multiple of 8 bytes wide (multiple of 8 pixels in an 8bpp bitmap, multiple of 16 pixels in a 4bpp bitmap, and so on) for a screen bitmap, and a multiple of 4 bytes in a non-screen bitmap.

The maximum width and height of the bitmap are 2048 pixels and 2048 lines.

This function also resets the current position to 0,0 (relative to the newly defined bitmap), resets the clipping rectangle to the size of the bitmap, and enables all planes for update (see the HSBP function), but does not clear the bitmap memory.

This function is available only in the XGA and Image Adapter/A AIs.

Related functions are HQBMAP, HSAFP, HSDW, and all drawing functions.

HSBP

Enables/disables bit planes for updating and displaying. The parameter information is as follows:

Byte offset	Type and value	Description
0	WORD = 12 or 26	Size of the remaining parameter block
2	DWORD	Plane enable for graphics
6	DWORD	Plane enable for alphanumerics
10	DWORD	Plane enable for display
14	BYTE	Flags (reserved, must be set to 0)
15	BYTE	Reserved (set to 0)*

continued...

...from previous page

Byte offset	Type and value	Description
16	DWORD	Green bits mask*
20	DWORD	Red bits mask*
24	DWORD	Blue bits mask*

* Available only in the XGA and Image Adapter/A versions of the AI.

This function can be used to disable planes from being written or displayed. Each bit in the plane determines the access or display of a plane. In a 4 bit per pixel mode, only the low order four bits are valid, and in an 8 bit per mode, the low order eight bits are valid. If the bit corresponding to a particular plane is set, access to that plane is enabled. This function overrides all other graphical modifiers, including mixes and the color compare.

Byte offset 2 (plane enable for graphics) controls all writes to the graphics device memory for drawing and regular text operations.

Byte offset 6 (plane enable for alphanumerics) controls all writes to display memory for all alphanumeric operations.

Byte offset 10 (plane enable for display) controls which planes are displayable on the attached monitor.

The three primary color bit masks are used when a fixed palette is being emulated in software (i.e., emulating a Direct Color 3:3:2) fixed palette while in an 8bpp display mode). By setting the proper bits in each color bits mask, arithmetic mix operations will operate properly for each color component of the pixel without overflowing or underflowing into adjacent color components within the pixel.

You should note that these plane enables in no way prevent you from reading the contents of display memory, and that they all default to having all valid planes enabled.

HSCMP

Sets color compare information. The parameter information is as follows:

Byte offset	Type and value	Description
0	WORD = 5	Size of the remaining parameter block
2	DWORD	Color compare color
6	BYTE	Compare logic

This function will set the color compare color and compare logic. The purpose of the color compare is to provide a diverse mechanism that allows certain color values in display memory to be excluded from updates, based on a color value and a logical comparison with that color. If the result of the operation is true, then the pixel in memory is left unmodified.

The compare logic field contains information on what type of comparison should be performed with the color compare color (CC) and the destination pixel's color. The operations are defined as:

Value	Operation
0	TRUE
1	Destination > CC
2	Destination == CC
3	Destination < CC
4	FALSE
5	Destination CC
6	Destination != CC
7	Destination CC

Color compares do not work with alphanumeric commands.

HSCOL

Sets the foreground color. The parameter information is as follows:

Byte offset	Type and value	Description
0	WORD = 4	Size of the remaining parameter block
2	DWORD	The color

This function sets the foreground color on the XGA. Currently, only the x least significant bits (where x is the number of bits per pixel for the current mode) of the color value are used. Note that color 0FFFFFFFFH is a reserved value, used for color fonts.

The related function is HSBCOL.

HSCOORD

Sets coordinate types. The parameter information is as follows:

Byte offset	Type and value	Description
0	WORD = 3	Size of the remaining parameter block
2	BYTE	Absolute coordinate format
3	BYTE	Relative coordinate format
4	BYTE	Number of dimensions

This function sets the coordinate type for the adapter to use. The validity of the request should be determined by first calling HQCOORD with the data in the parameter block.

The absolute coordinate format specifies the amount of space consumed by absolute coordinates:

Bits	Definition
7–4	Number of bytes in each coordinate. Default = 2.
3–0	Number of fractional bytes per coordinate. Default = 0.

The relative coordinate formate specifies the amount of space consumed by relative coordinates:

Bits	Definition
7–4	Number of bytes in each coordinate. Default = 1.
3–0	Number of fractional bytes per coordinate. Default = 0.

The number of dimensions can be two, three, or four. The XGA AI supports only two dimensions at present.

The result field is set based on the interpretation of the other parameters by the AI:

Bit	Definition
7	If set, the absolute coordinate format requested is not supported
6	If set, the relative coordinate format requested is not supported
5	If set, the number of dimensions requested is not supported
4–0	Reserved

Note: In the current XGA AI, this call is ignored.

The related function is HQCOORD.

HSCP

Sets current position. The parameter information is as follows:

Byte offset	Type and value	Description
0	WORD = 4	Size of the remaining parameter block
2	WORD	New X position
4	WORD	New Y position

This function sets the current position for drawing functions to X, Y.

The related function is HQCP.

HSCS

Defines character set. The parameter information is as follows:

Byte offset	Type and value	Description
0	WORD = 4	Size of the remaining parameter block
2	FARPTR	Address of font definition.

This function defines which character set is to be used by the normal text functions.

The font definition, whose address is required by this function, can be one of three different font types: monochrome bitmapped, color bitmapped, and short stroke vector. For an example of how to use the latter with the regular text functions, refer to Chapter 7. For more detailed information about the font structure and definitions, refer to Appendix J.

Once this function is called, the font definition data area should not be changed in any way, since the AI may have extracted information from it. If you do need to change such data, call the HSCS function after such changes have been made.

Related functions are HCCHST, HCHST, and HXLATE.

HSDW

Sets display window. The parameter information is as follows:

Byte offset	Type and value	Description
0	WORD = 8	Size of remaining parameter block
2	WORD	X of new display origin
4	WORD	Y of new display origin
6	WORD	Window height
8	WORD	Window width

This function will set the display origin and size, to allow for panning and roaming within the graphics device's display memory.

The display origin is specified as the point in the current bitmap that is to appear in the upper-left corner of the display. The X position of the new display origin must be specified as a multiple of 8 bytes (8 pixels in 8bpp mode, 16 pixels in 4bpp mode, and so forth).

This function is available only in the XGA and Image Adapter/A AIs.

Related functions are HQBMAP, HSBMAP, HSMODE.

HSFPAL

Saves full palette. The parameter information is as follows:

Byte offset	Type and value	Description
0	WORD = Special	Size of remaining parameter block
2	WORD	Format (set to 8)
4	BYTE	The palette data

This function saves the full palette and display mask from the board to the parameter block. The size of the palette-save area is determined by a call to HQDPS. The palette is saved in the same format required for restoration by the HRFPAL command.

This function should be used over the HRPAL and HSPAL functions, since it saves the full palette, not just the most significant 6 bits of each entry.

This function is available only on XGA and Image Adapter/A versions of the AI. Related functions are HRFPAL, HRPAL, HSPAL.

HSGQ

Sets graphics quality information. The parameter information is as follows:

Byte offset	Type and value	Description
0	WORD = 2	Size of the remaining parameter block
2	WORD	Graphics quality flags

This function sets various internal AI flags that determine the quality of output. The definition of the flag's bits is:

Bit(s)	Definition
15	Reserved (set to 0)
14	0 = High precision, 1 = Low precision. Determines whether the AI or adapter approximates objects, thus drawing them faster, or performs calculations to draw objects to the nearest pixel position. This operation is ignored in the XGA AI, but set it to 0.
13	Reserved (set to 0)
12–11	00B = Last pixel in a line is not drawn 01B = Last pixel in a line is drawn 10B = Last pixel in a line is conditionally drawn

In the latter case, the issue of whether or not the last pixel in a line is drawn depends on the mix mode. In the following mix modes, the last pixel is drawn (Dst refers to the pixel in display memory, and Src is the pixel intended to update display memory):

Dst = 0

Dst = 1 (all bits set)

Dst = Dst

Dst = NOT Src

Dst = Src

Dst = NOT Src OR Dst

Dst = Src OR Dst

continued...

...from previous page

                Dst = Src AND Dst

                Dst = NOT Src AND Dst

                Dst = MINIMUM(Src, Dst)

                Dst = MAXIMUM(Src, Dst)

                Dst = Dst - Src [with saturate]

10   0 = Automatically close areas to be filled by connecting the first point to the last via a line.

               1 = Don't close areas to be filled, up to the application.

9–0   Reserved (set to 0)

HSHS

Sets the clipping rectangle. The parameter information is as follows:

Byte Offset	Type and Value	Description
0	WORD = 0, 8, or 13	Size of the remaining parameter block
2	WORD	Left limit (low X)
4	WORD	Right limit (high X)
6	WORD	Bottom limit (high Y)
8	WORD	Top limit (low Y)
10	FARPTR	Address of mask map*
14	BYTE	Reserved (must be set to 80H)*

* This function is valid only in the XGA version of the AI.

This function sets the XGA hardware clipping rectangle. The purpose of the clipping rectangle is to prevent drawing commands from drawing outside of a specific area.

If the parameter size field is 0, the default clipping rectangle is set. If the parameter field is 8, the specified limit values are used. If the left limit is greater than the right limit, or the top limit is greater than the bottom limit, nothing will be drawn.

Pixels that lie on the clipping rectangle boundary are drawn.

If the parameter size field is 13, then a mask map can be specified, in the dimensions specified by the clipping limits. The mask map is monochrome, with each 1 bit allowing the data in the device relative to that position to be updated. A 0 bit in the mask map prevents the corresponding destination pixel from being updated.

HSLPC

Saves the line pattern count. No parameters are required:

Byte offset	Type and value	Description
0	WORD = 0 or 2	Size of the remaining parameter block
2	WORD	Word area to store line pattern count in.*

* This field is available only in the XGA and Image Adapter/A versions of the AI.

This function saves the line pattern count for later use by the HRLPC command.

The line pattern count is a pointer into the line bit pattern. As pixels in a line are drawn, the index is incremented until the end of the pattern is reached, in which case it is reset to the beginning of the pattern.

If the parameter block size is 2, then this function will save the line pattern count in the work at offset 2 in the parameter block.

The related function is HRLPC.

HSLT

Sets the line drawing type. The parameter information is as follows:

Byte offset	Type and value	Description
0	WORD = 1 or 6	Size of the remaining parameter block
2	BYTE	Line pattern type
3	BYTE	Reserved
4	FARPTR	Address of user defined pattern

This function sets the line pattern to be used for drawing. The line pattern type is one of the following:

Value	Type and pattern
0	Use user-defined pattern (see below)
1	Dotted line: 1 On, 2 Off
2	Short dashed line: 5 On, 3 Off
3	Dash-dot line: 6 On, 4 Off, 2 On, 4 Off

continued...

...from previous page

4	Double dotted line: 2 On, 4 Off, 2 On, 8 Off
5	Long dash line: 9 On, 3 Off
6	Dash double dot line: 8 On, 4 Off, 2 On, 4 Off, 2 On, 4 Off
7	Solid line
8	Invisible line
9	Dotted line #2: 1 On, 1 Off*

* This option is available only in the XGA and Image Adapter/A versions of the AI.

The user-defined line pattern data consists of a number of byte pairs, the first of which indicates an "On" count of pixels, and the second of which is the "Off" count. The byte pairs are preceded by a word that indicates the number of pairs following it. The XGA AI allows for a user-defined pattern up to 48 pixels long. The format is:

Byte offset	Type	Description
0	WORD	Byte pair count (n)
2	BYTE	"On" count
3	BYTE	"Off" count
.		
.		
.		
n * 2 + 2	BYTE	"On" count
n * 2 + 3	BYTE	"Off" count

This function resets the line pattern count.

Related function are HRLPC, HSLPC.

HSLW

Sets the line drawing width. The parameter information is as follows:

Byte offset	Type and value	Description
0	WORD = 1	Size of the remaining parameter block
2	BYTE	Line width

This function sets the line width to be used for line drawing.

The XGA AI supports line widths of only 1 or 3 pixels. If the width is specified as 0 or 1, 1 is used. For a specified width greater than 1, a pixel width of 3 is used.

A line of width 3 is thickened by drawing an extra line to the left and right or above and below, depending on the angle of the line.

HSMARK

Defines a marker. The parameter information is as follows:

Byte offset	Type and value	Description
0	WORD = 10 or 14	Size of the remaining parameter block
2	BYTE	Mark width (in pixels)
3	BYTE	Mark height (in lines)
4	BYTE	Flags
5	BYTE	Reserved
6	WORD	Size of mark definition data
8	FARPTR	Address of mark definition
12	FARPTR	Address of mark color data

This function defines the marker used by the marker drawing commands. A marker is a rectangular block of binary data. The definition of the marker starts with bit 7 of the first byte in the block, and proceeds with sequential bytes until the entire marker is defined. There is no padding between the rows. The color data, if specified, consists of 1 byte containing a color value for each pixel in the marker definition (or as many pixels per byte as will fit, if selected via the flags below), regardless of bit pattern in the binary definition.

The flags are defined as follows:

Bit	Definition
7	0 = Use monochrome definition, 1 = Use color definition
6	For color data: 0 = 1 pixel per byte, 1 = packed pixel format*
5–0	Reserved (set to 0)

* Supported only by XGA and Image Adapter/A AIs.

The size of monochrome mark definition data is calculated by the following formula:

```
Size = ((Width * Height) + 7) / 8.
```

Related function are HCMRK and HMRK.

HSMODE

Sets a new mode. The parameter information is as follows:

Byte offset	Type and value	Description
0	WORD = 1 or 2	Size of the remaining parameter block
2	BYTE	Mode number
3	BYTE	Clear memory flag

This function sets a new mode for the XGA to operate in. Valid mode numbers are:

Mode	Screen size	Alpha text size	Text resolution
0	1024x768	12x20	85x38
1	640x480	8x14	80x34
2	1024x768	8x14	128x54
3	1024x768	7x15	146x52

If the parameter block size is 2, then the clear memory flag can be used to protect the XGA's display memory. A 00H means "clear all memory when this function is called," while an 80H will prevent the memory from being cleared.

All other modes are reserved for future use.

A call to this function resets the character grid origin to 0,0; resets the scissor/ clip rectangle to the size of the newly specified mode; sets the cursor to be invisible; resets the plane mask to its default; and sets the bits per pixel to the maximum supported by the mode/configuration.

Related functions are ASGO and HOPEN.

HSMX

Sets the mix modes. The parameter information is as follows:

Byte offset	Type and value	Description
0	WORD = 2	Size of the remaining parameter block
2	BYTE	Foreground mix
4	BYTE	Background mix

This function sets the foreground and background mix. A mix (also known as a raster operation) is used to logically or mathematically combine the source pixel (from the active color, PC data, or display data) with the destination pixel (the pixel already at the destination in display memory). The result of the mix is placed in the destination pixel position, pursuant to the setting of the plane enables, clipping rectangle, and color comparison. Valid mix values and their meanings are:

Mix value	Description
0	Keep existing mix
1	Src OR Dst
2	Src
3	Reserved
4	Src XOR Dst
5	Dst
6	MAXIMUM(Src, Dst)
7	MINIMUM(Src, Dst)
8	Src + Dst [with saturation]
9	Dst - Src [with saturation]
10	Src - Dst [with saturation]
11	(Src + Dst) / 2 [with overflow] (Average)
12	Reserved
13	Reserved
14	Reserved
15	Reserved
16	0, all bits cleared

continued...

...from previous page

17	Src AND Dst
18	Src AND NOT Dst
19	Src
20	NOT Src AND Dst
21	Dst
22	Src XOR Dst
23	Src OR Dst
24	NOT Src AND NOT Dst
25	NOT (Src XOR Dst)
26	NOT Dst
27	Src OR NOT Dst
28	NOT Src
29	NOT Src OR Dst
30	NOT Src OR NOT Dst
31	1, all bits set
32–255	Reserved

AND, OR, XOR, NOT are all bitwise binary operators. Saturate, as used above, means that the operations are bounded at 0 in the case of subtractions, or at the maximum pixel value (15 or 255) in the case of additions.

HSPAL

Saves the palette. The parameter information is as follows:

Byte offset	Type and value	Description
0	WORD = Special	Size of the remaining parameter block
2	BYTE	The palette data

This function saves into the parameter block the palette located on the board. The size of the palette save area is determined by a call to HQDPS. The palette is saved in a format appropriate for restoration using the HRPAL command.

The related function is HRPAL.

HSPATT

Defines an area pattern. The parameter information is as follows:

Byte offset	Type and value	Description
0	WORD=10 or 14	Size of the remaining parameter block
2	BYTE	Pattern width (in pixels)
3	BYTE	Pattern height (in lines)
4	BYTE	Flags
5	BYTE	Reserved
6	WORD	Size of pattern definition data
8	FARPTR	Address of pattern definition
12	FARPTR	Address of pattern color data

This function defines the pattern used by the area fill and rectangle drawing commands. An area pattern is a rectangular block of binary data. The definition of the pattern starts with bit 7 of the first byte in the block and proceeds with sequential bytes until the entire pattern is defined. There is no padding between the rows. The color data, if specified, consists of 1 byte containing a color value for each pixel in the pattern definition (unless the packed pixel mode is selected via the flags field; see below), regardless of bit settings in the binary definition.

The area pattern also has a reference point specified by the HSPATTO command.

The flags are defined as follows:

Bit	Definition
7	0 = Use monochrome definition, 1 = Use color definition
6	For color data: 0 = 1 pixel per byte, 1 = packed pixel format*
5–0	Reserved

* Supported only in XGA and Image Adapter/A AIs.

The size of the monochrome pattern definition data is calculated by the following formula:

```
Size = ((Width * Height) + 7) / 8
```

A solid fill pattern is specified by using a width and height of 1. The maximum pattern size is 32 by 32 for the 8514/A AI. There is no real limit in XGA and Image Adapter/A versions of the AI.

The related function is HSPATTO.

HSPATTO

Sets the pattern reference point. The parameter information is as follows:

Byte offset	Type and value	Description
0	WORD = 4	Size of the remaining parameter block
2	WORD	X
4	WORD	Y

This function sets the pattern reference point for functions that use the pattern. The reference point refers to the upper-left corner of the pattern.

The related function is HSPATT.

HSPRITE

Positions hardware sprite. The parameter information is as follows:

Byte offset	Type and value	Description
0	WORD = 4	Size of remaining parameter block
2	WORD	Display position of Sprite's X hot spot
4	WORD	Display position of Sprite's Y hot spot

Positions the hardware sprite's hot spot at the specified position on the display, relative to the origin of the display (0,0 in the upper left).

The sprite is defined and enabled/disabled via the HSSPRITE function.

This function is available only in the XGA version of the AI.

The related function is HSSPRITE.

HSSPRITE

Defines and enables/disables hardware sprite. The parameter information is as follows:

Byte offset	Type and value	Description
0	WORD = 1 or 24	Size of remaining parameter block
2	BYTE	Flags
3	BYTE	Reserved (set to 0)
4	BYTE	X hot spot offset
5	BYTE	Y hot spot offset
6	FARPTR	Address of sprite definition data buffer
10	WORD	Sprite width (in pixels)
12	WORD	Sprite height (in lines)
14	WORD	Color 0, red component
16	WORD	Color 0, green component
18	WORD	Color 0, blue component
20	WORD	Color 1, red component
22	WORD	Color 1, green component
24	WORD	Color 1, blue component

The sprite is enabled/disabled via the flag byte:

Bits	Description
7	0 = disabled; 1 = enabled (and visible)
6-0	Reserved (set to zero)

Once a sprite definition has been made, the sprite may be enabled or disabled by using a parameter block size of 1, and the appropriate flag byte.

The sprite must be a multiple of 4 pixels wide, and may be as large as 64x64 pixels in size.

The sprite data is defined as a 2bpp packed pixel bitmap, where each 2-bit pixel has the following definition:

Bit 1	Bit 0	Definition
0	0	Sprite color 0
0	1	Sprite color 1
1	0	Transparent (allows underlying pixel data to show through)
1	1	Complement (1's complement of underlying pixel data)

The sprite is positioned via the HSPRITE function.

This function is available only in the XGA version of the AI.

The related function is HSPRITE.

HSYNC

Synchronizes the AI with a task. The parameter information is as follows:

Byte offset	Type and value	Description
0	WORD = 2	Size of the remaining parameter block
2	WORD	Task buffer segment

This function updates the task dependent portion of the AI with the task information located at offset 0 of the segment specified in the parameter block. This command can be used to implement task switching.

The related function is HINIT.

HXLATE

Sets a translate table for multicolor text font. The parameter information is as follows:

Byte offset	Type and value	Description
0	WORD = 32	Size of the remaining parameter block
2	DWORD	8 color values

This function sets up a translation table for the multiplane bitmapped fonts (see Appendix J) you draw with the HCCHST and HCHST functions. Multiplane fonts can consist of eight different colors, and hence the 8 color values in the parameter block.

Chapter 7

Tutorial: the AI

Since it's difficult to determine how to properly use something like the AI without examples, this chapter will give a number of programming examples in C. We assume that you have a good understanding of C, and won't go over any of the basics here. All the code shown here was developed using Microsoft C v5.1; other C compilers may require minor changes in the code. If you would like the code in magnetic form and didn't purchase a disk with this book, you can find obtain the disk by calling MIS:Press customer service at 1-800-488-5233.

In addition to the C compiler, you need a couple of include files, AFIDATA.H and IBMAFI.H, and an object file, CALLAFI.OBJ, which is linked with all AI code. All three of these files are supplied with the IBM XGA adapter.

AFIDATA.H contains the data structures used to define the parameter blocks and things like the font file headers. I have provided my version of AFIDATA.H in Appendix L for your reference.

IBMAFI.H contains definitions for all the AI functions, as well as a line that includes ADIDATA.H. This means that your C source files need to have only the following line to be able to use the AI definitions:

```
#include "AFIDATA.H"
```

325

Make sure that both AFIDATA.H and IBMAFI.H are located in your include file directory so that the C preprocessor can locate them. A listing of my version of IBMAFI.H can be found in Appendix K.

CALLAFI.OBJ contains code that checks for the existence of the AI, as well as a routine that is used to make calls to the AI. My version of the source code, CALLAFI.ASM, is provided in Appendix M.

In the example code, I also use a slightly different convention of declaring and casting variables. The definitions for my convention are in Listing 7.1. I have found that this convention helps when communicating with assembly language subroutines and working under other operating systems, since you always know what size your parameters are (8, 16, or 32 bits). It also clarifies structure sizes.

Also, please note that all the code in this chapter is designed to work across the least common denominator, namely the 8514/A AI.

What's First?

With the IBM XGA, the supplied installation program will set up directories on your disk with the AI files and fonts. The AI is contained in a file called XGAAIDOS.SYS, and can usually be found in the \XGAPCDOS directory of your system. This program needs to be loaded prior to running any programs that use the AI (see Chapter 6).

The first thing your program needs to do when it wants to use the AI is to check that the AI is installed. You don't need to check for the presence of the graphics board, since the AI will not allow itself to be installed if an appropriate board isn't present.

The following code snippet will perform the check to see if the AI has been installed; getafi() is defined in CALLAFI.ASM.

```
/*
    Sample C code to determine if AI is loaded, and if so,
    get the pointer to the jump table. The jump table pointer
    is stored internal to the C binding.
*/
    if (!getafi())
        {
        printf("AI not loaded!\n");
        exit(1);
        }
```

Opening the Graphics Device

As discussed in Chapter 5, you treat the AI similar to the way you would deal with a disk file. The check for the AI above is like checking to see if the file you want to open exists. Once you have determined that it does, it's time to open it.

The first step in opening the AI is to use the HQDPS command to determine the sizes of the palette save area and the task state buffer. Using this information, blocks of memory can be allocated to store the data.

The next thing to do is actually open the AI for use, via the HOPEN command. The HOPEN command returns information that can be used to determine if any errors occurred while trying to open the AI.

The final step in getting the AI set up for general use is a call to the HINIT function, which loads the state information into the state buffer allocated earlier.

The definitions in Listing 7.1 are used in all the listings to reference certain data types. This is done to help make the code more readable, and to assist later translation and communication with assembly language.

Listing 7.1. Jake's C conventions (located in IBMAFI.H)

```
#define  FALSE      0
#define  TRUE       !(FALSE)
#define  BYTE       char
#define  WORD       short
#define  DWORD      long
#define  UBYTE      unsigned BYTE
#define  UWORD      unsigned WORD
#define  UDWORD     unsigned DWORD
#define  FAR        far
#define  HUGE       huge
#define  VOID       void
```

Listing 7.2. Opening the AI—SKELETON.C

```
/*

      This program can be run by compiling it with the following line
      CL SKELETON.C CALLAFI.OBJ

      Make sure to include a routine called DoSomething() in
      order to get a clean compile and see some results.

*/
/*─────────────────────────────────────


      Include file section

      Some of these are required by the examples in Chapter 7.

─────────────────────────────────────────*/

#include <stdio.h>
#include <stdlib.h>
#include <string.h>
#include <errno.h>
#include <fcntl.h>
#include <dos.h>
#include <conio.h>
#include <io.h>
#include <malloc.h>
#include <sys\types.h>
#include <sys\stat.h>
#include "ibmafi.h"     /* Used for AI info              */

/*─────────────────────────────────────


    Code

─────────────────────────────────────────*/
main(argc, argv)

WORD  argc;

BYTE  **argv;

{
```

```
/*
```

　　Allocate the data areas for the HQDPS, HOPEN, and HINIT
　　commands. The non-zero values for initialization are
　　the parameter block sizes as defined in Chapter 7. The
　　structure definitions for HQDPS_DATA, HOPEN_DATA, and
　　HINIT_DATA are located in AFIDATA.H.

```
*/

static HQDPS_DATA        stateInfo = { 6, 0, 0, 0 };

static HOPEN_DATA        openData = { 3, 0, 0 };

static HINIT_DATA        stateData = { 2, 0 };

/*
```

　　Allocate the data area for the HCLOSE command.

```
*/

static HCLOSE_DATA       closeData = { 2, 1 };

     BYTE FAR        *statAddr;    /* Pointer to task buffer */

   if(!getafi())                   /* Is AI loaded? */

       {

       printf("Error! No Adapter Interface Loaded.\n");

       exit(1);

       }
/*
```

　　Get the size of the state buffer. The C call "HQDPS" is
　　actually a macro definition in IBMAFI.H. This applies
　　to all the other AI calls as well.

```
*/
```

continued...

...from previous page

```
HQDPS(&stateInfo);

/*
    Use the state buffer size to dynamically allocate
    memory for the state buffer. The "+ 15" is necessary
    because HINIT requires the segment of the state buffer,
    and the buffer is assumed to start at offset 0 of that
    segment. By adding 15 to the size, we make sure that we
    have allocated enough space for the buffer even in the
    worst case situation in which the segment alignment is
    furthest off. Remember that segment alignment occurs at
    16 byte intervals where the linear address' least
    significant nibble is 0.

*/

statAddr = (BYTE FAR *) malloc(stateInfo.size + 15);

/*

    Get the segment of the state buffer. Make sure to
    account for an allocation that is not segment boundary
    aligned.

*/

stateData.segment = FP_SEG(statAddr) + ((FP_OFF(statAddr) + 15) >> 4);

/*

    Initialize the parameters for the HOPEN command and
    make the call. The HOPEN command opens the AI for use.
    After the call has returned, check the return flags for
    an error condition.
*/

openData.oflags = 0x00;

openData.mode = 0;    /* Set the 1024x768 mode */

HOPEN(&openData);
```

```
if (openData.iflags)

        {

        printf("An error occurred while trying to open the AI!\n");

        exit(2);

        }

/*

    No error occurred, so get the state information so we
    can start drawing.

*/

HINIT(&stateData);

/*

    The following call has been included to indicate that
    this is the point at which you can insert your own
    graphics code, or many of the examples in this chapter.

*/

DoSomething();

getch());           /* Wait until the display has been viewed */
    getch();
/*
    Now that we have done something, it's time to clean up
    after ourselves. This includes closing the AI and
    deallocating the state buffer.
*/
HCLOSE(&closeData);
free(statAddr);
return(0);

}
```

As you may notice from the code, several references are made to macros and structures defined in the IBM-supplied files. To make things easier, we have provided a better documented version of the macros and structures in Listing 7.3.

Listing 7.3. The structures and macros used in Listing 7.2

```
/*

    The following are the macro definitions used by the program in
Listing 7-2. The integer passed to "callafi" is the function number
for the given command. The "X" in the macro definition is a pointer
to the parameter block for the function being called.

*/

extern VOID FAR callafi(WORD, BYTE FAR *);

#define HQDPS(X)    callafi(31, (BYTE FAR *) X)

#define HOPEN(X)    callafi( 8, (BYTE FAR *) X)

#define HINIT(X)    callafi(48, (BYTE FAR *) X)

#define HCLOSE(X)   callafi(34, (BYTE FAR *) X)

/*

    Here we have the four different structures used in Listing 7.2. The
    complete list and definition of AI structures can be be found in
    Appendix L.

*/

typedef struct
    {
    UWORD       length;
    WORD            size;
    WORD            stack;
    WORD            palbufsize;
    } HQDPS_DATA;
```

```
typedef struct
    {
    UWORD       length;
    UBYTE       oflags;
    UBYTE       mode;
    UBYTE       iflags;
    } HOPEN_DATA;

typedef struct
    {
    UWORD       length;
    UWORD       segment;
    } HINIT_DATA;

typedef struct
    {
    UWORD       length;
    UBYTE       flags;
    } HCLOSE_DATA;
```

> **NOTE:** In the code in this chapter, we assume that the AI and the graphics board will properly support the 1024x768 mode, but that is not necessarily a good assumption. If you want to make sure that your AI programs work at any resolution, you should use the HQMODE command after HOPEN, to determine the current resolution. Once you have the resolution, your program should automatically adapt.

Closing the Graphics Device

Closing the AI is much easier than opening it, since only one call, namely to HCLOSE, is required. The use of the HCLOSE command is shown at the end of Listing 7.2.

Let's Get Graphical

Now you know everything you need to know about setting up an AI program. All that's left is putting some things up on the screen. Actually, it's not that trivial, but it is pretty straightforward. Before we actually start drawing, there are some things that need to be considered, namely environmental variables, such as color, mixes, color compares, plane masks, and clipping rectangles. Also not to be forgotten is the current drawing position.

Let's go through each of these.

Color

The color of a pixel depends on two things: the digital value of the pixel in memory, and the contents of the look-up table (LUT) for that value.

Using the AI, the value of the pixel is generally set using the HSCOL or HSBCOL commands. These commands set the color for future drawing commands. In a 4 bit per pixel (bpp) configuration, the color value can range from 0 to 15. In an 8bpp system, the values run from 0 to 255.

These color values are then run through the LUT and converted into three values: red, green, and blue. These three values control the intensities of the three respective color guns for a given pixel on the display. Figure 7.1 shows a diagram of this operation.

The default palette on the XGA has the first 16 entries set to the same IRGB combination used in color text modes, and the remaining 240 entries are set up in a similar pattern (see below for a list). The AI palette functions are HLDPAL, HRPAL, and HSPAL. Drawing colors are selected by HSCOL and HSBCOL, for foreground and background colors, respectively.

What this all boils down to is that you can assign a specific color to a pixel value. The color applies to all pixels of that value on the screen.

All other operations, such as HSMIX, HSCMP, and HSBP, deal only with the value of a pixel, not its color.

The initial LUT definitions are listed in the following table.

Entry	**Color**
0	Black
1	Dark blue
2	Dark green
3	Dark cyan
4	Dark red
5	Dark magenta
6	Dark yellow/brown
7	Gray
8	Dark gray (almost black)
9	Bright blue
10	Bright green
11	Bright cyan
12	Bright red
13	Bright magenta
14	Bright yellow
15	White
16–31	Dark blue
32–47	Dark green
48–63	Dark cyan
64–79	Dark red
80–95	Dark magenta
96–111	Dark yellow/brown
112–127	Gray
128–143	Dark gray (almost black)
144–159	Bright blue
160–175	Bright green
176–191	Bright cyan
192–207	Bright red
208–223	Bright magenta
224–239	Bright yellow
240–255	White

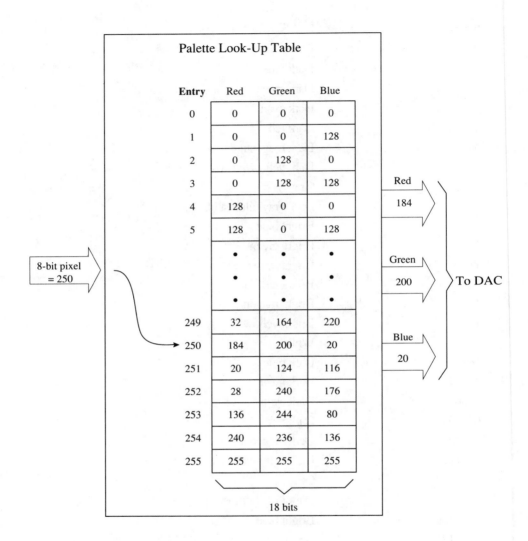

Figure 7.1. This figure shows how the palette Lock-Up Table (LUT) works inside a RAMDAC chip. In this example, the LUT is processing 8-bit pixels, with the current pixel having a value of 250. The pixel value is then used as an index (or "look up") into the LUT. The LUT, in turn, sends out the red, green, and blue data corresponding to the entry. These RGB digital levels are then translated in analog signals by the DAC.

Mixes

Mixes are used to manipulate the values of pixels before they are placed in display memory. Many operations can be performed on the pixel (see the explanation of the HSMX function in Chapter 6). When the AI is initialized (via HINIT), the foreground mix is set to replace/overpaint mode, and the background mix is left alone.

Color Compares

The color compare function built into the XGA and supported by the AI allows for specific pixels in display memory to be excluded from updating. The pixels protected in this way are selected by a comparison to the color compare value. The color compare takes precedence over the mix operation on a pixel. In other words, if the result of the color compare operation is such that a pixel can be updated, then the result of the mix operation is placed in that pixel. The color compare value is not set at initialization of the AI, but the color compare function is set to FALSE to enable the update of all pixel values. See the section on the HSCMP function in Chapter 6 for a more detailed explanation.

Plane Masks

Plane masks, specifically the write mask, also affect how pixels are updated in display memory. The write mask affects updates to display memory by controlling the ability to update the individual planes of a pixel (see the description of HSBP in Chapter 6). The write mask is set to all planes enabled upon AI initialization.

Clipping Rectangles

A clipping rectangle allows a program to limit the update of display memory to a specific rectangular subset of memory. This is very useful in windowing environments, since it ensures that drawing operations won't extend beyond the clipping rectangle (see HSHS in Chapter 6). When the AI is initialized, the clipping rectangle is set to the screen dimensions.

Current Position

As with many graphics interfaces, the AI supports both relative and absolute X, Y addressing of display memory. Relative points are signed 8-bit values, relative to the current position. The current position is set directly by the HSCP command, or indirectly by a number of drawing commands. It may also help to review the coordinate system used by the XGA & AI, described in Chapter 6. The current position is initialized to 0, 0.

For more information on how things are initialized by the AI, refer to the description of HINIT in Chapter 6.

Back to the Drawing Board

Now that we have covered the operation environment for drawing functions, lets look at some of these functions.

Line Drawing

Drawing lines is the first thing most people want to try on a graphics board, and we won't divert that instinct. Lines are easy to draw using any of four AI commands: HLINE, HCLINE, HCRLINE, and HRLINE. The *C*s in the command names indicate that they use the current position as the first point in the line, and the *R*s signify that those commands support relative coordinates. All four of these commands are polyline commands. That means that they can draw any number (less than 32K) of connected lines. Listing 7.4 shows four routines based on the four line commands that each draw a box at the point specified upon entry to the routine.

Listing 7.4. Four line drawing examples

```
/*─────────────────────────────────────

  DrawBox1(x, y)

  Draw a 10x10 box with the upper left corner at x,y using HCLINE.
  Assume CP is already set to x,y. Use current drawing environment.

─────────────────────────────────────*/

VOID  DrawBox1(x, y)
WORD  x, y;
{
    HCLINE_DATA(4)   line;              /* Define the data structure   */
    line.length = 16;                   /* 4 point pairs = 16 bytes    */
```

```
    line.coords[0].x_coord = x + 10;      /* Define the polyline        */
    line.coords[0].y_coord = y;           /* Upper right corner         */
    line.coords[1].x_coord = x + 10;
    line.coords[1].y_coord = y + 10;      /* Lower right corner         */
    line.coords[2].x_coord = x;
    line.coords[2].y_coord = y + 10;      /* Lower left corner          */
    line.coords[3].x_coord = x;
    line.coords[3].y_coord = y;           /* Back to upper left corner  */
    HCLINE(&line);                        /* Draw the box               */
    return;
}
/*————————————————————————————————

    DrawBox2(x, y)

    Draw a 10x10 box with the upper left corner at x,y using HCRLINE.
    Assume CP is already set to x,y. Use current drawing environment.

————————————————————————————————*/

VOID  DrawBox2(x, y)
WORD  x, y;
{
    static HCRLINE_DATA(4) lineCR =


                    {


                        8,                /* 4 relative point pairs     */
                    10,   0,              /* Upper right corner         */
                     0,  10,              /* Lower right                */
                   -10,   0,              /* Lower left                 */
                     0, -10,              /* Back to upper left         */
}
    HCRLINE(&lineCR);                     /* Draw the box               */
    return;
}
```

continued...

...from previous page

```
/*————————————————————————————

   DrawBox3(x, y)
   Draw a 10x10 box with the upper left corner at x,y using  HLINE.
   Use current drawing environment.
————————————————————————————*/

VOID  DrawBox3(x, y)

WORD  x, y;

{
    HLINE_DATA(4)  line;               /* Define the data structure     */
    line.length = 20;                  /* 5 point pairs = 20 bytes       */
    line.coords[0].x_coord = x;        /* Define the polyline            */
    line.coords[0].y_coord = y;        /* Upper left corner              */
    line.coords[1].x_coord = x + 10;
    line.coords[1].y_coord = y;        /* Upper right corner             */
    line.coords[2].x_coord = x + 10;
    line.coords[2].y_coord = y + 10;   /* Lower right corner             */
    line.coords[3].x_coord = x;
    line.coords[3].y_coord = y + 10;   /* Lower left corner              */
    line.coords[4].x_coord = x;
    line.coords[4].y_coord = y;        /*Back to upper left corner       */
    HLINE(&line);                      /* Draw the box                   */
    return;
    }

/*————————————————————————————

   DrawBox4(x, y)
   Draw a 10x10 box with the upper left corner at x,y using HRLINE.
   Use current drawing environment.
————————————————————————————*/

VOID  DrawBox4(x, y)

WORD  x, y;

{
    static HRLINE_DATA(4) lineR =
                    {
```

```
                    8,              /* 4 relative point pairs     */
             0,    0,              /* Starting position          */
            10,    0,              /* Upper right corner          */
             0,   10,              /* Lower right                 */
           -10,    0,              /* Lower left                  */
             0,  -10,              /* Back to upper left          */
            };
    lineR.coord1.x_coord = x;
    lineR.coord1.y_coord = y;       /* Set the starting point      */
    HRLINE(&lineR);                 /* Draw the box                */
    return;
}


/*—————————————————————————————

    DoSomething()
    Code called from the AI skeleton code in Listing 7-2 (SKELETON.C)
    Draws boxes using the four box routines.
    ——————————————————————————————*/
VOID  DoSomething()
{
    HSCP_DATA    hscp;
    HSCOL_DATA   hscol;
    hscp.length = 4;                /* 2 point pairs = 4 bytes      */
    hscol.length = 4;               /* Color is 32 bits             */
    hscol.index = -1;               /* Set color to all bits set,   */
    HSCOL(&hscol);                  /*   means white in normal palette*/
    hscp.x_coord = 50;
    hscp.y_coord = 50;              /* Initial box position          */
    HSCP(&hscp);
    DrawBox1(50, 50);               /* Box using HCLINE              */
    hscp.x_coord = 70;              /* Second box position           */
    HSCP(&hscp);
    DrawBox2(70, 50);               /* Box using HCRLINE             */
    DrawBox3(50, 70);               /* Box using HLINE               */
    DrawBox4(70, 70);               /* Box using HRLINE              */
    return;
}
```

Note how the two relative commands can have their box-drawing information pre-defined. That's because of the way that relative coordinates operate. Also, DrawBox2(), which uses the HCRLINE function, doesn't actually require the start point as a parameter, since it draws relative to the current point. Finally, DrawBox1() also could have been recoded to use the HQCP command to get the current position, instead of requiring the position as a parameter.

These routines also demonstrate how dependent the AI is on the parameter blocks. In a situation where the same parameter block is going to be used over and over again, it's best to define it as a static or global and initialize as many fields as possible.

One thing you may notice in the AI command set is that there is no clear way to draw a single pixel. The easiest way to get around this problem is to use the line drawing routines to draw a one-pixel long line by specifying the same start and end point. It's not very efficient, but it's the quickest way to get it done in the AI.

The line commands also have a few line-specific modifiers, such as line pattern and line width.

The line width can be set (using the HSLW command) only to one or three pixels, and the three-pixel lines are not quite accurate, since they are drawn as three separate lines, set one pixel apart. This introduces errors when certain types of mixes are used, since there is usually some overlap between adjacent lines due to the pixel-oriented nature of the line drawing.

The line pattern is less flaky and more useful. The AI allows you to select eight different predefined line patterns, in addition to a user-defined pattern. These patterns can be selected using the HSLT command. As a line is drawn, a counter in the AI determines where in the pattern to read from for the next pattern information. When the counter reaches the end of the pattern, it cycles back to the beginning. This is important because some of the line drawing operations, namely HCRLINE and HRLINE, reset the counter to the start of the pattern, while the other line drawing functions continue using the counter from the previous operation. To preserve the counter, the AI has two functions, HRLPC and HSLPC, which restore and save the counter, respectively. One case in which you may want to do this is when highlighting a line-based object with "marching ants"—a line pattern that is continually shifting by one position.

Markers

Many graphics interfaces draw markers, which are graphical symbols that can be placed at any point. The symbol is defined with either a single-plane bitmap or a color bitmap that can be up 255 pixels square. The function used to define the symbol is HSMARK.

The marks are then BitBLTed onto the display with the HCMRK and HMRK. Both of these are actually polymark functions, and therefore multiple markers can be drawn with just one call.

Listing 7.5 shows how to use the marker commands. In the listing, we show only the use of monochrome bitmaps. Note that the most significant bit of the first byte is the first to be expanded and displayed. Color markers are left as an exercise to the reader.

Listing 7.5. Use of marks

```
/*————————————————————————————

    DoSomething()

    Code called from the AI skeleton code in Listing 7.1 (SKELETON.C)

    Defines a monochrome mark and draws it at points along a formula.
————————————————————————————————*/
VOID  DoSomething()
{
    static BYTE markBitmap[14][2] =
    {
                0xFF, 0xFF,  /* 1111111111111111 */
                0xC0, 0x03,  /* 1100000000000011 */
                0xA0, 0x05,  /* 1010000000000101 */
                0x90, 0x09,  /* 1001000000001001 */
                0x88, 0x11,  /* 1000100000010001 */
                0x87, 0xE1,  /* 1000011111100001 */
                0x84, 0x21,  /* 1000010000100001 */
                0x84, 0x21,  /* 1000010000100001 */
                0x87, 0xE1,  /* 1000011111100001 */
                0x88, 0x11,  /* 1000100000010001 */
                0x90, 0x09,  /* 1001000000001001 */
                0xA0, 0x05,  /* 1010000000000101 */
                0xC0, 0x03,  /* 1100000000000011 */
                0xFF, 0xFF   /* 1111111111111111 */
        };
```

continued...

...from previous page

```
HSMARK_DATA     hsMark;
HMRK_DATA(13)   marks;
HSCOL_DATA      hscol;
WORD            i, j;
hscol.length = 4;                            /* Color is 32 bits            */
hscol.index = 14;                            /* Set color to yellow         */
HSCOL(&hscol);                               /*  (in normal palette)        */
hsMark.length = 10;                          /* Size for monochrome mark    */
hsMark.width = 16;                           /* Width of the mark (in pixels) */
hsMark.height = 14;                          /* Height in lines             */
hsMark.flags = 0;                            /* Monochrome mark             */
hsMark.res = 0;                              /* Reserved words are always 0 */
hsMark.imlen = sizeof(markBitmap);           /* Length of mark data in bytes */
hsMark.image = (UBYTE FAR *)markBitmap;  /* Pointer to mark data        */
HSMARK(&hsMark);
marks.length = sizeof(marks) - 2;            /* Simple way to set length    */
j = 6;
i = 13;                                      /* Initialize some loop vars   */
while (i—)                                   /* Plot a facsimile of x**3    */
{
    marks.coords[i].x_coord = (j + 20) * 20;
    marks.coords[i].y_coord = j * j * j + 250;
}
HMRK(&marks);
return;
}
```

Rectangles

The XGA excels at a few drawing functions, and solid- and pattern-filled rectangles are among them. The AI command for drawing filled rectangles is HRECT. Area patterns are specified via the HSPATT and HSPATTO commands.

One thing you can use filled rectangles for is clearing the screen, or portions of it. If you want to clear the entire display, you may want to use the HEGS command. HEGS clears the display to 0, but just like HRECT, it has the drawback of being affected by the clipping rectangle and plane enable.

Listing 7.6 gives an example of how to fill solid and patterned rectangles.

Listing 7.6. Example of filled rectangles with and without patterns

```
/*————————————————————————

    DoSomething()
    Code called from the AI skeleton code in Listing 7-2 (SKELETON.C)
    Draws two rectangles, one solid filled and one pattern filled.
————————————————————————————*/
VOID  DoSomething()
{
                                        /* Psuedo-anti-aliased diamond   */
    static BYTE colorPattern[13][7] =
            {
            0, 0, 0, 9, 0, 0, 0,   /* ...B... */
            0, 0, 1, 9, 1, 0, 0,   /* ..bBb.. */
            0, 0, 9, 9, 9, 0, 0,   /* ..BBB.. */
            0, 1, 9, 9, 9, 1, 0,   /* .bBBBb. */
            0, 9, 9, 9, 9, 9, 0,   /* .BBBBB. */
            1, 9, 9, 9, 9, 9, 1,   /* bBBBBBb */
            9, 9, 9, 9, 9, 9, 9,   /* BBBBBBB */
            1, 9, 9, 9, 9, 9, 1,   /* bBBBBBb */
            0, 9, 9, 9, 9, 9, 0,   /* .BBBBB. */
            0, 1, 9, 9, 9, 1, 0,   /* .bBBBb. */
            0, 0, 9, 9, 9, 0, 0,   /* ..BBB.. */
            0, 0, 1, 9, 1, 0, 0,   /* ..bBb.. */
            0, 0, 0, 9, 0, 0, 0    /* ...B... */
            };
    HRECT_DATA      rect;
    HSCOL_DATA      hscol;
    HSPATT_DATA     pattInfo;
    HSPATTO_DATA    pattRef;WORD        i, j;
    hscol.length = 4;                   /* Color is 32 bits         */
```

continued...

...from previous page

```
hscol.index =  9;                        /* Set color to blue         */
HSCOL(&hscol);                           /*  (in normal palette)      */
rect.length = 8;
rect.width = 49;
rect.height = 42;                        /* Set fixed parts of rectangle  */
for (i = 0; i < 1000; i += 98)           /* Draw solid based checkerboard */
    for (j = 0; j < 700; j += 84)
       {
       rect.coord.x_coord = i;
       rect.coord.y_coord = j;
       HRECT(&rect);
       }
pattInfo.length = 14;                    /* Size for color pattern      */
pattInfo.width = 7;                      /* Width of the pattern (in pix)
*/
pattInfo.height = 13;                     /* Height in lines           */
pattInfo.flags = 0x80;                    /* Color patttern            */
pattInfo.reserved = 0;                    /* Reserved words are always 0  */
pattInfo.img_length = sizeof(colorPattern);                             /*
Size of pattern                  */
pattInfo.image = (UBYTE FAR *)colorPattern;                            /*
Pointer to pattern               */
HSPATT(&pattInfo);
pattRef.length = 4;
pattRef.coord1.x_coord = 0;               /* Reference is upper left corner */
pattRef.coord1.y_coord = 0;
HSPATTO(&pattRef);
for (i = 49; i < 1000; i += 98)           /* Used patterns in blank spots   */
for (j = 84; j < 700; j += 84)
        {
        rect.coord.x_coord = i;
        rect.coord.y_coord = j;
        HRECT(&rect);
        }
     return;
}
```

BitBLTs

Bit BLock Transfers (BitBLTs) are used to copy rectangular blocks of graphical data from one position to another. A proper BitBLT will handle overlap of the source and destination areas so that the source area will always be copied in full. Figure 7.2 shows some examples of how BLTs should and shouldn't work.

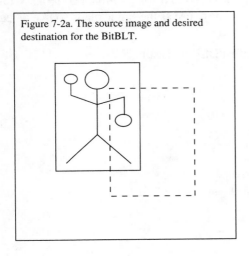

Figure 7-2a. The source image and desired destination for the BitBLT.

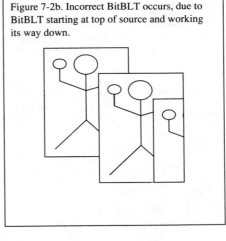

Figure 7-2b. Incorrect BitBLT occurs, due to BitBLT starting at top of source and working its way down.

Figure 7-2c. Correct BitBLT results from BitBLTting the source image from the bottom up.

Figure 7.2. How a BitBLT can go wrong if you don't take the direction of the BitBLT activity into account.

Two types of BLT operations are possible, all plane copy and single plane expansion. An all-plane copy BitBLT is what we would consider a normal BLT—all pixels from the source region are copied to the destination, persuant to the various mixes, clipping rectangles, and so forth.

A single plane expansion is generally used to take monochrome (single plane) data and expand it into the foreground color for bits that are set, and the background color for bits that are cleared. This capability is sometimes used to display bitmapped fonts. With respect to the AI, you must specify the source plane to use as the single plane source when doing the expansion BLT.

You will find an example of both types of BitBLTs in Listing 7.7 using the AI HBBC command.

Listing 7.7. Example usage of HBBC

```
/*────────────────────────────────

    DoSomething()
    Code called from the AI skeleton code in Listing 7.2 (SKELETON.C)
    Demonstrates the use of all plane and single plane BitBLTs.
────────────────────────────────*/
VOID  DoSomething()
{
    HRLINE_DATA(4)  lines =          /* Define the data structure    */
                        {
        14,                          /* 7 Points                     */
        0, 400,                      /* Initial point                */
        10,   0,   0,  10,           /* Top and right of box         */
        -10,  0,   0, -10,           /* Bottom and left of box       */
        10,  10,   0, -10,           /* First part of X, back to top */
        -10, 10                      /* Second part of X             */
        };
    HBBC_DATA     bltInfo;
    HRECT_DATA    rect;
    HSCOL_DATA    hscol;
    WORD          i, j;
    hscol.length = 4;                /* Color is 32 bits             */
```

```
rect.length = 8;
rect.width = 100;
rect.height = 100;                    /* Set fixed parts of rectangle   */
    /*
    Set up something that we can do an all plane BLT on. In this case,
    it's a 4x4 block of different colored rectangles.
*/

for (i = 0; i < 4; i++)
    for (j = 0; j < 4; j++)
        {
        hscol.index =  j * 4 + i;       /* Set color                      */
        HSCOL(&hscol);
        rect.coord.x_coord = i * 100;
        rect.coord.y_coord = j * 100;
        HRECT(&rect);                   /* Draw the rectangle             */
        }
bltInfo.length = 16;                    /* Size of HBBC parameter block   */
bltInfo.format = 8;                     /* All plane copy                 */
bltInfo.width = 400;                    /* Size of block                  */
bltInfo.height = 400;
bltInfo.plane = 0;                      /* Plane is irrelevant in all pln */
bltInfo.reserved = 0;                   /* Golden rule                    */
bltInfo.source.x_coord = 0;             /* Source block position          */
bltInfo.source.y_coord = 0;
bltInfo.dest.x_coord = 400;             /* Destination of BLT             */
bltInfo.dest.y_coord = 0;
HBBC(&bltInfo);                         /* Do the BitBLT                  */
    /*
Now we need to demonstrate the single plane expansion. Let's do so
by simulating a single plane source. We'll draw a box with an X in
it in plane 2, and then do a BLT expansion of the object into a
array of multi-colored versions of the object.
    */
```

continued...

```
hscol.index =  4;                      /* Set color for drawing plane 2  */
HSCOL(&hscol);
HRLINE(&lines);                        /* Draw the object                */
bltInfo.format = 0;                    /* Single plane expansion         */
bltInfo.width = 10;                    /* Size of object                 */
bltInfo.height = 10;
bltInfo.plane = 2;                     /* Plane is #2                    */
bltInfo.source.x_coord = 0;            /* Source block position          */
bltInfo.source.y_coord = 400;
    for (i = 0; i < 16; i++)
        for (j = 0; j < 16; j++)
        {
        hscol.index =  i;              /* Set foreground color           */
        HSCOL(&hscol);
        hscol.index =  j;              /* Set background color           */
          HSBCOL(&hscol);
        bltInfo.dest.x_coord = i * 10 + 100; /*Destination of BLT        */
        bltInfo.dest.y_coord = j * 10 + 400;
        HBBC(&bltInfo);                    /*Do the BitBLT                */
        }
    return;
}
```

Data Transfer

An extension of the XGA BitBLT function is the ability to transfer data to and from the XGA. The AI supports this functionality via HBBW, HCBBW, and HBBCHN for writing data to the board, and via HBBR and HBBCHN for reading data from the board. As with normal BitBLTs, these data transfer operations support the all-plane copy and single-plane expansion modes.

You may notice that HBBCHN is used for both reading and writing data. This is because these transfer operations are two step operations. The first step is the set-up of the operation—this is when HBBR, HBBW, or HCBBW are used. The second step is the use of the HBBCNH function, which actually does the transfer of data. The HBBCHN is used as often as needed to transfer all of the specified data. This is the only way to transfer bitmap information to or from the board.

An example of both reading and writing board data in the all-plane mode is given in Listing 7.8. The single plane version of this code is left as an exercise. A derivative of the code in Listing 7.8 can be used to load image files to the board.

Listing 7.8. Example of data transfer between PC and board

```
/*—————————————————————————————

   DoSomething()
   Code called from the AI skeleton code in Listing 7-2 (SKELETON.C)
   Demonstrates the use of all plane read and write transfers.
   ——————————————————————————————*/
VOID  DoSomething()
{
    HBBR_DATA        readInfo;
    HBBW_DATA        writeInfo;
    HBBCHN_DATA      chainInfo;
    HRECT_DATA       rect;
    HSCOL_DATA       hscol;
    WORD             i, j;
    UBYTE            *tmpBuffer;
    hscol.length = 4;                   /* Color is 32 bits            */
    rect.length = 8;
    rect.width = 10;
    rect.height = 10;                   /* Set fixed parts of rectangle */
/*
        Set up something that we can read from the board. In this case,
        it's a 4x4 block of different colored rectangles.
*/
for (i = 0; i < 4; i++)
    for (j = 0; j < 4; j++)
        {
        hscol.index =  j * 4 + i;      /* Set color                    */
        HSCOL(&hscol);
        rect.coord.x_coord = i * 10;
```

continued...

...from previous page

```
        rect.coord.y_coord = j * 10;
        HRECT(&rect);                      /* Draw the rectangle        */
        }
tmpBuffer = (BYTE *)malloc(40 * 40);    /* Allocate memory for storage  */
/*
    First we need to set up the read operation. This tells the AI
    and board how much data and what kind of data we want to read,
    as well as where we want to read it from. It is an option to read
    the data into a rectangular region in PC memory. For this example,
    we are just doing a simple transfer.
*/
readInfo.length = 12;                   /* Size of HBBR parameter block  */
readInfo.format = 8;                    /* All plane copy                */
readInfo.width = 40;                    /* Size of block                 */
readInfo.height = 40;

readInfo.plane = 0;                     /* Plane is irrelevant in all pln */
readInfo.reserved = 0;                  /* Golden rule                   */
readInfo.coord.x_coord = 0;             /* Source block position         */
readInfo.coord.y_coord = 0;
HBBR(&readInfo);                        /* Set up the Read operation     */

/*
    Next, we need to read the data from the board via the HBBCHN command.
    We'll do this one line at a time. A line is 40 pixels, ergo 40 bytes.
*/
chainInfo.length = 6;
chainInfo.len = 40;                     /* Non-changing info             */
for (i = 0; i < 40; i++)                /* Read all forty lines          */
    {
    chainInfo.address = (UBYTE FAR *)&tmpBuffer[i * 40];
    HBBCHN(&chainInfo);
    }
    if (!getch())
        getch();
/*
```

Now let's write the same back up to the board, but at a different
location. Again, we want to start with a command to tell the AI
that we want to start a write transfer. Data is referenced as
linear data, not rectangular, on the PC side. (We could have use
the "readInfo" structure here instead of the "writeInfo," since
they are identical.)
For a better effect, let's clear the screen first.
*/

```
HEGS();
writeInfo.length = 12;              /* Size of HBBW parameter block  */
                                    /* (Also means simple transfer)  */
writeInfo.format = 8;               /* All plane copy                */
writeInfo.width = 40;               /* Size of block                 */
writeInfo.height = 40;
writeInfo.plane = 0;                /* Plane is irrelevant in all pln */
writeInfo.reserved = 0;             /* Golden rule                   */
writeInfo.coord.x_coord = 200;      /* Source block position         */
writeInfo.coord.y_coord = 200;
HBBW(&writeInfo);                   /* Set up the write operation    */
/*
```

Next, we need to write the data to the board via the HBBCHN command.
This time we'll transfer it all at once.
*/

```
chainInfo.len = 40 * 40;            /* Buffer size                   */
chainInfo.address = (UBYTE FAR *)tmpBuffer;
HBBCHN(&chainInfo);                 /* Write it all                  */
/* (Also means simple transfer)       */
return;
}
```

Text

The AI supports text through three different font types: short stroke, monochrome bitmap, and
multiplane bitmap. Text can be displayed via the AI using one of two methods.

The first is using the normal text commands: HSCS, which is used to tell the AI about
a loaded font, and HCCHST and HCHST, which draw text strings. The normal text

commands allow for positioning of text at any pixel location. All text colors are controlled by the standard means, except for the multiplane bitmap fonts, whose color is specified by the HXLATE command.

The second method for displaying text involves the AI commands that start with "A." These are the alphanumeric commands. They are based on a specific font cell size, determined by the current mode (see HOPEN, HSMODE, and ASCELL). Using the cell size as a measure, the screen is then addressed as a series of character rows and columns. This limits the positioning of the text characters, but on the other hand, you can specify the colors and text attributes for each character that is displayed without having to use separate AI commands. This approach is somewhat similar to the way that the standard CGA, EGA, and VGA text modes work.

Therefore, we will concentrate on the normal text commands in our example, which can be found in Listing 7.9. The font loading routine is the same one you would use for loading the font for alphanumeric operations. This is because the fonts used for both display methods are identical, and as such, can be loaded in the same fashion.

Listing 7.9. Using fonts via the AI text routines.

```
/*————————————————————————

    LoadFont(name)
    This routine loads fonts from the files supplied by IBM with the XGA.
    The function requires the file name of the AI compatible font file, and
    if the font is successfully loaded, returns a pointer to the character
    set definition, as required by the AI. If the return value is 0, an
    error occurred while trying to load the file. Also, if you really want
    to be neat about things, the memory allocated for the font should be
    freed prior to exiting to DOS. Refer to Appendix J for more information
    on font files.
    NOTE: FFDEF and CHARSET are defined in our version of AFIDATA.H but not
          in IBMs.

————————————————————————*/

CHARSET  *LoadFont(name)
BYTE   *name;
{
static  FFDEF    *ioAddr;         /* Address to load font to    */
        UWORD    fontLen;         /* Size of font to load       */
        WORD     fontHdl;         /* Font file handle           */
        CHARSET  *pCSD;           /* Pointer to Char Set Def    */
```

```c
                                       /* Open the Font file            */
      if ((fontHdl = open(name, O_RDONLY|O_BINARY)) == -1)
        {
        printf("Could not open font file '%s'!!!\n", name);
        return(0);
        }
                                       /* Get size of font file         */
fontLen = (UWORD) lseek(fontHdl, 0L, SEEK_END);
ioAddr = (FFDEF *) malloc(fontLen);    /* Allocate enough space for file */
if (!ioAddr)
        {
        printf("Not enough memory to load font!\n");
        return(0);
        }
    lseek(fontHdl, 0L, SEEK_SET);       /* Return to start of file       */
read(fontHdl, (BYTE *)ioAddr, fontLen); /* Load the whole file into mem. */
                                       /* Point to start of def. font   */
pCSD = (CHARSET *) (((BYTE *) ioAddr) +
        ioAddr->page_array[ioAddr->def_page].csd_offset);
        /* Update all address fields with load address             */
pCSD->chardef1 = ((UBYTE FAR *) ioAddr) + ((DWORD) pCSD->chardef1);
pCSD->chardef2 = ((UBYTE FAR *) ioAddr) + ((DWORD) pCSD->chardef2);
pCSD->chardef3 = ((UBYTE FAR *) ioAddr) + ((DWORD) pCSD->chardef3);
pCSD->indextbl = (word FAR *)
        (((UBYTE FAR *) ioAddr) + ((DWORD) pCSD->indextbl));
    pCSD->enveltbl = ((UBYTE FAR *) ioAddr) + ((DWORD) pCSD->enveltbl);
    close(fontHdl);                     /* Close the font handle         */
    return(pCSD);                       /* Return pointer to the font    */
}

/*_____

   DoSomething()
   Code called from the AI skeleton code in Listing 7.2 (SKELETON.C)
   Demonstrates the use of the normal text commands.
_____*/
```

continued...

```
VOID  DoSomething()
{
    HSCS_DATA         setChar;
    HCHST_DATA(80)    strInfo;
    HSCOL_DATA        hscol;
    hscol.length = 4;                    /* Color is 32 bits            */
setChar.length = 4;                      /* Load the font - makes an    */
                                         /* assumption about file name  */
setChar.address = (CHARSET FAR *) LoadFont("\\hdipcdos\\stan1220.fnt");
HSCS(&setChar);                          /* Set the character set       */
hscol.index = -1;                        /* Default to white color      */
HSCOL(&hscol);
strInfo.coord.x_coord = 200;
strInfo.coord.y_coord = 100;             /* Let's put it some place     */
    /*
strcpy(strInfo.string, "Hello World!"); /*
Sample string :-)                        */
strInfo.length = strlen(strInfo.string) + 4; /* Sneaky way to get length */
HCHST(&strInfo);                         /* Display the string          */
```

NOTE: Short stroke fonts, which the FONT????.DLD files happen to
   contain, do not clear the background when displayed. This means that
   you need to do a filled rectangle to clear an area before displaying
   short stroke font characters. This can have some positive uses as
   well, especially if you don't want to alter the background of the
   character cell.
*/

```
    free(ioAddr);                        /* Free up the font buffer     */
    return;
}
```

Summary

In this chapter you learned how to begin using the AI in your graphics programs. If you
would like additional information, we recommend that you purchase the IBM documents listed in the bibliography and at the beginning of Chapter 6. The disk that comes
with the IBM Programmer's Guide contains a number of useful utilities that may aid
you in debugging your AI programs.

   If you are interested in using assembly language with the AI, refer to GETAFI.ASM,
shown in Appendix F.

Appendix A

Addresses

T his appendix contains the addresses and phone numbers of companies with XGA products and support mentioned in this book

Cirrus Logic, Inc.
3100 West Warren Avenue
Fremont, CA 94538
Telephone: 510/226-8300
FAX: 510/226-2250

IBM
1000 NW 51st Street
Boca Raton, FL 33429
Telephone: 407/443-2000

Integrated Information Technology, Inc.
2445 Mission College Blvd.
Santa Clara, CA 95054
Telephone: 408/727-1885
FAX: 408/980-0432

Panacea Inc.
Post Office Square
24 Orchard View Drive
Londonderry, NH 03053
Telephone: 603/437-5022
FAX: 603/434-2461

Radius, Inc.
1710 Fortune Drive
San Jose, CA 95131
Telephone: 408/434-1010

SGS-Thomson Microelectronics/Inmos
2055 Gateway Place, Suite 300
San Jose, CA 95110
Telephone: 408/452-9122
FAX: 408/452-0218

ULSI Systems
58 Daggett Drive
San Jose, CA 95134
Telephone: 408/943-0562
FAX: 408/943-0106

VESA
2150 N. First Street
San Jose, CA 95131
Telephone: 408/435-0333
FAX: 408/435-8225

VESA ® VXE 1.0 Standard

Video Electronics Standards Association

2150 North First Street, Suite 440
San Jose, CA 95131-2020

Phone: (408) 435-0333
FAX: (408) 435-8225

VESA XGA* Extensions Standard

Standard # VXE 1.0
May 8, 1992

PURPOSE

To standardize a software interface to XGA-compatible video subsystems, independent of the system bus type, in order to provide uniform driver and application access to XGA-compatible products.

SUMMARY

This standard defines a set of register and bit functions which allow software developers to write a single version of an application or driver for XGA-compatible video subsystems in EISA, Micro Channel Architecture® and ISA Personal Computer Systems. It also defines a set of functions accessible via INT 10h as an extension to the BIOS video services. The functions defined provide information about capabilities and characteristics of a specific hardware implementation and provide control of video mode setting and video buffer access. The defined functions explicitly do not address any drawing engine functionality.

Specific areas covered include bus master support for all three industry standard PC buses, video subsystem setup requirements, and issues related to multiple video subsystems. Special attention is given to ISA resource limitations with respect to XGA-compatible configurations.

VESA is a registered trademark of Video Electronics Standards Association.
*XGA is a registered trademark of International Business Machines Corporation.

Trademarks

The trademarks mentioned in this document are credited to the respective corporations listed below:

Trademark	Corporation
IBM®	IBM Corporation
VGA	IBM Corporation
XGA®	IBM Corporation
Micro Channel Architecture®	IBM Corporation
Personal System/2®	IBM Corporation
EISA	Compaq
Microsoft	Microsoft Corporation
MS-DOS	Microsoft Corporation
INMOS®	INMOS Limited
iAPX	Intel Corporation
VESA®	Video Electronics Standards Association

Revision History

1.0   Initial release: May 8, 1992

Table of Contents

1. Introduction

This document contains a specification for a standardized interface to XGA video modes and functions. The specification consists of mechanisms for supporting standard and extended video modes and functions that have been approved by the VESA General Membership, in a uniform manner that application software can utilize without having to understand the intricate details of the particular XGA hardware. In particular, the interface is intended to allow a single application or driver to run on the three standard PC platforms: ISA, EISA and Micro Channel Architecture.

The primary topics of this specification are the definitions of the interface to XGA video hardware and the definitions necessary for application software to understand the characteristics of the video modes and manipulate the memory associated with the video modes.

Readers of this document should already be familiar with programming XGAs at the hardware level and Intel iAPX real mode assembly language. Readers who are unfamiliar with programming the XGA should first read the *Update for the PS/2 Hardware Interface Technical Reference: Common Interfaces, Video Subsystems* published by IBM Corporation.

1.1. Recommended Reference Documents

EISA reference: *EISA Specification*, BCPR Services, 1201 New York Ave, N.W., Suite 1225, Washington, D.C. 20005; (202) 962-8349.

Micro Channel reference: *Update for the PS/2 Hardware Interface Technical Reference: Architectures*, September 1991 (IBM document number S04G-3282-00, may be obtained from (800) IBM-PCTB).

ISA reference: *IBM AT Technical Reference* (IBM document number 1502494).

Feature Connector references: *VESA 8514/A Standard* (VS890802) and *VGA Pass Through Connector Standard* (VS890803).

BIOS references: *Super VGA BIOS Extension* (VS911022) and *Super VGA Protected Mode Interface* (VS11020).

XGA and VGA references: *Update for the PS/2 Hardware Interface Technical Reference: Common Interfaces, Video Subsystems*, September 1991 (IBM document number S04G-3281-00, may be obtained from (800) IBM-PCTB).

1.2. Goals and Objectives

The IBM XGA has become the new high end graphics standard on the PS/2 platform. Several XGA-style graphics adapters will soon be coming to the marketplace, each one providing compatibility with the IBM XGA. These XGA-compatible products will implement various super sets of the XGA standard. These extensions range from higher resolutions and more colors to improved performance and support of other platforms besides the PS/2.

However, several problems face a software developer who intends to take advantage of these XGA graphics adapters. Because of the various hardware platforms, the developer is faced with disparate XGA implementations. Lacking a common software interface, designing applications for these environments would be costly and technically difficult. Except for applications supported by OEM-specific display drivers, very few software packages could take advantage of the power and capabilities of XGA products.

With the above issues in mind, the VESA XGA Technical Committee adopted the following set of objectives:

- Develop a standard for XGA-compatible subsystems on EISA, Micro Channel Architecture and ISA platforms.
- Remain IBM XGA-compatible.
- Provide equivalent functionality to IBM's Micro Channel based XGA.
- Provide a robust standard.
- Require only the minimum of environment specific software.
- Ensure that software which was written solely to the IBM XGA will operate, if possible.
- Allow expansion and product differentiation within the VESA XGA Standard.
- Define a standard access and/or ID function for any unique extensions or special requirements for any manufacturer.

2. Overview of Document

This document is broken into two major areas, including 1) the VESA XGA Hardware Specification and 2) the VESA XGA Real Mode BIOS Specification. The Hardware Specification is broken into XGA Architecture, Setup, EISA Systems, Micro Channel Systems, and ISA Systems sections. The Software Specification is broken into Software Goals and Objectives, OEM-Defined Mode Tags, and VESA XGA BIOS sections. This document also includes a Programming Considerations Appendix, an Adapter Identification Appendix and a Multiple Video Subsystem Appendix.

All addresses, register values and bit fields are in hexadecimal, unless otherwise noted. Byte order is low byte/high byte at increasing addresses. Bit definitions are assumed to start from zero (0). A logic high is defined as a one (1) and a logic low as zero (0). Reserved bits shown by a pound sign (#) **must** be read and have their values preserved during a write. Reserved bits shown by a dash (-) are reserved and should be written with a logic low, unless otherwise noted. Bits shown by a one (1) are reserved and must be written as a logic high.

I. VESA XGA Hardware Specification

3. XGA Architecture

3.1. Bus Architecture ID

Due to the differences among the three industry standard PC bus architectures, it may be necessary for software to identify the host bus at run time. The BIOS function calls defined in the XGA BIOS provide the necessary bus information. In addition, bits are provided in the XGA subsystem to identify the host bus type and width.

3.2. Hierarchical Compliance

VESA compliance requires compatibility with the IBM XGA as defined in IBM document number S04G-3281-00, with the exception of modifications defined in this specification, and one of the following two classes:

A. Products which are 100% IBM XGA-compatible, **with no extensions**, are not required to include the VESA items in section B below. These products must use the appropriate POS ID of the IBM XGA with which they are compatible.

OR

B. Compliance with all of the following:

1. The POS Enable mechanism defined for each bus type is required for that bus type. Only that mechanism required for a specific bus type may be used on that bus type.

2. The Micro Channel Architecture requires a unique POS ID number for each model of video subsystem. The POS ID number is assigned by IBM and may be obtained through VESA. A manufacturer's EISA and/or ISA products should use the same POS ID number as their corresponding Micro Channel Architecture products. Manufacturers without a Micro Channel Architecture POS ID should use the POS ID number of the IBM XGA product with which they are compatible.

3. External Memory Enable, POS 3 bit 1, is required.

4. VESA Manufacturer ID at POS Data 4, Index 1 is required and the value is assigned by VESA.

5. If the bytes at POS Data 4, Index 2 and XGA Index 75h do not contain ID information, these bytes must read back as zero (0).

6. The bits defined in the Auto Configuration register (XGA Index 4) are required. Not all bus types and sizes need to be supported.

7. DMA Channel Readback (XGA Index 74h) is required in ISA systems only. Not all DMA channels need to be supported.

8. XGA Index 76h and 77h are only used for manufacturer-specific extensions.

9. All XGA video subsystems supplied with a video BIOS must comply with the requirements in Section II, VESA XGA Real Mode BIOS Specification.

10. All XGA video subsystems supplied with a video BIOS must include four bytes of storage for the BIOS chain vector.

3.3. Manufacturer ID Mechanism

Each XGA video subsystem has up to seven bytes of manufacturer ID in hardware. The first two bytes are the POS ID at POS 0 and 1. IBM has allocated 1024 (1K) POS IDs for VESA-compliant Micro Channel XGA products.

VESA XGA POS IDs
0240h-027Fh
0830h-0A7Fh
0A90h-0BFFh

These IDs are available for Micro Channel systems only. Manufacturers developing Micro Channel and ISA/EISA subsystems must use the same ID for both systems. Assignment of POS IDs is controlled by IBM. IDs may be requested through VESA. Manufacturers designing only ISA/EISA subsystems should use the POS ID of the IBM XGA product with which they are compatible (8FD8h-8FDBh or 8FD0h-8FD3h).

Additional ID bytes are contained in POS 4, Index 1 and 2. Encoding for the ID byte at POS 4, Index 1 is assigned by VESA. The second ID byte is manufacturer-specific and optional. It is suggested that the silicon manufacturer use this byte to identify product type and revision. If this byte is not used, it must read back as zero (00h).

One or more bytes of subsystem vendor ID information is provided in the standard XGA index space (21xAh) at Index 75h. This byte is used for subsystem vendor identification and is assigned by the silicon supplier. If this byte is not used, it must read back as zero (00h). Two additional bytes at Indices 76h-77h are reserved for manufacturer-specific functions. These bytes are manufacturer-specific and optional.

4. Setup

The subsystem location mechanism is based on allowing the IBM-defined Micro Channel Architecture POS register definitions to be used in all three bus configurations. This allows a minimum of additional chip hardware and application software by encoding subsystem configuration information independently of the bus.

The extension registers in this document fall into several categories:

- Registers required to allow access to the POS information.
- Registers which contain configuration information required to support non-Micro Channel Architecture systems.
- Registers to support the identification of silicon manufacturer and subsystem vendor ID.

4.1. POS Mechanism

The POS Mechanism is used to locate the XGA subsystem in the system memory and I/O space. Registers are provided to control memory location and bus interface controls. These registers are enabled during the "setup" phase of system configuration and when software needs to determine the location of subsystem resources. The setup mechanism for each bus environment is as follows:

- Micro Channel Architecture: Use the IBM-prescribed method using the INT 15h BIOS call and register 94h to enable the POS registers.
- ISA: Use 108h-10Fh to enable the POS registers.
- EISA: Read the POS data from slot-specific addresses zC88h-zC8Fh or use the EISA Setup register to enable the POS registers.

4.2. Extension Register Descriptions

The following register descriptions list the extension registers for a VESA-compatible XGA subsystem. There has been no attempt to document registers which exist within an IBM XGA; therefore, all registers present in the IBM XGA documentation which are **not** described below are unchanged from the IBM XGA implementation. Also, these descriptions cover all system configurations (ISA, EISA, and Micro Channel Architecture) and a specific subsystem could omit registers or fields based on a desired configuration.

Extension registers have been added at POS Data 4, Indices 1-3 and to the XGA indexed registers at 21xAh, Indices 74h-77h. Indices 76h and 77h have been allocated for manufacturer expansion. Indices 72h and 73h are reserved for future expansion of the VESA XGA specification and may **not** be used for manufacturer expansion.

While they are not explicitly listed below, the POS registers implemented within the XGA are re-mapped to slot-specific addresses in EISA systems, starting at zC88h. This is shown in the register descriptions for POS 3, POS 6, POS 7, POS Data 3 and POS Data 4, discussed below.

4.3. POS Register Extensions

The following extensions have been added to the IBM defined POS register specification. Features include mechanisms to support Manufacturer ID and a VGA-style BIOS. These registers are present only during setup and are addressed at the POS locations of 100h-107h.

4.3.1. POS 3

Register Name: **POS 3** Register Address: 103h[1] or 0zC8B - Index 0							
bit 7	*bit 6*	*bit 5*	*bit 4*	*bit 3*	*bit 2*	*bit 1* External Memory Enable	*bit 0*
#	#	#	#	#	#		#

1 Setup Only

Bit 1: External Memory Enable

This bit is used to enable the 8KB XGA External Memory space. When it's value is 1, access to the external memory is enabled. The memory address is determined by the value in the POS 2 register. Note that XGA subsystems do not necessarily contain an 8KB ROM. This bit has no effect on the accessibility of the XGA memory registers.

Bits 7-2 & 0: Manufacturer Reserved

The function of these bits are bus-type and manufacturer-specific. If this register is written, the value contained in these bits **must** be preserved.

4.3.2. POS 3, 4, 6 & 7

POS registers 3, 4, 6 and 7 are used to access one of 128K possible 8-bit registers. The index to the registers is placed in POS 6 (low byte) and POS 7 (high byte). The registers are then visible through the data ports at POS 3 and 4.

The implementation of POS 3, Index 0 and POS 4, Index 0 is fully compatible with the function of POS 3 and POS 4 in the IBM XGA product.

At this time only Index 0 is defined for POS Data 3. For POS Data 4, only Indices 0 through 3 are defined. In order to maintain compatibility with future specifications, the full 16-bit index value **must** be used.

4.3.3. POS 6

Register Name: **POS 6** Register Address: 106h[1], zC8Eh[2]							
bit 7	*bit 6*	*bit 5*	*bit 4*	*bit 3*	*bit 2*	*bit 1*	*bit 0*
			POS Index Low				

1 Setup Mode only

2 EISA systems only

4.3.4. POS 7

Register Name: **POS 7** Register Address: 107h[1], zC8Fh[2]							
bit 7	*bit 6*	*bit 5*	*bit 4*	*bit 3*	*bit 2*	*bit 1*	*bit 0*
POS Index High							

1 Setup Mode only

2 EISA systems only

POS 7 & 6: Index High and Low

These two fields define a 16-bit register index value. Values 0004h through 000Fh are RESERVED and should not be used, all greater values are undefined. The entire 16-bit value **must** be used to access the data registers at POS 3 and POS 4. POS 7 is the high order 8 bits and POS 6 is the low order 8 bits. The reset value of POS 6 and POS 7 must be 0.

4.3.5. POS Data 3

Register Name: **POS Data 3** Register Address: 103h[1], zC8Bh[2]							
bit 7	*bit 6*	*bit 5*	*bit 4*	*bit 3*	*bit 2*	*bit 1*	*bit 0*
POS Data 3							

1 Setup Mode only

2 EISA systems only

4.3.6. POS Data 4

Register Name: **POS Data 4** Register Address: 104h[1], zC8Ch[2]							
bit 7	*bit 6*	*bit 5*	*bit 4*	*bit 3*	*bit 2*	*bit 1*	*bit 0*
POS Data 4							

1 Setup Mode only

2 EISA systems only

POS 4 & 3: Data Registers

POS Data 3 and POS Data 4 are the data registers used to access the POS extensions. POS Data 3 is undefined for non-zero index values. POS Data 4 is currently defined for indices 0-3 only.

4.3.7. Manufacturer ID

bit 15	bit 14	bit 13	bit 12	bit 11	bit 10	bit 9	bit 8

Register Name: **Manufacturer ID**
Register Address: POS Data 4 - Index 1-2[1]

bit 15	bit 14	bit 13	bit 12	bit 11	bit 10	bit 9	bit 8
			Manufacturer ID 15-8[2]				
bit 7	bit 6	bit 5	bit 4	bit 3	bit 2	bit 1	bit 0
			Manufacturer ID 7-0[3]				

1 Setup Mode only

2 Optional

3 Required, VESA assigned

This 2-byte field contains the Manufacturer ID. Only the first byte (Index 1, bits 7-0) of the ID is required and the value read from this field is assigned by the VESA organization. The second byte (Index 2, bits 7-0) is manufacturer-specific and will read back the value 0 if it does not contain ID information. Since this field may be implemented as read/write or read only, software should take care to assure that this field is not written.

4.3.8. VGA BIOS Configuration

Register Name: **VGA BIOS Configuration**
Register Address: POS Data 4 - Index 3

bit 7	bit 6	bit 5	bit 4	bit 3	bit 2	bit 1	bit 0
-	-	-	-	VGA BIOS ROM Decode Location			VGA BIOS ROM Decode Enable

Bit 0: VGA BIOS ROM Decode Enable

This bit enables decoding of the VGA BIOS ROM within the XGA subsystem. This bit has no effect on the XGA-compatible relocatable 8KB ROM Aperture. When this bit is 1, the VGA BIOS is decoded at the location determined by the VGA BIOS ROM Decode Location field (see below). When this bit is 0, the XGA subsystem does not respond to VGA BIOS accesses. This bit does not affect accessibility to the XGA memory registers.

Bits 3-1: VGA BIOS ROM Decode Location

This field determines the VGA BIOS addresses to which the XGA subsystem responds. If the VGA BIOS and the XGA external memory are decoded at the same location, the XGA external memory has priority. The starting address of the 32KB VGA BIOS is encoded as follows:

Value	Starting Address
000	C000:0
001	C800:0
010	D000:0
011	D800:0
100	E000:0
101	E800:0
110	Reserved for future VESA use
111	Reserved for future VESA use

Note that if the 8KB External Memory space is programmed to overlap with the 32KB VGA BIOS space, accesses to the overlapping locations will access the 8KB External Memory.

4.4. XGA Index Register Extensions

The following extensions have been added to the IBM defined XGA register set. Features include: Bus Identification, Subsystem Vendor ID, Manufacturer Expansion and VESA-reserved registers. These registers are accessed through the standard XGA index and data space at 21xAh and 21xBh through 21xFh, respectively.

4.4.1. Auto-Configuration

Register Name: **Auto-Configuration**							
Register Address: 21xAh, Index 4							
bit 7	*bit 6*	*bit 5*	*bit 4*	*bit 3*	*bit 2*	*bit 1*	*bit 0*
-	-	Subsystem Interface Configuration		Bus Size 1	-	-	Bus Size 0

The bits in this register may be configured at power up by strapping options. This register must not be written.

Bits 3 & 0: Bus Size 1 & 0

These bits indicate the bus size as defined below:

Bits	Bus Size
00	16-bit
01	32-bit
10	8-bit
11	RESERVED

Bits 5-4: Subsystem Interface Configuration

This 2-bit field is used to read the configuration of the XGA subsystem's host interface. The system bus selection bits are encoded below.

Value	System Bus Type
00	Micro Channel
01	ISA
10	RESERVED
11	EISA

4.4.2. Index 72h-73h

XGA Index registers 72h and 73h are reserved by VESA for future expansion of the VESA XGA standard and may not be used.

4.4.3. DMA Channel Readback (ISA Only)

Register Name: **DMA Channel Readback**							
Register Address: 21xAh, Index 74h[1]							
bit 7	bit 6	bit 5	bit 4	bit 3	bit 2	bit 1	bit 0
-	-	-	-	DMA Channel Select			DMA Channel Enable

1 ISA Systems only

This register is read only. Application software must not attempt to write this register.

Bit 0: DMA Channel Enable

This bit is used to indicate whether the DMA Channel is enabled for bus mastering.

Bits 3-1: DMA Channel Select

This field encodes which DMA channel is selected for bus master arbitration in an ISA system bus. This field is encoded as follows:

Value	ISA DMA Channel Number
000	Channel 0
001	Channel 1
010	Channel 2
011	Channel 3
100	RESERVED
101	Channel 5
110	Channel 6
111	Channel 7

4.4.4. Subsystem Vendor ID

Register Name: **Subsystem Vendor ID**							
Register Address: 21xAh, Index 75h							
bit 7	bit 6	bit 5	bit 4	bit 3	bit 2	bit 1	bit 0
			Subsystem Vendor ID				

Bits 7-0: Subsystem Vendor ID

This byte is used to identify the subsystem (board or mother board) vendor. A write to the XGA Index Register (21xAh) initializes this register. After initializing the register, the first read will return one of three sets of values:

Value Description

00h   The Subsystem Vendor ID mechanism has not been implemented.

01-FEh Chip manufacturer-assigned subsystem vendor ID. All further subsequent reads are undefined, and may be used by either the chip manufacturer or the subsystem vendor.

FFh   The software must read this register twice more to get a 16-bit, VESA-allocated subsystem vendor ID. The first subsequent read is the low-order byte of the 16-bit VESA assigned ID, while the second subsequent read is the high-order byte. All further subsequent reads are undefined, and may be used by either the chip manufacturer or the subsystem vendor. (Note that this definition is optional, but if not implemented, then the FFh value is reserved and should not be assigned by the chip manufacturer).

This register may be implemented as RAM or ROM and software other than initialization software must not write to this register.

4.4.5. Manufacturer Expansion

XGA Index registers 76h and 77h are allocated for manufacturer expansion. These two registers are manufacturer-specific and cannot be relied upon to be consistent across different products. Note that these registers should not be accessed without knowledge of the manufacturer's implementation.

4.4.6. BIOS Chain Function

For those XGA subsystems supplied with a BIOS, four 8-bit storage locations are required for storage of a double word value. These locations are used to store the double word value for the startup video subsystem's INT 10h vector. The location and implementation of this BIOS Chain function is manufacturer-specific and cannot be relied upon to be consistent across product lines.

5. EISA Systems

This section discusses issues related to implementation of an IBM XGA-compatible video subsystem in the EISA bus structure, including:

- Bus Hardware Interface
- EISA Registers
- EISA Implementation of POS Registers for XGA

5.1. Bus Hardware Interface

5.1.1. Address Range and Data Range

Both EISA and Micro Channel Architecture have 32-bits of address and 32-bits of data. Therefore, EISA XGA implementation have the same address range capabilities as the Micro Channel Architecture XGA.

5.1.2. I/O Address and Data Range

Because of the slot-specific implementation of the EISA bus, there are some limitations of addressing the full range of the XGA I/O address. In particular, Instance 0 and 7 are not recommended to be implemented in the EISA system. The Instance 0, if implemented in the EISA system, causes potential conflict of I/O registers with other products. Instance 7 has potential conflict with the CPU. Although the XGA hardware specification indicates Instance 0 and 7 may be used, the IBM XGA is not configured to use Instances 0 and 7. Therefore, the limitation of the EISA system has no effect on the current software that supports the IBM XGA.

The EISA bus requires a set of I/O registers (four bytes) for manufacturers to specify their product identification. The I/O register address is 0zC80h to 0zC83h, where the "z" is the slot number.

5.1.3. Bus Mastership

EISA allows bus mastership by the expansion board. The EISA bus master arbitrator uses a rotational arbitration, whereas the Micro Channel Architecture has priority level based arbitration. This is a hardware implementation which is not seen by software; therefore, EISA versions of XGA can perform bus master without any change.

5.1.4. POS Registers

The POS registers are available through the EISA slot-specific addresses at all times. They are accessible through I/O addresses 100h-107h when enabled by the EISA Setup register described below.

5.1.5. EISA Setup

Register Name: **EISA Setup**							
Register Address: zC85h[1]							
bit 7	*bit 6*	*bit 5*	*bit 4*	*bit 3*	*bit 2*	*bit 1*	*bit 0*
-	-	-	-	-	-	-	Setup Mode Enable

1 EISA systems only

This register is only accessible in systems using the EISA bus, as identified by the Subsystem Interface Configuration. In these systems, this register is located at a slot-specific address. Thus, this register may be located at any one of 16 addresses in the EISA I/O address space, depending on the system bus slot to which the XGA subsystem is configured to respond.

Bit 0: Setup Mode Enable

This bit is used to enable access to the POS registers. When Setup Mode Enable is 1 and EISA Access Enable Arm is 1, the CPU may access the POS registers through addresses 100h-107h.

5.1.6. EISA Implementation of POS Registers for XGA

The EISA version of XGA has POS registers in order to tell the host of its configuration. The POS registers reside after the EISA ID and EISA Control registers, following the same order as in the IBM XGA. The following table shows the address correspondence:

EISA XGA I/O Address	IBM XGA I/O Address
0zC80h (EISA ID)	
0zC81h (EISA ID)	
0zC82h (EISA ID)	
0zC83h (EISA ID)	
0zC84h (Expansion Board Control Bits)	
0zC85h (Setup Control)	
0zC88h	100h (POS 0)
0zC89h	101h (POS 1)
0zC8Ah	102h (POS 2)
0zC8Bh	103h (POS 3)
0zC8Ch	104h (POS 4)
0zC8Dh	105h (POS 5)
0zC8Eh	106h (POS 6)
0zC8Fh	107h (POS 7)

The location for the POS registers is used because 0zCxx in the EISA bus is a slot-specific address range designed not to overlap with the ISA I/O alias or equivalent locations on other EISA adapters.

6. Micro Channel Systems

Products which are 100% IBM XGA compatible, with no extensions, may use the product ID of 8FD8h-8FDBh or 8FD0h-8FD3h, based on the ID of the IBM XGA with which they are compatible. All other subsystems use one of the 1K reserved XGA IDs. The reserved XGA values are 0240h-027Fh, 0830h-0A7Fh and 0A90h-0BFFh. A valid POS ID must be requested from IBM or through VESA.

7. ISA Systems

This section describes the bus master and memory mapping functions of XGA on the 16-bit ISA bus. The ISA XGA implementation outlined in this section provides full programming interface compatibility with the Micro Channel Architecture and EISA XGA platforms. This compatibility is achieved by implementing a POS mechanism for ISA adapters and by the POS register settings themselves.

This standard defines a single instance of XGA in an ISA system. The current Instance number is limited to a value of one (1). There is nothing in this standard which precludes multiple instances.

7.1. ISA POS Enable

The mechanism to enable the POS registers on the ISA bus requires that the Instance number be used as both data and address. The address is computed as (108h + Instance). The data written to the lower nibble must also match the Instance + 8 to enable setup. If the Instance number fields in the address and data do not match, the XGA subsystem will not recognize the access.

Register Name: **ISA POS Enable**							
Register Address: 108h + Instance[1]							
bit 7	*bit 6*	*bit 5*	*bit 4*	*bit 3*	*bit 2*	*bit 1*	*bit 0*
-	-	-	-	Setup Mode Enable	Instance Number		

1 ISA systems only

Only Instance 1 is currently defined; therefore, **this register must be accessed at location 109h**.

Bits 2-0: Instance Number

These bits must match the Instance number of the subsystem (001b).

Bit 3: Setup Mode Enable

This bit is used to enable access to the POS registers. When Setup Mode Enable is 1, the CPU may access the POS registers. Setup mode should be disabled by writing this register with the value 01h (the Instance number and a 0 for Setup Mode Enable).

7.2. ISA Bus Mastership for XGA

7.2.1. ISA Bus Requirements

VESA-compliant subsystems support bus mastership. In order to run on the ISA platform this requires a 16-bit ISA architecture, which includes:

- 24-bit addressing
- 16-bit data and I/O
- 7 DMA channels
- Alternate bus master (cascade DMA) operation

7.2.2. DMA Channel Assignment

This standard allows any of the seven DMA channels called for in the 16-bit ISA bus to be made available to an ISA XGA. This standard does not require an ISA XGA to support the use of all DMA channels. The DMA Channel Readback register defines which DMA channel is used by a given XGA. It is read at XGA Index 74h.

II. VESA XGA Real Mode BIOS Specification

8. Software Goals and Objectives

By providing a common software interface to XGA graphics products, the primary objective is to enable application and system software to adapt to and exploit the wide range of features available on current and future XGAs.

Specifically, the VESA XGA BIOS attempts to address the following two main issues: a) return information about the video environment to the application and b) assist the application in initializing and programming the hardware.

8.1. Video Environment Information

The VESA XGA BIOS provides several functions to return information about the video environment. These functions return system level information as well as video mode specific details. Function 00h returns general system level information, including the number of XGAs installed in the system and a system OEM identification string. Function 01h returns board dependent information for each XGA installed in the system. The function also returns a pointer to a list of the video modes supported by the particular board. Function 02h may be used by the application to obtain information about each supported video mode. Function 04h returns the current video mode for a particular XGA.

8.2. Programming Support

Due to the fact that different XGA products have different hardware implementations, application software could have great difficulty in adapting to each environment. However, since each is based on the XGA hardware architecture, differences are most common in platform specific implementation issues and video mode initialization. The rest of the architecture is kept intact.

The VESA XGA BIOS provides several functions to interface to the different XGA hardware implementations. The most important of these is Function 03h, Set XGA Video Mode. This function isolates the application from the tedious and complicated task of setting up a video mode.

8.2.1. Compatibility

A primary design objective of the VESA XGA BIOS is to preserve maximum compatibility to the standard XGA and VGA environments. In no way should the BIOS compromise compatibility or performance. Another related concern is to minimize the changes necessary to an existing VGA BIOS. RAM- as well as ROM-based implementations of the VESA XGA BIOS should be possible.

8.2.2. Scope of VESA XGA BIOS Standard

The purpose of the VESA XGA BIOS is to provide support for XGA environments. Thus, the underlying hardware architecture is assumed to be an XGA. Graphics software that drives a VESA-compatible XGA board, will perform its graphics output in generally the same way it drives a standard XGA, i.e., writing directly to an XGA style frame buffer, manipulating graphic primitives registers, directly programming the palette, etc.

8.3. Support of Existing BIOS Standards

A primary design goal with the VESA XGA BIOS is to minimize the effects on the standard VGA BIOS and the VESA VGA BIOS Extensions. Standard VGA BIOS functions should not be affected in any way. Also, the VESA XGA BIOS should peacefully coexist with the VESA VGA BIOS Extensions. This is important since it is possible that all three standards will be implemented in a single BIOS ROM or in a RAM TSR.

8.3.1. INT 10h Vector Preservation

To facilitate compatibility, all VESA compatible-XGA video subsystems will contain 4 bytes of BIOS Chain storage that will be reserved for the BIOS to store the address of the INT 10h service handler that was present before the VESA XGA BIOS hooked the interrupt. The VESA XGA BIOS will pass any INT 10h service requests that do not apply to an XGA to the routine at this address.

8.3.2. XGA Board Resident VESA XGA BIOS Address Standardization

In a system environment that contains multiple XGAs, it may be desirable to request service from each of the different XGA's BIOS. This is accomplished by selectively enabling the target board's BIOS decode and then calling the BIOS at a predetermined address. In order to provide for such a feature, the ROM-based VESA XGA BIOS uses a standard entry point address for the INT 10h VESA XGA BIOS service routines. This address is at **offset 40h** within the target board's XGA ROM aperture.

8.3.3. XGA Board Resident VGA BIOS Address Standardization

In a system environment that contains multiple XGAs (and therefore VGAs), it may be desirable to request service from each of the different VGA's BIOS. This is accomplished by selectively enabling the target board's VGA BIOS decode and then calling the VGA BIOS at a predetermined address. In order to provide for such a feature, the XGA Board-Resident VGA BIOS uses a standard entry point address for the INT 10h VGA BIOS service routines. This address is at **offset 40h** within the target board's VGA ROM space.

8.4. OEM-Defined Mode Tags

The VESA XGA BIOS does not assign specific numbers to set resolutions. It provides an interface by which the application video driver may query the XGA display adapter and determine what resolutions, pixel depths and pixel formats are supported. The action required to set a video mode using the VESA XGA BIOS involves querying the BIOS about what mode tags the currently installed XGA's OEM has defined, then querying the BIOS to find out the resolution and pixel depth particulars for each mode tag returned, and finally, calling Function 03h (Set XGA Video Mode) with the mode tag representing the desired resolution and pixel format.

Due to the limitations of 7-bit mode numbers, VESA video mode tags are 15-bits wide. To initialize an XGA mode, its tag is passed in the BX register to VESA XGA BIOS Function 03h (Set XGA Video Mode).

The format of VESA XGA mode tags is as follows:

> D15= Reserved for Clear Memory flag
>
> D14-10= Reserved by VESA for future expansion (= 0)
>
> D9-0= Mode tag
>
> > If D9 == 0, this is not an XGA mode
> >
> > If D9 == 1, this is an XGA mode
> >
> > D8 = 0, Reserved by VESA for future expansion

Thus, VESA XGA mode tags begin at 200h.

8.5. VESA XGA BIOS

Several new BIOS calls have been defined to support XGA modes. For maximum compatibility with the standard VGA BIOS, these calls are grouped under one function number. This number is passed in the AH register to the INT 10h handler.

The designated VESA XGA extended function number is **4Eh**. This function number is presently unused in most, if not all, VGA BIOS implementations. A standard VGA BIOS performs no action when function call 4Eh is made. This standard defines subfunctions 00h through 06h. Subfunction numbers 07h through 0FFh are reserved for future use.

8.5.1. Status Information

Every function returns status information in the AX register. The format of the status word is as follows:

AL ==	4Eh:	Function is supported
AL !=	4Eh:	Function is not supported
AH ==	00h:	Function call successful
AH ==	01h:	Function call failed

Software should treat a non-zero value in the AH register as a general failure condition. In later versions of this standard, new error codes might be defined.

8.5.2. XGA Handles

It is possible to have more than one XGA installed in a system at a given time. Therefore the VESA XGA BIOS assigns a logical "handle" to each XGA currently installed. The first 16-bit handle assigned is 0000h and additional handles are assigned incrementally. Therefore, valid handles are 0 through (Number of XGAs Installed - 1). VESA XGA BIOS Functions 01h through 06h require that a valid handle be passed in the DX register.

8.5.3. Function 00h - Return XGA Environment Information

The purpose of this function is to provide information to the calling program about the general capabilities of the XGA environment. The function fills an information block structure at the address specified by the caller. The information block size is 256 bytes.

Input:

```
AH= 4Eh      ; XGA support
AL= 00h      ; Return XGA environment information
ES:DI= Pointer to buffer
```

Output:

```
AX= Status   ; If AX equals 014Eh upon return, then there is no XGA currently
               installed in the system.
```

All other registers are preserved.

The environment information block has the following structure:

```
EnvInfoBlock      struc
VESASignature     db    'VESA'        ; 4 signature bytes
VESAVersion       dw    100h          ; VESA version number
OEMStringPtr      dd    ?             ; pointer to system OEM string
EnvironmentFlag   dd    ?             ; capabilities of the system environment
NumXGAs           dw    ?             ; number of XGAs installed
Reserved          db    240 dup (?)   ; remainder of EnvInfoBlock
EnvInfoBlock      ends
```

The `VESASignature` field contains the ASCII characters 'VESA' if this is a valid block.

The `VESAVersion` is a binary field which specifies to what level of the VESA standard the VESA XGA BIOS conforms. The higher byte specifies the major version number. The lower byte specifies the minor version number. The current VESA XGA version number is 1.0. Applications written to use the features of a specific version of the VESA XGA BIOS, are **guaranteed** to work in later versions. The VESA XGA BIOS will be fully upwards compatible.

The OEMStringPtr is a 32-bit pointer (segment:offset) to a null terminated OEM-defined string. The string may be used to identify the system environment by system-specific display drivers. There are no restrictions on the format of the string.

The EnvironmentFlag field describes what general features are supported in the system environment. The bits are defined as follows:

> D31-3= Reserved by VESA for future expansion
>
> D2= Bus Mastering Capability
>
>> 0 = Bus Mastering not available in this system
>>
>> 1 = Bus Mastering is available in this system
>
> D1-0= System Bus Architecture ID[1]
>
>> 00 = Micro Channel Architecture Bus Platform
>>
>> 01 = ISA Bus Platform
>>
>> 10 = RESERVED
>>
>> 11 = EISA Bus Platform

The NumXGAs field indicates the total number of XGAs installed in the system. The VESA XGA BIOS recognizes handle values of 0 through (NumXGAs minus one).

Note that the VESA XGA BIOS will set to zero all unused fields in the environment information block, always returning exactly 256 bytes. This facilitates upward compatibility with future versions of the standard, as any newly-added fields will be designed such that values of zero will indicate nominal defaults or non-implementation of optional features. (For example, a field containing a bit-mask of extended capabilities would reflect the absence of all such capabilities.)

8.5.4. Function 01h - Return XGA Subsystem Information

The purpose of this function is to provide information to the calling program about the capabilities of a particular XGA in the system. The function fills an information block structure at the address specified by the caller. The information block size is 256 bytes. To obtain information for all of the XGAs present, the application should load the DX register with 0, and then call this function NumXGAs times, incrementing DX after each call.

Input:

```
AH= 4Eh      ; XGA support
AL= 01h      ; Return XGA subsystem information
DX= XGA Handle
ES:DI= Pointer to buffer
```

---

[1] The VESA XGA BIOS will determine the system's bus mastering capabilities during the POST, with diagnostic test routines.

Output:

```
AX= Status  ; If AX equals 014Eh upon return, then there is no XGA currently
              installed in the system.
```

All other registers are preserved.

The adapter information block has the following structure:

```
XgaInfoBlock       struc
OEMStringPtr       dd    ?    ; pointer to board OEM string
CapabilitiesFlag   dd    ?    ; capabilities of this XGA board
XGARomAddr         dd    ?    ; pointer to XGA's 8KB ROM Aperture
XGAMemRegAddr      dd    ?    ; pointer to XGA's memory mapped registers
XGAIORegAddr       dw    ?    ; base address of XGA's I/O registers
VidMemBaseAddr     dd    ?    ; base address of XGA's physical video memory
XGA4MBAddr         dd    ?    ; pointer to XGA's 4MB Aperture
XGA1MBAddr         dd    ?    ; pointer to XGA's 1MB Aperture
XGA64KBAddr        dd    ?    ; pointer to XGA's 64KB Aperture
OemAptrAddr        dd    ?    ; pointer to XGA's OEM defined Aperture
OemAptrSize        dw    ?    ; size of OEM defined Aperture, in 64KB units
VideoModePtr       dd    ?    ; pointer to supported XGA modes
TotalMemory        dw    ?    ; number of 64KB memory blocks on board
XGAManId           dd    ?    ; XGA Manufacturer's ID
Reserved           db    194 dup (?) ; remainder of XgaInfoBlock
XgaInfoBlock       ends
```

The `OEMStringPtr` is a 32-bit pointer (segment:offset) to a null terminated OEM-defined string. The string may be used to identify the XGA board to hardware-specific display drivers. There are no restrictions on the format of the string.

The `CapabilitiesFlag` field describes what features are supported on the XGA **board**. The bits are defined as follows:

> D31-8= Reserved by VESA for future expansion
>
> D7= DMA Channel Status[2]
>
>> 0 = Disabled
>>
>> 1 = Enabled
>
> D6-4= DMA Channel assigned for acquiring bus mastership[2]
>
> D3-2= Reserved by VESA for future expansion
>
> D1-0= Board Bus Architecture ID

---

[2] The information in this field is valid for ISA bus board architectures only.

00 = Micro Channel Architecture Bus Interface

01 = ISA Bus Interface

10 = RESERVED

11 = EISA Bus Interface

The XGARomAddr is a 32-bit pointer (segment:offset) that specifies the address at which this XGA's 8KB ROM resides. If this value is zero, then the 8KB ROM is not enabled.

The XGAMemRegAddr is a segment:offset pair that specifies the address at which this XGA's memory mapped registers reside.

The XGAIORegAddr is a word that specifies the base address of this XGA's I/O registers.

The VidMemBaseAddr is a 32-bit **absolute address** that specifies the physical address of this XGA's video memory.

The XGA4MBAddr is a 32-bit **absolute address** that specifies where this XGA's 4MB Aperture resides. If this value is zero, then the 4MB Aperture is not enabled.

The XGA1MBAddr is a 32-bit **absolute address** that specifies where this XGA's 1MB Aperture resides. If this value is zero, then the 1MB Aperture is not enabled.

The XGA64KBAddr is a segment:offset that specifies the address at which this XGA's 64KB Aperture resides. If this value is zero, then the 64KB Aperture is not enabled.

The OemAptrAddr is a 32-bit **absolute address** that specifies where this XGA's OEM defined Aperture resides. If this value is zero, then an OEM Aperture is not available. This field is provided to allow for the definition of apertures larger than 4MB.

The OemAptrSize is a word that specifies the size of the OEM defined aperture, in 64KB units.

The VideoModePtr points to a list of mode tags representing all the XGA modes supported by the current VESA XGA BIOS. Each mode tag occupies one word (16 bits). The list of mode tags is terminated by a -1 (0FFFFh). Please refer to the OEM-Defined Mode Tags section for a complete description of VESA XGA mode tags. The pointer could point into either ROM or RAM, depending on the specific implementation. Either the list would be a static string stored in ROM or the list would be generated at run-time in the information block (see above) in RAM. It is the application's responsibility to verify the current availability of any mode returned by this function through the Return XGA Mode Information (Function 02h) call. Some of the returned modes may not be available due to the video board's current memory and monitor configuration.

The TotalMemory field indicates the amount of memory installed on the XGA board. Its value represents the number of 64KB blocks of memory currently installed.

The XGAManId field indicates the content of POS Data 4, Index 1 (byte 0) and Index 2 (byte 1) and XGA Index 75h (byte 2). Byte 3 is undefined and reserved by VESA for future expansion.

Note that the VESA XGA BIOS will set to zero all unused fields in the adapter information block, always returning exactly 256 bytes. This facilitates upward compatibility with future versions of the standard, as any newly-added fields will be designed such that values of zero will indicate nominal defaults or non-implementation of optional features. (For example, a field containing a bit-mask of extended capabilities would reflect the absence of all such capabilities.)

8.5.5. Function 02h - Return XGA Mode Information

This function returns information about a specific XGA video mode, on a specific XGA, that was returned by Function 01h. The function fills a mode information block structure at the address specified by the caller. The mode information block size is 256 bytes.

Input:

```
AH= 4Eh       ; XGA support
AL= 02h       ; Return XGA mode information
CX= OEM video mode tag
DX= XGA Handle
ES:DI= Pointer to 256 byte buffer
```

Output:

```
AX= Status
```

All other registers are preserved.

The mode information block has the following structure:

```
ModeInfoBlock           struc
ModeAttributes          dw    ?    ; mode attributes
BytesPerScanLine        dw    ?    ; bytes per scan line
XResolution             dw    ?    ; horizontal resolution
YResolution             dw    ?    ; vertical resolution
XCharSize               db    ?    ; character cell width
YCharSize               db    ?    ; character cell height
NumberOfPlanes          db    ?    ; number of memory planes
BitsPerPixel            db    ?    ; bits per pixel
MemoryModel             db    ?    ; memory model type
NumberOfImagePages      db    ?    ; number of images
RedMaskSize             db    ?    ; number of red bits in a single pixel's
                                     data
RedFieldPosition        db    ?    ; position of red bits in a single pixel's
                                     data
GreenMaskSize           db    ?    ; number of green bits in a single pixel's
                                     data
GreenFieldPosition      db    ?    ; position of green bits in a single
                                     pixel's data
```

```
BlueMaskSize            db      ?       ; number of blue bits in a single pixel's
                                          data
BlueFieldPosition       db      ?       ; position of blue bits in a single
                                          pixel's data
ReservedMaskSize        db      ?       ; number of reserved bits in a single
                                          pixel's data
ReservedFieldPosition   db      ?       ; position of reserved bits in a single
                                          pixel's data
Reserved                db      234 dup (?)  ; remainder of ModeInfoBlock
ModeInfoBlock           ends
```

The `ModeAttributes` field describes certain important characteristics of the video mode. Bit D0 specifies whether this mode can be initialized in the present video configuration. This bit can be used to block access to a video mode if it requires a certain monitor type and that this monitor is presently not connected. Bit D2 indicates whether the BIOS has support for output functions like TTY output, scroll, pixel output, etc., in this mode.

The field is defined as follows:

D15-5= Reserved by VESA for future expansion

D4= Mode type

      0 = Text mode (VGA registers active, XGA registers inactive)

      1 = Graphics mode (VGA registers inactive, XGA registers active)

D3= Reserved by VESA for future expansion

D2= Output functions supported by BIOS

      0 = Output functions not supported by BIOS

      1 = Output functions supported by BIOS

D1= Reserved by VESA for future expansion

D0= Mode supported in current hardware configuration

      0 = Mode not supported in present configuration

      1 = Mode supported in present configuration

The `BytesPerScanline` field specifies how many bytes are contained within each logical scanline. The logical scanline could be equal to or larger than the displayed scanline.

The `XResolution` and `YResolution` specify the width and height of the video mode. In graphics modes, this resolution is in units of pixels. In text modes this resolution is in units of characters. Note that text mode resolutions, in units of pixels, can be obtained by multiplying `XResolution` and `YResolution` by the cell width and height.

The `XCharSize` and `YCharSize` specify the size of the character cell in pixels.

The `NumberOfPlanes` field specifies the number of bit planes available to software in that mode. For XGA packed pixel modes, the field is set to one.

The `BitsPerPixel` field specifies the total number of bits that define the color of one pixel. The number of bits per pixel per plane can normally be derived by dividing the `BitsPerPixel` field by the `NumberOfPlanes` field.

The `MemoryModel` field specifies the general type of memory organization used in this mode. The following models have been defined:

00h=	Text mode
01h=	CGA graphics
02h=	Hercules graphics
03h=	4-plane planar
04h=	Packed pixel
05h=	Non-chain 4, 256 color
06h=	Direct Color
07h=	YUV-24
08h-0FFh=	Reserved by VESA for future expansion

The `NumberOfImagePages` field specifies the number of complete display images (minus 1) that will fit into the XGA's memory, at one time, in this mode. The application may load more than one image into the XGA's memory if this field is non-zero and flip the display between.

The remaining fields in the `ModeInfoBlock` contain valid data only when the `MemoryModel` equals 06h (Direct Color) or 07h (YUV-24).

The `RedMaskSize` specifies the number of bits in a single pixel's data field that contain the Red component information, when in a Direct Color mode. When in a YUV mode, this field contains the number of bits used by the V component. (E.g., in the standard 640 x 480 x 65536 XGA mode, this field would contain a five.)

The `RedFieldPosition` specifies the location of the least significant bit of the Red component within a single pixel's data field. When in a YUV mode, this field contains the bit location of the first bit of the V component. (E.g., in the standard 640 x 480 x 65536 XGA mode, this field would contain a 0Bh.)

The `GreenMaskSize` specifies the number of bits in a single pixel's data field that contain the Green component information, when in a Direct Color mode. When in a YUV mode, this field contains the number of bits used by the Y component. (E.g., in the standard 640 x 480 x 65536 XGA mode, this field would contain a six.)

The `GreenFieldPosition` specifies the location of the least significant bit of the Green component within a single pixel's data field. When in a YUV mode, this field contains the bit location of the first bit of the Y component. (E.g., in the standard 640 x 480 x 65536 XGA mode, this field would contain a 05h.)

The `BlueMaskSize` specifies the number of bits in a single pixel's data field that contain the Blue component information, when in a Direct Color mode. When in a YUV mode, this field contains the number of bits used by the U component. (E.g., in the standard 640 x 480 x 65536 XGA mode, this field would contain a five.)

The `BlueFieldPosition` specifies the location of the least significant bit of the Blue component within a single pixel's data field. When in a YUV mode, this field contains the bit location of the first bit of the U component. (E.g., in the standard 640 x 480 x 65536 XGA mode, this field would contain a 00h.)

The `ReservedMaskSize` specifies the number of bits in a single pixel's data field that do not contain color component information. (E.g., in a 32-bit per pixel, 16.7 million color mode, this field might contain an 08h.)

The `ReservedFieldPosition` specifies the location of the least significant bit of the field that does not contain color component information, within a single pixel's data field. (E.g., in a 32-bit per pixel, 16.7 million color mode, this field might contain an 18h.)

Note that the VESA XGA BIOS will set to zero all unused fields in the mode information block, always returning exactly 256 bytes. This facilitates upward compatibility with future versions of the standard, as any newly-added fields will be designed such that values of zero will indicate nominal defaults or non-implementation of optional features. (For example, a field containing a bit-mask of extended capabilities would reflect the absence of all such capabilities.)

8.5.6. Function 03h - Set XGA Video Mode

This function initializes a video mode. The BX register contains the OEM tag for the mode to set. The format of VESA XGA mode tags is described in the OEM-Defined Mode Tags section. The DX register contains the virtual handle of the XGA to which the mode set request applies. If the mode cannot be set, the BIOS will leave the video environment unchanged and return a failure error code. This function should be used to set all graphics modes on the desired XGA adapter, including VGA modes. It **must** be used to switch between XGA and VGA modes on the given adapter.

Input:

```
AH= 4Eh      ; XGA support
AL= 03h      ; Set XGA video mode
BX= OEM Video mode tag
     D15= Clear memory flag
               0 = Clear video memory
               1 = Don't clear video memory
     D14-0= Video mode
CX= Other command flags
     D15-1= Reserved (0)
     D0= Feature connector flag
               0 = Set Feature connector to default state³
```

---

[3] In single monitor systems utilizing a VGA that is not on the XGA board, the VGA's output will usually be fed to the XGA through the feature connector, for display on the XGA's monitor. In default mode in this configuration, the VESA XGA BIOS will disable the feature connector when switching to an XGA mode and enable it when switching to a VGA mode. This action can be overridden by setting bit D0 of the CX register when making the Set XGA Video Mode BIOS call (see Function 05h - Enable Feature Connector).

```
                        1 = Do not change state of feature connector
DX= XGA Handle
```

Output:

```
AX= Status
```

All other registers are preserved.

8.5.7. Function 04h - Return Current Video Mode

This function returns the OEM tag for the current video mode in BX. The format of VESA XGA video mode tags is described in the OEM-Defined Mode Tags section.

Input:

```
AH= 4Eh       ; XGA support
AL= 04h       ; Return current video mode
DX= XGA Handle
```

Output:

```
AX= Status
BX= OEM mode tag or VGA mode number for current video mode
```

All other registers are preserved.

8.5.8. Function 05h - Set Feature Connector State

This function enables or disables the transmission of video data through the XGA board's feature connector and sets the direction in which the data is transferred.

Input:

```
AH= 4Eh       ; XGA support
AL= 05h       ; Set feature connector state
BX= Feature Connector state
     D15-2= Reserved (0)
     D1= Feature connector Input/Output control
          0 = Set feature connector to input mode
          1 = Set feature connector to output mode
     D0= Feature connector enable
          0 = Disable feature connector
          1 = Enable feature connector
DX= XGA Handle
```

Output:

```
AX= Status
```

All other registers are preserved.

8.5.9. Function 06h - Get Feature Connector State

This function returns the current state of the feature connector.

Input:

```
AH= 4Eh      ; XGA support
AL= 06h      ; Get feature connector state
DX= XGA Handle
```

Output:

```
AX= Status
BX=Feature Connector state
     D15-2= Reserved (0)
     D1= Feature connector Input/Output state
          0 = Feature connector is in input mode
          1 = Feature connector is in output mode
     D0= Feature connector enable
          0 = Feature connector is disabled
          1 = Feature connector is enabled
```

All other registers are preserved.

III. Appendices

A. Programming Considerations Appendix

The following sequence illustrates how an application interfaces to the VESA XGA BIOS. The hypothetical application is VESA XGA-aware and calls the VESA XGA BIOS functions.

The application first allocates a 256-byte buffer. This buffer is used by the VESA XGA BIOS to return information about the video environment. Some applications will statically allocate this buffer, while others will use system calls to temporarily obtain buffer space.

The application then calls VESA XGA BIOS Function 00h (Return XGA Environment Information). If the AX register does not contain 004Eh on return from the function call, the application can determine that either the VESA XGA BIOS or an XGA is not present and handle such a situation.

If no error code is returned in AX, the function call was successful. The buffer has been zeroed and then filled by the VESA XGA BIOS with various information, including the number of XGAs installed in the system. The application can verify that it is a valid VESA block by identifying the characters 'VESA' in the beginning of the block. The application can inspect the `VESAVersion` field to determine whether the VESA XGA BIOS has sufficient functionality. The application may use the `OEMStringPtr` to determine system OEM-specific information.

The application then creates a new 256-byte buffer for each XGA in the system. Then the application calls VESA XGA BIOS Function 01h (Return XGA Subsystem Information) for each XGA present. If the AX register does not contain 004Eh on return from the function call, the application can determine that either the VESA XGA BIOS or an XGA is not present and handle such a situation.

If no error code is returned in AX, the function call was successful. The buffer has been filled by the VESA XGA BIOS with information about the adapter indicated by the virtual handle passed in the DX register, including its access address. The application may use the `OEMStringPtr` to determine board OEM-specific information.

Finally, the application can obtain a list of the supported XGA modes, by using the `VideoModePtr`. This field points to a list of OEM defined tags, representing the video modes supported by the specified XGA adapter.

The application then creates and clears new buffers and calls VESA XGA BIOS Function 02h (Return XGA Mode Information) to obtain information about the supported video modes on each XGA. Stepping through the tags pointed to by the `VideoModePtr`, obtained in the previous step, the application calls this function with a new tag until a suitable video mode is found. If no appropriate video mode is found, it is up to the application to handle the situation.

The Return XGA Mode Information function fills a buffer specified by the application with information describing the features of the video mode. The data block contains all the information an application needs to take advantage of the video mode.

To verify that the mode is supported, the application inspects bit D0 of the `ModeAttributes` field. If D0 is cleared, then the mode is not supported by the hardware. This might happen if a specific mode requires a certain type of monitor, but that monitor is not present.

After the application has selected a video mode, the next step is to initialize the mode. However, the application should save the present video mode. When the application exits, this mode should be restored. To obtain the present video mode, the VESA XGA BIOS Function 04h (Get XGA Video Mode) is used. If a non-VESA (standard VGA) mode is in effect, only the lower byte in the mode number is filled. The upper byte is cleared.

To initialize the video mode, the application would use VESA XGA BIOS Function 03h (Set XGA Video Mode). From this point on the application has full access to the XGA hardware and video memory.

When the application terminates, it should restore the prior video mode. The prior video mode, obtained above, could be either a standard VGA mode or an OEM-specific mode. It reinitializes the video mode by calling VESA XGA BIOS Function 03h (Set XGA Video Mode). The application would then exit.

B. Adapter Identification Appendix

In order to differentiate between the original IBM XGA and VESA compatible systems, the following mechanism is suggested:

1. Check the POS ID to determine if the POS ID is within the 1K set of POS ID numbers. If it is, then the product is a VESA compliant XGA. If not, then step (2).

2. Check for POS ID=8FD8h through 8FDBh or 8FD0h through 8FD3h. If not found, then the product is not XGA. If found, then step (3).

3. Determine if indexing of POS registers is supported. This could be determined by writing multiple values to the POS Index registers (POS 6 and POS 7), and verifying that the values read back correctly. Note that values larger than 3 are not guaranteed to read back correctly. If indexing is not supported, the product is an original IBM XGA or 100% compatible. If indexing is supported, then step (4).

4. Read Manufacturer ID and save.

5. Check for revision number at POS 4, Index 2. If zero (0), no revision numbering is supported, otherwise save.

6. Check for vendor subsystem ID at XGA Index 75h. If zero (0), no vendor ID is supported, otherwise save.

C. Multiple Video Subsystems Appendix

XGA/XGA Combination

In the case of two coexisting XGA subsystems, the standard IBM mechanism using the POS registers and subsystem-specific Instance numbers will keep the I/O locations from conflicting. However, VESA XGA subsystems will usually contain a VGA BIOS within them. This means that some mechanism will be required to allow coexistence of the VGA BIOS ROMs. The register bits in the VGA BIOS Configuration register allow coexistence of multiple VESA compatible BIOSes. The only requirement is that a subsystem disable its own VGA BIOS prior to enabling the next subsystem. This can be achieved by locating the executable code which performs the switch in the 8KB relocatable ROM area.

Multiple XGAs from multiple manufacturers will create special problems. This issue will not be addressed in this standard.

XGA/VGA Combination

There are three cases of coexistence which must be handled by an XGA subsystem, as follows:

- XGA Adapter in a system with a VGA using an E000h BIOS
- XGA Adapter in a system with a VGA using a C000h BIOS
- XGA subsystem coexisting with another XVGA (an XGA subsystem in a VGA compatibility mode) subsystem

XGA/E000 VGA Combination

If the VGA subsystem is a properly constructed mother board subsystem (using 3C3h for sleep and an E000h segment VGA BIOS), then an XGA adapter (using 46E8h for sleep control and a C000h segment VGA BIOS) will coexist as a by-product of VGA compatibility.

If the VGA subsystem uses 46E8h for sleep, or does not respond to sleep, then the XGA subsystem's VGA compatibility may be disabled, and the pass-through mechanism used from the existing VGA.

XGA/C000 VGA Combination

If the VGA subsystem is logically an adapter design (46E8h sleep, C000h VGA BIOS), regardless of whether it is physically on the mother board, there are two solutions:

- If the system in which the XGA Adapter is installed allows a device on the system bus to decode the E000h segment, then the XGA subsystem can be configured as a mother board subsystem (3C3h sleep and E000h VGA BIOS). This will allow the two subsystems to coexist. However, since most system BIOSes will not recognize an E000h VGA BIOS as a video BIOS, the C000h VGA BIOS will be POSTed first (rather than second) and will be in control following POST.

- If this is not possible, then a pass-through mechanism from the VGA could be used. This would allow the VGA to be used for VGA modes, with the XGA used solely for Extended Graphics mode. This would be compatible for applications that do not take advantage of 132 Column Text mode and which do not make assumptions about the overlap between the VGA and XGA video buffer.

XGA/EGA Combination

The addressing issues are similar to those associated with XGA/VGA, except that there is no POS mechanism or equivalent available, and most EGAs cannot be software disabled. This issue will not be addressed in this standard.

XGA/CGA or MDA Combination

The issues are the same as a VGA with CGA/Mono and will not be addressed in this standard.

D. Obtaining VESA Identification Numbers Appendix

To obtain a VESA identification number, contact the Video Electronics Standards Association at 2150 North First Street, Suite 440, San Jose, CA 95131-2020 or phone (408) 435-0333.

The IBM XGA-NI

I n mid-1992, IBM announced the XGA-NI (NI stands for Non-Interlaced), its first extension to the original XGA architecture.

XGA-NI extends the base XGA with the following features:

- A Non-Interlaced 1024x768 resolution with a 70Hz refresh, designed to work with the near-simultaneous release of the IBM 8517 monitor.

- The XGA-NI ships standard with 1MB of VRAM. The original XGA was available with 512 kilobytes.

- A PLL (Phase Locked Loop) integrated into the XGA's RAMDAC/VRAM Serializer chip, which allows the XGA to synthesize a wide range of frequencies for display purposes. Pixel rates up to 90MHz can be generated by the PLL. This means resolutions up to 1024x768x8bpp by 75Hz non-interlaced, and 800x600x16bpp by 60Hz.

- A new mechanism for better future monitor identification (documented Appendix C in some detail).

- The RAMDAC has been enhanced to support 8 bits per color gun. The original XGA supported only 6 bits per gun. The difference is that the XGA-NI has a palette of 2^{8+8+8} (16,777,216 different colors) versus the original XGA's 2^{6+6+6}

(only 262,144 colors). This means that all 8 bits of the Sprite Color x and Palette Data registers are valid on the XGA-NI, instead of just the high order 6 bits.

- Drawing support for 16bpp maps. Previously you could display only 16bpp, but with the XGA-NI, you can define a 16bpp map, and use the XGA drawing engine to draw in it.

- A new character mode called Main Frame Interactive (MFI), which, as its name applies, is used for Main Frame color text terminal emulation. The IBM terminals that use this MFI mode are the 3270 and 5250

- The 132-column mode supports 9-bit wide fonts, in addition to the original XGA's 8-bit wide font support.

The DMQS specification presented in Appendix C was a result of IBM getting ready to introduce the XGA-NI, since older register-based XGA software will not support the higher refresh rates of the XGA-NI.

The XGA-NI can be identified as such through its POS ID (POS registers 100H and 101H), which is 8FDAH (the original XGA ID is 8FDBH).

The new/enhanced registers for the XGA-NI are documented on the following pages, using the notation from Chapter 4. The new field and registers that appear here are not available on the original XGA.

I/O   21x0 Operating Mode Register

Read/Write, 8 bits

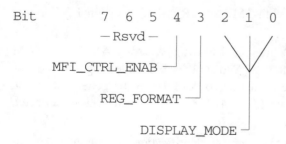

MFI_CTRL_ENAB

This bit, when set, enables the use of the MFI Control register (index 6DH) documented below. When cleared, the XGA-NI acts just like an original XGA. This bit is undefined on reads.

REG_FORMAT
Same as on original XGA.

DISPLAY_MODE
Same as on original XGA.

Comments
The reserved bits must be set to 0 when writing this register.

Mnemonic
OP_MODE

Index   54H Clock Select 1

Read/Write, 8 bits

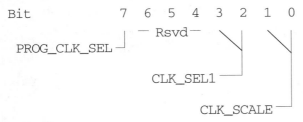

PROG_CLK_SEL
When the CLK_SEL1 field in this register and the CLK_SEL2 bit in the CLOCK_SEL2 register (index 70H) are cleared to 0s and this bit is set, the PLL in the XGA-NI is selected as the clock signal source for display frequency generation. This bit should be cleared when CLK_SEL1 and CLK_SEL2 are non-zero.

CLK_SEL1
Same as on original XGA.

CLK_SCAL
Same as on original XGA.

Comments
Both the CLOCK_SEL1 and CLOCK_SEL2 registers need to be set in order for a video clock to properly set for a given mode.

Mnemonic
CLOCK_SEL1

Index   58H PLL Program Register

Read/Write, 8 bits

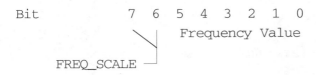

```
Bit            7  6  5  4  3  2  1  0
                        Frequency Value

     FREQ_SCALE
```

FREQ_SCALE

This field sets the frequency scale used to determine the frequency synthesized by the XGA-NI's PLL. The bits have the following meaning:

Bit 7	Bit 6	Description
0	0	Sets a division factor of 4, allowing a pixel clock frequency range of 16.25MHz to 32.00MHz, in 0.25MHz increments.
0	1	Sets a division factor of 2, allowing a pixel clock frequency range of 32.50MHz to 64.00MHz, in 0.50MHz increments.
1	0	Sets a division factor of 1, allowing a pixel clock frequency range of 65.00MHz to 128.00MHz, in 1.00MHz increments.
1	1	Reserved.

Frequency Value

This field sets the frequency value used to determine the frequency synthesized by the XGA-NI's PLL. The frequency value can be calculated as follows:

```
FrqValue = (DesiredPixClkFrq * DivisionFactor) - 65
```

Comments

The XGA-NI's PLL should only be driven as high as 90MHz. Anything beyond that will cause unpredicable results.

Mnemonic

PLL_PROGRAM

Index 59H Direct Color Control

Read/Write, 8 bits

```
Bit  7  6  5  4  3  2  1  0
     ──Reserved──       \  /
                         \/
              DC_MODIF ──┘
```

DC_MODIF

This field modifies the way Direct Color 5:6:5 pixels are displayed, particularly how the low order Red and Blue bits (the ones you can't access in a 16-bit pixel) are to be set to simulate a true DC 6:6:6 display.

Bit 2	Bit 1	Bit 0	Description
0	0	0	No change from the original XGA 16bpp display mode. This is called the Zero Intensity Black mode. The missing red and blue bits are set to 0.
0	0	1	The missing red and blue bits are set to 1 unless all other color bits are 0. IBM calls this the Non-Zero Color mode.
0	1	0	The missing red and blue bits are set to 0, same as option 000b.
0	1	1	The missing red and blue bits are set to 1, which IBM refers to as the Full Intensity White mode.
1	0	0	The missing red and blue bits are set to the value of the red and blue most significant bits (Bit 4 of each), which IBM calls the Linearized Color mode.

All other combinations are undefined.

Comments

The reserved bits are undefined on reads, and should be set to 0 on writes.

Mnemonic

DC_CTRL

Index   6CH Miscellaneous Control

Read/Write, 8 bits

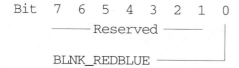

BLNK_REDBLUE

Setting this bit to 1 forces the output of the red and blue signals coming out of the DAC to 0, for simplified use with a monochrome display. Otherwise, you would have to load all red and blue palette entries with 0 to achieve the same effect as on the original XGA. When this bit is set to 0, the DAC output is left unaffected.

Comments

The reserved bits are undefined on reads, and should be set to 0 on writes.

Mnemonic

DC_CTRL

Index   6DH MFI Control

Read/Write, 8 bits

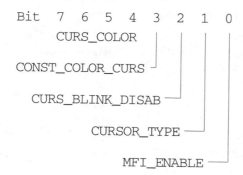

CURS_COLOR

This field contains the color of the cursor (using the standard IRGB format standard for VGA text characters), which is used if the CONST_CURS_COLOR bit is set.

CONST_COLOR_CURS

If this bit and the MFI_ENABLE bit are set, the constant color cursor is enabled, using the color specified by the CURS_COLOR field. If this bit is cleared, and the MFI_ENABLE bit is set, the cursor takes its color from the foreground color of the character underneath it.

CURS_BLINK_DISAB

If this bit and the MFI_ENABLE bit are set, a nonblinking cursor will be displayed. If this bit is cleared and the MFI_ENABLE bit is set, the cursor will blink at 1/32nd the speed of the vertical refresh (that is, as fast as characters blink in VGA text mode).

CURSOR_TYPE

If this bit and the MFI_ENABLE bit are set, the cursor highlights the character it is on by reversing its foreground and background colors. If cleared while the MFI_ENABLE bit is set, the cursor adopts the foreground of the character it is on.

MFI_ENABLE

If this bit is set, all other bits in this register go into use, and the display of text is controlled via the methods defined by the MFI (Main Frame Interactive).

XGA's MFI support works only in the VGA and 132-column text modes of the XGA-NI. The MFI support means that the attribute byte of an attribute/character pair takes on a different meaning than its typical VGA behavior. The attribute byte in MFI mode is as follows:

Bit(s)	Description
7	This bit is similar in function to the same bit in the VGA attribute byte. When set, the character to which it is relative will either blink (if the VGA character blink is enabled) or set the character's background color to 8. MFI characters, when blinking, remain on 75 percent of the time, as compared to VGA blinking characters, which are on 50 percent of time.
6	When set, the character is displayed in reverse video mode. When cleared, display of the character is normal.
5	If set, the associated character is underlined.
4	This bit, if set, enables the display of "column separator" pixels that appear in the first and last column of the character on the same scan line as would an underline (Bit 5, above). If the underline is enabled for the character, then setting this bit would clear the two-column separator pixels.
3-0	Set the character foreground color, just like in the VGA character modes.

If this bit is cleared, then regular VGA-style attributes take control.

Comments

IBM recommends that you call INT 10H with AH=12H, BL=37H, and AL=1 to Enable MFI attributes or AL=0 to disable MFI attributes instead of twiddling the registers, to preserve future compatibility. This call will return AL=12H if it is implemented.

Mnemonic

DC_CTRL

Memory   09H Auxiliary Status Register

Read Only, 8 bits

```
Bit          7  6  5  4  3  2  1  0
                 ┌──────── Reserved ────────┐
   AUX_BUSY ─┘
```

AUX_BUSY

If this bit is set during a read, then the XGA drawing engine is in the process of executing some type of drawing operation. While this bit is set, you should not write to any memory registers. If this bit is 0 on a read, then the XGA memory registers can be written to, and an XGA operation can be initiated.

Comments

The AUX_BUSY bit should be used instead of the BUSY bit in the Control register, because reading the BUSY bit causes the XGA drawing engine to suspend drawing operations while it services the register read request. The same is not true for this register, which is why you should use it instead if you're running on an XGA-NI. See the description of the XGAWAIT macro in Chapter 5 for more information.

Mnemonic

AUX_STAT_REG

Memory   1CH Pixel Map *n* Format

Write Only, 8 bits

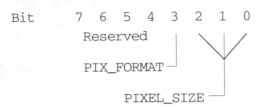

```
Bit     7  6  5  4  3  2  1  0
            Reserved
        PIX_FORMAT
            PIXEL_SIZE
```

PIX_FORMAT

Same as on original XGA.

PIXEL_SIZE

These three bits select the pixel size of the selected map:

Bit 2	Bit 1	Bit 0	Pixel Size
0	0	0	1 bit
0	0	1	2 bits
0	1	0	4 bits
0	1	1	8 bits
1	0	0	16 bits
1	0	1	Reserved
1	1	0	Reserved
1	1	1	Reserved

This field is used to tell the XGA's drawing engine about the size of a pixel for drawing operations. The IBM XGA-NI supports drawing operations in 1, 2, 4, 8, and 16 bit per pixel modes.

Comments

For the Mask Map, only the PIX_FORMAT field can be set. The PIXEL_SIZE field for the Mask Map should always be set for 1 bit per pixel. This rule also applies to whichever map (A, B, or C) you choose to use as a pattern map in drawing operations.

Mnemonic

MAP_FORMAT

The XGA Registers

POS (Programmable Option Select) Registers

Address[1]	Mnemonic[2]	Name
100H	POS_ID_LO	Identification Word, Low Byte
101H	POS_ID_HI	Identification Word, High Byte
102H	POS_CONFIG	XGA Configuration register
103H	POS_ARBITRATE	Bus Arbitration register
104H	POS_DISPMEMBASE	Display Memory Base Address
105H	POS_BASE_1MB	1 MB Aperture Base Address

1. This is the hexadecimal port address of the POS register. All POS registers are 8-bit. POS registers are available only at certain times. See the next chapter for information on when to access the POS registers.

2. The mnemonics for use with the C and ASM include files used in the XGA programming examples.

I/O Registers

Address[1]	Mnemonic	Name
21x0	OP_MODE	Operating Mode register
21x1	MEMWIN_CTRL	Aperture Control register
21x4	INT_ENABLE	Interrupt Enable register
21x5	INT_STATUS	Interrupt Status register
21x6	VIRT_MEM_CTRL	Virtual Memory Control register
21x7	VIRT_MEM_INT_STAT	Virtual Memory Interrupt Status register
21x8	MEMWIN_INDEX	Aperture Index register
21x9	MEM_ACCESS_MODE	Memory Access Mode
21xA	IO_INDEX	Index register
21xB	IO_DATA	Data register
21xC-F[2]	IO_MOREDATA	Supplemental Data registers

1. The port in hexadecimal notation for I/O register addresses. The XGA instance number is represented by *x*. All of these registers are 8-bits wide.

2. These registers are actually the IO-DATA register mapped at four additional byte locations, 21xC through 21xF, so that byte, word, or even double-word (32-bit) writes and reads can be made to/from the I/O registers.

Index Registers (addressed via the Index Register)

Index[1]	Access[2]	Mnemonic	Name
00H	RW	MEM_CONFIG0	Memory Configuration 0
01H	RW	MEM_CONFIG1	Memory Configuration 1
02H	RW	MEM_CONFIG2	Memory Configuration 2
04H	RO	AUTO_CONFIG	Auto-Configuration register
0CH	RW	STATE_A_DATA	State A Data
0DH	RW	STATE_B_DATA	State B Data
10H	RW	HTOTAL_LO	Horizontal Total Low
11H	RW	HTOTAL_HI	Horizontal Total High.
12H	RW	HDISP_END_LO	Horizontal Display End Low

13H	RW	HDISP_END_HI	Horizontal Display End High
14H	RW	HBLANK_START_LO	Horizontal Blank Start Low
15H	RW	HBLANK_START_HI	Horizontal Blank Start High
16H	RW	HBLANK_END_LO	Horizontal Blank End Low
17H	RW	HBLANK_END_HI	Horizontal Blank End High
18H	RW	HSYNC_START_LO	Horizontal Sync Start Low
19H	RW	HSYNC_START_HI	Horizontal Sync Start High
1AH	RW	HSYNC_END_LO	Horizontal Sync End Low
1BH	RW	HSYNC_END_HI	Horizontal Sync End High
1CH	WO	HSYNC_POS1	Horizontal Sync Position 1
1EH	WO	HSYNC_POS2	Horizontal Sync Position 2
20H	RW	VTOTAL_LO	Vertical Total Low
21H	RW	VTOTAL_HI	Vertical Total High
22H	RW	VDISPLAY_END_LO	Vertical Display End Low
23H	RW	VDISPLAY_END_HI	Vertical Display End High
24H	RW	VBLANK_START_LO	Vertical Blank Start Low
25H	RW	VBLANK_START_HI	Vertical Blank Start High
26H	RW	VBLANK_END_LO	Vertical Blank End Low
27H	RW	VBLANK_END_HI	Vertical Blank End High
28H	RW	VSYNC_START_LO	Vertical Sync Start Low
29H	RW	VSYNC_START_HI	Vertical Sync Start High
2AH	RW	VSYNC_END	Vertical Sync End
2CH	RW	VLINE_COMP_LO	Vertical Line Compare Low
2DH	RW	VLINE_COMP_HI	Vertical Line Compare High
30H	RW	SPRITE_POSX_LO	Sprite Position X Low
31H	RW	SPRITE_POSX_HI	Sprite Position X High
32H	RW	SPRITE_HOTX	Sprite Hotspot X
33H	RW	SPRITE_POSY_LO	Sprite Position Y Low
34H	RW	SPRITE_POSY_HI	Sprite Position Y High
35H	RW	SPRITE_HOTY	Sprite Hotspot Y
36H	RW	SPRITE_CTRL	Sprite Control
38H	RW	SPRITE_COLOR0_RED	Sprite Color 0 Red

continued...

...from previous page

39H	RW	SPRITE_COLOR0_GREEN	Sprite Color 0 Green
3AH	RW	SPRITE_COLOR0_BLUE	Sprite Color 0 Blue
3BH	RW	SPRITE_COLOR1_RED	Sprite Color 1 Red
3CH	RW	SPRITE_COLOR1_GREEN	Sprite Color 1 Green
3DH	RW	SPRITE_COLOR1_BLUE	Sprite Color 1 Blue
40H	RW	DISP_ADDR_LO	Display Start Low
41H	RW	DISP_ADDR_MID	Display Start Middle
42H	RW	DISP_ADDR_HI	Display Start High
43H	RW	BUFFER_PITCH_LO	Display Buffer Pitch Low
44H	RW	BUFFER_PITCH_HI	Display Buffer Pitch High
50H	RW	DISP_CTRL1	Display Control 1
51H	RW	DISP_CTRL2	Display Control 2
52H	RO	MON_ID_GUN_OUT	Monitor ID & Gun Output
54H	RW	CLOCK_SEL_1	Clock Select 1
55H	RW	BORDER_COLOR	Border Color
60H	RW	SPRITE_INDEX_LO	Sprite Index Low
60H[3]	RW	PALETTE_INDEX	Palette Index
61H	RW	SPRITE_INDEX_HI	Sprite Index High
62H	RW	SPRITE_INDEX_LO_PREF	Sprite Index Low with Prefetch
62H[3]	RW	PALETTE_INDEX_LO_PREF	Palette Index Low with Prefetch
63H	RW	SPRITE_INDEX_HI_PREF	Sprite Index High with Prefetch
64H	RW	PALETTE_MASK	Palette Mask
65H	RW	PALETTE_DATA	Palette Data
66H	RW	PALETTE_SEQUENCE	Palette Sequence
67H	RW	PALETTE_RED_PRE	Palette Red Prefetch
68H	RW	PALETTE_GREEN_PRE	Palette Green Prefetch
69H	RW	PALETTE_BLUE_PRE	Palette Blue Prefetch
6AH	RW	SPRITE_DATA	Sprite Data
6BH	RW	SPRITE_DATA_PRE	Sprite Data Prefetch
70H	RW	CLOCK_SEL_2	Clock Select 2

1. This is the index value, in hexadecimal notation, set in the IO-INDEX register to access the specified register. Data is written to this register via the IO-DATA or IO-MOREDATA registers.

2. RO = Read Only (should not be written), WO = Write Only (should not be read), and RW = Readable and Writable.

3. These registers control both the palette and sprite data indexing mechanism. I/O to the Palette and Sprite Data registers determine the meaning that the Sprite and Palette index and control registers take on.

Memory-Based Registers

Offset[1]	Access[2]	Mnemonic	Name
00H	WO32	PAGE_DIR_BASE_ADDR	Page Directory Base Address
04H	RO32	CURR_VIRT_ADDR	Current Virtual Address
0CH	RO8	STATE_A_LEN	State A Length
0DH	RO8	STATE_B_LEN	State B Length
11H	RW8	CTRL_REG	Control register
12H	WO8	MAP_INDEX	Pixel Map Index
14H	WO32	MAP_BASE	Pixel Map n Base Pointer
18H	WO16	MAP_WIDTH	Pixel Map n Width
1AH	WO16	MAP_HEIGHT	Pixel Map n Height
1CH	WO8	MAP_FORMAT	Pixel Map n Format
20H	RW16	BRES_ERROR	Bresenham Error Term
24H	WO16	BRES_K1	Bresenham Constant 1
28H	WO16	BRES_K2	Bresenham Constant 2
2CH	WO32	SHORT_STROKE	Short Stroke register
48H	WO8	FORE_MIX	Foreground Mix
49H	WO8	BACK_MIX	Background Mix
4AH	WO8	CC_FUNC	Color Compare Function
4CH	WO32	CC_COLOR	Color Compare Color
50H	WO32	PLANE_MASK	Plane Mask
54H	WO32	CARRY_CHAIN_MASK	Carry Chain Mask
58H	WO32	FORE_COLOR	Foreground Color
5CH	WO32	BACK_COLOR	Background Color
60H	WO16	DIM1	Operation Dimension 1
62H	WO16	DIM2	Operation Dimension 2

continued....

...from previous page

6CH	WO16	MASK_ORG_X	Mask Map Origin X Offset
6EH	WO16	MASK_ORG_Y	Mask Map Origin Y Offset
70H	RW16	SRC_X	Source Map X
72H	RW16	SRC_Y	Source Map Y
74H	RW16	PATT_X	Pattern Map X
76H	RW16	PATT_Y	Pattern Map Y
78H	RW16	DEST_X	Destination Map X
7AH	RW16	DEST_Y	Destination Map Y
7CH	WO32	CMD_REG	Command register

1. The Offset is a hexadecimal number reflecting the byte offset into the 128 byte page of register memory, assuming Intel format.

2. RO = Read Only (should not be written), WO = Write Only (should not be read), RW = Readable and Writable, 8 = Should be accessed as a byte, 16 = access as a word, 32 = access as a double word, if possible.

The XGA.H C Include File

T his appendix contains the C include file XGA.H, which is used in many of the examples throughout Chapter 5. Included in this file are all the XGA related definitions you'll need to write XGA register-specific C code.

```
/**********************************************************************
   XGA.H — "C" Include file for the "Power Programming the IBM XGA".

   Written by Jake Richter

   Copyright (C) 1990-1992 Panacea Inc. - All Rights Reserved

   NOTICE:

   This include file may be freely used and incorporated in your code,
   providing that this header, including the copyright notice, remains
   unchanged.

 **********************************************************************/
/*---------------------------------------------------------------------

   TYPE DEFINITIONS

   The following definitions are used in all the listings to
   reference certain data types. This is done to help make
   the code more readable, and to assist later translation
   and communication with assembly language.

---------------------------------------------------------------------*/

#define  FALSE      0
#define  TRUE       !(FALSE)
#define  BYTE       char
#define  WORD       short
#define  DWORD      long
#define  UBYTE      unsigned BYTE
#define  UWORD      unsigned WORD
#define  UDWORD     unsigned DWORD
#define  FAR        far
#define  HUGE       huge
#define  VOID       void

/*---------------------------------------------------------------------

   MACROS

---------------------------------------------------------------------*/

/*

   IOREGREAD

   Reads the byte size I/O register in the XGA pointed to by "regNum".
   Assumes that the ioRegBaseAddr variable has been loaded with a valid
   XGA I/O register base address.

*/

#define IOREGREADB(regNum)    inp(ioRegBaseAddr + (regNum))
```

```
/*

   IOREGREADW
   Reads the word size I/O register in the XGA pointed to by "regNum".
   Assumes that the ioRegBaseAddr variable has been loaded with a valid
   XGA I/O register base address.

*/

#define IOREGREADW(regNum)    inpw(ioRegBaseAddr + (regNum))

/*

   IOREGWRITEB

   Writes a byte to the I/O register in the XGA pointed to by "regNum".
   Assumes that the ioRegBaseAddr variable has been loaded with a valid
   XGA I/O register base address.

*/

#define IOREGWRITEB(regNum, value)   outp(ioRegBaseAddr + (regNum),
(value))

/*

   IOREGWRITEW

   Writes AX to the I/O register in the XGA pointed to by "regNum".
   Destroys DX. Assumes that _ioRegBaseAddr has already been
   initialized to point to the right address.

*/

#define IOREGWRITEW(regNum, value)   outpw(ioRegBaseAddr + (regNum),
(value))

/*

   XGAWAIT

   Waits until the XGA processor done with the current operation,
   by polling the processor in a tight loop.
   Assumes that memRegBaseAddr points to the base address of the
   XGA memory register page.
   If this macro is not used, then XGA operation may be corrupted and
   even hung. Also, on the current XGA rev, this polling will slow
   down the graphics operation.

*/

#define XGAWAIT  while (memRegBaseAddr[CTRL_REG] & BUSY)

/*
```

continued...

...from previous page

```
  SENDD

  Sends a DWORD value to an XGA memory register.
  Assumes that memRegBaseAddr points to the base address of the
  XGA memory register page.

*/

#define SENDD(address, valueH, valueL)  \
          *(UDWORD FAR *)(memRegBaseAddr + (address)) = \
                        (((UDWORD)(valueH) << 16) | (valueL))

/*

  SENDW

  Sends a WORD value to an XGA memory register.
  Assumes that memRegBaseAddr points to the base address of the
  XGA memory register page.

*/

#define SENDW(address, value)  \
                  *(UWORD FAR *)(memRegBaseAddr + (address)) = (value)


/*

  SENDB

  Sends a BYTE value to an XGA memory register.
  Assumes that memRegBaseAddr points to the base address of the
  XGA memory register page.

*/

#define SENDB(address, value)  (memRegBaseAddr[(address)] = (value))

/*----------------------------------------------------------------------

  EQUATES

  ----------------------------------------------------------------------*/

/*

  POS Registers

*/

#define  POS_ID_LO           0x100  /* Identification Word, Low Byte */
#define  POS_ID_HI           0x101  /* Identification Word, High Byte */
#define  POS_CONFIG          0x102  /* XGA Configuration Register */
#define  POS_ARBITRATE       0x103  /* Bus Arbitration Register */
#define  POS_DISPMEMBASE     0x104  /* Display Memory Base Address */
#define  POS_BASE_1MB        0x105  /* 1 MB Aperture Base Address */
```

```
/*

    I/O Registers (used as offsets from base I/O address)

*/
#define   OP_MODE              0x00    /* Operating Mode Register */
#define   MEMWIN_CTRL          0x01    /* Aperture Control Register */
#define   INT_ENABLE           0x04    /* Interrupt Enable Register */
#define   INT_STATUS           0x05    /* Interrupt Status Register */
#define   VIRT_MEM_CTRL        0x06    /* Virtual Memory Control Register */
#define   VIRT_MEM_INT_STAT    0x07    /* Virtual Memory Interrupt Status Reg. */
#define   MEMWIN_INDEX         0x08    /* Aperture Index Register */
#define   MEM_ACCESS_MODE      0x09    /* Memory Access Mode */
#define   IO_INDEX             0x0A    /* Index Register */
#define   IO_DATA              0x0B    /* Data Register */
#define   IO_MOREDATA          0x0C    /* Supplemental Data Registers */

/*

    Index Registers (accessed via the IO_INDEX register

*/
#define   MEM_CONFIG0          0x00    /* Memory Configuration 0 */
#define   MEM_CONFIG1          0x01    /* Memory Configuration 1 */
#define   MEM_CONFIG2          0x02    /* Memory Configuration 2 */
#define   AUTO_CONFIG          0x04    /* Auto-Configuration Register */
#define   STATE_A_DATA         0x0C    /* State A Data */
#define   STATE_B_DATA         0x0D    /* State B Data */
#define   HTOTAL_LO            0x10    /* Horizontal Total Low */
#define   HTOTAL_HI            0x11    /* Horizontal Total High */
#define   HDISP_END_LO         0x12    /* Horizontal Display End Low */
#define   HDISP_END_HI         0x13    /* Horizontal Display End High */
#define   HBLANK_START_LO      0x14    /* Horizontal Blank Start Low */
#define   HBLANK_START_HI      0x15    /* Horizontal Blank Start High */
#define   HBLANK_END_LO        0x16    /* Horizontal Blank End Low */
#define   HBLANK_END_HI        0x17    /* Horizontal Blank End High */
#define   HSYNC_START_LO       0x18    /* Horizontal Sync Start Low */
#define   HSYNC_START_HI       0x19    /* Horizontal Sync Start High */
#define   HSYNC_END_LO         0x1A    /* Horizontal Sync End Low */
#define   HSYNC_END_HI         0x1B    /* Horizontal Sync End High */
#define   HSYNC_POS1           0x1C    /* Horizontal Sync Position 1 */
#define   HSYNC_POS2           0x1E    /* Horizontal Sync Position 2 */
#define   VTOTAL_LO            0x20    /* Vertical Total Low */
#define   VTOTAL_HI            0x21    /* Vertical Total High */
#define   VDISPLAY_END_LO      0x22    /* Vertical Display End Low */
#define   VDISPLAY_END_HI      0x23    /* Vertical Display End High */
#define   VBLANK_START_LO      0x24    /* Vertical Blank Start Low */
#define   VBLANK_START_HI      0x25    /* Vertical Blank Start High */
```

continued...

...from previous page

```
#define  VBLANK_END_LO           0x26   /* Vertical Blank End Low */
#define  VBLANK_END_HI           0x27   /* Vertical Blank End High */
#define  VSYNC_START_LO          0x28   /* Vertical Sync Start Low */
#define  VSYNC_START_HI          0x29   /* Vertical Sync Start High */
#define  VSYNC_END               0x2A   /* Vertical Sync End */
#define  VLINE_COMP_LO           0x2C   /* Vertical Line Compare Low */
#define  VLINE_COMP_HI           0x2D   /* Vertical Line Compare High */
#define  SPRITE_POSX_LO          0x30   /* Sprite Position X Low */
#define  SPRITE_POSX_HI          0x31   /* Sprite Position X High */
#define  SPRITE_HOTX             0x32   /* Sprite Hotspot X */
#define  SPRITE_POSY_LO          0x33   /* Sprite Position Y Low */
#define  SPRITE_POSY_HI          0x34   /* Sprite Position Y High */
#define  SPRITE_HOTY             0x35   /* Sprite Hotspot Y */
#define  SPRITE_CTRL             0x36   /* Sprite Control */
#define  SPRITE_COLOR0_RED       0x38   /* Sprite Color 0 Red */
#define  SPRITE_COLOR0_GREEN     0x39   /* Sprite Color 0 Green */
#define  SPRITE_COLOR0_BLUE      0x3A   /* Sprite Color 0 Blue */
#define  SPRITE_COLOR1_RED       0x3B   /* Sprite Color 1 Red */
#define  SPRITE_COLOR1_GREEN     0x3C   /* Sprite Color 1 Green */
#define  SPRITE_COLOR1_BLUE      0x3D   /* Sprite Color 1 Blue */
#define  DISP_ADDR_LO            0x40   /* Display Start Low */
#define  DISP_ADDR_MID           0x41   /* Display Start Middle */
#define  DISP_ADDR_HI            0x42   /* Display Start High */
#define  BUFFER_PITCH_LO         0x43   /* Display Buffer Pitch Low */
#define  BUFFER_PITCH_HI         0x44   /* Display Buffer Pitch High */
#define  DISP_CTRL1              0x50   /* Display Control 1 */
#define  DISP_CTRL2              0x51   /* Display Control 2 */
#define  MON_ID_GUN_OUT          0x52   /* Monitor ID & Gun Output */
#define  CLOCK_SEL_1             0x54   /* Clock Select 1 */
#define  BORDER_COLOR            0x55   /* Border Color */
#define  SPRITE_INDEX_LO         0x60   /* Sprite Index Low */
#define  PALETTE_INDEX           0x60   /* Palette Index */
#define  SPRITE_INDEX_HI         0x61   /* Sprite Index High */
#define  SPRITE_INDEX_LO_PREF    0x62   /* Sprite Index Low with Prefetch */
#define  PALETTE_INDEX_LO_PREF   0x62   /* Palette Index Low with Prefetch */
#define  SPRITE_INDEX_HI_PREF    0x63   /* Sprite Index High with Prefetch */
#define  PALETTE_MASK            0x64   /* Palette Mask */
#define  PALETTE_DATA            0x65   /* Palette Data */
#define  PALETTE_SEQUENCE        0x66   /* Palette Sequence */
#define  PALETTE_RED_PRE         0x67   /* Palette Red Prefetch */
#define  PALETTE_GREEN_PRE       0x68   /* Palette Green Prefetch */
#define  PALETTE_BLUE_PRE        0x69   /* Palette Blue Prefetch */
#define  SPRITE_DATA             0x6A   /* Sprite Data */
#define  SPRITE_DATA_PRE         0x6B   /* Sprite Data Prefetch */
#define  CLOCK_SEL_2             0x70   /* Clock Select 2 */
```

```
/*
    Memory Based Registers (used as offsets from memory register base)
*/
#define    PAGE_DIR_BASE_ADDR      0x00    /* Page Directory Base Address */
#define    CURR_VIRT_ADDR          0x04    /* Current Virtual Address */
#define    STATE_A_LEN             0x0C    /* State A Length */
#define    STATE_B_LEN             0x0D    /* State B Length */
#define    CTRL_REG                0x11    /* Control Register */
#define    MAP_INDEX               0x12    /* Pixel Map Index */
#define    MAP_BASE                0x14    /* Pixel Map n Base Pointer */
#define    MAP_WIDTH               0x18    /* Pixel Map n Width */
#define    MAP_HEIGHT              0x1A    /* Pixel Map n Height */
#define    MAP_FORMAT              0x1C    /* Pixel Map n Format */
#define    BRES_ERROR              0x20    /* Bresenham Error Term */
#define    BRES_K1                 0x24    /* Bresenham Constant 1 */
#define    BRES_K2                 0x28    /* Bresenham Constant 2 */
#define    SHORT_STROKE            0x2C    /* Short Stroke Register */
#define    FORE_MIX                0x48    /* Foreground Mix */
#define    BACK_MIX                0x49    /* Background Mix */
#define    CC_FUNC                 0x4A    /* Color Compare Function */
#define    CC_COLOR                0x4C    /* Color Compare Color */
#define    PLANE_MASK              0x50    /* Plane Mask */
#define    CARRY_CHAIN_MASK        0x54    /* Carry Chain Mask */
#define    FORE_COLOR              0x58    /* Foreground Color */
#define    BACK_COLOR              0x5C    /* Background Color */
#define    DIM1                    0x60    /* Operation Dimension 1 */
#define    DIM2                    0x62    /* Operation Dimension 2 */
#define    MASK_ORG_X              0x6C    /* Mask Map Origin X Offset */
#define    MASK_ORG_Y              0x6E    /* Mask Map Origin Y Offset */
#define    SRC_X                   0x70    /* Source Map X */
#define    SRC_Y                   0x72    /* Source Map Y */
#define    PATT_X                  0x74    /* Pattern Map X */
#define    PATT_Y                  0x76    /* Pattern Map Y */
#define    DEST_X                  0x78    /* Destination Map X */
#define    DEST_Y                  0x7A    * Destination Map Y */
#define    CMD_REG                 0x7C    /* Command Register */

/*-----------------------------------
    Register Field Mnemonics (for all registers)
------------------------------------*/

/*
    POS  102H  -  XGA Configuration Register
*/
#define    EXT_MEM_ADDR            0xF0    /* Mask. * 200H + C0000H = 8KB ROM Base
*/
#define    INSTANCE                0x0E    /* Mask for instance number */
```

continued...

...from previous page

```
#define  INSTANCE_SHFT     1        /* Left shift to get instance into place */
#define  XGA_ENABLE        0x01     /* Value to enable XGA register access */

/*

   POS  103H  -  Bus Arbitration Register (MCA Only)

*/
#define  ARB_LEVEL         0x78     /* Mask for arbitration level */
#define  ARB_LEVEL_SHFT    3        /* Left shift for arbitration level */
#define  FAIR_ENABLE       0x04     /* Value to enable MCA fairness */
#define  EXT_MEM_ENABLE    0x02     /* Value to enable 8KB XGA ROM addressing */
*

   POS  104H  -  Display Memory Base Address

*/
#define  DISP_MEM_BASE     0xFE     /* Mask for XGA linear address base */
#define  DISP_MEM_ACCESS   0x01     /* Value to enable PC access to XGA mem. */

/*

   POS  105H  -  1 MB Aperture Base Address

*/
#define  BASE_1MB          0x0F     /* Mask. * 100000H = 1MB Aperture addr. */

/*

   I/O  21x0H  -  Operating Mode Register

*/
#define  REG_FORMAT_INTEL  0x01     /* Value to set Intel addressing */
#define  REG_FORMAT_MOTOR  0x08     /* Value to set Motorola addressing */
#define  DISPLAY_MODE      0x07     /* Mask for display mode */
#define  DISP_VGA_MODE     0x1      /* Normal VGA Mode */
#define  DISP_132_MODE     0x2      /* Normal 132 column mode */
#define  DISP_XGA_MODE     0x4      /* Normal XGA graphics mode */

/*

   I/O  21x1H  -  Aperture Control Register

*/
#define  MEMWIN_ACCESS     0x03     /* Mask for 64KB Mem. Win. access */
#define  MEMWIN_DISABLE    0x00     /* Value to disable the Mem Win */
#define  MEMWIN_ENABLE_A   0x01     /* Value to enable the Mem Win at A0000H */
#define  MEMWIN_ENABLE_B   0x02     /* Value to enable the Mem Win at B0000H */

/*

   I/O  21x4H  -  Interrupt Enable Register
```

```
*/
#define   CMD_DONE_ENAB       0x80    /* Value to enable Command Done interrupt
*/
#define   ACCESS_REJ_ENAB     0x40    /* Value to enable Access Reject interrupt
*/
#define   SPRT_DSPCMP_ENAB    0x04    /* Value to enable Sprite Disp. interrupt
*/
#define   START_PIC_ENAB      0x02    /* Value to enable Start Pict. interrupt */
#define   START_BLNK_ENAB     0x01    /* Value to enable End Pict. interrupt */
/*

   I/O  21x5H  -  Interrupt Status Register

*/
#define   CMD_DONE_STAT       0x80    /* Value to test Command Done interrupt */
#define   ACCESS_REJ_STAT     0x40    /* Value to test Access Reject interrupt */
#define   SPRT_DSPCMP_STAT    0x04    /* Value to test Sprite Disp. interrupt */
#define   START_PIC_STAT      0x02    /* Value to test Start Pict. interrupt */
#define   START_BLNK_STAT     0x01    /* Value to test End Pict. interrupt */
/*

   I/O  21x6H  -  Virtual Memory Control Register

*/
#define   PAGE_NP_ENAB        0x80    /* Value to enable Page Not Present int. */
#define   PROT_VIOL_ENAB      0x40    /* Value to enable Prot. Violation int. */
#define   USER_SUPER          0x04    /* Value to set user level privilege */
#define   ENAB_VIRT_LU        0x01    /* Value to enable MMU-style look-up */
/*

   I/O  21x7H  -  Virtual Memory Interrupt Status Register

*/
#define   PAGE_NP_ENAB        0x80     /* Value to test for Page Not Present int.
*/
#define   PROT_VIOL_ENAB       0x40   /* Value to test for Prot. Violation int.
*/

/*

   I/O  21x8H  -  Aperture Index Register

*/
#define   MEMWIN_BANK          0x3F    /* Mask for the Memory Window bank */
/*

   I/O  21x9H  -  Memory Access Mode

*/
#define   MEMPIX_FORMAT_INTEL  0x08    /* Value to set Intel format memory map
*/
```

continued...

...from previous page

```
#define  MEMPIX_FORMAT_MOTOR   0x08   /* Value to set Motorola format mem. map
*/
#define  MEMPIX_SIZE_1         0x00   /* Value for 1 bpp access */
#define  MEMPIX_SIZE_2         0x01   /* Value for 2 bpp access */
#define  MEMPIX_SIZE_4         0x02   /* Value for 4 bpp access */
#define  MEMPIX_SIZE_8         0x03   /* Value for 8 bpp access */
#define  MEMPIX_SIZE_16        0x04   /* Value for 16 bpp access */

/*

  Index  04H  -  Auto-Configuration

*/
#define  BUS_SIZE              0x01   /* Mask. If set, is 32 bit bus width */

/*

  Index  1CH  -  Horizontal Sync Pulse Position 1

*/
#define  SYNC_PULSE_DLY1_0     0x00   /* Value for 0 pixel Sync Pulse Delay */
#define  SYNC_PULSE_DLY1_4     0x40   /* Value for 4 pixel Sync Pulse Delay */

/*

  Index  1EH  -  Horizontal Sync Pulse Position 2

*/
#define  SYNC_PULSE_DLY2_0     0x00   /* Value for 0 pixel Sync Pulse Delay */
#define  SYNC_PULSE_DLY2_4     0x04   /* Value for 4 pixel Sync Pulse Delay */
/*

  Index  36H  -  Sprite Control

*/
#define  SPRITE_ENAB           0x01   /* Value used to enable Sprite display */

/*

  Index  50H  -  Display Control 1

*/
#define  SYNC_POLAR            0xC0   /* Mask for Sync Polarity */
#define  SYNC_POLAR_768        0x00   /* Value for 768 line Sync Polarity */
#define  SYNC_POLAR_400        0x40   /* Value for 400 line Sync Polarity */
#define  SYNC_POLAR_350        0x80   /* Value for 350 line Sync Polarity */
#define  SYNC_POLAR_480        0xC0   /* Value for 480 line Sync Polarity */
#define  DISP_CTRL1_PRESERVE   0x20   /* Mask to preserve necessary bit */
#define  FEATURE_ENAB          0x10   /* Mask/Value to enable Feature Conn. */
#define  INTERLACED            0x08   /* Mask/Value to enable interlacing */
#define  BLANK_DISP            0x03   /* Mask for blank display field */
#define  BLANK_DISP_CRTCRESET  0x00   /* Value to reset CRT Controller for
blank display field */
```

```
#define   BLANK_DISP_PREPCRTC    0x01   /* Value for CRTC reset preparation */
#define   BLANK_DISP_NORMAL      0x03   /* Value for normal display operation */

/*

   Index  51H  -  Display Control 2

*/
#define   VSCALE                 0xC0   /* Mask for the Vertical Scale Factor */
#define   VSCALE_1               0x00   /* Value for vertical scale of 1 */
#define   VSCALE_2               0x40   /* Value for vertical scale of 2 */
#define   VSCALE_4               0x80   /* Value for vertical scale of 4 */
#define   HSCALE                 0x30   /* Mask for the Horiztonal Scale Factor
*/
#define   HSCALE_1               0x00   /* Value for horizontal scale of 1 */
#define   HSCALE_2               0x10   /* Value for horizontal scale of 2 */
#define   HSCALE_4               0x20   /* Value for horizontal scale of 4 */
#define   DSPPIX_SIZE            0x07   /* Mask for the Display Pixel Size */
#define   DSPPIX_SIZE_1          0x00   /* Value for 1 bpp display */
#define   DSPPIX_SIZE_2          0x01   /* Value for 2 bpp display */
#define   DSPPIX_SIZE_4          0x02   /* Value for 4 bpp display */
#define   DSPPIX_SIZE_8          0x03   /* Value for 8 bpp display */
#define   DSPPIX_SIZE_16         0x04   /* Value for 16 bpp display */

/*

   Index  52H  -  Monitor ID and Gun Output

*/
#define   BLUE_OUT               0x80   /* Mask for Blue gun level */
#define   GREEN_OUT              0x40   /* Mask for Green gun level */
#define   RED_OUT                0x20   /* Mask for Red gun level */
#define   MONITOR_ID             0x0F   /* Mask for Monitor ID */

/*

   Index  54H  -  Clock Select 1

*/
#define   CLK_SEL1               0x0C   /* Mask for Clock Select 1 field */
#define   CLK_SCALE              0x03   /* Mask for Clock Scale */

/*

   Index  66H  -  Palette Sequence

*/
#define   COLOR_FORMAT           0x04   /* Mask for Color format */
#define   COLOR_FORMAT_RGB       0x00   /* Value for RGB color format */
#define   COLOR_FORMAT_RBGx      0x04   /* Value for RBGx color format */
#define   COLOR_COMPNT           0x03   /* Mask for color component sequence */
#define   COLOR_COMPNT_R         0x00   /* Value for the red color component */
```

continued...

...from previous page

```
#define   COLOR_COMPNT_G        0x01   /* Value for the green color
component */
#define   COLOR_COMPNT_B        0x02   /* Value for the blue color component
*/
#define   COLOR_COMPNT_x        0x03   /* Value for the discard color
component */

/*

   Index  70H  -  Clock Select 2

*/
#define   CLK_SEL2              0x80   /* Mask/Value for Clock Select 2 bit
*/

/*

   Memory  11H  -  Control Register

*/
#define   BUSY                 0x80   /* Mask for Busy bit */
#define   TERM_OPER            0x20   /* Mask/Value for Terminate Operation
bit */
#define   OPER_SUSPND          0x10   /* Mask for Operation Suspended bit
*/
#define   SUSPND_OPER          0x08   /* Mask/Value for Suspend Operation
bit */
#define   STATE_SAVRST         0x02   /* Mask/Value for State Save/Restore
bit */
/*

   Memory  12H  -  Pixel Map Index

*/
#define   MAP_INDEX_MASK       0x00   /* Value to set the mask map index */
#define   MAP_INDEX_A          0x01   /* Value to set the map A index */
#define   MAP_INDEX_B          0x02   /* Value to set the map B index */
#define   MAP_INDEX_C          0x03   /* Value to set the map C index */
/*
   Memory  1CH  -  Pixel Map n Format
*/
#define   PIX_FORMAT_INTEL     0x00   /* Value to set Intel mode for curr.
map */
#define   PIX_FORMAT_MOTOR     0x08   /* Value to set Motorola mode for map
*/
#define   PIXEL_SIZE_1         0x00   /* Value to set 1 bpp map depth */
#define   PIXEL_SIZE_2         0x01   /* Value to set 2 bpp map depth */
#define   PIXEL_SIZE_4         0x02   /* Value to set 4 bpp map depth */
#define   PIXEL_SIZE_8         0x03   /* Value to set 8 bpp map depth */
```

```
/*

   Memory  48H,49H  -  Foreground/Background Mix

*/
#define  MIX_ZEROS                 0x00   /* 0 (all bits cleared) */
#define  MIX_0                     0x00   /* 0 (all bits cleared) */

#define  MIX_AND                   0x01   /* Src AND Dst */
#define  MIX_SRC_AND_NOT_DST       0x02   /* Src AND NOT Dst */

#define  MIX_SRC                   0x03   /* Src */
#define  MIX_PAINT                 0x03   /* Src */

#define  MIX_NOT_SRC_AND_DST       0x04   /* NOT Src AND Dst */

#define  MIX_DST                   0x05   /* Dst */
#define  MIX_LEAVE_ALONE           0x05   /* Dst */

#define  MIX_SRC_XOR_DST           0x06   /* Src XOR Dst */
#define  MIX_XOR                   0x06   /* Src XOR Dst */

#define  MIX_SRC_OR_DST            0x07   /* Src OR Dst */
#define  MIX_OR                    0x07   /* Src OR Dst */

#define  MIX_NOT_SRC_AND_NOT_DST 0x08   /* NOT Src AND NOT Dst */
#define  MIX_NOR                   0x08   /* NOT Src AND NOT Dst */

#define  MIX_SRC_XOR_NOT_DST       0x09   /* Src XOR NOT Dst */

#define  MIX_NOT_DST               0x0A   /* NOT Dst */

#define  MIX_SRC_OR_NOT_DST        0x0B   /* Src OR NOT Dst */

#define  MIX_NOT_SRC               0x0C   /* NOT Src */

#define  MIX_NOT_SRC_OR_DST        0x0D   /* NOT Src OR Dst */

#define  MIX_NOT_SRC_OR_NOT_DST    0x0E   /* NOT Src OR NOT Dst */
#define  MIX_NAND                  0x0E   /* NOT Src OR NOT Dst */

#define  MIX_ONES                  0x0F   /* 1 (all bits set) */
#define  MIX_1                     0x0F   /* 1 (all bits set) */

#define  MIX_MAX                   0x10   /* MAXIMUM(Src, Dst) */

#define  MIX_MIN                   0x11   /* MINIMUM(Src, Dst) */

#define  MIX_PLUS_SAT              0x12   /* Src + Dst [with saturate] */

#define  MIX_DST_MINUS_SRC_SAT     0x13   /* Dst - Src [with saturate] */

#define  MIX_SRC_MINUS_DST_SAT     0x14   /* Src - Dst [with saturate] */

#define  MIX_AVERAGE               0x15   /* (Src + Dst) / 2 */

/*
```

continued...

...from previous page

```
Memory  4AH  -  Color Compare Function
*/
#define   CC_COND_TRUE          0x00  /* Always True */
#define   CC_COND_GT            0x01  /* Dst > CC */
#define   CC_COND_EQ            0x02  /* Dst == CC */
#define   CC_COND_LT            0x03  /* Dst < CC */
#define   CC_COND_FALSE         0x04  /* Always FALSE */
#define   CC_COND_GE            0x05  /* Dst >= CC */
#define   CC_COND_NE            0x06  /* Dst != CC */
#define   CC_COND_LE            0x07  /* Dst <= CC */

/*
   Memory  7CH  -  Command Register (Low Word)
*/
#define   PATT_SRC_A            0x1000 /* Pattern source is Map A */
#define   PATT_SRC_B            0x2000 /* Pattern source is Map B */
#define   PATT_SRC_C            0x3000 /* Pattern source is Map C */
#define   PATT_SRC_FORESRC      0x8000 /* Pattern source is Foreground
Source */
#define   PATT_SRC_SRCDATA      0x9000 /* Pattern source is source data */
#define   MASK_MODE_DISAB       0x0000 /* Mask Map is disabled */
#define   MASK_MODE_CLIP        0x0040 /* Mask Map boundary enabled
(clipping) */
#define   MASK_MODE_ENAB        0x0080 /* Mask Map is fully enabled */
#define   DRAW_MODE_ALL         0x0000 /* Draw all pixels in line/vector */
#define   DRAW_MODE_NOT_FIRST   0x0010 /* Draw all but the first pixel */
#define   DRAW_MODE_NOT_LAST    0x0020 /* Draw all but the last pixel */
#define   DRAW_MODE_BOUNDARY    0x0030 /* Draw area boundary for fill */
#define   DEC_X                 0x0004 /* Draw in Negative X direction */
#define   DEC_Y                 0x0002 /* Draw in Negative Y direction */
#define   YMAJOR                0x0001 /* Y axis is major axis */
/*
   Memory  7EH  -  Command Register (High Word)
*/
#define   BACK_SRC_COLOR        0x0000 /* Background Source is Background
Color */
#define   BACK_SRC_SRCMAP       0x8000 /* Background Source is Source Pixel
Map */
#define   FORE_SRC_COLOR        0x0000 /* Foreground Source is Foreground
Color */
#define   FORE_SRC_SRCMAP       0x2000 /* Foreground Source is Source Pixel
Map */
#define   CMD_SSV_READ          0x0200 /* Short Stroke Vector Read Command
```

```
*/
#define  CMD_LINE_READ          0x0300 /* Line Draw Read Command */
#define  CMD_SSV                0x0400 /* Short Stroke Vector Draw Command
*/
#define  CMD_LINE               0x0500 /* Line Draw Command */
#define  CMD_BITBLT             0x0800 /* BitBLT Command */
#define  CMD_INVERT_BITBLT      0x0900 /* Inverted BitBLT Command */
#define  CMD_AREA_FILL          0x0A00 /* Area Fill Command */
#define  SRC_MAP_A              0x0010 /* Use Map A as source map */
#define  SRC_MAP_B              0x0020 /* Use Map B as source map */
#define  SRC_MAP_C              0x0030 /* Use Map C as source map */
#define  DST_MAP_A              0x0001 /* Use Map A as destination map */
#define  DST_MAP_B              0x0002 /* Use Map B as destination map */
#define  DST_MAP_C              0x0003 /* Use Map C as destination map */
```

ASM Include File

This appendix contains the assembly language include file XGA.INC, which is used in some of the examples throughout Chapter 5. Included in this file are all the XGA-related definitions you'll need to write XGA register-specific assembly language code.

```
;*********************************************************************
;
; XGA.INC — ASM Include file for the "Power Programming the IBM XGA".
;
; Written by Jake Richter
;
; Copyright (C) 1990-1992 Panacea Inc. - All Rights Reserved
;
; NOTICE:
;       This include file may be freely used and incorporated in your code,
;       providing that this header, including the copyright notice, remains
;       unchanged.
;
;*********************************************************************
;
;-------------------------------------------------------------------
;
;       MACROS
;
;-------------------------------------------------------------------
;
; MEMREGBASE
;
; Loads ES with the memory register base segment.
; Assumes that CS:memRegBaseAddr has already been
; initialized to point to the right address.
;
MEMREGBASE    macro
              mov       ES, _memRegBaseAddr
              endm
;
;
; IOREGREADB
;
; Reads the byte size I/O register in the XGA pointed to by "regNum".
; Destroys DX, and returns result in AL. Assumes that _ioRegBaseAddr
; has already been initialized to point to the right address.
;
IOREGREADB    macro     regNum
              mov       DX, _ioRegBaseAddr
              add       DL, regNum
              in        AL, DX
              endm
```

```
;
;
; IOREGREADW
;
; Reads the word I/O register in the XGA pointed to by "regNum".
; Destroys DX, and returns result in AX. Assumes that _ioRegBaseAddr
; has already been initialized to point to the right address.
;
IOREGREADW macro        regNum
           mov          DX, _ioRegBaseAddr
           add          DX, regNum
           in           AX, DX
           endm
;
;
; IOREGWRITEB
;
; Writes AL to the I/O register in the XGA pointed to by "regNum".
; Destroys DX. Assumes that _ioRegBaseAddr has already been
; initialized to point to the right address.
;
IOREGWRITEB macro       regNum
           mov          DX, _ioRegBaseAddr
           add          DX, regNum
           out          DX, AL
           endm
;
;
; IOREGWRITEW
;
; Writes AX to the I/O register in the XGA pointed to by "regNum".
; Destroys DX. Assumes that _ioRegBaseAddr has already been
; initialized to point to the right address.
;
IOREGWRITEW macro       regNum
           mov          DX, _ioRegBaseAddr
           add          DX, regNum
           out          DX, AX
           endm
;
;
; XGAWAIT
;
; Waits until the XGA processor done with the current operation,
; by polling the processor in a tight loop.
; Assumes that ES is pointing to the memory registers.
; If this macro is not used, then XGA operation may be corrupted and
```
continued...

...from previous page

```
; even hung. Also, on the current XGA rev, this polling will slow
; down the graphics operation.
;
XGAWAIT     macro
            local     loop
loop:
            test      byte ptr ES:[CTRL_REG], BUSY
            jnz       short loop
            endm
;
;
; SENDD
;
; Sends a DWORD value to an XGA memory register. Assumes
; ES points to the memory register page. No registers trashed.
;
SENDD       macro     address, valueH, valueL
            mov       word ptr ES:[address], valueL
            mov       word ptr ES:[address+2], valueH
            endm
;
;
; SENDW
;
; Sends a WORD value to an XGA memory register. Assumes
; ES points to the memory register page. No registers trashed.
;
SENDW       macro     address, value
            mov       word ptr ES:[address], value
            endm
;
;
; SENDB
;
; Sends a BYTE value to an XGA memory register. Assumes
; ES points to the memory register page. No registers trashed.
;
SENDB       macro     address, value
            mov       byte ptr ES:[address], value
            endm
;
;
;-----------------------------------------------------------------------
;
;   EQUATES
;
;-----------------------------------------------------------------------
```

```
;
; POS Registers
;
POS_ID_LO              equ      100H    ; Identification Word, Low Byte
POS_ID_HI              equ      101H    ; Identification Word, High Byte
POS_CONFIG             equ      102H    ; XGA Configuration Register
POS_ARBITRATE          equ      103H    ; Bus Arbitration Register
POS_DISPMEMBASE        equ      104H    ; Display Memory Base Address
POS_BASE_1MB           equ      105H    ; 1 MB Aperture Base Address
;
;
; I/O Registers (used as offsets from base I/O address)
;
OP_MODE                equ      00H     ; Operating Mode Register
MEMWIN_CTRL            equ      01H     ; Aperture Control Register
INT_ENABLE             equ      04H     ; Interrupt Enable Register
INT_STATUS             equ      05H     ; Interrupt Status Register
VIRT_MEM_CTRL          equ      06H     ; Virtual Memory Control Register
VIRT_MEM_INT_STAT      equ      07H     ; Virtual Memory Interrupt Status Reg.
MEMWIN_INDEX           equ      08H     ; Aperture Index Register
MEM_ACCESS_MODE        equ      09H     ; Memory Access Mode
IO_INDEX               equ      0AH     ; Index Register
IO_DATA                equ      0BH     ; Data Register
IO_MOREDATA            equ      0CH     ; Supplemental Data Registers
;
;
; Index Registers (accessed via the IO_INDEX register
;
MEM_CONFIG0            equ      00H     ; Memory Configuration 0
MEM_CONFIG1            equ      01H     ; Memory Configuration 1
MEM_CONFIG2            equ      02H     ; Memory Configuration 2
AUTO_CONFIG            equ      04H     ; Auto-Configuration Register
STATE_A_DATA           equ      0CH     ; State A Data
STATE_B_DATA           equ      0DH     ; State B Data
HTOTAL_LO              equ      10H     ; Horizontal Total Low
HTOTAL_HI              equ      11H     ; Horizontal Total High
HDISP_END_LO           equ      12H     ; Horizontal Display End Low
HDISP_END_HI           equ      13H     ; Horizontal Display End High
HBLANK_START_LO        equ      14H     ; Horizontal Blank Start Low
HBLANK_START_HI        equ      15H     ; Horizontal Blank Start High
HBLANK_END_LO          equ      16H     ; Horizontal Blank End Low
HBLANK_END_HI          equ      17H     ; Horizontal Blank End High
HSYNC_START_LO         equ      18H     ; Horizontal Sync Start Low
HSYNC_START_HI         equ      19H     ; Horizontal Sync Start High
HSYNC_END_LO           equ      1AH     ; Horizontal Sync End Low
HSYNC_END_HI           equ      1BH     ; Horizontal Sync End High
HSYNC_POS1             equ      1CH     ; Horizontal Sync Position 1
```

continued...

...from previous page

```
HSYNC_POS2               equ    1EH    ; Horizontal Sync Position 2
VTOTAL_LO                equ    20H    ; Vertical Total Low
VTOTAL_HI                equ    21H    ; Vertical Total High
VDISPLAY_END_LO          equ    22H    ; Vertical Display End Low
VDISPLAY_END_HI          equ    23H    ; Vertical Display End High
VBLANK_START_LO          equ    24H    ; Vertical Blank Start Low
VBLANK_START_HI          equ    25H    ; Vertical Blank Start High
VBLANK_END_LO            equ    26H    ; Vertical Blank End Low
VBLANK_END_HI            equ    27H    ; Vertical Blank End High
VSYNC_START_LO           equ    28H    ; Vertical Sync Start Low
VSYNC_START_HI           equ    29H    ; Vertical Sync Start High
VSYNC_END                equ    2AH    ; Vertical Sync End
VLINE_COMP_LO            equ    2CH    ; Vertical Line Compare Low
VLINE_COMP_HI            equ    2DH    ; Vertical Line Compare High
SPRITE_POSX_LO           equ    30H    ; Sprite Position X Low
SPRITE_POSX_HI           equ    31H    ; Sprite Position X High
SPRITE_HOTX              equ    32H    ; Sprite Hotspot X
SPRITE_POSY_LO           equ    33H    ; Sprite Position Y Low
SPRITE_POSY_HI           equ    34H    ; Sprite Position Y High
SPRITE_HOTY              equ    35H    ; Sprite Hotspot Y
SPRITE_CTRL              equ    36H    ; Sprite Control
SPRITE_COLOR0_RED        equ    38H    ; Sprite Color 0 Red
SPRITE_COLOR0_GREEN      equ    39H    ; Sprite Color 0 Green
SPRITE_COLOR0_BLUE       equ    3AH    ; Sprite Color 0 Blue
SPRITE_COLOR1_RED        equ    3BH    ; Sprite Color 1 Red
SPRITE_COLOR1_GREEN      equ    3CH    ; Sprite Color 1 Green
SPRITE_COLOR1_BLUE       equ    3DH    ; Sprite Color 1 Blue
DISP_ADDR_LO             equ    40H    ; Display Start Low
DISP_ADDR_MID            equ    41H    ; Display Start Middle
DISP_ADDR_HI             equ    42H    ; Display Start High
BUFFER_PITCH_LO          equ    43H    ; Display Buffer Pitch Low
BUFFER_PITCH_HI          equ    44H    ; Display Buffer Pitch High
DISP_CTRL1               equ    50H    ; Display Control 1
DISP_CTRL2               equ    51H    ; Display Control 2
MON_ID_GUN_OUT           equ    52H    ; Monitor ID & Gun Output
CLOCK_SEL_1              equ    54H    ; Clock Select 1
BORDER_COLOR             equ    55H    ; Border Color
SPRITE_INDEX_LO          equ    60H    ; Sprite Index Low
PALETTE_INDEX            equ    60H    ; Palette Index
SPRITE_INDEX_WRITE_HI    equ    61H    ; Sprite Index High
SPRITE_INDEX_LO_PREF     equ    62H    ; Sprite Index Low with Prefetch
PALETTE_INDEX_LO_PREF    equ    62H    ; Palette Index Low with Prefetch
SPRITE_INDEX_HI_PREF     equ    63H    ; Sprite Index High with Prefetch
PALETTE_MASK             equ    64H    ; Palette Mask
PALETTE_DATA             equ    65H    ; Palette Data
PALETTE_SEQUENCE         equ    66H    ; Palette Sequence
```

```
PALETTE_RED_PRE       equ     67H     ; Palette Red Prefetch
PALETTE_GREEN_PRE     equ     68H     ; Palette Green Prefetch
PALETTE_BLUE_PRE      equ     69H     ; Palette Blue Prefetch
SPRITE_DATA           equ     6AH     ; Sprite Data
SPRITE_DATA_PRE       equ     6BH     ; Sprite Data Prefetch
CLOCK_SEL_2           equ     70H     ; Clock Select 2
;
;
; Memory Based Registers (used as offsets from memory register base)
;
PAGE_DIR_BASE_ADDR    equ     00H     ; Page Directory Base Address
CURR_VIRT_ADDR        equ     04H     ; Current Virtual Address
STATE_A_LEN           equ     0CH     ; State A Length
STATE_B_LEN           equ     0DH     ; State B Length
CTRL_REG              equ     11H     ; Control Register
MAP_INDEX             equ     12H     ; Pixel Map Index
MAP_BASE              equ     14H     ; Pixel Map n Base Pointer
MAP_WIDTH             equ     18H     ; Pixel Map n Width
MAP_HEIGHT            equ     1AH     ; Pixel Map n Height
MAP_FORMAT            equ     1CH     ; Pixel Map n Format
BRES_ERROR            equ     20H     ; Bresenham Error Term
BRES_K1               equ     24H     ; Bresenham Constant 1
BRES_K2               equ     28H     ; Bresenham Constant 2
SHORT_STROKE          equ     2CH     ; Short Stroke Register
FORE_MIX              equ     48H       Foreground Mix
BACK_MIX              equ     49H     ; Background Mix
CC_FUNC               equ     4AH     ; Color Compare Function
CC_COLOR              equ     4CH     ; Color Compare Color
PLANE_MASK            equ     50H     ; Plane Mask
CARRY_CHAIN_MASK      equ     54H     ; Carry Chain Mask
FORE_COLOR            equ     58H     ; Foreground Color
BACK_COLOR            equ     5CH     ; Background Color
DIM1                  equ     60H     ; Operation Dimension 1
DIM2                  equ     62H     ; Operation Dimension 2
MASK_ORG_X            equ     6CH     ; Mask Map Origin X Offset
MASK_ORG_Y            equ     6EH     ; Mask Map Origin Y Offset
SRC_X                 equ     70H     ; Source Map X
SRC_Y                 equ     72H     ; Source Map Y
PATT_X                equ     74H     ; Pattern Map X
PATT_Y                equ     76H     ; Pattern Map Y
DEST_X                equ     78H     ; Destination Map X
DEST_Y                equ     7AH     ; Destination Map Y
CMD_REG               equ     7CH     ; Command Register
;
;
;
```

continued...

...from previous page

```
; Register Field Mnemonics (for all registers)
;
;
;
; POS  102H  -  XGA Configuration Register
;
EXT_MEM_ADDR             equ    0F0H    ; Mask. * 200H + C0000H = 8KB ROM
                                         Base
INSTANCE                 equ    00EH    ; Mask for instance number
INSTANCE_SHFT            equ    1       ; Left shift to get instance into
                                         place
XGA_ENABLE               equ    001H    ; Value to enable XGA register access
;
;
; POS  103H  -  Bus Arbitration Register (MCA Only)
;
ARB_LEVEL                equ    078H    ; Mask for arbitration level
ARB_LEVEL_SHFT           equ    3       ; Left shift for arbitration level
FAIR_ENABLE              equ    004H    ; Value to enable MCA fairness
EXT_MEM_ENABLE           equ    002H    ; Value to enable 8KB XGA ROM
                                         addressing
;
;
; POS  104H  -  Display Memory Base Address
;
DISP_MEM_BASE            equ    0FEH    ; Mask for XGA linear address base
DISP_MEM_ACCESS          equ    001H    ; Value to enable PC access to XGA
                                         mem.
;
;
; POS  105H  -  1 MB Aperture Base Address
;
BASE_1MB                 equ    00FH    ; Mask. * 100000H = 1MB Aperture
                                         addr.
;
;
; I/O  21x0H  -  Operating Mode Register
;
REG_FORMAT_INTEL         equ    001H    ; Value to set Intel addressing
REG_FORMAT_MOTOR         equ    008H    ; Value to set Motorola addressing
DISPLAY_MODE             equ    007H    ; Mask for display mode
DISP_VGA_MODE            equ    01H     ; Normal VGA Mode
DISP_132_MODE            equ    02H     ; Normal 132 column mode
DISP_XGA_MODE            equ    04H     ; Normal XGA graphics mode
;
;
```

```
; I/O  21x1H  -  Aperture Control Register
;
MEMWIN_ACCESS          equ     003H     ; Mask for 64KB Mem. Win. access
MEMWIN_DISABLE         equ     000H     ; Value to disable the Mem Win
MEMWIN_ENABLE_A        equ     001H     ; Value to enable the Mem Win at
                                          A0000H
MEMWIN_ENABLE_B        equ     002H     ; Value to enable the Mem Win at
                                          B0000H
;
;
; I/O  21x4H  -  Interrupt Enable Register
;
CMD_DONE_ENAB          equ     080H     ; Value to enable Command Done
                                          interrupt
ACCESS_REJ_ENAB        equ     040H     ; Value to enable Access Reject
                                          interrupt
SPRT_DSPCMP_ENAB       equ     004H     ; Value to enable Sprite Disp.
                                          interrupt
START_PIC_ENAB         equ     002H     ; Value to enable Start Pict.
                                          interrupt
START_BLNK_ENAB        equ     001H     ; Value to enable End Pict. interrupt
;
;
; I/O  21x5H  -  Interrupt Status Register
;
CMD_DONE_STAT          equ     080H     ; Value to test Command Done
                                          interrupt
ACCESS_REJ_STAT        equ     040H     ; Value to test Access Reject
                                          interrupt
SPRT_DSPCMP_STAT       equ     004H     ; Value to test Sprite Disp.
                                          interrupt
START_PIC_STAT         equ     002H     ; Value to test Start Pict. interrupt
START_BLNK_STAT        equ     001H     ; Value to test End Pict. interrupt
;
;
; I/O  21x6H  -  Virtual Memory Control Register
;
PAGE_NP_ENAB           equ     080H     ; Value to enable Page Not Present
                                          int.
PROT_VIOL_ENAB         equ     040H     ; Value to enable Prot. Violation
                                          int.
USER_SUPER            equ     004H     ; Value to set user level privilege
ENAB_VIRT_LU          equ     001H     ; Value to enable MMU-style look-up
;
;
```

continued...

...from previous page

```
; I/O  21x7H  -  Virtual Memory Interrupt Status Register
;
PAGE_NP_ENAB            equ     080H    ; Value to test for Page Not Present
                                        int.
PROT_VIOL_ENAB         equ     040H    ; Value to test for Prot. Violation
                                        int.
;
;
; I/O  21x8H  -  Aperture Index Register
;
MEMWIN_BANK            equ     03FH    ; Mask for the Memory Window bank
;
;
; I/O  21x9H  -  Memory Access Mode
;
MEMPIX_FORMAT_INTEL    equ     008H    ; Value to set Intel format memory
                                        map
MEMPIX_FORMAT_MOTOR    equ     008H    ; Value to set Motorola format mem.
                                        map
MEMPIX_SIZE_1          equ     000H    ; Value for 1 bpp access
MEMPIX_SIZE_2          equ     001H    ; Value for 2 bpp access
MEMPIX_SIZE_4          equ     002H    ; Value for 4 bpp access
MEMPIX_SIZE_8          equ     003H    ; Value for 8 bpp access
MEMPIX_SIZE_16         equ     004H    ; Value for 16 bpp access
;
;
; Index  04H  -  Auto-Configuration
;
BUS_SIZE               equ     001H    ; Mask. If set, is 32 bit bus width
;
;
; Index  1CH  -  Horizontal Sync Pulse Position 1
;
SYNC_PULSE_DLY1_0      equ     000H    ; Value for 0 pixel Sync Pulse Delay
SYNC_PULSE_DLY1_4      equ     040H    ; Value for 4 pixel Sync Pulse Delay
;
;
; Index  1EH  -  Horizontal Sync Pulse Position 2
;
SYNC_PULSE_DLY2_0      equ     000H    ; Value for 0 pixel Sync Pulse Delay
SYNC_PULSE_DLY2_4      equ     004H    ; Value for 4 pixel Sync Pulse Delay
;
;
; Index  36H  -  Sprite Control
;
SPRITE_ENAB            equ     001H    ; Value used to enable Sprite display
```

```
;
;
; Index  50H  -  Display Control 1
;
SYNC_POLAR              equ    0C0H    ; Mask for Sync Polarity
SYNC_POLAR_768          equ    000H    ; Value for 768 line Sync Polarity
SYNC_POLAR_400          equ    040H    ; Value for 400 line Sync Polarity
SYNC_POLAR_350          equ    080H    ; Value for 350 line Sync Polarity
SYNC_POLAR_480          equ    0C0H    ; Value for 480 line Sync Polarity
DISP_CTRL1_PRESERVE     equ    020H    ; Mask to preserve necessary bit
FEATURE_ENAB            equ    010H    ; Mask/Value to enable Feature Conn.
INTERLACED              equ    008H    ; Mask/Value to enable interlacing
BLANK_DISP              equ    003H    ; Mask for blank display field
BLANK_DISP_CRTCRESET    equ    003H    ; Value to reset CRT Controller for
                                         blank display field
BLANK_DISP_PREPCRTC     equ    003H    ; Value for CRTC reset preparation
BLANK_DISP_NORMAL       equ    003H    ; Value for normal display operation
;
;
; Index  51H  -  Display Control 2
;
VSCALE                  equ    0C0H    ; Mask for the Vertical Scale Factor
VSCALE_1                equ    000H    ; Value for vertical scale of 1
VSCALE_2                equ    040H    ; Value for vertical scale of 2
VSCALE_4                equ    080H    ; Value for vertical scale of 4
HSCALE                  equ    030H    ; Mask for the Horiztonal Scale
                                         Factor
HSCALE_1                equ    000H    ; Value for horizontal scale of 1
HSCALE_2                equ    010H    ; Value for horizontal scale of 2
HSCALE_4                equ    020H    ; Value for horizontal scale of 4
DSPPIX_SIZE             equ    007H    ; Mask for the Display Pixel Size
DSPPIX_SIZE_1           equ    000H    ; Value for 1 bpp display
DSPPIX_SIZE_2           equ    001H    ; Value for 2 bpp display
DSPPIX_SIZE_4           equ    002H    ; Value for 4 bpp display
DSPPIX_SIZE_8           equ    003H     Value for 8 bpp display
DSPPIX_SIZE_16          equ    004H    ; Value for 16 bpp display
;
;
; Index  52H  -  Monitor ID and Gun Output
;
BLUE_OUT                equ    080H    ; Mask for Blue gun level
GREEN_OUT               equ    040H    ; Mask for Green gun level
RED_OUT                 equ    020H    ; Mask for Red gun level
MONITOR_ID              equ    00FH    ; Mask for Monitor ID
;
;
```

continued...

...from previous page

```
; Index   54H  -  Clock Select 1
;
CLK_SEL1                equ     00CH    ; Mask for Clock Select 1 field
CLK_SCALE               equ     003H    ; Mask for Clock Scale
;
;
; Index   66H  -  Palette Sequence
;
COLOR_FORMAT            equ     004H    ; Mask for Color format
COLOR_FORMAT_RGB        equ     000H    ; Value for RGB color format
COLOR_FORMAT_RBGx       equ     004H    ; Value for RBGx color format
COLOR_COMPNT            equ     003H    ; Mask for color component sequence
COLOR_COMPNT_R          equ     000H    ; Value for the red color component
COLOR_COMPNT_G          equ     001H    ; Value for the green color component
COLOR_COMPNT_B          equ     002H    ; Value for the blue color component
COLOR_COMPNT_x          equ     003H    ; Value for the discard color
                                          component
;
;
; Index   70H  -  Clock Select 2
;
CLK_SEL2                equ     080H    ; Mask/Value for Clock Select 2 bit
;
;
; Memory   11H  -  Control Register
;
BUSY                    equ     080H    ; Mask for Busy bit
TERM_OPER               equ     020H    ; Mask/Value for Terminate Operation
                                          bit
OPER_SUSPND             equ     010H    ; Mask for Operation Suspended bit
SUSPND_OPER             equ     008H    ; Mask/Value for Suspend Operation
                                          bit
STATE_SAVRST            equ     002H    ; Mask/Value for State Save/Restore
                                          bit
;
;
; Memory   12H  -  Pixel Map Index
;
MAP_INDEX_MASK          equ     000H    ; Value to set the mask map index
MAP_INDEX_A             equ     001H    ; Value to set the map A index
MAP_INDEX_B             equ     002H    ; Value to set the map B index
MAP_INDEX_C             equ     003H    ; Value to set the map C index
;
;
; Memory   1CH  -  Pixel Map n Format
;
```

```
PIX_FORMAT_INTEL        equ     000H    ; Value to set Intel mode for
                                          curr. map
PIX_FORMAT_MOTOR        equ     008H    ; Value to set Motorola mode for
                                          map
PIXEL_SIZE_1            equ     000H    ; Value to set 1 bpp map depth
PIXEL_SIZE_2            equ     001H    ; Value to set 2 bpp map depth
PIXEL_SIZE_4            equ     002H    ; Value to set 4 bpp map depth
PIXEL_SIZE_8            equ     003H    ; Value to set 8 bpp map depth
;
;
; Memory  48H,49H  -  Foreground/Background Mix
;
MIX_ZEROS              equ     00H     ; 0 (all bits cleared)
MIX_0                 equ     00H     ; 0 (all bits cleared)

MIX_AND               equ     01H     ; Src AND Dst

MIX_SRC_AND_NOT_DST    equ     02H     ; Src AND NOT Dst

MIX_SRC               equ     03H     ; Src

MIX_PAINT             equ     03H     ; Src

MIX_NOT_SRC_AND_DST    equ     04H     ; NOT Src AND Dst

MIX_DST               equ     05H     ; Dst
MIX_LEAVE_ALONE        equ     05H     ; Dst

MIX_SRC_XOR_DST        equ     06H     ; Src XOR Dst
MIX_XOR               equ     06H     ; Src XOR Dst

MIX_SRC_OR_DST         equ     07H     ; Src OR Dst
MIX_OR                equ     07H     ; Src OR Dst

MIX_NOT_SRC_AND_NOT_DST equ    08H     ; NOT Src AND NOT Dst
MIX_NOR               equ     08H     ; NOT Src AND NOT Dst

MIX_SRC_XOR_NOT_DST    equ     09H     ; Src XOR NOT Dst

MIX_NOT_DST            equ     0AH     ; NOT Dst

MIX_SRC_OR_NOT_DST     equ     0BH     ; Src OR NOT Dst

MIX_NOT_SRC            equ     0CH     ; NOT Src

MIX_NOT_SRC_OR_DST     equ     0DH     ; NOT Src OR Dst

MIX_NOT_SRC_OR_NOT_DST equ     0EH     ; NOT Src OR NOT Dst
MIX_NAND              equ     0EH     ; NOT Src OR NOT Dst

MIX_ONES              equ     0FH     ; 1 (all bits set)
MIX_1                 equ     0FH     ; 1 (all bits set)

MIX_MAX               equ     10H     ; MAXIMUM(Src, Dst)

MIX_MIN               equ     11H     ; MINIMUM(Src, Dst)
```

continued...

...from previous page

```
MIX_PLUS_SAT             equ     12H     ; Src + Dst [with saturate]

MIX_DST_MINUS_SRC_SAT    equ     13H     ; Dst - Src [with saturate]

MIX_SRC_MINUS_DST_SAT    equ     14H     ; Src - Dst [with saturate]

MIX_AVERAGE              equ     15H     ; (Src + Dst) / 2

;
;
; Memory   4AH   -   Color Compare Function
;
CC_COND_TRUE             equ     000H    ; Always True
CC_COND_GT               equ     001H    ; Dst > CC
CC_COND_EQ               equ     002H    ; Dst == CC
CC_COND_LT               equ     003H    ; Dst < CC
CC_COND_FALSE            equ     004H    ; Always FALSE
CC_COND_GE               equ     005H    ; Dst >= CC
CC_COND_NE               equ     006H    ; Dst != CC
CC_COND_LE               equ     007H    ; Dst <= CC
;
;
; Memory   7CH   -   Command Register (Low Word)
;
PATT_SRC_A               equ     01000H  ; Pattern source is Map A
PATT_SRC_B               equ     02000H  ; Pattern source is Map B
PATT_SRC_C               equ     03000H  ; Pattern source is Map C
PATT_SRC_FORESRC         equ     08000H  ; Pattern source is Foreground Source
PATT_SRC_SRCDATA         equ     09000H  ; Pattern source is source data
MASK_MODE_DISAB          equ     00000H  ; Mask Map is disabled
MASK_MODE_CLIP           equ     00040H  ; Mask Map boundary enabled
                                                (clipping)
MASK_MODE_ENAB           equ     00080H  ; Mask Map is fully enabled
DRAW_MODE_ALL            equ     00000H  ; Draw all pixels in line/vector
DRAW_MODE_NOT_FIRST      equ     00010H  ; Draw all but the first pixel
DRAW_MODE_NOT_LAST       equ     00020H  ; Draw all but the last pixel
DRAW_MODE_BOUNDARY       equ     00030H  ; Draw area boundary for fill
DEC_X                    equ     00004H  ; Draw in Negative X direction
DEC_Y                    equ     00002H  ; Draw in Negative Y direction
YMAJOR                   equ     00001H  ; Y axis is major axis
;
;
; Memory   7EH   -   Command Register (High Word)
;
BACK_SRC_COLOR           equ     00000H  ; Background Source is Background
                                                Color
BACK_SRC_SRCMAP          equ     08000H .; Background Source is Source Pixel
                                                Map
```

```
FORE_SRC_COLOR       equ    00000H  ; Foreground Source is Background
                                       Color
FORE_SRC_SRCMAP      equ    02000H  ; Foreground Source is Source Pixel
                                       Map
CMD_SSV_READ         equ    00200H  ; Short Stroke Vector Read Command
CMD_LINE_READ        equ    00300H  ; Line Draw Read Command
CMD_SSV              equ    00400H  ; Short Stroke Vector Draw Command
CMD_LINE             equ    00500H  ; Line Draw Command
CMD_BITBLT           equ    00800H  ; BitBLT Command
CMD_INVERT_BITBLT    equ    00900H  ; Inverted BitBLT Command
CMD_AREA_FILL        equ    00A00H  ; Area Fill Command
SRC_MAP_A            equ    00010H  ; Use Map A as source map
SRC_MAP_B            equ    00020H  ; Use Map B as source map
SRC_MAP_C            equ    00030H  ; Use Map C as source map
DST_MAP_A            equ    00001H  ; Use Map A as destination map
DST_MAP_B            equ    00002H  ; Use Map B as destination map
DST_MAP_C            equ    00003H  ; Use Map C as destination map
```

The 8514/A AI versus the XGA AI

T he XGA AI is basically a superset of the 8514/A AI. However, there are also a few areas in which the XGA AI cannot perform the same functions as the 8514/A:

1. The 8514/A architecture implied that a separate VGA device, and hence frame buffer, was available for access, both for data storage and dual screen display. With the XGA, since it has built-in VGA compatibility (which is mutually exclusive with the XGA's graphics mode), this is not possible without an additional XGA or VGA device in the same system. Hence, the dual display or single display/dual source scenario can no longer be counted on.

2. The use of the off-screen space has changed. The 8514/A AI used off-screen memory for certain functions, such as area fills. The XGA AI uses a separate area fill plane for such purposes. This means that any software that counted on the contents of the 8514/A AI's off-screen memory to be set or used a certain way will no longer function properly with the XGA AI. See the new HSAFP and HSBMAP functions in Chapter 6 for details on the new way things are done.

3. There was a little-known mode in the 8514/A hardware that allowed a 512KB 8514/A to display a 640x480 by 8bpp mode by writing the low-order nibble (4 bits) of a pixel to one area, and the four high-order bits to another. By combining the AI and some direct hardware manipulation, an AI-based application could accomplish this as well. Since the XGA has the ability to support a regular 8bpp, 640x480 bitmap in its 512KB configuration, this technique is no longer necessary, nor will it work.

Outside of these reasonably minor incompatibilities, the XGA AI supplies the following functions in addition to those provided by the 8514/A AI:

ASGO	Sets alphanumeric character grid origin
HBMC	Copies bitmap block data
HCPSTEP	Draws short stroke–style at current position
HDLINE	Draws disjoint line(s) at given position, with absolute coordinates
HPEL	Draws pixel string at given position
HPSTEP	Draws short stroke–style at given position
HQBMAP	Queries bitmap attributes
HQDEVICE	Queries device-specific information
HRFPAL	Restores full palette
HRPEL	Reads pixel string at given position
HRSTEP	Reads short stroke–style at current position
HRWVEC	Reads/writes vector draw data
HSAFP	Sets area fill plane
HSBMAP	Sets bitmap attributes
HSDW	Sets display window
HSFPAL	Saves full palette
HSPRITE	Displays/positions sprite
HSSPRITE	Sets sprite shape

The following 8514/A AI–compatible functions have changed slightly to encompass the features of the XGA:

ABLOCKMFI	Draws block of alphanumeric characters (MFI encoded)
HBBC	Bit block—copies block on-board

HBBR	Bit block—reads image data from board
HBBW	Bit block—writes image data from host
HCBBW	Bit block—writes at current position from host
HCLOSE	Closes adapter
HINT	Waits for event
HQDPS	Queries drawing process state size
HQMODE	Queries mode
HRECT	Draws a filled rectangle
HRLPC	Restores line-pattern count
HSBCOL	Sets background color
HSCOL	Sets foreground color
HSHS	Sets clipping rectangle
HSLPC	Saves line-pattern count
HSLT	Sets line type
HSMARK	Sets marker shape
HSMODE	Sets mode
HSPATT	Sets pattern shape

Finally, a closing comment about the differences between the two AIs: If you are going to be writing an application that uses the AI, I recommend sticking as much as possible to the original 8514/A definition, because otherwise you will be limiting the platforms on which your software can run. You can also write your application so that it detects which version of the AI is available to it, and then uses whatever features it needs for that version. But in any event, don't limit your horizons if you plan to use the AI.

AI Functions

AI Functions Sorted Alphabetically

ABLOCKCGA	Draws block of characters (CGA encoded)
ABLOCKMFI	Draws block of alphanumeric characters (MFI encoded)
ACURSOR	Sets character cursor position
AERASE	Erases block of characters
ASCELL	Sets default character cell size
ASCROLL	Scrolls a block of characters
ASCUR	Sets character cursor shape
ASFONT	Sets alphanumeric character set
ASGO[1]	Sets alphanumeric character grid origin
AXLATE	Assigns alphanumeric color index table
HBAR	Begins area definition
HBBC	Bit block—copies block on-board
HBBCHN	Bit block—transfers (chain) data
HBBR	Bit block—reads image data from board

HBBW	Bit block—writes image data from host
HBMC[1]	Copies bitmap block data
HCBBW	Bit block—writes at current position from host
HCCHST	Draws a string at current position
HCHST	Draws a string at given position
HCLINE	Draws line(s) at current position, with absolute coordinates
HCLOSE	Closes adapter
HCMRK	Draws marker at current position
HCPSTEP[1]	Draws short stroke–style at current position
HCRLINE	Draws line(s) at current position, with relative coordinates
HDLINE[1]	Draws disjoint line(s) at given position, with absolute coordinates
HEAR	Ends area definition
HEGS	Erases graphics screen
HESC	Escape—aborts current operation
HINIT	Initializes state
HINT	Waits for event
HLDPAL	Loads palette
HLINE	Draws line(s) at given position, with absolute coordinates
HMRK	Draws marker at given position
HOPEN	Opens adapter
HPEL[1]	Draws pixel string at given position
HPSTEP[1]	Draws short stroke–style at given position
HQBMAP[1]	Queries bitmap attributes
HQCOORD	Queries coordinate type
HQCP	Queries current position
HQDEVICE[1]	Queries device-specific information
HQDFPAL	Queries default palette
HQDPS	Queries drawing process state size
HQMODE	Queries mode
HQMODES	Queries adapter modes
HRECT	Draws a filled rectangle
HRFPAL[1]	Restores full palette
HRLINE	Draws line(s) at given position, with relative coordinates

HRLPC	Restores line pattern count
HRPAL	Restores a palette
HRPEL[1]	Reads pixel string at given position
HRSTEP[1]	Reads short stroke–style at current position
HRWVEC[1]	Reads/writes vector draw data
HSAFP[1]	Sets area fill plane
HSBCOL	Sets background color
HSBMAP[1]	Sets bitmap attributes
HSBP	Sets bit plane controls
HSCMP	Sets "Color Comparison" register
HSCOL	Sets foreground color
HSCOORD	Sets coordinate type
HSCP	Sets current position
HSCS	Sets text character set
HSDW[1]	Sets display window
HSFPAL[1]	Saves full palette
HSGQ	Sets graphics quality
HSHS	Sets clipping rectangle
HSLPC	Saves line pattern count
HSLT	Sets line type
HSLW	Sets line width
HSMARK	Sets marker shape
HSMODE	Sets mode
HSMX	Sets mix
HSPAL	Saves a palette
HSPATT	Sets pattern shape
HSPATTO	Sets pattern reference point
HSPRITE[2]	Displays/positions sprite
HSSPRITE[2]	Sets sprite shape
HSYNC	Synchronizes adapter
HXLATE	Assigns multi-plane text color index table

AI Functions Sorted by Function Type

Alphanumeric Functions

ABLOCKCGA	Draws block of characters (CGA encoded)
ABLOCKMFI	Draws block of alphanumeric characters (MFI encoded)
ACURSOR	Sets character cursor position
AERASE	Erases block of characters
ASCELL	Sets default character cell size
ASCROLL	Scrolls a block of characters
ASCUR	Sets character cursor shape
ASFONT	Sets alphanumeric character set
ASGO[1]	Sets alphanumeric character grid origin
AXLATE	Assigns alphanumeric color index table

Drawing Functions

HBAR	Begins area definition
HBBC	Bit block—copies block on-board
HBBCHN	Bit block—transfers (chain) data
HBBR	Bit block—reads image data from board
HBBW	Bit block—writes image data from host
HBMC[1]	Copies bitmap block data
HCBBW	Bit block—writes at current position from host
HCCHST	Draws a string at current position
HCHST	Draws a string at given position
HCLINE	Draws line(s) at current position, with absolute coordinates
HCMRK	Draws marker at current position
HCPSTEP[1]	Draws short stroke-style at current position
HCRLINE	Draws line(s) at current position, with relative coordinates
HDLINE[1]	Draws disjoint line(s) at given position, with absolute coordinates
HEAR	Ends area definition
HEGS	Erases graphics screen

HLINE	Draws line(s) at given position, with absolute coordinates
HMRK	Draws marker at given position
HPEL[1]	Draws pixel string at given position
HPSTEP[1]	Draws short stroke-style at given position
HRECT	Draws a filled rectangle
HRLINE	Draws line(s) at given position, with relative coord.
HRPEL[1]	Reads pixel string at given position
HRSTEP[1]	Reads short stroke–style at current position

Control Functions

HCLOSE	Closes adapter
HESC	Escape—aborts current operation
HINIT	Initializes state
HINT	Waits for event
HOPEN	Opens adapter
HRWVEC[1]	Reads/writes vector draw data
HSDW[1]	Sets display window
HSCS	Sets text character set
HSMODE	Sets mode
HSPRITE[2]	Displays/positions sprite
HSSPRITE[2]	Sets sprite shape
HSYNC	Synchronizes adapter

Palette Functions

HLDPAL	Loads palette
HRFPAL[1]	Restores full palette
HRPAL	Restores a palette
HSFPAL[1]	Saves full palette
HSPAL	Saves a palette

Query Functions

HQBMAP[1]	Queries bitmap attributes
HQCOORD	Queries coordinate type
HQCP	Queries current position
HQDEVICE[1]	Queries device-specific information
HQDFPAL	Queries default palette
HQDPS	Queries drawing process state size
HQMODE	Queries mode
HQMODES	Queries adapter modes

Drawing Environment Functions

HRLPC	Restores line pattern count
HSAFP[1]	Sets area fill plane
HSBCOL	Sets background color
HSBMAP[1]	Sets bitmap attributes
HSBP	Sets bit plane controls
HSCMP	Sets Color Comparison register
HSCOL	Sets foreground color
HSCOORD	Sets coordinate type
HSCP	Sets current position
HSGQ	Sets graphics quality
HSHS	Sets clipping rectangle
HSLPC	Saves line pattern count
HSLT	Sets line type
HSLW	Sets line width
HSMARK	Sets marker shape
HSMX	Sets mix
HSPATT	Sets pattern shape
HSPATTO	Sets pattern reference point
HXLATE	Assigns multi-plane text color index table

AI Functions Sorted by Number

0	HLINE	Draws line(s) at given position, with absolute coordinates
1	HCLINE	Draws line(s) at current position, with absolute coordinates
2	HRLINE	Draws line(s) at given position, with relative coordinates
3	HCRLINE	Draws line(s) at current position, with relative coordinates
4	HSCP	Sets current position
5	HBAR	Begins area definition
6	HEAR	Ends area definition
7	HSCOL	Sets foreground color
8	HOPEN	Opens adapter
9	HSMX	Sets mix
10	HSBCOL	Sets background color
11	HSLT	Sets line type
12	HSLW	Sets line width
13	HEGS	Erases graphics screen
14	HSGQ	Sets graphics quality
15	HSCMP	Sets Color Comparison register
16	HINT	Waits for event
17	HSPATTO	Sets pattern reference point
18	HSPATT	Sets pattern shape
19	HLDPAL	Loads palette
20	HSHS	Sets clipping rectangle
21	HBBW	Bit block—writes image data from host
22	HCBBW	Bit block—writes at current position from host
23	HBBR	Bit block—reads image data from board
24	HBBCHN	Bit block—transfers (chain) data
25	HBBC	Bit block—copies block on-board
26	HSCOORD	Sets coordinate type
27	HQCOORD	Queries coordinate type
28	HSMODE	Sets mode

29	HQMODE	Queries mode
30	HQMODES	Queries adapter modes
31	HQDPS	Queries drawing process state size
32	HRECT	Draws a filled rectangle
33	HSBP	Sets bit plane controls
34	HCLOSE	Closes adapter
35	HESC	Escape—aborts current operation
36	HXLATE	Assigns multi-plane text color index table
37	HSCS	Sets text character set
38	HCHST	Draws a string at given position
39	HCCHST	Draws a string at current position
40	ABLOCKMFI	Draws block of alphanumeric characters (MFI encoded)
41	ABLOCKCGA	Draws block of characters (CGA encoded)
42	AERASE	Erases block of characters
43	ASCROLL	Scrolls a block of characters
44	ACURSOR	Sets character cursor position
45	ASCUR	Sets character cursor shape
46	ASFONT	Sets alphanumeric character set
47	AXLATE	Assigns alphanumeric color index table
48	HINIT	Initializes state
49	HSYNC	Synchronizes adapter
50	HMRK	Draws marker at given position
51	HCMRK	Draws marker at current position
52	HSMARK	Sets marker shape
53	HSLPC	Saves line pattern count
54	HRLPC	Restores line pattern count
55	HQCP	Queries current position
56	HQDFPAL	Queries default palette
57	HSPAL	Saves a palette
58	HRPAL	Restores a palette
59	HSAPF[1]	Sets area fill plane
60	ASCELL	Sets default character cell size

61	ASGO[1]	Sets alphanumeric character grid origin
62	HDLINE[1]	Draws disjoint line(s) at given position, with absolute coordinates
64	HPEL[1]	Draws pixel string at given position
65	HRPEL[1]	Reads pixel string at given position
66	HPSTEP[1]	Draws short stroke–style at given position
67	HCPSTEP[1]	Draws short stroke–style at current position
68	HRSTEP[1]	Reads short stroke–style at current position
69	HSBMAP[1]	Sets bitmap attributes
70	HQBMAP[1]	Queries bitmap attributes
71	HBMC[1]	Copies bitmap block data
72	HSDW[1]	Sets display window
73	HSPRITE[2]	Displays/positions sprite
74	HSSPRITE[2]	Sets sprite shape
75	HRWVEC[1]	Reads/writes vector draw data
78	HSFPAL[1]	Saves full palette
79	HRFPAL[1]	Restores full palette
80	HQDEVICE[1]	Queries device-specific information

[1]These functions exist in both the Image Adapter/A AI and XGA AI, but not in the 8514/A AI.

[2]These functions appear only in the XGA AI.

AI-Compatible Character Definitions

T he Adapter Interface supports three types of fonts:

1.   Short Stroke Vector fonts,

2.   Monochrome bitmapped fonts, and

3.   Color bitmapped fonts.

Short Stroke Vector (or SSV) fonts are made up of a number of lines or vectors that are no more than 15 pixels in length. Each SSV must be drawn at an angle that is a multiple of 45 degrees; therefore, only vertical, horizontal, and diagonal lines can be drawn. For each SSV in a font-character definition, you can indicate whether or not it should draw. The latter case is handy for moving the drawing pointer without having to actually draw pixels.

Coincidentally, both the 8514/A and the XGA can take in short stroke vector information directly via their Short Stroke Vector registers.

The benefit of the SSV font type is that it is very quick to draw, and reasonably easy to size, since it is a vector defintion and not a raster definition. Also, SSV fonts can have odd cell dimension, which means they do not have to be aligned to certain memory positions and widths, a drawback of some raster font implementations. On the other hand, SSV fonts can be rather space consuming, and require that you clear the cell in which the character is to be drawn, since otherwise you will end up with overwritten characters that probably will not be legible.

IBM supplies only SSV fonts with the 8514/A, but both raster and SSV fonts with the XGA.

The second type of font the AI supports, monochrome bitmapped fonts, have been around for a long time. In the PC environment, these fonts are used in the graphics modes on all industry standard graphics boards (CGA, EGA, MCGA, and VGA). This is basically a predefined block of bits, with set bits indicating pixels that are to drawn in the foreground color, and cleared bits indicating pixels that should be drawn in the background color.

The cell width of monochrome bitmapped fonts must be a multiple of 4, and the height a multiple of 2.

The third type of font available, color bitmapped fonts, consist of three monochrome bitmaps; therefore each pixel in a color font can have one of eight colors. The actual colors are determined by the HXLATE call in the AI.

When using the AI text functions to display color bitmapped fonts, there are two ways in which the text can be displayed, and both depend on the foreground color in which the text is to be drawn.

1. If the foreground color is 0xFFFFFFFF (all bits set), the three monochrome bitmaps will be ORed together, and the result will be treated as the monochrome bitmapped font usually is.

2. If the foreground color is anything but 0xFFFFFFFF, then the three planes will determine in which of the eight colors defined by the HXLATE function a given pixel will be drawn.

This font type cannot be used with the AI's alphanumeric functions.

All the fonts share the same header structure, but with variations in the contents. You pass a pointer to the header to functions like HSCS and ASFONT. The header is usually part of a larger font file that contains several variations of a given font for different languages. The header of the font file contains information that points to the proper character set header. The file header looks like this:

Offset	Type	Description
0	WORD	Number of font variations (code pages) in file
2	WORD	The default code page number
4	WORD	Alternate default code page number

The following is repeated once for every code page:

Offset	Type	Description
6	BYTE	Code page ID, contains IBM-specific code page info
10	WORD	Offset from start of file to character set header for this page

Once the proper code page has been located, and the address of the appropriate character set header has been determined, use the following structure. Note that the offset value is a reference only from the start of the header, not from the start of the file:

Offset	Type	Description
0	BYTE	Reserved
1	BYTE	Type of font:
		0= Bitmapped (monochrome and/or color)
		3= Short stroke vector
		All others are reserved
2	BYTE	Reserved
3	DWORD	Reserved
7	BYTE	Character width
8	BYTE	Character height
9	BYTE	Reserved
10	WORD	Character area in bytes
		Calculated by: *(width + 7) / 8) * height*
		Applies to bitmapped fonts only

continued...

...from previous page

12	WORD	Flags
		Bit 15 is reserved
		Bit 14
		0 = Monochrome bitmapped font
		1 = Color bitmapped font
		Bit 13
		0 = Fixed spaced
		1 = Proportional spaced
		Bits 12–0 are reserved
14	DWORD	Offset of index table
18	DWORD	Offset of proportional-spacing table
22	BYTE	ASCII value of first character in font
23	BYTE	ASCII value of last character in font
24	DWORD	Offset of character definition 1
28	WORD	Reserved
30	DWORD	Offset of character definition 2
34	WORD	Reserved
36	DWORD	Offset of character definition 3

All offsets are unsigned absolute byte offsets from the start of the file.

Character definitions 2 and 3 are used only by color bitmapped fonts, and contain the second and third planes of the font, respectively.

The address of the actual bitmap or SSV definition for a given font character is calculated by using the ASCII character value as a word offset (after normalizing with the first character in the font) into the index table. The contents of the location in the index table are then added to the offset of the appropriate character definition, resulting in the address of the font definition for the character in question.

Each character definition starts on a byte boundary. For SSV fonts, each SSV component request occupies one byte (see Chapter 4 for a discussion of the Short Stroke register), and terminates with a byte whose value is 0. Bitmapped fonts have the width rounded up to the nearest byte count *(byte count = (width + 7) / 8)* for each line in the definition.

The proportional spacing table is used to properly space variable width fonts. There are two bytes for each proportionally spaced character in a font: the first contains the left adjustment, and the second contains the right adjustment. The left adjustment should be subtracted from the X position at which the character is being drawn, and the right adjustment should be subtracted from the font width to determine where to place the next character.

IBMAFI.H

This appendix contains the C include file IBMAFI.H, which is used in many of the examples in Chapter 7. This file automatically "includes" AFIDATA.H (appendix L), and provides some core structure definitions, as well as all of the function macros for the AI.

IBMAFI.M—C Include file for *Power Programming the IBM XGA.* Written by Jake Richter. Copyright (C) 1989-1992 Panacea Inc. All Rights Reserved. This include file may be freely used and incorporated in your code, providing that this header, including the copyright notice, remains unchanged.

This file contains definitions used by programs writing to the 8514/A Adapter Interface.

```
/*————————————————————————————

    TYPE DEFINITIONS
    The following definitions are used in all the listings to reference
    certain data types. This is done to help make the code more readable,
    and to assist later translation and communication with assembly
    language.
————————————————————————————*/

#define FALSE           0
#define TRUE            !(FALSE)
#ifndef NULL
#define NULL            (void *)0
#endif
#define BYTE            char
#define WORD            short
#define BOOL            short
#define DWORD           long
#define UBYTE           unsigned BYTE
#define UWORD           unsigned WORD
#define UDWORD          unsigned DWORD
#define FAR             far
#define HUGE            huge
#define VOID            void

#define MIN(a,b)        ((a) > (b) ? (b) : (a))
#define MAX(a,b)        ((a) < (b) ? (b) : (a))

/*————————————————————————————

    Standard AI Definitions
————————————————————————————*/

typedef struct
    {
    WORD        x_coord;
    WORD        y_coord;
    } coord_pr;
```

```
typedef struct
    {
    BYTE        rx_coord;
    BYTE        ry_coord;
    } rcoord_pr;

typedef struct
    {
    coord_pr coord;
    WORD        width;
    WORD        height;
    } rect_def;

typedef struct
    {
    coord_pr    coord;
    WORD        pel_count;
    } pel_pr;

typedef struct
    {
    WORD        x_start;
    WORD        y_start;
    WORD        x_end;
    WORD        y_end;
    } dcoord;

struct afi_entries
    {
    VOID(FAR *array[84])();
    };

/*
```

The following structure is used to allow multiple AIs, and/or multiple AI-capable devices, and accessed at the same time. The address of the structure can be found by calling GetAFIL(). Then, you need to parse through each link block to see if it is the adapter type you want to use. If it isn't, look at the next AI info block via the link_ptr. Once the right block has been found, copy the afi_tbl_ptr into the afi_ptr variable defined externally. You'll then be ready to make CallAFI calls.

```
*/
```

```
struct afi_list_entry          /* For AI linked lists */
    {
    struct afi_entries FAR     *afi_tbl_ptr;
    BYTE                       adapter_type;
    BYTE                       instance;
    struct afi_list_entry FAR *link_ptr;
    };
/*————————————————————————————

    Externals — defined in CALLAFI.ASM
————————————————————————————*/

extern struct afi_entries FAR *afi_ptr;
extern VOID FAR CallAFI(WORD, UBYTE FAR *);
extern struct afi_entries FAR *(FAR GetAFI(VOID));
extern struct afi_list_entry FAR * (FAR GetAFIL(VOID));

*————————————————————————————

    Macro Function Definitions - sorted by command number.
————————————————————————————*/

#define HLINE(X)      CallAFI( 0,  (UBYTE FAR *) X)
#define HCLINE(X)     CallAFI( 1,  (UBYTE FAR *) X)
#define HRLINE(X)     CallAFI( 2,  (UBYTE FAR *) X)
#define HCRLINE(X)    CallAFI( 3,  (UBYTE FAR *) X)
#define HSCP(X)       CallAFI( 4,  (UBYTE FAR *) X)
#define HBAR()        CallAFI( 5,  (UBYTE FAR *) 0L)
#define HEAR(X)       CallAFI( 6,  (UBYTE FAR *) X)
#define HSCOL(X)      CallAFI( 7,  (UBYTE FAR *) X)
#define HOPEN(X)      CallAFI( 8,  (UBYTE FAR *) X)
#define HSMX(X)       CallAFI( 9,  (UBYTE FAR *) X)
#define HSBCOL(X)     CallAFI(10,  (UBYTE FAR *) X)
#define HSLT(X)       CallAFI(11,  (UBYTE FAR *) X)
#define HSLW(X)       CallAFI(12,  (UBYTE FAR *) X)
#define HEGS()        CallAFI(13,  (UBYTE FAR *) 0L)
#define HSGQ(X)       CallAFI(14,  (UBYTE FAR *) X)
#define HSCMP(X)      CallAFI(15,  (UBYTE FAR *) X)
#define HINT(X)       CallAFI(16,  (UBYTE FAR *) X)
#define HSPATTO(X)    CallAFI(17,  (UBYTE FAR *) X)
#define HSPATT(X)     CallAFI(18,  (UBYTE FAR *) X)
```

```
#define HLDPAL(X)      CallAFI(19,  (UBYTE FAR *) X)
#define HSHS(X)        CallAFI(20,  (UBYTE FAR *) X)
#define HBBW(X)        CallAFI(21,  (UBYTE FAR *) X)
#define HCBBW(X)       CallAFI(22,  (UBYTE FAR *) X)
#define HBBR(X)        CallAFI(23,  (UBYTE FAR *) X)
#define HBBCHN(X)      CallAFI(24,  (UBYTE FAR *) X)
#define HBBC(X)        CallAFI(25,  (UBYTE FAR *) X)
#define HSCOORD(X)     CallAFI(26,  (UBYTE FAR *) X)
#define HQCOORD(X)     CallAFI(27,  (UBYTE FAR *) X)
#define HSMODE(X)      CallAFI(28,  (UBYTE FAR *) X)
#define HQMODE(X)      CallAFI(29,  (UBYTE FAR *) X)
#define HQMODES(X)     CallAFI(30,  (UBYTE FAR *) X)
#define HQDPS(X)       CallAFI(31,  (UBYTE FAR *) X)
#define HRECT(X)       CallAFI(32,  (UBYTE FAR *) X)
#define HSBP(X)        CallAFI(33,  (UBYTE FAR *) X)
#define HCLOSE(X)      CallAFI(34,  (UBYTE FAR *) X)
#define HESC()         CallAFI(35,  (UBYTE FAR *) 0L)
#define HXLATE(X)      CallAFI(36,  (UBYTE FAR *) X)
#define HSCS(X)        CallAFI(37,  (UBYTE FAR *) X)
#define HCHST(X)       CallAFI(38,  (UBYTE FAR *) X)
#define HCCHST(X)      CallAFI(39,  (UBYTE FAR *) X)
#define ABLKMFI(X)     CallAFI(40,  (UBYTE FAR *) X)
#define ABLKCGA(X)     CallAFI(41,  (UBYTE FAR *) X)
#define AERASE(X)      CallAFI(42,  (UBYTE FAR *) X)
#define ASCROLL(X)     CallAFI(43,  (UBYTE FAR *) X)
#define ACURSOR(X)     CallAFI(44,  (UBYTE FAR *) X)
#define ASCUR(X)       CallAFI(45,  (UBYTE FAR *) X)
#define ASFONT(X)      CallAFI(46,  (UBYTE FAR *) X)
#define AXLATE(X)      CallAFI(47,  (UBYTE FAR *) X)
#define HINIT(X)       CallAFI(48,  (UBYTE FAR *) X)
#define HSYNC(X)       CallAFI(49,  (UBYTE FAR *) X)
#define HMRK(X)        CallAFI(50,  (UBYTE FAR *) X)
#define HCMRK(X)       CallAFI(51,  (UBYTE FAR *) X)
#define HSMARK(X)      CallAFI(52,  (UBYTE FAR *) X)
#define HSLPC(X)       CallAFI(53,  (UBYTE FAR *) X)
#define HRLPC(X)       CallAFI(54,  (UBYTE FAR *) X)
#define HQCP(X)        CallAFI(55,  (UBYTE FAR *) X)
```

```
#define HQDFPAL(X)      CallAFI(56,  (UBYTE FAR *) X)
#define HSPAL(X)        CallAFI(57,  (UBYTE FAR *) X)
#define HRPAL(X)        CallAFI(58,  (UBYTE FAR *) X)
#define HSAFP(X)        CallAFI(59,  (UBYTE FAR *) X)
#define ASCELL(X)       CallAFI(60,  (UBYTE FAR *) X)
#define ASGO(X)         CallAFI(61,  (UBYTE FAR *) X)
#define HDLINE(X)       CallAFI(62,  (UBYTE FAR *) X)
        /* There is no function number 63 */
#define HPEL(X)         CallAFI(64,  (UBYTE FAR *) X)
#define HRPEL(X)        CallAFI(65,  (UBYTE FAR *) X)
#define HPSTEP(X)       CallAFI(66,  (UBYTE FAR *) X)
#define HCPSTEP(X)      CallAFI(67,  (UBYTE FAR *) X)
#define HRSTEP(X)       CallAFI(68,  (UBYTE FAR *) X)
#define HSBMAP(X)       CallAFI(69,  (UBYTE FAR *) X)
#define HQBMAP(X)       CallAFI(70,  (UBYTE FAR *) X)
#define HBMC(X)         CallAFI(71,  (UBYTE FAR *) X)
#define HSDW(X)         CallAFI(72,  (UBYTE FAR *) X)
#define HSPRITE(X)      CallAFI(73,  (UBYTE FAR *) X)
#define HSSPRITE(X)     CallAFI(74,  (UBYTE FAR *) X)
#define HRWVEC(X)       CallAFI(75,  (UBYTE FAR *) X)
        /* There is no function number 76 */
        /* There is no function number 77 */
#define HSFPAL(X)       CallAFI(78,  (UBYTE FAR *) X)
#define HRFPAL(X)       CallAFI(79,  (UBYTE FAR *) X)
#define HQDEVICE(X)     CallAFI(80,  (UBYTE FAR *) X)
/*—————————————————————————————

    Other include files
—————————————————————————————*/

    #include "afidata.h"
/*—————————————————————————————

    End of IBMAFI.H
—————————————————————————————*/
```

AFIDATA.H

T his appendix contains the C include file AFIDATA.H, which is used in many of the examples in Chapter 7. This file is automatically included via IBMAFI.H (in Appendix K), and provides all of the structures required to interface with the Adapter Interface functions.

```
/*********************************************************************

   AFIDATA.H -- "C" Include file for "Power Programming the IBM XGA".

   Written by Jake Richter.

   Copyright (C) 1989-1992 Panacea Inc. -- All Rights Reserved

   NOTICE:

      This include file may be freely used and incorporated in your code,
      providing that this header, including the copyright notice, remains
      unchanged.

   This file contains structures used by programs writing to the
   8514/A Adapter Interface. This file is included by IBMAFI.H

   Note: In some cases it is necessary to have defitions that differ
   between the 4 and 8 bit per pixel modes of the AI. In such
   cases, the definitions for the 4 bit per pixel mode start with "B4_",
   and the 8 bit per pixels start with "B8_".

*********************************************************************
/*-------------------------------------------------------------------

AI Constant Definitions

-------------------------------------------------------------------*/
/*
Color values for 4 and 8 bits per pixel using standard palette.
*/
#define        B4_RED          0x000CL
#define        B4_GREEN        0x000AL
#define        B4_BLUE         0x0009L
#define        B4_WHITE        (B4_RED | B4_GREEN | B4_BLUE)
#define        B4_CYAN         (B4_GREEN | B4_BLUE)
#define        B4_YELLO        (B4_RED | B4_GREEN)
#define        B4_MAGEN        (B4_RED | B4_BLUE)

#define        B8_RED          0x0049L
#define        B8_GREEN        0x0092L
#define        B8_BLUE         0x0024L
#define        B8_WHITE        (B8_RED | B8_GREEN | B8_BLUE)
#define        B8_CYAN         (B8_GREEN | B8_BLUE)
#define        B8_YELLO        (B8_RED | B8_GREEN)
#define        B8_MAGEN        (B8_RED | B8_BLUE)

/*

   Bit level definitions for each color (and intensity in case of 4bpp).
   Used to control the individual bits that control a given color.
```

When in 4 bit per pixel (bpp) mode, the colors are based on an IRGB
palette similar to that of the CGA color text mode.
When in 8bpp mode, 3 bits each are allocated to the Red and Green
components, and 2 bits to the Blue.
```
*/
#define         B4_R0           0x004L
#define         B4_B0           0x001L
#define         B4_G0           0x002L
#define         B4_IN           0x008L

#define         B8_R0           0x001L
#define         B8_R1           0x008L
#define         B8_R2           0x040L
#define         B8_B0           0x004L
#define         B8_B1           0x020L
#define         B8_G0           0x002L
#define         B8_G1           0x010L
#define         B8_G2           0x080L


/*

Standard MIXes.

*/
#define         MIX_NOC         0x00    /* No change            */
#define         MIX_OR          0x01    /* Src OR Dst           */
#define         MIX_OVER        0x02    /* Src (overpaint)      */
#define         MIX_XOR         0x04    /* Src XOR Dst          */
#define         MIX_LEAVE       0x05    /* Dst (leave alone)    */
#define         MIX_ADD         0x08    /* Src + Dst            */
#define         MIX_SUB         0x09    /* Dst - Src            */
#define         MIX_MEAN        0x0B    /* (Src + Dst) / 2      */


/*

Flags for CharSetDef structure.

*/
#define MULTIPLANE 0x4000       /* single or multi plane       */
#define PROPSPACE  0x2000       /* single or multi plane       */


/*-----------------------------------------------------------

    AI Structures and Typedefs

-------------------------------------------------------------*/

typedef         coord_pr        APOINT; /* Absolute point (IBMAFI.H)*/
typedef         rcoord_pr       RPOINT; /* Relative point (IBMAFI.H)*/
```

continued...

...from previous page

```
/*
Font file header
*/
typedef struct CharSetDef   /* Character Set Def. block */
    {
    UBYTE        reserve1;
    UBYTE        type;
    DWORD        reserve2;
    UBYTE        reserve3;
    UBYTE        cellwidth;
    UBYTE        cellheight;
    UBYTE        reserve4;
    WORD         cellnbytes;
    WORD         flags;
    WORD FAR     *indextbl;
    UBYTE FAR    *enveltbl;
    UBYTE        cdpt1st;
    UBYTE        cdptlast;
    UBYTE FAR    *chardef1;
    WORD         reserve5;
    UBYTE FAR    *chardef2;
    WORD         reserve6;
    UBYTE FAR    *chardef3;
    }  CHARSETDEF;

typedef struct FontFileDefn
    {
    WORD   no_pages; /* # of code pages in the file (size of page_array)*/
    WORD   def_page; /* default page index (into page_array) */
    WORD   alt_page; /* alternate default page index (into page_array) */
    struct
        {
        BYTE    code_page_id[4];
        WORD    csd_offset;
        } page_array[1];
    } FFDEF;

/*-------------------------------------------------------------------
```

AI Parameter Definition—sorted by AI command number.

Some commands, such as HEGS, do not have data structs. All commands that do are listed here. They can be found by searching for the command name followed by "_DATA". Hence, the data structure for HINIT is called HINIT_DATA.

```
    -------------------------------------------------------------------*/
```

```
/*
    Define structures for HLINE, HCLINE, HRLINE, and HCRLINE. They are
    set up as macros because they require a size parameter.
*/
#define HLINE_DATA(SIZE)    struct\
                                {\
                                UWORD   length;\
                                APOINT  coords[SIZE];\
                                }

#define HCLINE_DATA(SIZE)   struct\
                                {\
                                UWORD   length;\
                                APOINT  coords[SIZE];\
                                }

#define HRLINE_DATA(SIZE)   struct\
                                {\
                                UWORD   length;\
                                APOINT  coord1;\
                                RPOINT  rcoords[SIZE];\
                                }

#define HCRLINE_DATA(SIZE)  struct\
                                {\
                                UWORD   length;\
                                RPOINT  rcoords[SIZE];\
                                }

typedef struct
    {
    UWORD   length;
    APOINT  coord1;
    } HSCP_DATA;

typedef struct
    {
    UWORD   length;
    UBYTE   flags;
    } HEAR_DATA;

typedef struct
    {
    UWORD   length;
    DWORD   index;
    } HSCOL_DATA;
```

continued...

...from previous page

```c
typedef struct
    {
    UWORD    length;
    UBYTE    oflags;
    UBYTE    mode;
    UBYTE    iflags;
    } HOPEN_DATA;

typedef struct
    {
    UWORD    length;
    UBYTE    foremix;
    UBYTE    backmix;
    } HSMX_DATA;

typedef struct
    {
    UWORD    length;
    DWORD    index;
    } HSBCOL_DATA;

typedef struct
    {
    UWORD    length;
    UBYTE    index;
    UBYTE    reserved;
    UBYTE FAR  *def;
    } HSLT_DATA;

typedef struct
    {
    UWORD    length;
    UBYTE    index;
    } HSLW_DATA;

typedef struct
    {
    UWORD    length;
    UWORD    index;
    } HSGQ_DATA;

typedef struct
    {
    UWORD    length;
    DWORD    col;
    UBYTE    function;
    } HSCMP_DATA;
```

```
typedef struct
     {
     UWORD    length;
     DWORD    eventid;
     } HINT_DATA;

typedef struct
     {
     UWORD    length;
     APOINT   coord1;
     } HSPATTO_DATA;

typedef struct
     {
     UWORD    length;
     UBYTE    width;
     UBYTE    height;
     UBYTE    flags;
     UBYTE    reserved;
     UWORD    img_length;
     UBYTE FAR  *image;
     UBYTE FAR  *colour;
     } HSPATT_DATA;

typedef struct
     {
     UWORD    length;
     UBYTE    pal_id;
     UBYTE    res1;
     WORD     first;
     WORD     count;
     UBYTE FAR *address;
     } HSLDPAL_DATA;

typedef struct
     {
     UWORD    length;
     WORD     l;
     WORD     r;
     WORD     b;
     WORD     t;
     BYTE FAR *address;    /* New for XGA & Image Adapter/A AIs */
     BYTE     flags;       /* ditto */
     } HSHS_DATA;
```

continued...

...from previous page

```
typedef struct
    {
    UWORD   length;
    UWORD   format;
    UWORD   width;
    UWORD   height;
    APOINT  coord;
    WORD    l;
    WORD    t;
    WORD    w;
    WORD    h;
    } HBBW_DATA;

typedef struct
    {
    UWORD   length;
    UWORD   format;
    UWORD   width;
    UWORD   height;
    WORD    l;
    WORD    t;
    WORD    w;
    WORD    h;
    } HCBBW_DATA;

typedef struct
    {
    UWORD   length;
    UWORD   format;
    UWORD   width;
    UWORD   height;
    UBYTE   plane;
    UBYTE   reserved;
    APOINT  coord;
    WORD    l;
    WORD    t;
    WORD    w;
    WORD    h;
    HBBR_DATA;

typedef struct
    {
    UWORD   length;
    UBYTE FAR *address;
    UWORD   len;
    } HBBCHN_DATA;
```

```
typedef struct
    {
    UWORD    length;
    UWORD    format;
    UWORD    width;
    UWORD    height;
    UBYTE    plane;
    UBYTE    reserved;
    APOINT   source;
    APOINT   dest;
    } HBBC_DATA;

typedef struct
    {
    UWORD    length;
    UBYTE    acformat;
    UBYTE    rcformat;
    UBYTE    ndimens;

    } HSCOORD_DATA;

typedef struct
    {
    UWORD    length;
    UBYTE    acformat;
    UBYTE    rcformat;
    UBYTE    ndimens;
    UBYTE    result;
    } HQCOORD_DATA;

typedef struct
    {
    UWORD    length;
    UBYTE    scformat;
    UBYTE    flags;            /* New for XGA & Image Adapter/A AIs */
    } HSMODE_DATA;

typedef struct
    {
    UWORD    length;
    UBYTE    mode;
    UBYTE    clvl[2];
    UBYTE    atype;
    UBYTE    dtype;
    UBYTE    ac_w;
    UBYTE    ac_h;
    UBYTE    nplanes;
    UBYTE    width;
    UBYTE    height;
```

continued...

...from previous page

```
    UBYTE    h_pitch;
    UBYTE    v_pitch;
    UBYTE    moco;
    UBYTE    n_i_lvls;
    UBYTE    areafp;          /* New for XGA & Image Adapter/A AIs */
    UBYTE    vga;             /* ditto */
    } HQMODE_DATA;

typedef struct
    {
    UWORD    length;
    UBYTE    atype;
    UBYTE    modes[32];
    } HQMODES_DATA;

typedef struct
    {
    UWORD    length;
    WORD     size;
    WORD     stack;
    WORD     palbufsize;
    UDWORD   vramsize;        /* New for XGA & Image Adapter/A AIs */
    UDWORD   areafpsize;      /* ditto */
    } HQDPS_DATA;

typedef struct
    {
    UWORD    length;
    APOINT   coord;
    WORD     width;
    WORD     height;
    } HRECT_DATA;

#define HRECTS_DATA(SIZE) struct /* Only in XGA and Image Adapter/A AIs
                          */\
                          {\
                          UWORD      length;\
                          rect_def rect[SIZE];\
                          }

typedef struct
    {
    UWORD    length;
    UDWORD   grupdate;
    UDWORD   alupdate;
    UDWORD   display;
    UBYTE    flags;          /* Only in XGA and Image Adapter/A AIs */
```

```
     UBYTE    reserved;      /* ditto */
     UDWORD  green_msk;      /* ditto */
     UDWORD  red_msk;        /* ditto */
     UDWORD  blue_msk;       /* ditto */
     } HSBP_DATA;

typedef struct
     {
     UWORD    length;
     UBYTE    flags;
     }HCLOSE_DATA;

typedef struct
     {
     UWORD    length;
     UDWORD   table[8];
     } HXLATE_DATA;

typedef struct
     {
     UWORD    length;
     CHARSETDEF FAR *address;
     } HSCS_DATA;

#define HCHST_DATA(LEN)     struct\
                              {\
                              UWORD   length;\
                              APOINT  coord;\
                              BYTE    string[LEN];\
                              }

#define HCCHST_DATA(LEN)    struct\
                              {\
                              UWORD   length;\
                              BYTE    string[LEN];\
                              }

typedef struct
     {
     UWORD    length;
     UBYTE    colm;
     UBYTE    row;
     UBYTE    across;
     UBYTE    down;
     UBYTE FAR *chars;
     UBYTE    width;
     } ABLKMFI_DATA;
```

continued...

...from previous page

```
typedef struct
    {
    UWORD       length;
    UBYTE       colm;
    UBYTE       row;
    UBYTE       across;
    UBYTE       down;
    UBYTE FAR *chars;
    UBYTE       width;
    UBYTE       hilite;
    } ABLKCGA_DATA;

typedef struct
    {
    UWORD       length;
    UBYTE       colm;
    UBYTE       row;
    UBYTE       across;
    UBYTE       down;
    UBYTE       colour;
    } AERASE_DATA;

typedef struct
    {
    UWORD       length;
    UBYTE       sor_colm;
    UBYTE       sor_row;
    UBYTE       across;
    UBYTE       down;
    UBYTE       des_colm;
    UBYTE       des_row;
    } ASCROLL_DATA;

typedef struct
    {
    UWORD       length;
    UBYTE       colm;
    UBYTE       row;
    } ACURSOR_DATA;

typedef struct
    {
    UWORD       length;
    UBYTE       start;
    UBYTE       stop;
    UBYTE       attr;
    } ASCUR_DATA;
```

```
typedef struct
    {
    UWORD       length;
    UBYTE       font;
    UBYTE       res;
    CHARSETDEF FAR *address;
    } ASFONT_DATA;

typedef struct
    {
    UWORD       length;
    UDWORD      foreTable[16];
    UDWORD      backTable[16];
    } AXLATE_DATA;

typedef struct
    {
    UWORD       length;
    UWORD       segment;
    } HINIT_DATA;

typedef struct
    {
    UWORD       length;
    UWORD       segment;
    } HSYNC_DATA;

#define HMRK_DATA(SIZE)     struct\
                                {\
                                UWORD  length;\
                                APOINT coords[SIZE];\
                                }

#define HCMRK_DATA(SIZE)    struct\
                                {\
                                UWORD  length;\
                                APOINT coords[SIZE];\
                                }

typedef struct
    {
    UWORD   length;
    UBYTE   width;
    UBYTE   height;
    UBYTE   flags
    UBYTE   res;
    WORD    imlen;
    UBYTE FAR *image;
    UBYTE FAR *colour;
    } HSMARK_DATA;
```

continued...

...from previous page

```
typedef struct
    {
    WORD    length;
    WORD    count;
    } HSLPC_DATA;          /* Only in XGA and Image Adapter/A AIs */

typedef struct
    {WORD    length;
    WORD    count;
    }
    HRLPC_DATA;            /* Only in XGA and Image Adapter/A AIs */

typedef struct
    {
    UWORD   length;
    APOINT  coord1;
    } HQCP_DATA;

typedef struct
    {
    UWORD   length;
    DWORD   table[16];
    } HQDFPAL_DATA;

typedef struct
    {
    UWORD   length;
    BYTE    paldata[1028];   /* 1028 is worst case, but the   */
    } HSPAL_DATA;            /* actual size is in HQDPS.      */

typedef struct
    {
    UWORD   length;
    BYTE    paldata[1028];   /* 1028 is worst case, but the   */
    } HRPAL_DATA;            /* actual size is in HQDPS.      */

typedef struct
    {
    UWORD   length;
    UBYTE FAR    *address;
    UBYTE   flags;
    } HSAFP_DATA

typedef struct
    {
    UWORD   length;
    UBYTE   width;
    UBYTE   height;
    } ASCELL_DATA;
```

```
typedef struct
    {
    UWORD   length;
    APOINT  coord;
    } ASGO_DATA;            /* Only in XGA and Image Adapter/A AIs */

#define HDLINE_DATA(SIZE)  struct /* Only in XGA and Image Adapter/A AIs */\
                    {\
                    UWORD           length;\
                    dcoord          dcoords[SIZE];\
                    }

#define HPEL_DATA(SIZE)    struct /* Only in XGA and Image Adapter/A AIs */\
                    {\
                    UWORD           length;\
                    pel_pr          coord[SIZE];\
                    }

typedef struct
    {
    UWORD   length;
    UBYTE FAR *address;
    APOINT  coord;
    WORD    pel_count;
    } HRPEL_DATA;       /* Only in XGA and Image Adapter/A AIs */

typedef struct
    {
    UWORD   length;
    APOINT  coord;
    UBYTE FAR *def_address;
    UBYTE FAR *src_address;
    } HPSTEP_DATA;      /* Only in XGA and Image Adapter/A AIs */

typedef struct
    {
    UWORD   length;
    UBYTE FAR *def_address;
    UBYTE FAR *src_address;
    } HCPSTEP_DATA;     /* Only in XGA and Image Adapter/A AIs */

typedef struct
    {
    UWORD   length;
    APOINT  coord;
    UBYTE FAR *def_address;
    UBYTE FAR *tgt_address;
    } HRSTEP_DATA;          /* Only in XGA and Image Adapter/A AIs */
```

...continued

...from previous page

```
typedef struct
    {
    UWORD    length;
    UBYTE    flags;
    UBYTE    format;
    UBYTE FAR  *bmap_addr;
    WORD     width;
    WORD     height;
    } HSBMAP_DATA;              /* Only in XGA and Image Adapter/A AIs */

typedef struct
    {
    UWORD    length;
    UBYTE    flags;
    UBYTE    format;
    UBYTE FAR *bmap_addr;
    WORD     width;
    WORD     height;
    APOINT   coord;
    UWORD    wind_width;
    UWORD    wind_height;
    } HQBMAP_DATA;              /* Only in XGA and Image Adapter/A AIs */

typedef struct
    {
    UWORD         length;
    UWORD         flags;
    WORD          blk_width;
    WORD          blk_height;
    BYTE          dst_format;
    BYTE          reserved1;
    UBYTE FAR *dst_addr;
    WORD          dst_width;
    WORD          dst_height;
    APOINT        dst_coord;
    BYTE          src_format;
    BYTE          reserved2;
    UBYTE FAR *src_addr;
    WORD          src_width;
    WORD          src_height;
    APOINT        src_coord;
    BYTE          pat_format;
    BYTE          reserved3;
    UBYTE FAR *pat_addr;
    WORD          pat_width;
    WORD          pat_height;
```

```
    APOINT      pat_coord;
    } HBMC_DATA;              /* Only in XGA and Image Adapter/A AIs */

typedef struct
    {
    UWORD   length;
    APOINT  coord;
    } HSPRITE_DATA;           /* Only in XGA and Image Adapter/A AIs */

typedef struct
    {
    UWORD   length;
    UBYTE   flags;
    BYTE    res;
    BYTE    hotx;
    BYTE    hoty;
    BYTE FAR *image;
    WORD    width;
    WORD    height;
    WORD    col1_green;
    WORD    col1_red;
    WORD    col1_blue;
    WORD    col2_green;
    WORD    col2_red;
    WORD    col2_blue;
    } HSSPRITE_DATA;     /* Only in XGA and Image Adapter/A AIs */

typedef struct
    {
    UWORD   length;
    APOINT  coord;
    WORD    width;
    WORD    height;
    HSDW_DATA;               /* Only in XGA and Image Adapter/A AIs */

#define HRWVEC_DATA(SIZE)  struct /* Only in XGA and Image Adapter/A AIs
                           */\
                           {\
                           UWORD      length;\
                           UBYTE      flags;\
                           BYTE       reserved;\
                           UBYTE FAR *buffer;\
                           APOINT     coords[SIZE];\
                           }
```

continued...

...from previous page

```
typedef struct   /* Only in XGA and Image Adapter/A AIs */
    {
    UWORD    length;
    UWORD    format;
    BYTE     paldata[1028];    /* 1028 is worst case, but the*/
    } HSFPAL_DATA;             /* actual size is in HQDPS.*/

typedef struct   /* Only in XGA and Image Adapter/A AIs */
    {
    UWORD    length;
    UWORD    format;
    BYTE     paldata[1028];    /* 1028 is worst case, but the*/
    } HRFPAL_DATA;             /* actual size is in HQDPS.*/

/*-----------------------------------------------------------------------

    End of AFIDATA.H

------------------------------------------------------------------------*/
```

Appendix L

CALLAFI.ASM

This appendix contains the assembly language source code for my version of CALLAFI.OBJ, which is the program you need to link with in order to run Adapter Interface based programs, such as those presented in Chapter 7.

```
;*********************************************************************
;
; CALLAFI.ASM - AI call interface for "Power Programming the IBM XGA".
;
; Written by Jake Richter
;
; Copyright (C) 1992 Panacea Inc. - All Rights Reserved
;
; NOTICE:
;               This include file may be freely used and incorporated in your
;               code,
;               providing that this header, including the copyright notice,
;               remains
;               unchanged.
;
;*********************************************************************
;
               .MODEL      SMALL        ; Our code is Small Model
;
;-------------------------------------------------------------------
;
;   EQUATES
;
;-------------------------------------------------------------------
;
FP_ARG1        equ         [BP + 6]     ; Location of 1st arg, far func.
FP_ARG2        equ         [BP + 8]     ; Second Arg.
;
;-------------------------------------------------------------------
;
;   DATA
;
;-------------------------------------------------------------------
;
               .DATA                    ; Set up data segment
               public      _afi_ptr     ; AI header table addr.

_afi_ptr       label       dword        ; Set to 0, initially
_afiPtrLo      dw          0
_afiPtrHi      dw          0
;
;
;-------------------------------------------------------------------
;
;   CODE
;
;-------------------------------------------------------------------
;
```

```
            .CODE                       ; Set up code segment
;
;
            public      _GetAFI, _GetAFIL, _CallAFI
;
;
; BYTE FAR * (FAR GetAFI())
;
; This function allows a calling program to get the address of
; the AI jump table. The function returns the 32 bit segment:offset
; address of the jump table in DX:AX.
;
; NOTE: This routine is called as a FAR routine from 'C'.
;
; Registers trashed: AX, BX, CX, DX, and ES.
;
_GetAFI     proc        far
            push        SI              ; Save registers.
            push        DI

            mov         AX, 357FH       ; Get contents of INT 7FH vector
            int         21H             ; Returns result in ES:BX

            mov         AX, ES
            or          AX, BX          ; If vector data = 0, no AI
            jz          GetAFI_NoAI

            mov         AX, 105H        ; AI might be present, check it
            int         7FH
            jc          GetAFI_NoAI     ; If carry set, no valid AI

            mov         _afiPtrLo, DX   ; If AI valid, CX:DX has jump
            mov         _afiPtrHi, CX   ;   table address
            mov         AX, DX          ; Also need to return the data in
            mov         DX, CX          ;   DX:AX
            jmp         short GetAFI_Done

GetAFI_NoAI:                            ; If we get here, no valid AI
            xor         AX, AX          ; Return a jump table addr of 0:0
            mov         DX, AX
GetAFI_Done:
            cld                         ; Clear carry and dir. flags
            clc
            pop         DI
            pop         SI
            ret
_GetAFI     endp
;
;
```
continued...

...from previous page

```
; struct afi_list_entry FAR *(FAR GetAFIL())
;
; This function returns the 32-bit segment:offset address of the AI
; Linked List. This function is a post-8514/A AI function, which allows
; multiple AI-supported devices to each have their own AI interface, all
; in one system. The structure of the linked list is in IBMAFI.H in
; Appendix K.
;
; NOTE: This routine is called as a FAR routine from 'C'.
;
; Registers trashed: AX, BX, CX, DX, and ES.
;
_GetAFIL   proc     far
           push     SI
           push     DI               ; Save regs.

           mov      AX, 357FH        ; Get INT 7FH vector data
           int      21H              ; Result of call in ES:BX

           mov      AX, ES
           or       AX, BX           ; Check for vector not set
           jz       GetAFIL_NoAI     ; Jump if vector data is 0

           mov      AX, 113H         ; Assume AI loaded, call to get
           xor      BX, BX           ;  address of AI linked list
           int      7FH
           jc       GetAFIL_NoAI     ; If carry set, then not available

           mov      AX, DX           ; Otherwise, address in CX:DX
           mov      DX, CX           ; Copy into DX:AX for return
           jmp      short GetAFIL_Done

GetAFIL_NoAI:
           xor      AX, AX
           mov      DX, AX           ; Return 0:0

GetAFIL_Done:
           cld               ; Clear direction flag
           pop      DI
           pop      SI
           ret
_GetAFIL   endp
;
;
; VOID FAR CallAFI(funcNum, far byte *parmBlock)
;
; This is the entry point for programs to call the AI. The function
; number is passed as a 16 bit integer. The parameter block's 32 bit
; address (segment:offset) is passed as the second parameter.
```

```
;
; NOTE: This routine is called as a FAR routine from 'C'.
;
; Registers trashed: AX, BX, CX, DX, and ES.
;
_CallAFI   proc      far
           push      BP
           mov       BP, SP              ; Set stack frame
           push      SI
           push      DI                  ; Saved trashed registers

           mov       AX, FP_ARG1         ; Load function number
           les       BX, FP_ARG2         ; Get parm block pointer

           push      ES                  ; Push parm ptr onto stack
           push      BX

           shl       AX, 1               ; Get DWORD ptr from func #
           shl       AX, 1

           les       BX, _afi_ptr        ; Get ptr to AI call table
           add       BX, AX              ; Index to proper function
           call      dword ptr ES:[BX]   ; Do the call

           pop       DI                  ; Restore regs and return
           pop       SI
           pop       BP
           ret
_CallAFI   endp

           end
```

132-Column Mode

This appendix contains all the code (combined with XGAFIND.ASM from Chapter 5) that you will need to switch your XGA into 132-column text mode and back into VGA mode. It is included here an appendix instead of as part of Chapter 5 because it is not really a XGA graphics function. Instead, it exercises the VGA portion of the XGA chip.

There are three source code files shown here:

VGATO132.C   The main program used to switch an XGA that is already in VGA mode into 132-column text display mode.

SETXG132.ASM   The assembly language routine call from VGATO132.C that actually performs the 132 mode switch.

132TOVGA.C   The program used to switch you back from 132-column text mode into the XGA's VGA mode.

```
/*-----------------------------------------------------------------------

   VGATO132.C - Shows how to initialize an XGA into 132-column mode

   This program can be run by compiling it with the following lines:

        CL -c -Zp VGATO132.C
        LINK VGATO132 SETXG132 XGAFIND;
-----------------------------------------------------------------------*/

/*-----------------------------------------------------------------------

   Include file section

   (the fail safe approach, include everything you might need later)
-----------------------------------------------------------------------*/
#include <stdio.h>
#include <stdlib.h>
#include <string.h>
#include <errno.h>
#include <fcntl.h>
#include <dos.h>
#include <conio.h>
#include <io.h>
#include <malloc.h>
#include <sys\types.h>
#include <sys\stat.h>
#include "xga.h"
/*-----------------------------------------------------------------------

   Structures

-----------------------------------------------------------------------*/
typedef struct XGA_Info
   {
   BYTE         xiMonitor;      /* Monitor type */
   UBYTE        xiMode;         /* Native or VGA mode */
   UWORD        xiBaseVRML;     /* Base VRAM address (low) */
   UWORD        xiBaseVRMH;     /* Base VRAM address (high) */
   UWORD        xiIOReg;        /* I/O Reg address */
   UWORD        xiMemReg;       /* Mem Reg address */
   UWORD        xiMemSize;      /* Memory Size for board (in 256Ks) */
   } XGA_INFO;
/*-----------------------------------------------------------------------

   Externals (all in XGAFIND.ASM)

-----------------------------------------------------------------------*/
extern    XGA_INFO  xgaList[];         /* Contains XGA information */
extern    UWORD     xgaCount;          /* Number of XGAs found */
extern    VOID      GetBoardConfig();  /* Function to find XGAs */
```

```
/*---------------------------------------------------------------------

   Locally Defined Variables

--------------------------------------------------------------------*/
union REGS  inRegs, outRegs;   /* Used for reinit'ing video mode */

UWORD       ioRegBaseAddr;      /* The I/O register base address */
WORD        selectXGA = -1;     /* Index to selected XGA in xgaList */
/*---------------------------------------------------------------------

   Code

--------------------------------------------------------------------*/
/*----------------------------------

WORD  main(argc, argv)

This is the main entry point into the program.

_____*/
WORD  main(argc, argv)
WORD  argc;
BYTE  **argv;
{
   UWORD      i;               /* Loop counter */

   GetXGAList();               /* Are any XGAs present? */
   if (!xgaCount)              /* Check the count */
      {
      printf("No XGAs found in system!\n");
      return(1);              /* Abort with an error code */
      }
   /*
      If we get this far, at least one XGA has been found.
      Let's switch the one that's in VGA mode into 132-column
      mode. If there isn't one in VGA mode, we'll need to avoid
      memory conflicts, and just report we can't go into 132
      column mode. Note that we also need a monitor on the XGA.
   */
   for (i = 0; i < xgaCount; i++)
      {
      if (xgaList[i].xiMonitor < 0)
         continue;            /* Ignore XGAs with no monitor */
      if (xgaList[i].xiMode == DISP_XGA_MODE)
         continue;            /* Ignore XGAs in XGA graphics mode */
      selectXGA = i;
      break;
      }
```

continued...

...from previous page

```c
  if (selectXGA == -1)
     {
     /*
        If we get here, no valid XGA found.
     */
     printf("None of the XGAs in the system are in a valid mode!\n");
     return(2);               /* Return with an error */
     }

  /*
     Once we get here, it means we have found a valid XGA to use.
     First, if it's already in 132-column mode, we don't need to
     do anything.
  */
  if (xgaList[selectXGA].xiMode < DISP_VGA_MODE)
     {
     printf("The XGA is already in 132-column mode.\n");
     return(0);              /* Return with no error */
     }

  /*
     Now we're clear. Let's initialize the XGA in VGA mode into
     132-column text mode.
  */

  ioRegBaseAddr = xgaList[selectXGA].xiIOReg;

  SetXGA132();                   /* Located in SETXG132.ASM */

  return(0);  /* Return with no error */
}
```

```asm
;**********************************************************************
;
; SETXG132.ASM - Contains XGA 132-column init code
;
;
; This file should be assembled via the following line:
;
;      MASM -ml SETXG132;
;
; This will produce a file called SETXG132.OBJ which should be linked
; with XGA132.OBJ and XGAFIND.OBJ.
;
;**********************************************************************
```

```
        include     XGA.INC

                    .MODEL      SMALL
                    .DATA

                    extrn       _ioRegBaseAddr:word

stateTable  db      64 dup (?)          ; Place to store VGA state info.

                    .CODE
;
; SetXGA132
;
; Sets the given XGA (selected by _ioRegBaseAddr) into a 132-column
; text mode. This code also shows how to avoid using the IOREGxxxxx
; macros to decrease code size by allows word writes which set
; both an index and data at the same time.
;
                    public      _SetXGA132
_SetXGA132 proc
                    push        ES
                    push        DI                  ; Save important registers.
;
; First step, force the XGA into a proper VGA mode (in case something
; was screwey at first), and set display mode 3 (80x25 color).
;
            mov         DX, _ioRegBaseAddr
            add         DX, IO_INDEX        ; Point to I/O Index reg.
            mov         AL, DISP_CTRL1      ; Low byte (to index reg)
            mov         AH, 15H             ; Data for high byte
            out         DX, AX              ; Send both at once
            mov         AH, 14H             ; Finish the CRTC reset
            out         DX, AX

            mov         AL, CLOCK_SEL_1     ; Select the VGA clock.
            mov         AH, 04H
            out         DX, AX              ; Send to Index regs.

            mov         AX, 1202H           ; Set 400 line mode via BIOS
            mov         BL, 30H
            int         10H

            mov         AX, 3               ; Set Color 80x25 mode.
            int         10H
;
; Now we're really ready for the 132-column mode. IBM has indicated
; that some day this mode will end up as INT 10H BIOS mode 14H, so
; let's first see if that mode is available, so we can just use
; the BIOS instead and make life easy.
;
```

continued…

...from previous page

```
                mov       AX, DS            ; Our data segment
                mov       ES, AX
                lea       DI, stateTable    ; Point to stateTable
                mov       AH, 1BH           ; Read VGA BIOS func/state
                mov       BX, 0             ; Implementation type
                int       10H               ; Get the data
                les       DI, ES:[DI]       ; Point to the fixed data
                test      byte ptr ES:[DI+2], 10H ; Bit for Mode 14H
                jz        Set132_Manual     ; Jump if mode not in BIOS
Set132_BIOS:
                mov       AX, 14H           ; It exists, use BIOS.
                int       10H               ; Do it. Simple, huh?
                jmp       Set132_Exit       ; We're done.
;
; If we get here, the BIOS was of no help (the most likely situation).
; This means we have to twiddle lots of registers.
;
Set132_Manual:
                IOREGWRITEB IO_INDEX, DISP_CTRL1
                IOREGREADB  IO_DATA         ; Prepare CRTC for reset.
                and       AL, NOT BLANK_DISP
                or        AL, BLANK_DISP_PREPCRTC
                out       DX, AL            ; We know DX is set for IO_DATA
                and       AL, NOT BLANK_DISP
                out       DX, AL            ; Actually reset it.
                                            ; Set the 132-column mode.
                IOREGWRITEB OP_MODE, DISP_132_MODE
                                            ; Set Clock scale of 2x
                IOREGWRITEW IO_INDEX, <CLOCK_SEL_1 OR (1 SHL 8)>
                                            ; Set 132-column clock
                IOREGWRITEW IO_INDEX, <CLOCK_SEL_2 OR (80H SHL 8)>

                mov       AL, DISP_CTRL1
                out       DX, AL            ; Point to DISP_CTRL1
                inc       DX                ; Bump up to IO_DATA
                in        AL, DX            ; Get Mode value
                and       AL, NOT FEATURE_ENAB
                out       DX, AL            ; Disable feature connector
;
; The following code modifies the VGA defaults for the VGA CRTC registers
; in order to accomodate the 132-column mode. These are IBM recommended
; values, and if you want to know exactly what's going on, check out a
; VGA programming book for details.
;
                mov       DX, 03D4H         ; Point to VGA CRTC index register
                mov       AL, 11H
```

```
out     DX, AL
inc     DX
in      AL, DX
and     AL, 07FH
out     DX, AL
dec     DX

mov     AX, 0A400H
out     DX, AX

mov     AX, 08301H
out     DX, AX

mov     AX, 08402H
out     DX, AX

mov     AX, 08303H
out     DX, AX

mov     AX, 09004H
out     DX, AX

mov     AX, 08005H
out     DX, AX

IOREGWRITEW IO_INDEX, <HSYNC_END_LO OR (0A3H SHL 8)>
inc     AL                   ; Point to HSYNC_END_HI
xor     AH, AH               ; Set to 0
out     DX, AX               ; Send it.

mov     AL, HSYNC_POS1  ; Point to new reg.
out     DX, AL
inc     DX
in      AL, DX           ; Read it
and     AL, 9FH          ; Mask off some bits.
out     DX, AL           ; Send it back out.

dec     DX
mov     AL, HSYNC_POS2  ; Same thing here.
out     DX, AL
inc     DX
in      AL, DX
and     AL, 0F9H
out     DX, AL

mov     DX, 03D4H        ; Another VGA register
mov     AX, 04213H
out     DX, AX

mov     AL, 11H
out     DX, AL
inc     DX
```

continued...

...from previous page

```
            in        AL, DX              ; Read it.
            or        AL, 80H             ; Disable VGA CRTC update
            out       DX, AL

            IOREGWRITEB IO_INDEX, DISP_CTRL1
            inc       DX
            in        AL, DX
            or        AL, BLANK_DISP_NORMAL
            out       DX, AL              ; Reenable the CRTC

            mov       DX, 3C4H            ; More VGA control
            mov       AL, 1
            out       DX, AL
            inc       DX
            in        AL, DX
            or        AL, 1               ; 8-bit characters
            out       DX, AL

            mov       DX, 3DAH
            in        AL, DX              ; Reset Attribute Controller Flip/Flop

            mov       DX, 3C0H            ; Point to Attr. Controller
            mov       AL, 13H
            out       DX, AL              ; Index 13H
            mov       AL, 0
            out       DX, AL              ; Set to 0
            mov       AL, 20H
            out       DX, AL              ; Restore Palette
            mov       AX, 40H
            mov       ES, AX              ; Point to BIOS area, set screen width
            mov       byte ptr ES:[4AH], 132 ; Necessary for DOS work.
Set132_Exit:
            pop       DI                  ; Restore Regs.
            pop       ES
            ret
_SetXGA132 endp

            end
```

```
/*----------------------------------------------------------------------

   132TOVGA.C - Shows how to reset an XGA from 132-column mode into VGA

   This program can be run by compiling it with the following lines:

       CL -c -Zp 132TOVGA.C
       LINK 132TOVGA XGAFIND;

----------------------------------------------------------------------*/
```

```
/*-------------------------------------------------------------------------

   Include file section
   (the fail safe approach, include everything you might need later)

   -----------------------------------------------------------------------*/
#include <stdio.h>
#include <stdlib.h>
#include <string.h>
#include <errno.h>
#include <fcntl.h>
#include <dos.h>
#include <conio.h>
#include <io.h>
#include <malloc.h>
#include <sys\types.h>
#include <sys\stat.h>
#include "xga.h"
/*-------------------------------------------------------------------------

   Structures

   -----------------------------------------------------------------------*/
typedef struct XGA_Info
   {
   BYTE      xiMonitor;                /* Monitor type */
   UBYTE     xiMode;    /* Native or VGA mode */
   UWORD     xiBaseVRML;               /* Base VRAM address (low) */
   UWORD     xiBaseVRMH;               /* Base VRAM address (high) */
   UWORD     xiIOReg;  /* I/O Reg address */
   UWORD     xiMemReg; /* Mem Reg address */
   UWORD     xiMemSize;                /* Memory Size for board (in 256Ks)
                                          */

   } XGA_INFO;

/*-------------------------------------------------------------------------

   Externals (all in XGAFIND.ASM)

   -----------------------------------------------------------------------*/
extern     XGA_INFO  xgaList[];    /* Contains XGA information */
extern     UWORD     xgaCount;     /* Number of XGAs found */
extern     VOID      GetBoardConfig();  /* Function to find XGAs */

/*-------------------------------------------------------------------------

   Locally Defined Variables

   -----------------------------------------------------------------------*/
```
continued...

...from previous page

```
union REGS   inRegs, outRegs;          /* Used for reinit'ing video mode */

UWORD        ioRegBaseAddr;            /* The I/O register base address */
WORD         selectXGA = -1;           /* Index to selected XGA in xgaList */

/*------------------------------------------------------------------------

    Code

---------------------------------------------------------------------------*/
/*-------------------------------------

WORD    main(argc, argv)

This is the main entry point into the program.

---------------------------------------*/
WORD    main(argc, argv)
WORD    argc;
BYTE    **argv;
{
    UWORD        i;                     /* Loop counter */

    GetXGAList();                       /* Are any XGAs present? */
    if (!xgaCount)                      /* Check the count */
        {
        printf("No XGAs found in system!\n");
        return(1);                      /* Abort with an error code */
        }

    /*
        If we get this far, at least one XGA has been found.
        Let's switch the one that's in 132-column mode into VGA
        mode. If there isn't one in 132-column mode, we'll report
        an error. Note that we also need a monitor on the XGA.
    */
    for (i = 0; i < xgaCount; i++)
        {
        if (xgaList[i].xiMonitor < 0)
        continue;                       /* Ignore XGAs with no monitor */
    if (xgaList[i].xiMode != DISP_132_MODE)
        continue;                       /* Ignore XGAs in non-132 col. mode */
    selectXGA = i;
    break;
        }

    if (selectXGA == -1)
        {
        /*
        If we get here, no valid XGA found.
```

```
        */
        printf("None of the XGAs in the system are in a 132-column
mode!\n");
        return(2);                            /* Return with an error */
        }

  /*
        Now we're clear. Let's initialize the XGA in 132-column mode
        into VGA (80x25) mode.
  */

  ioRegBaseAddr = xgaList[selectXGA].xiIOReg;

  IOREGWRITEB(IO_INDEX, DISP_CTRL1);
  IOREGWRITEB(IO_DATA, 0x15);          /* Prepare CRTC for Reset */
  IOREGWRITEB(IO_DATA, 0x14);          /* Reset CRTC */
  IOREGWRITEB(IO_INDEX, DISP_CTRL2);
  IOREGWRITEB(IO_DATA, 0);             /* Prepare for VGA mode */
  IOREGWRITEB(IO_INDEX, CLOCK_SEL_1);
  IOREGWRITEB(IO_DATA, 4);             /* Select VGA Clock */
  IOREGWRITEB(IO_INDEX, CLOCK_SEL_2);
  IOREGWRITEB(IO_DATA, 0x7F);          /* Select VGA Clock */
  IOREGWRITEB(IO_INDEX, VSYNC_END);
  IOREGWRITEB(IO_DATA, 0x20);          /* Load expected value */
  IOREGWRITEB(OP_MODE, DISP_VGA_MODE); /* Set it! */
  outp(0x3C3, 1);                      /* Enable as VGA */
  inRegs.x.ax = 0x03;                  /* Mode 0x03 */
  int86(0x10, &inRegs, &outRegs);      /* Restore previous mode */

  return(0);                           /* Return with no error */
}
```

IBM DMQS Standard

T his appendix has been supplied by IBM Corporation with the kind assistance of James Wilkinson, Graeme Dougal, and Ed Eilbeck of the Visual Subsystems Development department in IBM Boca Raton, Florida.

XGA Adapter Identification, Location, and Mode Setting

A new mechanism for identifying XGA family subsystems has been introduced with the XGA-NI adapter, which is described in the "XGA Display Mode Query and Set (DMQS)" section of this appendix. DMQS will identify XGA family adapters, provide information for Extended Graphics Mode setting, and ensure migration for applications and drivers on future XGA hardware and displays.

Since the original XGA subsystem did not support DMQS, device drivers written to run on both XGA and XGA-NI subsystems must incorporate both mechanisms, attempting first to identify and locate the XGA-NI subsystem using DMQS, and, failing that, to use the original XGA-specific mechanism described in the "Locating and Initializing the XGA Subsystem without DMQS" section of this appendix.

DMQS may be implemented on original XGA level subsystems, so software should not assume that the existence of DMQS capability is proof of XGA-NI level of function.

In a system with multiple XGA subsystems, if any one XGA subsystem has DMQS capability, it will provide DMQS services for all XGA subsystems recognized. Software should not use the original XGA identification procedure if DMQS BIOS services are supported (see the "DMQS BIOS Interface" section of this appendix).

XGA Display Mode Query and Set (DMQS)

DMQS Architecture Overview

DMQS will identify XGA family adapters, provide information for Extended Graphics Mode setting, and ensure migration for applications and drivers on future hardware and displays.

DMQS is comprised to two types of data: DMQS primary data and DMQS display information, contained in the display information files.

The primary data is returned to the software via the INT 10 Video BIOS code point.

The DMQS primary data contains the following information for each XGA instance:

- XGA implementation level identifier.
- Location of XGA I/O registers or ports in I/O space.
- Location of memory mapped XGA registers in system address space.
- Location of 1 Meg memory mapped XGA aperture.
- Location of 4 Meg memory mapped XGA aperture.
- System address at which the XGA accesses video memory.
- The composite ID of the attached display (see the "Composite Display ID" section of this appendix).
- Amount of video memory available.

The Adapter POST "hooks" the INT 10 Video BIOS to point to two new code points. One code point returns the total size of the DMQS data array for all XGA instances. The other code point returns the DMQS data to the caller's buffer.

Software accesses the new BIOS code points to obtain the DMQS data stored by POST. Using the information from the composite ID field in the DMQS data, the device driver generates the DMQS display information file name. The DMQS display file is stored in a reserved directory named XGA$DMQS, or in the directory named in the DMQSPATH environment variable.

NOTE: In some operation systems, an alternative directory or path may be necessary.

Software should first look for the DMQSPATH environment variable to locate the directory containing the DMQS display information files. If the DMQSPATH environment does not exist, software should then look for a directory named XGA$DMQS on the boot disk.

The DMQS display information file contains the following data:

- Display-specific data, including physical display dimensions and display type (color, mono, LCD, CRT, and so on)

- The number of distinct Extended Graphics modes available on this display

- For each such mode available, the mode dimensions, the minimum level of XGA Adapter that supports this mode, XGA standard register settings to place the XGA Adapter in that particular mode.

Using the data contained in both the XGA DMQS primary data and the DMQS display information file, the Device Driver/Application can determine:

- The capability and physical characteristics of the XGA family adapter and display, including XGA implementation level, video memory size, physical display dimensions, and color/mono/LCD display information

- The location of all XGA registers and display buffers

- List of the modes available on the adapter/display combination

- Mode setting data for each mode

With this information, software can set the XGA and attached display into any available Extended Graphics mode without any hard-coded dependencies on displays or adapters.

If the DMQS display information file cannot be located, software should revert to direct mode setting as described in the "Locating and Initializing the XGA Subsystem without DMQS" section of this appendix.

DMQS BIOS Interface

The following two Video Int 10h code points are required to pass DMQS data to the software.

```
Video BIOS Int 10h Software Interrupt function

(AH) + 1FH - XGA Display Mode Query and Set (DMQS)

(AL) = 00H - Read DMQS Data Length

On Return:
     (AL) = 1FH - function supported
     (BX) = Number of bytes of DMQS data

Video BIOS Int 10h Software Interrupt function

(AL) = 01H - Read DMQS Data
     (ES:DI) - User buffer pointer for return of information

On Return:
     User buffer contains DMQS data
     (AL) = 1FH - function supported
```

As many as eight instances of XGA are possible. One copy of the following data structure exists for every instance:

(DI+00H) word	– Offset in bytes to DMQS data for next XGA instance
(DI+02H) byte	– Slot number
(DI+03H) byte	– XGA implementation function level identifier
(DI+04H) byte	– XGA implementation resolution level identifier
(DI+05H) word	– Vendor identifier – identifies card vendor
(DI+07H) word	– Vendor defined field
(DI+09H) word	– XGA Adapter I/O register base address
(DI+0BH) word	– XGA Coprocessor register base address – The location of memory mapped XGA coprocessor registers in system address space. Multiply the value of this field by 10h to get the physical address.
(DI+0DH) word	– 1 Megabyte System Video Memory Aperture – The location of 1 meg memory mapped XGA aperture in physical address space. A value of 0 indicates that the aperture is not allocated. Multiply the value of this field by 100000h to get the physical address
(DI+0FH) word	– 4 Megabyte System Video Memory Aperture — The location of 4 meg memory mapped XGA aperture in physical address space. A value of 0 indicates that the aperture is not allocated. Multiply the value

	of this field by 100000h to get the physical address
(DI+11H) word	– Video Memory Base Address — The location of video memory in the XGA system address space. Multiply the value of this field by 100000h to get the physical address
(DI+13H) word	– Composite ID of the attached display.
(DI+15H) byte	– Amount of video memory available, in multiples of 256K bytes
(DI+16H) dword	– Alternate XGA Coprocessor register base address — The location of alternative memory mapped XGA coprocessor registers in protect mode system address space. A value of 0 indicates that the alternative register location does not exist. A non-zero value is the physical location in system address space. If present, higher performance is available using the registers at this location.
(DI+??) misc	– DMQS Data for further XGA Instances.

Although the bits per pixel information has been omitted from the BIOS interface, it can be inferred from the XGA level (current level has 16 bits per pixel maximum), the video memory size, and the number of pixels on the screen in a particular mode (pixel height times pixel width) to get the maximum possible bits per pixel. Round off or down to the nearest supported bits per pixel value.

All fields will be coded in Intel format (low order byte first in word).

These calls return DMQS primary data for all XGA subsystems present in the system, both XGA and XGA-NI. XGA-NI subsystems recognize and provide DMQS services for non–DMQS-capable XGA subsystems.

DMQS Display Information Files

Software should expect to find the DMQS display information files in the XGA$DMQS directory on the boot disk or in the directory specified in the PATH environment variable. The section on DMQS display information file installation is included for information only.

Adapter and System Diskettes

Configuration information for future video subsystems must include a composite DMQS display file, made up of the individual DMQS display information files for all displays available at that time. The file is made by merging the individual display information files into a composite file. The individual files can be merged in any order.

The naming convention for the composite display file is the adapter ID followed by the letter M, with the extension DGS. For an adapter with a POS ID of hex 8FD9, the filename for the composite file is 8FD9M.DGS.

Future systems with the XGA subsystem integrated on the system board will provide the composite file on the Reference Diskette. Adapters will provide the file on the Option Diskette.

Display Diskette

Future displays that support new functions will ship with a display diskette to support the adapter in the extended graphics modes. The display diskette contains the DMQS display information file. The diskette will be a DOS format (FAT) diskette.

The naming convention for the display information file is the letters MON followed by a four-character alphanumeric string that would typically be an ASCII representation on the composite Display ID. These files use the file extension DGS. For a display with an ID of hex 001C, the filename for the display information file is MON001C.DGS.

Information in the DMQS display information file helps identify levels of hardware support. The revision level for the DMQS display information file allows an update to the file to replace an earlier version. And within the individual mode table, a field identifies the minimum level of XGA hardware that must be present to use that mode.

DMQS Display Information Files Installation

The installation of the display information files is operating-system specific. The display files may be installed during device driver installation. Both the composite display file and any necessary individual display information files would be copied to a subdirectory named XGA$DMQS. The DMQSPATH environment variable may also be used to locate DMQS display information files in an alternative directory. The path to the XGA$DMQS directory and the means of finding the path are operating-system specific.

In a LAN Server environment using remote IPL, the boot disk for such systems is on the server. Display information files are included with the boot image for diagnostics. For other environments, the location of the display files is operating-system specific.

DMQS Display Information File Structure

The DMQS display information files are stored in the XGA$DMQS directory of the boot drive unless the user chooses to store the XGA$DMQS subdirectory on another path. These files can be used by applications to determine the display characteristics, the available modes, and the register values to use in setting modes.

The XGA$DMQS directory contains a number of individual files, one for each display available.

As described in the "DMQS Customization File" section of this appendix, the composite ID returned in the DMQS Primary Data Area may be overridden under user control.

If the DMQS display information file cannot be located, software should revert to direct mode setting, as described in the "Locating and Initializing the XGA Subsystem without DMQS" section of this appendix.

Figure N.1 shows the structure of the directory and the individual display information files.

C:\XGA$DMQS\.

```
┌─────────────────────────────────────────────┐
│ ETC.                                         │
│  ┌─────────────────────────────────────────┐│
│  │ MON0002.DGS                             ││
│  │  ┌─────────────────────────────────────┐││
│  │  │ MON0001.DGS                         │││
│  │  │  ┌────────────────────────────────┐ │││
│  │  │  │ MON0000.DGS                    │ │││
│  │  │  │   ┌──────────────────────────┐ │ │││
│  │  │  │   │ Etc.                     │ │ │││
│  │  │  │   │  ┌──────────────────────┐│ │ │││
│  │  │  │   │  │ 1024 X 768 mode      ││ │ │││
│  │  │  │   │  │ Size of mode data    ││ │ │││
│  │  │  │   │  ┌──────────────────────┐ │ │││
│  │  │  │   │  │ 640 x 480 mode       │ │ │││
│  │  │  │   │  │ Size of mode data    │ │ │││
│  │  │  │   │  ├──────────┬───────────┤ │ │││
│  │  │  │   │  │ Register │ Value     │ │ │││
│  │  │  │   │  │  . .     │  . .      │ │ │││
│  │  │  │   │  │  . .     │  . .      │ │ │││
│  │  │  │   │  ├──────────┴───────────┤ │ │││
│  │  │  │   │  │ No. Modes supported  │ │ │││
│  │  │  │   │  │ Display phys. info.  │ │ │││
│  │  │  │   │  │ Color/Mono/LCD info  │ │ │││
│  │  │  │   │  └──────────────────────┘ │ │││
│  │  │  │   └──────────────────────────┘ │││
│  │  │  └────────────────────────────────┘│││
│  │  └─────────────────────────────────────┘││
│  └─────────────────────────────────────────┘│
└─────────────────────────────────────────────┘
```

Figure N.1. The DMQS display information file structure.

Details

The following table shows the detailed layout of the DMQS display information file. All fields are in hexadecimal, Intel format (low order byte first in work).

Offset	Data type	Description
00h	Bytes	DGS header data. The header must be hardcoded in hex to the following value: EB1B 901D 0045 4453 5900 0000 0000 2020 2000 0022 00EB 0690 FE01 0101 00EB 0190 F8CB.
		This should be ignored by software.
22h	Word	Total length of data in the file, in bytes. This field is used to unpack multiple display information files from a composite file.
24h	Word	Composite ID—used for unpacking a composite display file.
26h	Byte	Revision level—used to control file update.
27h	Byte	Number of modes supported by this display.
28h	Word	Display type
		00h Mono CRT
		01h Color CRT
		02h Mono LCD
		03h Color LCD
		04h Mono borderless capable
		05h Color borderless capable
2Ah.	Word	Width of screen in millimeters.
2Ch.	Word	Height of screen in millimeters.
2Eh	Bytes	Null terminated ASCII string that describes the display in user-friendly terms. The length of this field is 80 bytes. The string may be less than 80 bytes.
7Eh	Word	Offset of Individual Mode Data from the beginning of this file.
80h	Word	Length of first optional extension, including identifier. A length value of 0 indicates that no optional extensions exist. A nonzero value indicates that one or more optional extensions are present. Each optional extension consists of a length field, a 16-bit identifier, and the optional extension data. A zero length field terminates the chain of optional extensions.
82h	Word	First optional extension identifier (if present).
84h	Bytes	First optional extension data (if present).
xxh	Individual mode	First of multiple tables of variable length mode-specific data. See the following table for layout.

The following table shows the DMQS display data for individual modes. Multiple instances of this data may exist within the display file, one for each mode available on the applicable display.

Offset	Data type	Description
00h	Word	Length of Individual Mode Data (bytes in this table).
02h	Word	Screen pixel width of mode.
04h	Word	Screen pixel height of mode.
06h	Word	Minimum XGA implementation levels on which this mode is supported. A display may be capable of more modes than an earlier adapter implementation may be capable of supporting. See the "XGA Level Identifier" section of this appendix.
08h	Word	Vendor ID. For modes that are unique to a specific vendor, this field must be set. Currently reserved, this field will be set to zero.
0Ah	Word	Reserved. This field is intended to be used as a vendor-defined field. It will be activated when the Vendor ID field is set, and may be defined by the vendor to specify unique modes of operation.
0Ch	Word	Mode function type flags. This field identifies any special capabilities the mode may have: Bit 0 0 = Normal, 1 = borderless Bit 1 0 = Interlaced, 1 = Non-interlaced Bits 2-15 Reserved
0Eh	Word	N = Offset in bytes to mode set data from beginning of this table.
10h	Word	Mode Pixel Rate. This 16-bit value is four times the mode pixel rate in megaHertz. For example, a value of 360 indicates a mode pixel rate of 90 MHz.
12h	Word	Mode Line Rate. This 16-bit value is ten times the mode line rate in kiloHertz. For example, a value of 315 indicates a mode line rate of 31.5 kHz.
14h	Word	Mode Frame Rate. This 16-bit value is ten times the mode frame rate in Hertz. For example, a value of 750 indicates a frame refresh rate of 75 Hz.
16h	Word	Length of the first optional extension, including identifier. A length value of 0 indicates that no optional extensions exist. A nonzero value indicates that one or more optional extensions are present. Each optional extension consists of a length field, a 16-bit identifier, and the optional extension data. A zero length field terminates the chain of optional extensions.
18h	Word	First optional extension identifier (if present).
1Ah	Bytes	First optional extension data (if present).

Multiple repetitions of mode setting register value "triplets," as follows:

Offset	Data type	Description
N+00h, N+03h, etc.	Byte	Resister type

00h Write to XGA Direct Access I/O register.
01h Write to XGA Indexed Access I/O register.
02h OR with XGA Indexed Access I/O register.
03h OR with XGA Direct Access I/O register.
04h AND with XGA Indexed Access I/O register.
05h AND with XGA Direct Access I/O register.

Offset	Data type	Description
N+01h, N+04h, etc.	Byte	Register offset from Base I/O

Direct 0-Fh
Indexed 0-FFh

Offset	Data type	Description
N+02h, N+05h, etc.	Byte	Register value

NOTE: The "mode set data" section is a sequence of register settings required to place the hardware in the desired mode.

Mode Setting from the DMQS Display Information File

The "mode set data" section of the DMQS display information file Individual Mode Data includes only the section of the mode setting code that is display-specific, such as CRT Controller settings.

The complete XGA subsystem DMQS mode set sequence consists of:

1. Initial XGA subsystem display-independent initialization.
2. Display-dependent mode-specific initialization, using the mode set data from the display information file.
3. Final XGA subsystem display-independent initialization.

The complete XGA subsystem mode set sequence is as shown in Figure N.2.

XGA Register Name	XGA Register ID	Value	Comments
Interrupt Enable	21x4	00	Initial Value
Interrupt Status	21x5	FF	
Operating Mode	21x0	04	Set Extended Graphics Mode
Palette Mask	64	00	Blank Display
Video Mem Aperture Ctl	21x1	00	Initial Value
Video Mem Aperture Index	21x8	00	Initial Value
Virt Mem Ctl	21x6	00	Initial Value
Memory Access Mode	21x9	As required	Mode Depth (no. colors)

NOTE:

1. At this point XGA subsystem mode setting becomes display- and mode-specific, and the "mode set" register settings read from the Display Configuration file should be written to the appropriate XGA registers.

2. The initial palette should then be loaded, by writing to the appropriate XGA subsystem palette/sprite registers.

3. The video memory should also be initialized at this point, to avoid random data appearing when the palette mask is set to make the current display PEL map contents visible.

Sprite Control	36	00	Initial Value
Start Addr Low	40	00	Initial Value
Start Addr Me	41	00	Initial Value
Start Addr High	42	00	Initial Value
Display Pel Map Width Low	43	A0	As required
Display Pel Map Width High	44	00	As required
Display Mode 2	51	04	As required
Border Color	55	00	Initial Value
Palette Mask	64	FF	Make visible

Figure N.2. DMQS Extended Graphics Mode register settings.

Composite Display ID

The composite ID of the attached display is derived during POST, and is made available to the software in the DMQS Primary Data Area, as described in the "DMQS BIOS interface" section of this appendix.

Each display with a unique function or characteristics, and therefore a unique display information file, has a unique display ID. The display presents the display ID through pins on the display connector. The details of its derivation are shown in the "Display Type Detection" section of this appendix.

XGA Level Identifier

The XGA level identifier is returned as part of the BIOS interface, as described in the "DMQS BIOS Interface" section of this appendix. The XGA level identifier field consists of two bytes. One is the functional level identifier, which identifies the level of the Display Controller chip. The other is the resolution level identifier, which identifies the level of the Serializer Palette DAC chip.

Functional Level Identifier   Identifies the level of the Display Controller chip.

     '03'x   Base XGA implementation (XGA Display Adapter/A)

     '05'x   XGA-NI implementation level of function

Resolution Level Identifier   Identifies the level of the Serializer Palette DAC chip.

     '00'x   Base XGA implementation (XGA Display Adapter/A) (Maximum 45 MHz Pel rate)

     '03'x   XGA-NI Serializer Palette DAC (Maximum 90 MHz Pel rate)

DMQS Customization File

An additional file in the DMQS file directory should be consulted to ascertain additional XGA customization parameters, prior to reading the DMQS display configuration file. This file, called XGASETUP.PRO (if present), contains system customization information, as follows:

- Specifies a display ID alias for a particular slot. This overrides the display ID physically presented by the display, and specifies an alternate DMQS Display Configuration filename to be used instead.

- Identifies the slot to be used as the primary graphics display. In a multiple XGA system, the software normally chooses which XGA subsystem to use based on factors such as screen size, XGA subsystem, and so on. This entry overrides the software default, and forces the nominated slot—rather than the one chosen arbitrarily by the software—to be the primary XGA subsystem.

DMQS Customization File Example

Here is an example DMQS customization file:

```
/****************************************************************
/*
/* FILENAME: XGASETUP.PRO
/*
/* DESCRIPTION: Profile to set XGA DMQS preferences on current system.
/*
/* LAST MODIFIED: 04/09/92 at 16:13:38
/*
/****************************************************************
/****************************************************************
<SLOT, NUMBER=5, MONITOR_ID=F0FF>IBM 8515, 8516
/****************************************************************
<SLOT, NUMBER=8, MONITOR_ID=EXMP> Special DMQS DIF file
/****************************************************************
<STARTUP, NUMBER=5>
```

The profile above does the following:

1. Informs the software that the display in slot 5 is a display of type F0FF and the display information file MONF0FF.DGS should be used to obtain information about the installed display.

2. Informs the software that the display in slot 8 is a display of type EXMP and the display information file MONEXEMP.DGS should be used to obtain information about the installed display.

3. Identifies the slot (5 in this example) that holds the XGA subsystem to be used as the primary graphics display.

NOTE: If any of the slot numbers and/or display IDs are invalid when read, then the tag will be ignored and it will have no effect on how the XGA subsystem hardware is initialized.

XGA Subsystem DMQS Customization Tags

The syntax for the generalized DMQS Customization tag is shown in Figure N.3.

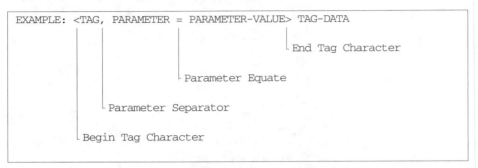

Figure N.3. DMQS Customization Tag Syntax

- Any number of blanks and/or new lines can be used to separate the begin tag character, the end tag character, tags, parameters, and parameter values. So, you can flow a single tag with many parameter values over multiple lines, and space out the elements within the tag for readability.

- The tag is the first text item following the begin tag character (<) and ending with the first comma (,) or end tag character (>).

- If any parameters exist, they are always separated by a comma (,). If no parameters exist for the tag, then the tag is immediately followed by an end tag character (>).

- Parameters are always assigned a value via the parameter equate character (=),

In the **SLOT** Syntax Diagram, the tag is defined as follows:

```
<SLOT, NUMBER=[slot number],MONITOR_ID=[display ID]>Text
```

Its parameters are:

- **NUMBER=[slot number]** (required). An integer value that indicates the system slot number that the XGA subsystem occupies. If this is an invalid number or there is no XGA subsystem in the specified slot, this tag will be ignored.

- **MONITOR_ID=[display ID]** (required). A four-character alphanumeric string that will be used to construct the name of the DMQS Display Configuration file to be loaded in place of the default file. This value will be used to generate a filename of the form MONXXXX.DGS, where XXXX will be the display ID value specified in the tag.

- **Text** (optional). A comment field that should be ignored by software.
- **Description.** This tag allows the user to specify a display ID override for display(s) attached to XGA subsystems with DMQS support. The display ID value in this customization file will override the physical value read from the display by the XGA subsystem.

In the **STARTUP** Syntax Diagram, the tag is defined as follows:

```
<STARTUP, NUMBER=[slot number]>Text
```

Its parameters are:

- **NUMBER=[slot number]** (required). An integer value that indicates the system slot number that the XGA subsystem occupies. If this is an invalid number or there is no XGA subsystem in the specified slot, this tag will be ignored.
- **Text** (optional). A comment field that should be ignored by software.
- **Description.** This tag allows the user to specify which XGA subsystem is to be used by an XGA mode application, where the default chosen by the application is inconvenient.

Locating and Initializing the XGA Subsystem without DMQS

Software should initially attempt to identify the XGA subsystem using DMQS, as described in the "XGA Display Mode Query and Set (DMQS)" section of this appendix. Only when DMQS has been found to be unsupported in the system, or if a DMQS display information file cannot be found, should software resort to the method of XGA subsystem identification and mode setting described in this section.

Software should not attempt to use this method in addition to DMQS, as DMQS (if not found) will provide support for both XGA and XGA-NI subsystems.

The procedure is as outlined here; more detail is given later in this section.

1. Identify if XGA subsystem is present by examining the system adapter's POS IDs one by one.
2. Locate the various I/O spaces of the XGA subsystem(s) spaces by decoding the XGA subsystem POS data.
3. Read the display ID to determine the attached display type.
4. Determine the amount of VRAM installed on the XGA subsystem.

5. Determine the modes available on the attached display.

6. Set the XGA subsystem into the required XGA mode, either 640x480 or 1024x768 resolution.

7. Handle any VGA primary adapter considerations, as described earlier in this book.

This procedure should be repeated, if necessary, until sufficient XGA subsystems in the system have been identified.

XGA Subsystem Identification

To identify all XGA subsystems, put every adapter in the system, including the system board video subsystem, into the setup mode in turn, and examine their POS IDs to locate any XGA adapters in the system.

For option cards, the procedure is described in System Services BIOS call INT 15h, AH=C4h Programmable Option Select in the *IBM Personal System/2 and Personal Computer BIOS Interface Technical Reference*.

For the system board video subsystem, a different procedure is necessary. To place the system board video subsystem in setup mode, write hex 0DF to port 94H; to enable it, write hex 0FF to port 94H.

Interrupts must be disabled for the entire period of time that each adapter is in setup mode.

The POS IDs for all adapters in the system must be read and examined to locate all of the XGA adapters in the system.

The following POS IDs have been preallocated to the XGA subsystem and follow-on XGA register compatible subsystems:

- 8FD8h to 8FDBh inclusive
- 8FD0h to 8FD3h inclusive
- VESA reserved IDs:
  —0240h to 027Fh inclusive
  —0830h to 0A7Fh inclusive
  —0A90h to 0BFFh inclusive

Check for these POS IDs when determining the existence of the XGA subsystem in the system.

After successfully matching POS IDs, read the remainder of the POS data bytes for that subsystem. This data is used to calculate the location of the XGA subsystem registers and display buffers in the I/O and physical system memory address space.

Location of XGA Subsystem I/O Spaces

ROM Address

Calculate the ROM address from POS data as follows:

```
ROM Address = (ROM Address field x hex 2000) + hex 0C0000
```

The ROM Address field is read from POS Register 2, bits 4 to 7.

XGA Coprocessor Registers

The XGA coprocessor registers are referenced from a base address. This address depends on the Instance (0–7) of the XGA subsystem and the ROM address calculated as shown above. The Coprocessor Register Base Address is calculated as follows:

```
(((128 x Instance) + hex 1C00) + ROM address)
```

The instance is read from POS Register 2, bits 1 to 3. For example:

```
Assuming Instance = 6 and ROM address = hex 0C0000, the Coprocessor Base
Address is hex 0C1F00.
```

I/O Registers

The XGA I/O registers are referenced from a base I/O address. The I/O address is calculated as follows:

```
Hex 21x0 (where x is the Instance)
```

The Instance is read from POS Register 2, bits 1 to 3.

The Video Memory Base Address

The Video Memory Base Address is calculated from the Video Memory Base Address field in POS Register 4, and the Instance.

Figures N.4 and N.5 show how these two values combine to give the Video Memory Base Address.

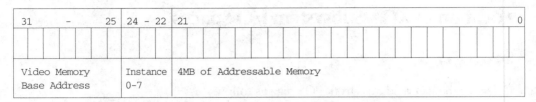

31 – 25	24 – 22	21																		0
Video Memory Base Address	Instance 0-7	4MB of Addressable Memory																		

Figure N.4. XGA video memory base address.

		Address (hex)	Virtual Memory Base Address
	4096MB	FFFFFFFF	127
	72MB	04800000	2
INSTANCE 1	68MB	04400000	2
INSTANCE 0	64MB	04000000	2
INSTANCE 7	60MB	03C00000	1
INSTANCE 6	56MB	03800000	1
INSTANCE 5	52MB	03400000	1
INSTANCE 4	48MB	03000000	1
INSTANCE 3	44MB	02C00000	1
INSTANCE 2	40MB	02800000	1
INSTANCE 1	36MB	02400000	1
INSTANCE 0	32MB	02000000	1
	16MB		
			0
	1MB		
ROM			
A000/B000			
SYSTEM RAM	0MB	0000000	0

Figure N. 8 The XGA Video Memory Base Address diagram.

The Video Memory Base Address field defines a 32MB address range and the Instance defines a 4 MB address range within the 32 MB range. For example:

```
Assuming Instance = 6 and the Video Memory Base Address field = 1, the
Video Memory Base Address is hex 03800000.
```

The Video Memory Base Address, when calculated, serves two purposes:

- **4MB System Video Memory Aperture.** If enabled (read from bit 0 in POS Register 4 to determine if the aperture is enabled), the 4MB system video memory aperture is located at this address in physical system address space. If virtual addressability to this range of physical address space can be achieved, the entire video memory can be accessed through this aperture at this address.

- **Video Memory Location in XGA Address Space.** This address is used to identify video memory to the XGA coprocessor.

- **1MB Aperture Base Address.** The 1MB aperture base address is calculated from the 1MB Aperture Base Address field in POS Register 5, bits 0 to 3.

```
If (1MB Base field)    0)
    1MB Aperture Base Address = 1MB Base field x hex 100000.

If (1MB Base field = 0) 1MB Aperture is disabled.
```

Display Type Detection

In order to determine what type of display is attached to the Video Subsystem, it is necessary to read the display's identification number. This ID is used to obtain information about the display, such as the resolutions supported, whether it is monochrome or color, and possibly the size of the screen.

The ID for each display is a 16-bit number, and usually uniquely identifies the display type. Some displays that have similar characteristics but are not the same model, have the same ID.

The recommended method of obtaining the display ID is by using a BIOS call:

```
Int 10h, (AH) + 1Fh-XGA Display Mode Query and Set (DMQS)
```

See the "XGA Display Mode Query and Set (DMQS)" section in this appendix. If it is necessary to read the display ID explicitly, the following procedure must be followed.

The display ID is read from the Display ID and Comparator register, which returns four ID bits at a time. Four reads must be performed in order to obtain all sixteen bits. The components of the ID are selected by manipulating the values of Horizontal Sync and Vertical Sync that are output to the display. Therefore, the ID may be read only when disruption of these signals may be tolerated, such as power-on time, or when changing display modes.

After setting the required Sync Polarity (SP field in Display Control 1 Register) to any of the various combinations of Horizontal and Vertical Sync listed below, it is necessary to wait for fifteen microseconds for this change to take effect before display ID may be read. This is best achieved by doing five consecutive reads or writes to any byte-wide XGA I/O port.

The display ID Reading sequence is as follows:

1. Prepare the CRTC for reset (Display Control 1 Register – Index 50 – DB field = '01'b)

2. Reset the CRTC (Display Control 1 Register DB field = '00'b)

3. Set Sync Polarity (SP field in Display Control 1 Register) to '01'b. This Sets VSYNC to '0'b and HSYNC to '1'b.

4. After a fifteen microsecond wait, read the display ID bits from Display ID and Comparator Register (Index 52). Place them in a hex variable A.

5. Set SP to '10'b. This sets VSYNC to '1'b and HSYNC to '0'b.

6. After a fifteen microsecond wait, read the display ID bits again. Place them in a hex variable B.

7. Set SP to '00'b. This sets VSYNC to '0'b and HSYNC to '0'b.

8. After a fifteen microsecond wait, read the display ID bits again. Place them in a hex variable C.

9. Set SP to '11'b. This sets VSYNC to '1'b and HSYNC to '1'b.

10. After a fifteen microsecond wait, read the display ID bits again. Place them in a hex variable D.

Assemble the 16 bits into four nibbles, one for each MID pin, from MSB to LSB, as shown in Figure N.6. The resulting four-hex-digit number (from MID bit 3 to bit 0) is the display ID.

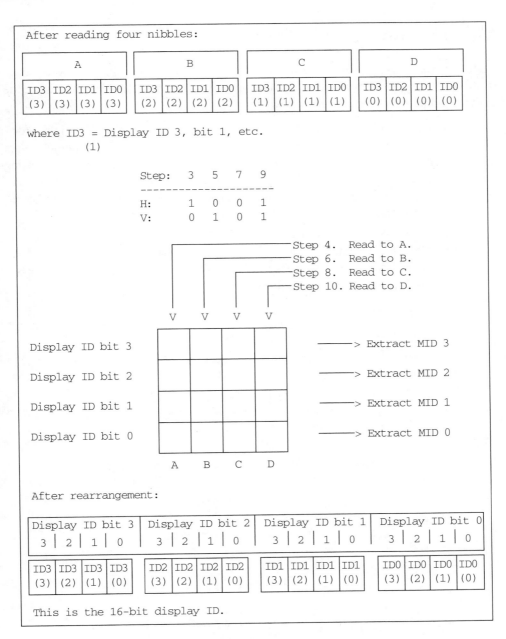

```
After reading four nibbles:
```

where ID3 = Display ID 3, bit 1, etc.
         (1)

This is the 16-bit display ID.

Figure N.9. Reading the display ID.

Video Memory Size Determination

There are two ways to determine the size of video memory installed. Both rely on a write-readback-check, in which a particular value is written to a key location. This value is then read to determine whether the written value has persisted.

- Use the XGA subsystem PxBIt capability to perform a test similar to the previous example. Transfer a constant color to the location in video memory, then transfer that value back from video memory to system memory using busmastership. This technique works regardless of the availability of a system video memory aperture. However, it requires physical addressability to a location in system memory for the busmastership operation.

- Use the system processor to write a value through an aperture to the word at offset 768KB into video memory. This technique assumes that the system video memory real mode aperture is available. The following sample code shows a list of displays and their associated IDs.

```
;* Assume GS points to start of A0000 Real mode aperture
;* and VGA adapter is in text mode so A0000 Real mode
;* aperture is available for this operation.
;* Where registers are shown as (for instance 21x0h), this should
;* be filled in with the appropriate IO port address after determining
;* the location of the XGA subsystem in IO space
;*
;* First put the adapter PARTIALLY in extended graphics mode
;* to allow use of the system video memory Aperture
        mov     al,0
        mov     dx,21x4h        ; disable XGA interrupts
        out     dx,al
;
        mov     ax,0064h
        mov     dx,21xAh        ; Blank palette
        out     dx,ax           ; indexed XGA register 64h
;
        mov     ax,04h
        mov     dx,21x0h        ; Set adapter in Extended Graphics Mode
        out     dx,al
;
        mov     al,01h
        mov     dx,21x1h        ; Locate video memory Aperture at A0000
        out     dx,al
;
        mov     dx,21x8h        ; System video memory indx reg.
        mov     al,0ch          ; Offset 768K
        out     dx,al           ;
;
        mov     byte ptr gs:[0],0A5h  ; Set byte to A5h
        mov     byte ptr gs:[1],0h    ; Avoid shadows on data lines
```

```
;
        cmp     byte ptr gs:[0],0A5h    ; Test against value written
        jne     vram_512k               ; 512k video memory only
;
        mov     byte ptr gs:[0],5Ah     ; Set byte to 5Ah
        mov     byte ptr gs[1],0h       ; Avoid shadows on data lines
;
        cmp     byte ptr gs:[0],0A5h    ; Test against value written
        je      vram_1Meg               ; 1 Meg if still matches
        jmp     vram_512K               ; Otherwise 1/2 meg found
```

Extended Graphics Modes Available

Figure N.7 shows the list of modes available according to the display type and size of video memory configured on the XGA subsystem.

Composite display ID (hex)	Example displays	Size (in.)	Color	Max address	512KB memory	1MB memory
FFFF	None				None	None
FF0F	8503	12	Mono	640x480	640x480x64 Grays	640x480x64 Grays
FFF0	8513	12	Color	640x480	640x480x256 Colors	640x480x256 Colors
	8512	14				640x480x65536 Colors
	8518					
F0FF	8515	14	Color	1024x768	640x480x256 Colors	640x480x256 Colors
	8516				1024x768x16 Colors	640x480x65536 Colors
						1024x768x16 Colors
						1024x768x256 Colors
F00F	8604	15	Mono	1024x768	640x480x64 Grays	640x480x64 Grays
	8507	19			1024x768x16 Grays	1024x768x16 Grays
						1024x768x64 Grays
F0F0	8514	16	Color	1024x768	640x480x256 Colors	640x480x256 Colors
					1024x768x16 Colors	640x480x65536 Colors
						1024x768x16 Colors
						1024x768x256 Colors
90F0	8517	17	Color	1024x768	640x480x256 Colors	640x480x256 Colors
					1024x768x16 Colors	640x480x65536 Colors
						1024x768x16 Colors
						1024x768x256 Colors

Figure N.7. The Availability of Extended Graphics Modes.

To set the XGA subsystem into Extended Graphics Mode, the configuration must be capable of supporting the required mode as listed above. The Extended Graphics Mode register settings are listed in Figure N.8.

XGA Register Name	XGA Reg. ID	Oper	Color Mode Value (hex) 1024x768 x256	1024x768 x16	640x480 x256	640x480 x65536	Comments
Interrupt Enable	21x4	=	00	00	00	00	Initial Value
Interrupt Status	21x5	=	FF	FF	FF	FF	
Operating Mode	21x0	=	04	04	04	04	Set Extended Graphics Mode
Palette Mask	64	=	00	00	00	00	Blank Display
Video Mem Aperture Ctl	21x1	=	00	00	00	00	Initial Value
Video Mem Aperture Index	21x8	=	00	00	00	00	Initial Value
Virt Mem Ctl	21x6	=	00	00	00	00	Initial Value
Memory Access Mode	21x9	=	03	02	03	04	Initial Value
Disp Mode 1	50	=	01	01	01	01	Prepare for reset
Disp Mode 1	50	=	00	00	00	00	Reset CRT Ctrl
Horiz Total Low	10	=	9D	9D	63	63	)
Horiz Total High	11	=	00	00	00	00	)
Horiz Display End Low	12	=	7F	7F	4F	4F	)
Horiz Display End High	13	=	00	00	00	00	)
Horiz Blank Start Low	14	=	7F	7F	4F	4F	)
Horiz Blank Start High	15	=	00	00	00	00	)
Horiz Blank End Low	16	=	9D	9D	63	63	)
Horiz Blank End High	17	=	00	00	00	00	)
Horiz Sync Start Low	18	=	87	87	55	55	)
Horiz Sync Start High	19	=	00	00	00	00	)
Horiz Sync End Low	1A	=	9C	9C	61	61	)
Horiz Sync End High	1B	=	00	00	00	00	)
Horiz Sync Posn	1C	=	40	40	00	00	)
Horiz Sync Posn	1E	=	04	04	00	00	)
Vert Total Low	20	=	30	30	0C	0C	)
Vert Total High	21	=	03	03	02	02	) XGA CRT
Vert Disp End Low	22	=	FF	FF	DF	DF	) Controller
Vert Disp End High	23	=	02	02	01	01	) param
Vert Blank Start Low	24	=	FF	FF	DF	DF	)
Vert Blank Start High	25	=	02	02	01	01	)
Vert Blank End Low	26	=	30	30	0C	0C	)
Vert Blank End High	27	=	03	03	02	02	)
Vert Sync Start Low	28	=	00	00	EA	EA	)
Vert Sync Start High	29	=	03	03	01	01	)
Vert Sync End	2A	=	08	08	EC	EC	)
Vert Line Comp Low	2C	=	FF	FF	FF	FF	)
Vert Line Comp High	2D	=	FF	FF	FF	FF	)
Sprite Control	36	=	00	00	00	00	Initial Value
Start Addr Low	40	=	00	00	00	00	Initial Value
Start Addr Me	41	=	00	00	00	00	Initial Value
Start Addr High	42	=	00	00	00	00	Initial Value
Buffer Pitch Low	43	=	80	40	50	A0	
Buffer Pitch High	44	=	00	00	00	00	
Clock Sel	54	=	0d	0d	00	00	
Display Mode 2	51	=	03	02	03	04	
Ext Clock Sel	70	=	00	00	00	00	
Display Mode 1	50	=	0F	0F	C7	C7	

NOTE: Initial palette loading must be done at this point, by writing to the appropriate XGA subsystem palette/sprite registers. The video memory must also be initialized at this point, to avoid random data appearing when the palette mask is set to make the current display PEL map contents visible.

| Border color | 55 | = | 00 | 00 | 00 | 00 | Initial value |
| Palette mask | 64 | = | FF | FF | FF | FF | Make visible |

Figure N.8. The Extended Graphics Mode register settings.

Glossary

Accelerated VGA

Also known as XVGA, accelerated VGAs are a new breed of VGA, which combine VGA compatibility with graphics acceleration, such as line drawing or BitBLTing capability. The key differences between such devices and other graphics coprocessors are that XVGAs integrate the capabilities into a single chip, and their acceleration features function in VGA and SVGA graphics modes.

Adapter

See **Controller**.

Adapter Interface

The Adapter Interface, or AI, was introduced in 1987 in conjunction with the IBM 8514/A as a software interface to IBM's advanced graphics architectures. For two years, the AI was the only way to access the capabilities of the 8514/A. Most graphics boards claiming to be 8514/A compatible are, in fact, only 8514/A AI compatible, and not compatible at the hardware register level. IBM has since introduced AIs for both its Image Adapter/A and the XGA Display Adapter/A, since both of these graphics devices are 8514/A hardware compatible.

Address Space

The address space of a computer defines the range of memory that can be addressed at any one time by the processor upon which the computer is based. The original IBM PC had an address space of 1024KB (or 1MB), while the Apple II had an address space of 64KB. New PCs based on the 386 or 486 processors have an address space of 1MB in **real mode** operation, and 4 gigabytes (4096MB) in **protected mode** operation.

AI

See **Adapter Interface**.

Area Fill

Also called a "flood fill," an area fill is a type of graphical primitive generally used to fill bounded areas on a graphics display. A **bounded area** normally consists of a single color that is completely surrounded (or **bounded**) by pixels of a different color. An area may also be bounded by multiple colors that are different from the surrounded color, or a single bounding color surrounding a variety of others.

Bank

A contiguous block of memory, usually 16KB or 64KB, that can be moved, or switched, around in the address space of a computer.

Bank Switching

In the IBM PC–compatible environment, in which free memory locations are scarce, graphics boards (which typically have at least 512KB of display memory) use bank switching to allow software to access all of their display memory. For example, a Super VGA may allow one bank of 64KB to be switched into the PC address space at a time. Software which draws into display memory must determine which bank it needs to access in order to affect the desired portion of the display. See also **Bank**.

BIOS

Basic **I**nput/**O**utput **S**ystem; a collection of hardware-specific routines that usually reside in ROM. The BIOS is used by low-level software to access the PC's peripheral devices. Each PC comes with a BIOS, and some peripheral boards, such as graphics adapters and drive controllers, may contain additional BIOS ROMs with routines designed to allow access to the devices on which they reside.

BitBLT

BitBLT is an acronym for **Bit-BLock-Transfer**. A BitBLT is used to copy a block of graphical data from one location to another, generally on a graphics board. BitBLTs may occur to/from system memory as well. Another variant on a BitBLT is a color expansion BitBLT, which uses a monochromatic source (1 bit per pixel), in which each 1 bit is expanded to one color, and each 0 bit is expanded into another color—this type of BLT is frequently used to display raster fonts on a display. BitBLT operations are most commonly visible in windowing environments.

Bitmap

A bitmap is used to define a portion of memory in which graphical raster data is stored. A bitmap can reside in either system or graphics device memory.

Board

See **Controller.**

BPP

An acronym for **B**its **P**er **P**ixel. The number of bits per pixel defines the depth of the color space that can be used by a graphics device. The following table shows the relationship between bpp and colors:

BPP	Number of Available Colors
1	2
2	4
4	16
8	256
15	32, 768
16	65, 536
24	16, 777, 216

Bresenham

A computer scientist who created graphics algorithms that translate graphics primitives like lines and circles from a mathematical coordinate space to a pixel-oriented computer space. Bresenham line drawing is the most commonly known such algorithm, and is used in most graphics systems because it uses only integers; that is, no floating point operations are required.

CGA

Color Graphics Adapter, introduced by IBM in 1982, shortly after the release of the original IBM PC. The CGA was capable of either a 320x200x4 color resolution or a 640x200 monochrome resolution.

Character Cell

A character cell defines the dimensions, usually in units of pixels, of a character in a font. This is most commonly used with fixed-pitch fonts.

Clipping

Clipping, or scissoring, is used to limit the drawing area of a graphical object, such as a line or image. Objects can be clipped against a **clipping rectangle**, such as a viewport or window in a windowing environment, or against more complex objects, such as polygons or circles (generally known as **arbitrary clipping**). Clipping is useful for preventing graphical objects from overflowing into areas where such objects should not appear.

Clock

In computer terms, a clock is a chip level device that generates a voltage pulse at a certain frequency. For example, a 25MHz clock will issue 25 million pulses per second, equally spaced so that a pulse occurs every 40 nanoseconds. Clocks are an integral part of any computer system, since they are used to drive microprocessors, generate display signals, and control memory access.

Controller

A controller, also known as an "adapter," "controller board," or just a "board," is a peripheral, usually a circuit board or chip, that controls some type of device. Graphics-related sample usages include IBM's Professional Graphics Controller, the IBM Color Graphics Adapter, and TIGA graphics boards. The term **graphics controller** or **display controller** is also used to also refer to a graphics chip that generates display signals and controls graphics memory access.

Cropping

Cropping is a user's form of clipping, seen at the application level. See **Clipping**.

CRT

Cathode **R**ay **T**ube. Technical name for a display, screen, and/or monitor. Most commonly associated with computer displays.

CRTC

CRT Controller. The CRTC used to be a standalone computer chip that would generate the signals necessary to drive a CRT; that is, create the frequencies necessary for an image to be displayed at a specific resolution. CRTCs started becoming an integrated part of graphics controllers in the mid–1980s, and can now be found in chips and chip sets ranging from EGAs and VGAs to XGAs and TI 34020s.

Cursor

A cursor is an on-screen position indicator. In a text environment, the cursor is usually a rectangular block (such as a line at the base of text characters), usually highlighted or blinking. In a graphics environment, such as Microsoft Windows, a cursor is frequently represented as an arrow at an angle. Also see **Sprite.**

DAC

Digital to Analog Converter. A DAC is used to translate a digital (integer) input, such as a pixel value, into an analog (noninteger) voltage signal. DACs are used in CD players to convert CD data into sounds, and are also a key component of any graphics subsystem, since they convert the pixel values into colors on the screen. Graphics boards tend to use a chip known as a RAM DAC, which combines DACs with Look-Up Tables (LUTs). See **LUT** for more information.

Direct Color

Initially an IBM term for the 16 bpp in the XGA, Direct Color has now become the VESA method for differentiating between devices that use Indexed Color and ones in which pixel data is passed directly through the DAC, bypassing the LUT. Nonindexed graphics resolutions are referred to by the complete term *Direct Color A:R:G:B,* where *A* is the number of bits of the Alpha channel (optional), and *R, G,* and *B* specify the number of bits for the red, green, and blue components, respectively. For example, the XGA 16 bpp mode is referred to as Direct Color 5:6:5 (or DC 5:6:5), while the TARGA-standard 16 bpp mode is DC 1:5:5:5. True color devices that use 24 bpp can be specified as DC 8:8:8.

DGIS

Direct **G**raphics **I**nterface **S**pecification is a product of GSS (Graphics Software Systems), a division of Spectragraphics, Inc. DGIS is a software interface (similar in concept to the AI) designed to be used with a wide range of graphics boards. These days, the predominant type of graphics board shipping with DGIS is based on the TI 340 family of graphics processors. DGIS has been around since the mid–1980s, and is supported by many applications.

DPI

Dots **P**er **I**nch. The DPI of a display or other type of output device indicates the surface resolution of the device. For example, a monitor that has a horizontal display area of 14" and can show 1,024 pixels in that space has a DPI of 73.14. DPI is more commonly used as a measurement of detail for scanners and printers.

DRAM

Dynamic **R**andom **A**ccess **M**emory. DRAMs are the core type of silicon memory used in computer these days. It is "dynamic" because DRAM-stored data decays rapidly, unless it is dynamically refreshed. Refreshing is a process by which the electrical signals that maintain data in the DRAM are boosted periodically (every few hundreds of nano-seconds) in order to offset the natural decay. DRAMs have the benefit of being quite in-expensive compared to other types of memory, and hence are used prolifically, even in graphics designs. See also **SRAM** and **VRAM**.

8514/A

The 8514/A is a graphics architecture and board introduced by IBM in 1987. The 8514/A core is based on a graphics coprocessor with line drawing, BitBLT, and other abilities. A number of companies, including ATI, Western Digital Imaging, and Chips and Technologies have cloned the 8514/A. The core 8514/A supports resolutions of both 640x480 and 1024x768, at either 16 or 256 colors.

EGA

Enhanced **G**raphics **A**dapter. The EGA was the second PC color graphics adapter intro-duced by IBM (in 1985), and thus a successor to CGA. The EGA provided an increase in resolution over CGA to 640x350 by 16 colors (chosen out of a palette of 64 colors). The EGA was heavily cloned, and the resultant Super EGAs supported resolutions as high as 800x600 by 16 colors.

EMS

EMS is **E**xpanded **M**emory **S**pecification, a type of memory access mechanism used by real-mode PC applications as an alternative to the clunkier extended memory access mechanism. EMS-accessible memory is also known as "expanded" memory. The big benefit EMS provides is that it is paged memory, and can exist in locations in which there is traditionally no memory available (known as the high-memory area). Originat-ing as a hardware implementation, EMS became popular as a software solution on 386 and 486 based systems, since the paging approach could be simulated via the MMU (Memory Management Unit), without having to enter protected mode, as one would with pure extended memory. Software EMS is provided by a category of utilities known as EMMs (Expanded Memory Managers), which convert extended memory in expanded memory. See **Extended Memory** for further details.

Enhanced VGA

See **Extended VGA**.

EVGA

See **Extended VGA**.

Expanded Memory

See **EMS**.

Extended Memory

Extended memory is the memory in a PC that resides above the 1 MB address mark. It is typically used by protected mode applications, such as operating systems and enhanced software packages, like Paradox 386 or AutoCAD 386. In real mode, it can be used in two ways. The first is by allocating space in the real mode accessible portion of memory (below the 1MB address mark), going into protected mode, copying the desired data to/from the sub-1MB area, and returning to real mode. This is obviously quite time-consuming. Hence the second method (which only works on 386 and 486 based systems, as well as some types of 80286 based PCs), namely accessing extended memory via an EMM. See **EMS** for further details.

Extended VGA

This term has been used to refer to clone VGA boards that are capable of a resolution of 800x600 by 16 colors. The use of the EVGA acronym never became widespread because of the more general term **Super VGA**.

Flicker

Flicker refers to the repeated display/fade cycle present on monitors and displays. The amount of flicker present depends on a number of factors, including the individual viewing the display, the vertical refresh frequency of the display, lighting, and whether or not the display is operating in an interlaced or noninterlaced mode. It is generally agreed that a flicker-free display is one that is operating noninterlaced at a minimum vertical refresh rate of 70Hz.

Fixed Function Processor

A fixed function processor is a device that has a highly specific instruction set and purpose. A typical fixed function processor is a math coprocessor. In graphics terms, a fixed function processor (also known as a graphics *co*processor) can perform a fixed set of graphics primitives, and is not capable of executing a program (like a true processor can). Examples of fixed function graphics processors include the 8514/A and XGA.

Fixed-pitch

This term refers to a **font** in which each character has the same cell width. The counterpart of the fixed-pitch (or monospaced) font is the proportional font. An example of a fixed-pitch font can be found in any of the program linsings in Chapters 5 and 7.

Font

A font, or typeface, is a group of characters/letters that share similar visual characteristics. Commonly used fonts are Times-Roman or Helvetica.

Graphics Assist

A graphics assist is a device, or component, that enhances the graphics functionality of another device that typically does not have such additional functionality. XVGAs are an example of graphics assists, as they add drawing functions (the graphics assist portion) to VGAs, which have no innate drawing capability.

Graphics Coprocessor

See **Fixed Function Processor**.

Graphics Processor

A graphics processor differs from a graphics coprocessor in that it can execute full-fledged programs, and though it is much more flexible than a coprocessor, it tends to be a more complicated device for which to develop software support. Traditional graphics processors, such as the TI 34010, include low-level graphics functions, such as line drawing and BitBLTs, on top of a functional general-purpose command architecture.

GUI

Graphical **U**ser **I**nterface (pronounced "gooey"). A GUI is any type of software application that provides a graphical interface for manipulation and use. Examples include Microsoft Windows and Digital Research's GEM. GUIs are traditionally associated with windowing environments (which place heavy emphasis on BitBLT performance), although packages like AutoCAD, which are more vector-based, can rightly be considered GUIs as well.

Hardware Accelerator

This is a rather vague term, since it can mean either a device that makes existing hardware faster or a hardware device that makes something else run faster. In the graphics world, the latter definition is the one applied. A hardware accelerator, or more accurately, a graphics hardware accelerator, can be any graphics hardware device that increases the throughput of on-screen graphics, such as most graphics coprocessor–or processor–based graphics boards.

Hercules

This is the name of the only company outside of IBM to ever establish a PC graphics hardware standard, namely the Hercules Graphics Controller. Also see **HGC**.

Hertz (Hz)

A unit of measurement for the number of times an event is repeated in a second. For example, the second hand on a clock has a frequency of 1 Hz. In graphics, Hz is used to measure video signal frequency, processor speeds, and pixel rates. Also see **Clock**.

HGA

Hercules Graphics Adapter. Same as **HGC**.

HGC

One of the only non-IBM graphics board standards, the **Hercules Graphics Controller** added monchrome graphics support, with a 720x348 resolution, to an MDA-compatible core. It sold so well because it also supported existing MDA-compatible monitors.

High Color

This is a new term derived from Sierra Semiconductor's trademarked HiColor, used to refer to 15 bpp (32,768 color) and 16 bpp (65,536 color) display modes. A VESA suggested methodology for naming color modes, however, is **Direct Color**.

Horizontal Frequency

The number of horizontal passes the electron beam makes per second across the surface of a monitor. A television, for example has a horizontal frequency of 15.75KHz (a **KHz** is 1000 Hz), while a VGA text display has a horizontal frequency of 31.5KHz.

I/O

Input/Output; refers to anything related the flow of data. In programming terms, I/O implies that access to a device is achieved via I/O ports, instead of via memory access.

Instance

This term was coined by IBM to refer to a given XGA board in a system. Instance 6, for example, references an XGA board with ID #6.

Interlaced

Interlacing is a means by which inexpensive monitors can display higher resolutions. An interlaced display will generally have a longer persistence phosphor (meaning that it takes longer for the image to fade), so that it can put up all even scan lines of an image in one pass of the electron beam, and the odd scan lines in the next pass. Two such passes make up the display frame (the complete image). The drawback to interlaced displays is that they are very prone to flicker.

Interrupt

In computer terms, an interrupt is an external stimulus to a computer. When an interrupt signal is received by a computer, the computer executes a specialized software routine (called an Interrupt Service Routine or Interrupt Handler), which then determines the cause of the interrupt and takes appropriate actions. On your PC, for example, every time you press or release a key on the keyboard, an interrupt is issued. Graphically, interrupts are generated to signal several events; primarily, the start of a vertical retrace. Graphics coprocessor and processor boards add additional interrupt signals, including error conditions, command completion, and data requested.

KB

Kilobyte. 1024 bytes, where each byte consists of 8 bits of data.

KHz

Kilohertz. 1000 **Hz**.

LIM

Lotus Intel Microsoft specification. In the early days, this is what **EMS** was called, named after the companies that helped to create the specification.

Linear Address

A linear address is the address of a memory location as counted from the start of memory. For example, the byte at the 128KB mark in memory has a linear address of 131,072 (decimal) or 020000H (hexadecimal). For Intel 80x86–compatible systems, an alternate way of expressing addresses is to use a Segment:Offset (real mode) or Selector:Offset (protected mode) mechanism.

LUT

Look-Up Table. The LUT is the part of the output section of a graphics board that translates a pixel value (primarily in 4 or 8 bpp modes) into its red, green, and blue components (see Figure 7.1). Once the components have been determined, they are passed through the DAC to generate displayable signals.

Map

The map, or memory map, of a system designates at what address things reside in memory. Figure G.1, on the next page, shows a typical PC memory map.

Mapped

A memory-mapped device is one whose memory is mapped into system memory, and is accessible at some address by PC-resident software. Graphics boards, like the XGA, are frequently memory mapped. The XGA, for example, can be mapped for 64KB in high memory, 1MB in the first 16MB of memory, and/or for 4MB in the 386/486's 4 gigabyte address space. The XGA also supports memory-mapped registers, which means that the board can be controlled and used via normal system memory operations.

Mask

A mask, in computer terms, is a numerical (most commonly binary) pattern that covers/controls some other type of data. The XGA, for example, supports a "Map Mask," which inhibits graphical data from being updated for each 0 bit in the mask, but allows data to be written for each 1 in the mask. There is always a one-to-one correlation between an item in a mask and the data to which the mask controls access.

MB

Megabyte. 1 megabyte is equal to 1 KB * 1 KB = 1024 x 1024 = 1,048,576 bytes.

Linear Address	Contents	Additional Comments
108000	XMS area. Real mode programs can cheat and access this memory by using a segment of 0FFFFH	This is the 1MB mark, and the start of extended memory
100000		
F8000	PC BIOS ROMs	Sometimes swapped to fast RAM
F0000		
E8000	Location of IBM's ABIOS	Also used for EMS Page Frame and other High Memory needs
E0000		
D8000	This is where all your peripheral adapter ROMs go, including things like non-VGA graphics boards, disk controllers, network adapters, and much more.	Areas not used by ROM up here will tend to get used by memory managers to "load high" TSRs.
D0000		
C8000		
C0000	VGA ROM BIOS	"High Memory" starts here
B8000	CGA Frame Buffer	VGA Uses these area for text mode operations
B0000	MDA Frame Buffer	
A8000	Graphics Frame Buffer Area, used by EGA, VGA, XGA, TARGA, and others.	A0000H is the 640KB mark.
A0000		
98000		
90000		
88000		
80000		
78000		
70000		
68000		
60000		
58000	This is normal program memory	
50000		
48000		
40000		
38000		
30000		
28000		
20000		
18000		
10000	More of DOS, and all your boot-time TSRs and Device Drivers get loaded around here	
8000		
0	The DOS core goes down here	

Figure G.1. A typical PC memory map.

MCGA

Multi-Color Graphics Array. MCGA is a stepping stone between EGA and VGA, and was released by IBM at the same time as the VGA and 8514/A. The MCGA can be found only on the initial IBM PS/2 Model 30.

MDA

Monochrome Display Adapter. This was the first display option for the original IBM PC. The MDA was capable only of displaying text. No graphics modes existed. Some documents also referred to the MDA as the MDPA (Monochrome Display and Printer Adapter), since the MDA also had a built-in parallel printer port.

MGA

Monochrome Graphics Adapter. Same as **HGC**.

MGC

Monochrome Graphics Controller. Same as **HGC**.

Mix

See **Raster Operation**.

Monochrome

A single color. A monochromatic display shows both a color and the absence of that color. Typically, you will have a white, green, or amber monochrome display on which you either see white, green, or amber text or graphics over a black background. In raster terms, a monochromatic bitmap is one in which pixels are composed of only a single bit. Raster text bitmaps are examples of monochrome bitmaps.

Monospaced

See **Fixed-Pitch**.

Non-Interlaced

A noninterlaced monitor displays a full frame of image in one pass of the electron beam. See **Interlaced** for more information.

Overscan

Overscan is the region on a monitor that does not contain visual data, but can still be viewed by an observer, as shown in Figure G.2.

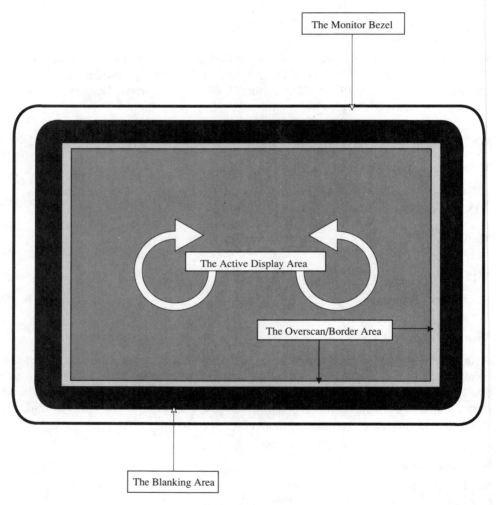

Figure G.2. An overscan on a monitor.

Packed-Pixel

Raster data can be stored in memory in one of two major ways. Packed-pixel means that all bits of a given pixel can be accessed as part of a regular data transfer. For example, in a 4 bpp packed-pixel representation, a one-byte transfer would affect two pixels (2 * 4 = 8). The other type of pixel access/storage is **planar**. See Figure G.3.

	Byte N								Byte N+1							
Line M	1	0	1	0	1	1	1	1	0	1	0	1	0	0	1	1
Line M+1	0	0	0	0	0	1	1	0	0	1	1	1	1	1	1	0

Figure G-3a. Above is a representation of graphical data in a packed pixel format.

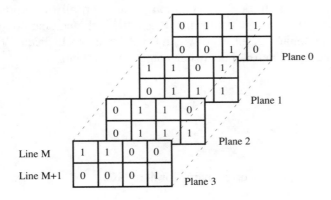

Figure G.3. Packed-pixel and planar displays.

Page Directory

The page directory (or page mapping table) in an i386 or i486 system is the list of all physical 4KB pages in memory, along with the corresponding remapped virtual address of that page (that is, the address that software has to use in order to access the physical memory). The page directory is part of the MMU (memory management unit) of the CPU.

Page Mapping

The act of using and modifying the page directory. This allows real-mode software to gain access to extended memory, and allows protected- mode software to virtualize memory (for better control under advanced operating systems).

Palette

The computer term "palette" is derived from the concept of an artist's palette, the flat piece of material upon which an artist selects and blends colors to create the desired shades. The palette on a graphics board specifies the range of colors available in any one pixel. For example, VGAs tend to have a palette of 262,144 colors, since every color in the palette is composed of 6 bits each of red, green, and blue, for a total of 18 bits (2^{18} = 262,144). However, since the VGA can display only 16 or 256 colors on-screen at any one time, it means that each one of these 16 or 256 colors must be chosen from the larger palette. See **LUT** for details.

Pass-through

A pass-through is a mechanism by which information can flow freely through a device. In PC graphics, a VGA pass-through is commonly found on all high-end graphics boards because it allows VGA display information and the high-end board output to be displayed on the same monitor. A software switch is used to control whether VGA data or high-end board data is in control of the display at any given time.

PEL

See **Pixel**.

PGA

Professional **G**raphics **A**dapter. Incorrect name for the **PGC**.

PGC

Professional **G**raphics **C**ontroller (also known as the PGA, or Professional Graphics Adapter). This 640x480 by 256 color display device was one of the first graphics controllers with a real processor (an Intel 8088) on the board. The 8088 was not directly programmable. Instead, a command language (known as PGL, or Programming Graphics Language) was used to drive the board. A few companies cloned it, but it has virtually disappeared from the market.

Pixel

Picture (**Pix**) **E**lement. A pixel is the smallest unit of display that a computer can access to display information. A resolution of 320x200, for example, means that a graphics display can show 200 lines, each consisting of 320 pixels horizontally. A pixel, in display memory, is represented as a numerical value. The pixel value is translated into a color by a DAC for display.

Pixel Clock

The pixel clock is a timing mechanism used to "clock" pixels out to the display. Generally, for one voltage pulse (or tick) of the clock, a pixel is sent to the display. See **Clock**.

Planar

Certain graphics devices store raster information in a planar mode, which means that each bit of a pixel is stored in a different location, or plane, of memory. For example, in the 4 bpp/16 color graphics mode of the VGA, Pixels are accessed and stored in a planar fashion. Access to the individual planes, in this case, is controlled by a number of control parameters that specify which bit planes can be updated and/or read. Some higher-end graphics boards also allow direct memory access to individual bit planes. See Figure G.3.

Plane

See **Planar**.

POS

Peripheral **O**peration **S**etup. Used in Micro Channel Architecture (MCA) and Extended Industry Standard Architecture (EISA) based systems as part of booting-up, initializing, and enabling various peripheral devices. In the MCA environment, each device has POS registers, accessed at I/O locations 100H-103H, which give control over the mapping and state of the device. The POS mechanism is used with the XGA in order to first locate all XGAs, and then assign each XGA its unique operating parameters.

Proportional Fonts

In proportional fonts, individual characters have proportional widths, meaning that, for instance, an "m" would be wider than an "i." The text used in this glossary, for instance, is proportionally spaced. The opposite of proportional spacing is fixed-pitch or mono-spacing.

RAMDAC

RAM Digital to Analog Converter. A RAMDAC is basically a DAC combined in one chip with a LUT.

Raster Operation

Frequently, in graphics operations, it is necessary to combine the data being drawn with the data already present in the destination area (such as the frame buffer). A very common combine function is the XOR (eXclusive OR), which is used to draw cursors. The XOR operation allows the same graphics data to be written once to contrast with existing data, and a second time to remove traces of the first drawing pass. These functions, which compute the result of a combination of source and destination data, are referred to as raster operations, ROPs, or MIXes.

Refresh Rate

The refresh rate of a monitor is the frequency at which complete frames of image are displayed. A television set has a refresh rate of 30Hz, while a VGA or XGA text screen refreshes at 70Hz (or 70 times a second).

Register

Data is placed in a register for temporary storage or, more often, to directly affect some part of the operation of a piece of hardware. Register-based software directly modifies the hardware. Programmers often desire direct access to registers because it permits faster operation. Registers can be I/O mapped or memory mapped.

Resolution

The resolution of a display device can be measured spatially or by color. Spatial resolution refers to the number of pixels that can be displayed horizontally and vertically on the monitor or display device. This type of resolution is specified as X by Y; for example, 640x480 or 1024x768. Color resolution is either added to the spacial resolution, as in 640x480x4 (bits per pixel) or 640x480x16 (# of colors), or by just by itself; for instance, a 24 bpp display.

ROM

Read-Only Memory. ROMs contain software (or more accurately firmware, since it can't be erased easily) that is burned into the core of the ROM chip. This supplies ROMs with a certain data permanence that RAM devices cannot achieve without some sort of power source. ROMs come built into computers (see **BIOS**), or on peripheral devices that need some basic software in order to start operation.

Scissoring

See **Clipping**.

Sprite

A sprite is a small bitmap that can be laid over the display of an image. Sprites tend to have limited color, and their own positioning mechanism. See **Cursor.**

SRAM

Static **RAM**. SRAM differs from DRAM in that it does not need to be refreshed periodically. Instead, SRAM needs only an electrical source, such as a battery, to keep data from deteriorating.

SVGA

See **Super VGA**.

Super VGA

Refers to all clone VGAs that provide better resolution than the original IBM VGA. Sample resolutions offered by SVGAs includes 1024x768 at 16 or 256 colors. This is also currently the dominant type of high-resolution graphics adapter on the market.

TARGA

TARGA stands for **T**ruevision **A**dvanced **R**aster **G**raphics **A**dapter, and is the name of the first Direct Color PC Graphics board, which set the standard for the 16 bit pixel (DC 1:5:5:5). The TARGA-compatible pixel breaks a 16 bit word into 5 bits (32 levels) of red, 5 bits of green, 5 bits of blue, and 1 bit for video use. Red, green, and blue are the primary colors used in color monitors.

TI 34010/TI 34020

The TI 34010 and 34020 are graphics processors developed by Texas Instruments. These chips have gained much popularity in the high-end graphics market because of their versatility. This same versatility makes them more difficult to use for mainstream environments, however. Most boards that use these chips provide a TIGA and/or DGIS interface for programmers and application support.

TIGA

Texas **I**nstruments **G**raphics **A**rchitecture (pronounced as "Tie-Gah"). TIGA is the interface developed by TI for all the graphics boards on the market that use TI's 34010 and 34020 graphics processors.

TLB

Table **L**ookaside **B**uffer. Part of the mechanism used by the Intel i386/i486 MMU for remapping memory. See **Page Directory**.

True Color

True color is a term used to describe high color content displays and images. Traditionally, 24 bpp and higher displays and images have been considered true color, as have 16 bpp images. The latter are rapidly becoming known as "high color" or "direct color" in the mass market, however.

VBE

VGA **B**IOS **E**xtension. VBE is a VESA standard software interface for SVGAs that allows software to determine what resolutions an SVGA (or other memory-mapped graphics controller) can support.

VDT

Video **D**isplay **T**erminal. These days, a VDT is virtually synonymous with a display or monitor, both of which are used to visually present computer data in either a textual or graphical format.

VESA

The **V**ideo **E**lectronics **S**tandards **A**ssociation, founded in 1989 to set monitor standards for the 800x600 resolution used by Super VGAs. VESA has since involved into an organization that sets standards in all aspects of the PC graphics industry. VESA is headquartered in San Jose, California.

Vector

A vector can be one of two things: First, an interrupt vector, which is the pointer to code which gets executed when an interrupt is received by a processor (see **Interrupt**), or second, a graphical element, also known as a line.

Vertical Frequency

See **Refresh Rate**.

VGA

Video **G**raphics **A**rray. The VGA was introduced at the same time as IBM's 8514/A and IBM's PS/2 line of computers in 1987. The IBM VGA supports maximum resolutions of 640x480 by 16 colors (out of 262,144) and 320x200 by 256 colors. The IBM VGA has also been extensively cloned and enhanced, resulting in SVGAs and AVGAs.

VGA Pass-Through

A mechanism by which a graphics board can take raw VGA display signals and pass them through its hardware in order to display VGA information on the monitor attached to the graphics board. The IBM 8514/A uses this mechanism, for example, in order to provide a single-screen solution. Software generally controls whether the VGA pass-through or the native graphics board information is viewed on a monitor.

Viewable Resolution

The viewable resolution of a graphics board is the physical resolution displayed by the board, measured in pixels. See **Virtual Resolution**.

Virtual Memory

Virtual memory is simulated memory, and occurs in systems that can swap RAM to another storage medium, such as a hard disk. For example, a 386 or 486 based PC may only have 4MB of RAM, but with a virtual memory manager and a large hard disk, programs can run as if they had many times more memory than the core 4MB. This approach stems back from early mainframes and minis, which had limited amounts of RAM (sometimes as little as 4KB) but quite a bit of disk storage. Physical memory is divided into small chunks, and control software keeps track of which chunks are used the least. These least-used chunks are then swapped out to disk when a program tries to access memory that is not loaded with the proper information.

Virtual Resolution

The virtual resolution of a graphics board is the resolution you can achieve using the board's video memory alone. For example, an XGA with 1MB of VRAM has virtual resolution of 1024x1024x8bpp, but a viewable resolution of only 640x480 or 1024x768.

VRAM

Video **RAM**, also known as Video DRAM, or dual-ported DRAM. VRAM was designed to eliminate the wait states that occurred when a CPU wanted to update a display while a display controller was reading the DRAM in order to display the information on the screen. The wait states occurred because only one processor/controller could access the DRAM at a time, forcing the other to wait, and since the display controller was more timing-sensitive, the CPU was always the one to wait. VRAM solves this problem by having a small additional memory area into which the current scan line of data is copied (or shifted). This additional buffer has its own read lines attached to it so that a display controller can fetch display data while the CPU accesses the main RAM.

XGA

IBM introduced the eXtended Graphics Array graphics device in 1990. The IBM XGA has the same resolution capabilities as the 8514/A, and roughly the same performance. The XGA, however, also has built-in VGA compatibility. The graphics coprocessor portion of the XGA is not compatible with the 8514/A.

XSVGA or XVGA

See **Accelerated VGA**.

Bibliography

Abrash, M., *Power Graphics Programming*. QUE, 1989.

Ferraro, R., *Programmer's Guide to the EGA and VGA Cards*. Addison-Wesley, 1988.

Foley, J., A. van Dam, S. Feiner, and J. Hughes, *Computer Graphics: Principles and Practice* (Second Edition). Addison-Wesley, 1990.

IBM Corporation, *IBM Personal System/2 Display Adapter 8514/A Adapter Interface Programmer's Guide*. P/N: 68X2279. IBM, 1987.

IBM Corporation, *IBM Personal System/2 Display Adapter 8514/A Technical Reference*. P/N: 68X2249. IBM, 1987.

IBM Corporation, *IBM Personal System/2 Image Adapter/A Technical Reference*. P/N: S15F2162. IBM, 1990.

IBM Corporation, *IBM Personal System/2 XGA Adapter Interface Technical Reference*. P/N: S15F2154. IBM, 1990.

IBM Corporation, *Update for the PS/2 Hardware Interface Technical Reference: Architectures*. P/N: S04G3282. IBM, 1991.

IBM Corporation, *Update for the PS/2 Hardware Interface Technical Reference: Common Interfaces, Video Subsystems*. P/N: S04G3281. IBM, 1991.

Kernighan, B. and D. Ritchie, *The C Programming Language*. Prentice Hall, 1978.

Richter, J. and B. Smith, *Graphics Programming for the 8514/A*. M&T Books, 1990.

Stevens, R., *Graphics Programming in C*. M&T Books, 1988.

Sutty, G. and S. Blair, *Advanced Programmer's Guide to the EGA/VGA*. Brady, 1988.

Wilton R., *Programmer's Guide to PC & PS/2 Video Systems*. Microsoft Press, 1987.

VESA XGA Extensions Standard. P/N: VXE 1.0. VESA, 1992.

Index

R

PROGRAM LISTINGS ON DISKETTE

MIS:PRESS

This diskette contains the complete listings for all programs and applications contained in this book—it eliminates the need to type in pages of program code.

Power Programming the IBM XGA
ISBN: 1-55828-212-2
MIS:PRESS

ADVANCED COMPUTER BOOKS

If you did not buy this book with a diskette, use this form to order now. *Only*

$29⁹⁵